ŽIŽEK'S ONTOLOGY

Northwestern University

Studies in Phenomenology

and

Existential Philosophy

Founding Editor †James M. Edie

General Editor Anthony J. Steinbock

Associate Editor John McCumber

ŽIŽEK'S ONTOLOGY

A Transcendental Materialist Theory of Subjectivity

Adrian Johnston

Northwestern University Press
Evanston, Illinois

Northwestern University Press
www.nupress.northwestern.edu

Printed in the United States of America

10 9 8 7 6 5 4 3 2 1

Library of Congress Cataloging-in-Publication Data

Johnston, Adrian, 1974–
     Žižek's ontology : a transcendental materialist theory of subjectivity / Adrian Johnston.
          p. cm. — (Northwestern University studies in phenomenology and existential philosophy)
     Includes bibliographical references and index.
     ISBN-13: 978-0-8101-2455-4 (cloth : alk. paper)
     ISBN-10: 0-8101-2455-6 (cloth : alk. paper)
     ISBN-13: 978-0-8101-2456-1 (pbk. : alk. paper)
     ISBN-10: 0-8101-2456-4 (pbk. : alk. paper)
     1. Žižek, Slavoj. 2. Subjectivity. 3. Transcendentalism. 4. Materialism. 5. Idealism, German. I. Title. II. Series: Northwestern University studies in phenomenology & existential philosophy.
B4870.Z594J64 2008
199'.4973—dc22

                                                                            2007042951

For wonderful Kathryn—the beautiful grace of the event of love

Like plants, most men have hidden properties that chance
alone reveals.
　　—François, duc de La Rochefoucauld

A man, whoever he is, always and everywhere likes to act as
he chooses, and not at all according to the dictates of reason
and self-interest; it is indeed possible, and sometimes *positively
imperative* (in my view), to act directly contrary to one's own best
interests. One's own free and unfettered volition, one's own
caprice, however wild, one's own fancy, inflamed sometimes to
the point of madness—that is the one best and greatest good,
which is never taken into consideration because it will not fit
into any classification, and the omission of which always sends
all systems and theories to the devil. Where did all the sages
get the idea that a man's desires must be normal and virtuous?
Why did they imagine that he must inevitably will what is
reasonable and profitable? What a man needs is simply and
solely *independent* volition, whatever that independence may cost
and wherever it may lead.
　　—Fyodor Dostoyevsky

Contents

Preface: Reinventing the Psychopathology of Everyday Life

One of Slavoj Žižek's favorite recent references is a short 1997 book on Gilles Deleuze by Alain Badiou (*Deleuze: The Clamor of Being*).[1] In this text, Badiou contends that the typical first impressions arising from a reading of Deleuze's works tend to reinforce a misinterpretation of him as philosophically celebrating the flourishing of heterogeneous multiplicities and the mad dance of "nomadic rhizomes" chaotically branching out in every possible direction, with no guiding trajectory either shaping this philosophical program or governing its objects of descriptive inquiry. Deleuze is all too often cast as a theoretical anarchist of desire, as a schizophrenic troublemaker disrupting the organized structures operative within both political and libidinal economies. In short, much of Deleuzean thought is exegetically filtered through the lens of his joint "anti-Oedipal" endeavor with Félix Guattari. Badiou maintains that a pronounced discrepancy exists in Deleuze's oeuvre between, on the one hand, its superficial style, whose baroque, ornate intricacies encourage the view that this is a philosophy of explosive fragmentation, and, on the other hand, its basic, underlying content, its endlessly reiterated thesis. Beneath the scintillating stylistic façade of a "rhizomatic" prose, Deleuze tirelessly and monotonously underscores the same essential point again and again: Everything exists on one ontological level alone; everything is to be situated on a single "plane of immanence": therefore, the temptation to posit split tiers of existence (such as Plato's division between the visible and intelligible realms and Kant's noumenal-phenomenal opposition) must be resisted. The heterogeneity of appearances belies the homogeneity of being: "the moment we introduce 'thriving multitude,' what we effectively assert is the exact opposite: underlying all-pervasive Sameness" (Žižek 2002c, 73). Thus, according to Badiou, the frenzied multiplication of the "Many" in Deleuze's philosophy ultimately serves better to reveal the all-inclusive "One" of an ontology of absolute immanence.[2]

A similar observation should be made regarding Žižek's own work. His frenetic accumulation of an ever-growing number of cultural examples and his famed forays into the twisting nooks and crannies of the popular imagination are liable to mislead readers into viewing him as an anti-systematic thinker (a thinker who seeks to compromise the ostensible purity of philosophical thought by forcing it into being dialectically contaminated through a symbiotic fusion with the disorganized domain of contemporary quotidian culture). Faced with the "pyrotechnics" and "fireworks" of his extended, elaborate asides concerning art, literature, film, and daily life in late-capitalist societies, readers are susceptible to being dazzled to the point of giddy, overstimulated incomprehension, of being stunned like the proverbial deer caught in the glare of blinding headlights.[3] Žižek's rhetorical flair and various features of his methodology are in danger of creating the same unfortunate sort of audience as today's mass media (with its reliance upon continual successions of rapid-fire, attention-grabbing sound bites), namely, consumers too easily driven to distraction. The extent of this risk can be mitigated if one keeps in mind that Badiou's warning about Deleuze (i.e., don't let the heterogeneous style distract from and thereby obscure the homogeneous content) is equally applicable to Žižek himself. When Žižek declares that he employs, for instance, popular culture as a subservient vehicle for the (re)deployment of late-modern philosophy—with the "Many" of Žižek's examples ultimately serving the "One" of a project aiming at the "reactualization" (as Žižek himself puts it) of Kantian and German idealist thought through the mediation of Freudian-Lacanian psychoanalytic metapsychology[4]—he is quite serious. The chain Kant-Schelling-Hegel, knotted together vis-à-vis Lacan himself as this chain's privileged *point de capiton* (quilting point), is the underlying skeletal structure holding together the entirety of the Žižekian theoretical edifice.

Nonetheless, much like Deleuze (and Derrida too), Žižek, whether deliberately or otherwise, seems to extend an invitation to read his texts in at least two ways. On the one hand, he proclaims himself to be a critic of various postmodernist trends, calling for a psychoanalytically informed return to modern philosophy. On the other hand, his almost schizoid jumping from topic to topic, his dizzying rampage through any and every disciplinary area and level of conceptual analysis, comes across as an approach strikingly different from that of such careful system-builders as Kant and Hegel. Perhaps the imagined, hypothetical figure of the cultural studies reader of Žižek, aesthetically inclined toward heterogeneity instead of homogeneity (and consequently favoring the second of the two aspects of his writings), can't resist asking why he resorts to so many extra-theoretical points of reference: Why would he expend this much authorial effort on objects of culture if they really are, as he sometimes maintains, mere window dressing in relation to the philosophical superstructure under whose heading they're supposedly subsumed? Isn't it justifiable to suspect that Žižek is being a bit disingenuous when he downplays this dimension of his work, when he plays the part of a fallen philosopher who is unable to resist the temptation to use high theory as a rationalization for wallowing in the obscene stupidity of American popular culture and telling dirty, off-color jokes?

What could be dubbed the "cultural studies Žižek" is something of a caricature resulting from an engagement with his corpus that, for whatever reasons, chooses to grant itself the low-effort luxury of being distracted by this corpus's numerous illustrative examples (examples mobilized therein precisely for the purpose of reinforcing the concepts at stake). The suggestion has even been made that Žižek himself has no central theoretical point to make, with this lack being hidden behind a flurry of references and a multitude of engagements with different fields.[5] However, why shouldn't the plethora of examples utilized by Žižek be construed, in their plurality, as adding all the more confirmatory force to the unifying theses on whose behalf these examples are assembled and marshaled as evidence? In other words, why, against the standard "scientific" perspective (one wholeheartedly embraced by Freudian analysis), should one conclude that the multiplication of sociocultural instantiations detracts from (rather than adds to) the persuasively coherent singularity of a conceptual configuration for which these instantiations are representative instances? Freud (especially the Freud favored by Lacan) is convinced that his accumulation of a formidable number of empirical illustrations—*The Interpretations of Dreams, The Psychopathology of Everyday Life,* and *Jokes and Their Relation to the Unconscious* (among other texts) hammer home Freud's central analytic claims through a veritable deluge of data—serves no other end than that of buttressing his overarching metapsychological framework.

What's more, in raising questions stemming from the suspicion that Žižek relates to cultural objects as more than just suggestive instantiations of philosophical and psychoanalytic concepts (i.e., that he seeks to fragment theory by routing it through extraneous domains), the cultural studies proponent of a Žižekianism compatible with reigning sensibilities in the postmodern humanities (if such a proponent exists) displays a failure to be faithful to the most fundamental and correct insights of his or her post-structuralist and deconstructionist masters. One of Derrida's crucial contributions to philosophical methodology, particularly apropos the technique of reading texts as itself a driving motor of philosophy's historical progress, is his decisive demolition of the grounding assumptions behind traditional modes of exegetical praxis. Derrida offers argument after argument for why appeals to the authorial authority of an intention-to-signify are specious and utterly illegitimate; they rest upon convenient myths compensating for the irreparable lack of access to a meaningful presence behind or beyond the text itself.[6] Foucault moves along similar lines when he declares the "death of the author." The conclusion sometimes drawn from this, in indefensible haste, is that a limitless play of interpretations proliferates following the demise of the intentional agent who is usually assumed to underwrite ultimate textual sense. Freud's myth of the primal horde from *Totem and Taboo* cautions against immediately taking the parameters of this forced choice for granted: instead of uninhibitedly reveling in a Bacchanalian orgy after liquidating the oppressive primal father (akin here to the loathed Derridean/Foucauldian author as master of meaning; the *Urvater* prevents the free circulation of women, just as the author prevents the free circulation of significations[7]), the band of brothers immediately enact laws constraining themselves from enjoying their newfound libidinal liberty. Likewise, Lacan, paraphrasing Dostoyevsky, observes that "if God is dead, then nothing is permitted."[8] Anarchy doesn't automatically blossom in the wake of an old authority's implosion.

Behind this hasty deconstructive conclusion lurks a false dilemma: either a text/oeuvre is assigned an objectified, transcendent signification through the invocation of authorial intentionality, or a text/oeuvre is exploded into an ungovernable plurality of significations through the prohibition of any recourse to the fiction of authorial intentionality. The falsity of this dilemma is easily demonstrated with the case of Derrida himself. Despite the sometimes excessively ornate and meandering quality of his texts as well as his insistence that he isn't a systematic philosopher, doesn't Derrida's collection of writings exhibit an amazing degree of consistency, a sustained pursuit of a sort of inverse Kantian-critical project wherein the "conditions of impossibility" for philosophy ever achieving the smug satisfaction of a self-sufficient closure are delineated? Oddly enough, Derrida, who often reinforces his own claims by auto-reflexively applying them to himself (thus rendering these claims all the stronger as absolute universals brooking no exceptions), refrains from a self-application of his suspension of authorial authority with regard to his denials of having a system or method (or, on a more concrete level, there's the infamous case of his interview entitled "Philosopher's Hell," published in the collection *The Heidegger Controversy*—he threatened legal action against the editors of the collection if they wouldn't allow him to pull the piece so as to prevent its appearance in subsequent editions of the book[9]). If one brackets Derrida's vehement disavowals of his consistent systematic ambitions (thereby faithfully adhering to Derridean interpretive procedures), then the outcome of decoupling the authorial intention-to-signify and the extant textual body is the exact inverse of

what is normally assumed to happen by deconstructionists themselves
(this being an illustration of what Žižek alleges transpires when the rules
of a system are followed too closely by the system's subjects—the system is subverted as a result, since it tacitly relies on its subjects taking a
minimal degree of distance from its official rules by quietly obeying a
subterranean set of accompanying unofficial commandments[10]). Instead
of opening up the field of interpretation to a chaotic multitude of heterogeneous, disseminated meanings, the suspension of the author's authority, at least in the present case, results in the emergence of a surprisingly univocal structure. In all likelihood, the assumption that the "death
of the author" is inevitably followed by, so to speak, a thousand blooming
flowers takes for granted the arbitrary contingency that the text being
deconstructed is one that clearly harbors a desire for systematicity, one
with pretensions to master and control its own meaning (say, the canonical great books of the history of Western metaphysics). Put differently,
deconstruction's hypotheses about the "anarchic" consequences of reading texts independently of authorial intentionality might receive confir-
mation exclusively on the condition that the sample pool of writings is
selectively limited to those texts that invite the challenge of subversive
interpretations by virtue of their perceived resistance to opening out
onto multiple perspectives. Concealed by a veil of overt proclamations,
the unwritten shadow law of Derridean deconstruction, from a Žižekian
perspective, would involve the prohibition of deconstructing texts that
already attempt to deconstruct themselves, a ban on applying deconstruction to so-called polyvocal writings. Whether or not the abolition of
the figure of the author leads to a disruptive multiplication of meanings
in the canonical great books of philosophy is an open issue. But more
pressing questions, linked to the example of Derrida himself, present
themselves in this context: What if the text/oeuvre removed from the
author's intentional jurisdiction is, at least superficially, of a non/anti-
systematic sort? Wouldn't an inverse sequence ensue, wherein the brack-
eting of the author's intentions allows a rigorous, consistent conceptual
apparatus to come fully into view?

   Žižek is a perfect case in point here. At first glance, the majority of
his texts are disorganized, hyper-kinetic meditations on various and sun-
dry popular cultural phenomena. And maybe there is something to the
suspicion that these reflections are more than just superfluous, disposable examples pressed into the service of cold, hard theory. Before proceeding further, it's worth noting that, of course, both deconstruction
and psychoanalysis render the entertaining of these suspicions vain and
futile. According to deconstructive axioms of exegesis, Žižek's underlying authorial intentions (whether legibly explicit or subtly implicit) with

regard to these examples are, strictly speaking, irrelevant, to be held in permanent abeyance. And according to psychoanalytic principles of interpretation, even if it could somehow definitively be proven that Žižek secretly yet knowingly accords greater importance to his illustrative cultural objects than he usually lets on, this fails to demonstrate convincingly that they actually possess the importance he consciously invests in them. In short, authors aren't "masters of their own texts" (hence, the surmised underlying purposes of the intentional agent named "Slavoj Žižek" are out of play here). However, this knot of difficulties is easy to cut—these sorts of debates are needlessly distracting sideshows—so as to enable the relation between theory and culture in Žižekian thought to emerge into the illuminating light of serene comprehension.

In the self-interview forming the appendix to *The Metastases of Enjoyment,* Žižek describes his passage through the defiles of popular culture as a labor of translating theoretical notions into the easily understood vernacular of a "stupid" medium, a labor thereby granting firmer access to truths typically exhibiting an elusive abstractness (the ideas of thinkers such as Hegel and Lacan are usually considered to be so ephemerally complex as to be almost unemployable with respect to the banal details of mundane, everyday existence—an impression forever destroyed by Žižek's numerous and formidable analytic accomplishments). As he admits, "I am convinced of my proper grasp of some Lacanian concept only when I can translate it successfully into the inherent imbecility of popular culture" (Žižek 1994b, 175). In terms of the general theory-culture rapport informing his methodology, Žižek's avowed preference for the Hegelian dynamic of "tarrying with the negative" should be kept in mind here. Speaking of *Geist* in its effective vitality (in the same paragraph of the *Phenomenology of Spirit* where the phrase "tarrying with the negative" appears), Hegel declares that "the life of Spirit . . . wins its truth only when, in utter dismemberment, it finds itself" (Hegel 1977c, 19 [§32]). In an identical way, the life of the Žižekian theoretical apparatus wins its truth only when, in the utter dismemberment of being fragmented into a seemingly disparate jumble of popular cultural examples, it finds itself as System. Or, in the language of Badiou's reading of Deleuze, the "One" of the Žižekian project is the encompassing horizon/frame within which the "Many" of his eclectic collection of cultural objects exhausts itself, thereby yielding up its contribution to the truth of Theory itself.[11] This "tarrying with popular culture," as it could be designated, amounts to nothing less than the reinvention, on the fertile soil of a contemporary sociopolitical milieu, of Freud's turn-of-the-century "psychopathology of everyday life" (a "psychopathology" that cannot be left to secure its veracity solely in reference to a 1901 "everyday"—the insights of psychoanalysis must test themselves continually against the givens of the immediate present).

As the epigraph to the published version of his 1974 television interview, Lacan pronounces that "he who interrogates me also knows how to read me," and he elsewhere credits Jacques-Alain Miller with being "the at-least-one to have read me" (Lacan 1990c, 135). The "at-least-one to have read Žižek" would likewise need to be someone who knows where and when to take the right measure of critical distance from this alluring, almost overbearingly dominant intellect. Consequently, in what follows, Žižek's work is shamelessly and unapologetically used—as Žižek sometimes insists, "Friends are to be ruthlessly exploited!"—as the platform for launching a preliminary elaboration (a sketch or outline) of what could be called a transcendental materialist theory of subjectivity (articulated vis-à-vis a carefully calculated interweaving of modern philosophy and Freudian-Lacanian psychoanalysis). Interminably dwelling on the empirical-cultural dimension of his corpus is the most profoundly unjust violence that can be inflicted on this corpus itself. In fact, the only sort of militant fidelity (in Badiou's parlance) to Žižek involves the infidelity of apparent betrayal: ignoring the appetizing, titillating tidbits of his smorgasbord of examples and refusing to be seduced by the razzle-dazzle of his cultural exposés—sticking instead to the single-minded pursuit of the philosophical trajectory that runs like a continuous, bisecting diagonal line through the entire span of his writings (i.e., the retroactive Lacanian reconstruction of the chain Kant-Schelling-Hegel). On offer here is a Deleuzean "buggering" of an author, an attempt at engendering novel, monstrous offspring. In Žižek's enthusiastic spirit of impassioned intellectual confrontation—he often demands, "There must be blood!"—this project is convinced that, in proper Hegelian dialectical fashion, the truth emerges out of error. The process of critiquing crucial features of Žižekian philosophy is the key to unleashing the full theoretical potential of this very philosophy itself, of raising Žižek (sometimes with him, sometimes against him) to the philosophical dignity of his Notion.

Acknowledgments

Modified portions of this volume have appeared in several different venues: "Revulsion Is Not Without Its Subject: Kant, Lacan, Žižek and the Symptom of Subjectivity," *Pli: The Warwick Journal of Philosophy*, no. 15 (Spring 2004), pp. 199–228; "Against Embodiment: The Material Ground of the Immaterial Subject," *Journal for Lacanian Studies* 2, no. 2 (December 2004), pp. 230–54; "Substanca in duhovi njene preteklosti: Schelling, Lacan in denaturalizacija narave," trans. Tomaž Bezjak, *Problemi*, no. 1/2 (2005), pp. 33–85; "Ghosts of Substance Past: Schelling, Lacan, and the Denaturalization of Nature," in *Lacan: The Silent Partners*, ed. Slavoj Žižek (London: Verso, 2006), pp. 34–55; "Lightening Ontology: Slavoj Žižek and the Unbearable Lightness of Being Free," *Lacanian Ink: The Symptom*, no. 8 (Spring 2007), http://www.lacan.com/symptom8_articles/johnston8.html. I appreciate the editors' allowing these portions to reappear here. I also would like to thank Anthony Steinbock, the editor of the Studies in Phenomenology and Existential Philosophy series, for the considerable amount of time, effort, and support he generously has given to my work.

Introduction: The Immanent Genesis
of the Transcendent

One of Žižek's most startling claims is his assertion that the Cartesian conception of subjectivity à la the cogito (especially as radicalized by Kant, Schelling, and Hegel) is, contrary to the prevailing intellectual consensus, anything but obsolete and outdated. However, it must be acknowledged that the past century's worth of research in the humanities as well as both the natural and social sciences has succeeded in raising many serious challenges and objections to philosophical theories according to which a subject exempt from material mediation exists on one level or another. Is a compromise possible between the critics of the modern subject and those (such as Žižek) calling for a return to this notion of subjectivity?

A fruitful compromise is indeed possible starting from two premises (derived primarily from the findings of psychoanalysis). One, the subject described by late-modern (especially transcendental) philosophy is emergent in relation to the body—that is to say, such "immaterial" (or, more accurately, more-than-material) subjectivity immanently arises out of a material ground. And two, this body as material ground is, from the very beginning, shot through with various antagonisms, conflicts, and tensions—in other words, rather than being internally harmonized with itself, the human body is hard-wired for a certain dysfunctionality. The physical constitution of this body means that human nature is, one could say, naturally inclined toward the dominance of nurture over nature. This nature "short-circuits" itself, and in so doing, gives birth to processes of denaturalization. The infant's prolonged state of pre-maturational helplessness, coupled with the ways in which its libidinal economy interacts with its perceptual-mnemic apparatuses, propel this bodily being into dematerialized, disembodied forms of subjectivity (with these subject-positions being, in part, defensive reaction-formations catalyzed by the struggle to evade or tame an unruly corporeality, a "corpo-Real").

Succinctly stated, the basic thesis advocated and defended throughout this project, a thesis making possible the articulation of what could be called a transcendental materialist theory of subjectivity, is that the choice between either a disembodied subject or an embodied self is a false dilemma. Cogito-like subjectivity ontogenetically emerges out of an originally corporeal condition as its anterior ground, although, once generated, this sort of subjectivity thereafter remains irreducible to its material sources. Hence, in terms of its overall contribution to the theoretical humanities, this project aims to open up pathways allowing for productive cooperation between, on the one hand, the plethora of investigations into the somatic constitution of the human individual (including cognitive science, neurology, and phenomenological embodiment theory) and, on the other hand, accounts of identity insisting upon a more-than-corporeal dimension (particularly as found in certain philosophical and psychoanalytic traditions). The combination of a reconsideration of the nature of the human body with a temporal-genetic model of emergent subjectivity (a model charting the immanent material genesis of the thereafter more-than-material transcendent) has the potential to shift fundamentally the terms of today's ongoing debates over the relation between soma and psyche.

This book is organized around a psychoanalytically influenced retraversing of a path running from Kant through Schelling to Hegel, a traversal steering its way toward a transcendental materialist theory of subjectivity. In the course of pursuing this new theory of subjectivity, the three sections of this book extensively address in detail Žižek's Lacan-inspired theoretical appropriations of Kant, Schelling, and Hegel; Žižek plays a guiding role in this Lacanian journey back through late-modern German philosophy. Accordingly, the first part of the book focuses on Kant (and to a lesser extent on Fichte, Kant's immediate idealist successor). More specifically, this part involves a reinterpretation of the splitting of the subject between noumenal and phenomenal domains that is central to Kant's critical-transcendental framework. This reinterpretation stresses the important functions of the interconnected factors of embodiment and mortality (things generally neglected by Kant) in the splitting of the subject, factors that render this subject finite and partially opaque to itself in the manners described by Kant's transcendental philosophy. The first part concludes with the proposal that forms of subjectivity set against and resisting assimilation to material bodies (i.e., cogito-like forms of subjectivity) emerge out of the specific sorts of material bodies possessed by human beings. That is to say, the more-than-material subject is, in part, a reaction-formation ontogenetically conditioned by bodily materiality (as this materiality is conceived of by psychoanalysis in particular).

The second part of this book picks up right where the first part leaves off, both historically (moving from Kant and Fichte to Schelling) and conceptually. The first part argues that the transcendental subject of Kant-

ian idealist philosophy, rather than being an always already pre-given
a priori structure, is genetic as formed over time through an ensemble
of mechanisms and processes. Consequently, the second part seeks
to delineate, through a sustained engagement with Schelling's post-
Kantian philosophical reflections, the ontogenetic conditions of possibility for the genesis of the transcendental, cogito-like subject (i.e., the meta-
transcendental level underpinning transcendental subjectivity). The ultimate ontological status of material being as a substance divided against
itself—this ontology of (in Lacanian parlance) a "barred Real" is developed through analyses of Žižek's fashions of combining German idealism and psychoanalysis—is identified as the crucial precondition for
transcendental subjectivity genetically arising out of an immanent plane
of materiality. Furthermore, this part of the text, in juxtaposing Schellingian philosophy with Freudian-Lacanian psychoanalytic metapsychology,
also revisits the philosophical themes/topics of autonomy and temporality (the latter receives further sustained attention in the second half
of the third part). The place of freedom in psychoanalysis—analysis is
typically (and erroneously) viewed as a discourse of determinism articulating narratives in which individuals are reduced to being mere puppets
of unconscious influences operating beyond their control—is radically
reconceived here. The veil of repression cordoning off the unconscious
conceals not only the heteronomy of hidden determining forces but also
the true extent of one's defensively obfuscated autonomy, a freedom that
people surprisingly often find frightening and unsettling.

The third part of this book contains the philosophical climax of the
project as a whole. Thanks to Lacan and certain of his prominent inter-
preters (Žižek first and foremost), Hegel's thought is widely viewed as the
portion of late-modern German philosophy that is most crucial for and
compatible with psychoanalysis. The third part begins by showing the impossibility of properly appreciating Hegelian philosophy and its potential
connections with psychoanalytic metapsychology without grasping how
this philosophy grew out of and positioned itself with respect to Kant and
his immediate successors (specifically Fichte and Schelling); most studies of the Hegel-Lacan rapport fail to consider sufficiently Hegel's place
in this era of philosophical history. This historical analysis leads to the
meticulous elaboration of a novel Hegel-inspired theory of subjectivity,
a theory taking into account and consolidating components previously
assembled in the first two parts in dialogue with Kant and Schelling (the
genetic dimension of subject formation discerned in Kant and touched
upon by Schelling is much more richly elaborated by Hegel—transcendental materialism could also be described as a genetic transcendentalism). Herein, the subject is portrayed as a by-product generated by the

coming-into-being of several different forms of temporality—more specifically, temporal structures that are fundamentally incompatible with each other. Full-fledged subjectivity proper is able briefly to flash into existence at those moments when the disharmonious conflicts between these multiple-speed temporal tracks become audible.

The conclusion of this book fulfills a promise made in the second and third paragraphs of this introduction: through bringing European philosophy and Freudian-Lacanian psychoanalysis into conversation with Anglo-American philosophy of mind and cognitive neuroscience, the conclusion seeks to demonstrate the explanatory power and theoretical elegance of transcendental materialism's portrayal of subjectivity. It highlights two key virtues of this new paradigm: how this portrayal of subjectivity allows for a non-reductive account of the subject's relation to its body; and how it enables an affirmation of subjective autonomy that nonetheless acknowledges the degree to which such freedom is also compromised by the individual's position with respect to determining biological, historical, and socio-psychical variables. The book closes with an acknowledgment of the profound indebtedness of this transcendental materialist theory of subjectivity to Žižek's thought, a body of thought forming one of this theory's most essential conditions of possibility.

ŽIŽEK'S ONTOLOGY

In the Beginning Was the Void: Psychoanalytic Metapsychology and the Modern Philosophical Legacy

(Kant–Žižek)

1

Failure Comes First: Negativity and the Subject

Thinkers committed today to an ongoing explication of Kantian philosophy and its German idealist variants tend to see themselves as embattled guardians of the notion of subjectivity defending against a barbarous onslaught of postmodern attacks upon the very idea of any subject whatsoever. A certain antagonistic dehiscence, closely paralleling the fictitious border between nineteenth-century Germany and postwar France, seems to run through large sections of an intellectual domain loosely referred to under the heading of "continental philosophy." Those influenced by Kant and his immediate successors often accuse deconstructionists and their ilk of promoting an incoherent and nihilistic relativism—for which the only true remedy is a return to the modern subject and its accompanying set of Enlightenment principles. The preferred philosophical method of these sorts of scholars in the European tradition is immersion in careful textual/historical exegesis, thus studiously avoiding the temptation to engage in jargonized, *très chic* "fashionable nonsense." On the other hand, representatives of the various "post" movements in contemporary continental theory have accused the heroes of such traditionalists of everything from quasi-fascistic, logocentric "totalitarianism" to phallocratic "colonialism." Although this description of the current theoretical scene is highly selective as well as a gross oversimplification—in addition, of course, the mutual misunderstandings between advocates of these various philosophical stances are rife—a tension between the historically motivated retrieval of modern subjectivity and the recent set of suspicions and criticisms of this same sort of subject is nonetheless a palpable feature of the present intellectual climate.

A perfect example of precisely this conflict is Manfred Frank's critique of Jacques Lacan. In *What Is Neostructuralism?*, Frank engages in a sweeping survey of developments in twentieth-century European philosophy from Husserl up through Derrida. He observes that one of the distinguishing features of this period is the emergence of modes of analysis ostensibly dispensing with subjectivity as a central theoretical point of explanatory reference. The clearest instance of this trend is, obviously, classical structuralism à la Claude Lévi-Strauss, a system of thought aptly described by Paul Ricoeur as "Kantianism without a transcendental sub-ject" (a description that Lévi-Strauss himself endorses).[1] In place of an idealism positing certain subjective factors as necessary possibility condi-tions for the constitution of experiential reality itself, orthodox struc-turalism asserts that a trans-individual, socio-symbolic matrix of repre-sentations, practices, and institutions entirely overdetermines individual cognition and identity. In Lacanese, this would be to say that the subject is nothing more than a puppet of the "big Other," a mere slave of the symbolic order; subjectivity is effectively eclipsed, overshadowed in be-ing reduced to the epiphenomenal residue of, in Hegelian parlance, a purely objective (and objectifying) *Geist.*

According to Frank, Lacan is a "neostructuralist," that is to say, an inheritor of the Lévi-Straussian legacy (more recently, Judith Butler also succumbs to the temptation to read Lacan this way).[2] From Frank's point of view, the Lacanian distinction between the Symbolic *je* (i.e., the subject as subject of the signifier and of the unconscious) and the Imaginary *moi* (i.e., the reflected, specular ego tied to circumscribed conscious aware-ness), like so many other structuralist-inspired theoretical devices, is an inadequate, unsatisfying substitute for the German idealist conception of the self-reflective "I." Frank's position is grounded on the assumptions that reflexivity is an essential feature of subjectivity, and furthermore, that reflexivity is a property solely of the subject and nothing else—if it isn't self-reflexive/reflective, then it isn't a subject, and vice versa. Hence, Frank interprets Lacan's "I" (*je*) as a mere permutation of functions forming part of the trans-subjective symbolic-linguistic network in which the individual is embedded.[3] Given the structural, Symbolic status of the unconscious in classical Lacanian theory ("the unconscious is structured like a language," "desire is the desire of the Other," and so on), the phrase "subject of the unconscious" is, for Frank, a contradiction in terms. A feature of a trans-subjective order can only ever itself be trans-subjective too, rather than being genuinely subjective. Does Lacan's reference to the *moi* (ego), this being the product of the mirror stage as a psychical moment or process involving the effects of reflection, get him any closer to formulating a satisfactory account of subjectivity in Frank's eyes?

Frank contends that the Lacanian theory of the ego brings to the fore a circularity plaguing Lacan's entire discourse on subjectivity, as well as hampering nearly any possible variant on a structuralist or post-structur-alist notion of the subject as a by-product or aftereffect of a non-reflexive structural system consisting solely of a network of differences (this being a leitmotif throughout postwar French thought). The account of the mirror stage is, according to Frank's interpretation of it, an attempt to explain the emergence of a "self," the genesis of the "I." In a moment of specular recognition mediated by the reflective surface of the mirror, the infant suddenly acquires its *moi* as the ground for an enduring, conscious self-identity[4] (one should note, of course, that Lacan attaches a slew of qualifications to this idea, stipulating, for example, that this "recognition" is inherently a "misrecognition" [*méconnaissance*]).[5] For Frank, Lacan is stuck having surreptitiously to presuppose the preexistence of that which he is trying to explain the coming-into-being of—that is to say, a self cannot emerge ex nihilo. Frank's argument is that the "moment of recognition" in the Lacanian myth of the mirror cannot occur unless the individual is already previously acquainted with him or herself as a self. Why does the body image reflected by the mirror strike the child as being something exceptional, as different in kind compared with the array of other objects in his or her visual field? How can a particular fragment of experience be latched onto as representative of a "me" in the absence of a prior sense of "me-ness"? Frank maintains that Lacan simply ignores this circularity as it pertains to the Symbolic *je* as well as the Imaginary *moi:*

> To the realm of the *grand Autre*... Lacan attributes the mystical mode of Being of *s'être*, without either explaining or, what is more, justifying the use of the reflexive pronoun in this formulation. Either the true subject is absolutely irreflexive, in which case it is impossible to see how one can speak of it as though it were a subject at all, or else with the formulation *s'être* it is in fact ascribed a problematic familiarity with itself about which Lacan does not say a word. (Frank 1989, 309–10)

Elaborating on the consequences of this philosophical dilemma for Lacan's theory, Frank categorically states:

> All attempts to derive consciousness from whatever relation between elements, no matter how it is constituted, are philosophically out of the question insofar as they always already presuppose consciousness... one cannot possibly first want to destroy consciousness, only in order to reintroduce it later. The demolition of consciousness can result in many things, but it cannot generate consciousness, just as nothing comes out of nothing. If, however, in a circular manner one already presupposes consciousness, it becomes meaningless to talk about a derivation of this phenomenon. (Frank 1989, 313–14)

Frank tries to force a choice between, on the one hand, a theory of the subject in which both consciousness and reflexive self-consciousness are primitive phenomena incapable of any sort of derivation and, on the other hand, a blanket denial of the existence of such subjectivity. There is either no genetic emergence of a state of selfhood from a state devoid of self, or else there simply is no self at all. After staging this either-or situation, Frank advocates the desirability of the former position (basically, the idealism of the early nineteenth-century German idealists) by pointing to the explanatory shortcomings of the latter position (in his view, a bald rejection of reflective subjectivity simply flies in the face of numerous observable facts of cognitive life). The Lacanian "third way," involving a philosophical radicalization of Freudian psychoanalytic metapsychology (and, contra Frank's forced choice, arguably continuing a line of thought revealing itself in such unlikely sources as Schelling's engagements with Kant),[6] is ruled out by Frank as invalid: a genetic theory of subjectivity is untenable. An obvious bone of contention here is the question of whether or not subjectivity should be entirely identified with the activities of consciousness.

In a footnote to his essay "The Cartesian Subject Versus the Cartesian Theater," Žižek directly responds to Frank's critique of the circularity allegedly operative within Lacan's conception of the mirror stage. He insists that the only way in which this criticism could be plausible is if one totally ignores Lacan's distinction between *moi* and *je:*

> When . . . Manfred Frank . . . argues, against Lacan, that one cannot ground the subject in his identification with his mirror image (according to Frank, such an account "reifies" the subject, reduces him to an object of mirror-identification, and thus simply misses the proper dimension of subjectivity), one can only stare at this line of argumentation: as if Lacan's main point is not the distinction between the *ego* (*moi*), which is explicitly determined by Lacan as an object grounded in mirror-identification, and the *subject* of the signifier. (Žižek 1998c, 271)

At stake in this rebuke of Frank are some of the most essential features of Žižek's general philosophical endeavor. From a genuinely Lacanian perspective, all instances of (self-)recognition, any and every positive moment of identification, are ego-level misrecognitions. In other words, whenever one is dealing with the various determinant empirical-phenomenal contents latched onto as emblematic of selfhood or identity, one is engaged with the organization of the ego (and hence not the subject, given the split Lacan posits between the *moi* and the *je-sujet*).[7] In "Responses to Students of Philosophy Concerning the Object of Psychoanalysis," Lacan cautions his audience to be wary of "the danger of a reduction of the subject to the *ego*" (Lacan 1990b, 109). In the same text, Lacan clarifies that the ego to which the subject mustn't be reduced is "an imaginary identification, or more exactly, an enveloping series of such identifications" (Lacan 1990b, 110). The "enveloping series" evokes the familiar metaphorical image of the onion: the ego is like an onion, taking on its shape by virtue of a series of successive, sedimented layers. But what happens if one keeps peeling away layer after layer? Eventually, instead of reaching some hardened center at the onion's core, one is left with nothing. The removal of the final veiling layer is tantamount to the annihilation of the very object itself. For Frank, as far as subjectivity goes, this isn't the case—a primordial self-acquaintance, an irreducible and immediate ipseity, is an indissoluble kernel subsisting behind the façade of the shifting states of consciousness and mediated identity. For Žižek, on the contrary, the true subject is nothing other than this nothingness itself, this void, absence, or "empty spot" remaining after the innerworldly visages of the ego have been stripped away.

Frank's position directly implies that, in the beginning, the failure of selfhood (as absence of identity or self-acquaintance) is impossible. It absolutely must be there from the start, since it cannot legitimately be derived in the course of subsequent developments. Through a unique philosophical recasting of Lacanian thought, Žižek advances a diametrically opposed thesis as one of the axioms of his own theoretical system: as far as subjectivity is concerned, in the beginning was failure.[8] As Mladen Dolar wittily formulates it, "the subject is precisely the failure to become the subject" (Dolar 1993, 77–78). The *sujet,* as a dynamic negativity standing apart from the standard visual and linguistic mediators of selfhood, is forever incapable of attaining a perfect sense of ipseity vis-à-vis some kind of adequate and satisfactory reflective equivalence. Given a Lacanian conception of subjectivity, any form of self-acquaintance alienates the subject from itself, derailing this emptiness into the fleshed-out fullness of the ego and its embodied avatars. Since both Lacan and Žižek associate the philosophically loaded term *self* with what psychoanalysis calls the ego, self and subject are construed as two opposed poles. Žižek proclaims that the Lacanian matheme $ (for the "barred" or split subject) signifies this primordial failure, this "lost cause" of the search for selfhood. Subjectivity itself is, ultimately, the permanent tension between the phenomenal, experientially constituted ego and the quasi-noumenal, unrepresentable *manque-à-être* (lack of being) in relation to which every determinate identity-construct is a defensive, fantasmatic response: "The split subject . . . can never fully 'become himself,' he can never fully realize himself" (Žižek 1992a, 181). Elsewhere, Žižek clarifies matters as follows: "The intimate link between *subject* and *failure* lies not in the fact that 'external' material social rituals and/or practices forever fail to reach the subject's innermost kernel, to represent it adequately

. . . but, on the contrary, in the fact that the 'subject' itself is *nothing but the failure of symbolization, of its own symbolic representation*" (Žižek 2000b, 119–20). The Žižekian version of the distinction between subjectivity proper (as the permanent rift in $, the original lack, failure, or absence of self-identity) and "subjectification" (as the inherently futile and interminably repeated effort to "suture" $ to a series of privileged object-contents [a])[9] is an expression of the fundamental thesis that, so to speak, the obstacle (the "bone in the throat") to the placid, complacent closure of unsullied self-consciousness is primary. In a paradoxical logic, the impediment generates that in relation to which it is an impediment.

What makes this more than just an issue of classical German idealism versus post-structuralist psychoanalysis is the fact that Žižek, in pursuing the general idea of the subject as simultaneously the cause of and obstacle to egoistic ipseity, makes an interesting move in terms of strategies of historical interpretation. He claims that, prior to Freud and Lacan, Kant and the German idealists (departing from a certain twist on Descartes) are the first thinkers to advance this theme of subjectivity as cleaved into incompatible components, as fractured and self-alienated. He thus problematizes certain assumptions informing the typical sort of rallying cry for a "return to modernity" exemplified by Manfred Frank's attacks against a straw-man caricature of "neostructuralism." Žižek effectively turns the tables here in showing that Lacan brings to their logical conclusions the implications of the idealist philosophical legacy, thereby implying that the self-appointed protectors of Kantian and German idealist philosophy might indeed have misunderstood their favored authority figures to such an extent as to have rendered themselves incapable of recognizing and unleashing the explosive potentials contained within their own tradition.

In Idealism More Than Idealism Itself: The Extimate Material Kernel of Psychical Life

Perhaps the most striking feature of Žižek's fundamental theoretical stance, a feature that sets him apart from the vast majority of other contemporary theorists, is his conviction that supposedly outdated and unfashionably old-fashioned ideas deserve preserving. In fact, Žižek goes so far as to argue not only that a variety of intellectual approaches rooted in modern philosophy (transcendentalism, German idealism, dialectical materialism, etc.) still contain valuable and legitimate insights worth salvaging in the present, but that thinkers such as Descartes, Kant, Schelling, and Hegel are more relevant in current contexts than those who tend to offer themselves as the analysts of an ostensibly postmodern now.[1] Modernity's philosophical revolution, inaugurated with the uncovering of the Cartesian cogito, is, on the Žižekian account, better able to measure the status quo of human being than the plethora of recent efforts to displace, dissolve, or deconstruct subjectivity.

One of the hallmarks of Žižek's work is his revival of the cogito. The opening lines of his 1999 volume *The Ticklish Subject* proclaim (paraphrasing the famous opening of the *Communist Manifesto*): "A spectre is haunting western academia . . . the spectre of the Cartesian subject. All academic powers have entered into a holy alliance to exorcize this spectre" (Žižek 1999b, 1). Similarly, in his introduction to the 1998 collection of essays on *Cogito and the Unconscious*, Žižek praises Lacan for having returned to and retrieved a conception of subjectivity first formulated by Descartes and then radicalized by Kant and the German idealist tradition.[2] Against the predominant tendencies of various wings of today's academy, Žižek employs the modern subject of Descartes in order to combat all attempts to reduce subjectivity to the sum total of its particular, historical attributes stemming from its situated, innerworldly existence (i.e., the subject as inherently sexual, ethnic, cultural, and so on). In fact, a now-classic Žižekian move is to underscore a paradox at the heart of postmodern theories of identity: the more one insists upon subjectivity as a dispersed multitude of shifting and unstable identity-constructs, the more one is confronted with the necessity of positing a universal, empty, and contentless frame, a formal void, as the backdrop against which the "mad dance of identification" takes place. The postmodern struggle to surmount the Cartesian subject of modern philosophy only succeeds, oddly enough, in further highlighting the contours of such subjectivity.[3]

However, one shouldn't be fooled here—Descartes himself isn't, strictly speaking, the real point of departure for Žižek's Lacan-inspired reinsertion of the modern subject back into contemporary debates. In his *Meditations on First Philosophy,* Descartes, after establishing the indubitable existence of the cogito, mentions a still-lingering uncertainty: "But I do not yet understand sufficiently what I am—I, who now necessarily exist" (Descartes 1993, 18). At this juncture, Descartes already has demonstrated the fact that the "I" as thinker necessarily exists each and every time thought occurs (including the thought "I do not exist"). However, the nature of this "I," its positive characteristics, has yet to be determined. Descartes proceeds to stipulate that the cogito must not be equated with any of the contents cognized by it through its own thinking activity: "For I would indeed be simulating were I to 'imagine' that I was something, because imagining is merely the contemplating of the shape or image of a corporeal thing" (Descartes 1993, 20). In other words, the activity of thinking as a verb or process cannot imaginarily be captured or encapsulated, through mental representations, in any of the content-level products of thought (i.e., imagined or perceived phenomena) generated by this same activity.

In his criticisms of the illegitimate hypostatization leading to the standard notion of the Cartesian *res cogitans* as a reified substance, Kant is more Cartesian than Descartes himself. He develops the full implications of Descartes' prohibition of equivocating between the cogito as the active possibility condition for all cognitive states (i.e., Kant's transcendental subject or Lacan's *sujet*) and the self as a set of ideas, images, marks, and signs identified with as the emblems of a "personality" or "soul" (i.e., Kant's empirical, psychological self or Lacan's *moi*).[4] Žižek advances this interpretation when he notes that "the Cartesian subject . . . is 'brought to its notion' with Kant" (Žižek 1998a, 3). And according to Žižek's own narrative of the historical development of the concept of the subject from Descartes through Hegel, the step that Hegel takes is simply to ontologize Kant's epistemological portrait of subjectivity. That is to say, the subject literally "is," in its very being (rather than as a matter of finite, limited thought and the shortcomings of its consciousness of self), nothing other than the void of negativity forever irreducible to any and every instance of determinate, phenomenal actualization.[5] Hegel is hence, on this reading, "more Kantian than Kant himself," thus making Kant the "vanishing mediator" (to put it in language Žižek borrows from Fredric Jameson) between two of the essential figures (Descartes and Hegel) facilitating Žižek's Lacanian appropriation of modern philosophy in the construction of a theory of subjectivity.[6] As Žižek notes, "Hegel rails at Kant more than at any other philosopher . . . Hegel grows furious precisely because Kant was already there, within the speculative principle, yet radically misrecognized the true dimension of his own act, and espoused the worst metaphysical prejudices" (Žižek 1994b, 187).

The Žižekian project obviously could be depicted, in large part, as an effort to raise Lacan to the dignity of the philosophical tradition.[7] Furthermore, despite the apparent favoring of Hegel as Lacan's privileged interlocutor in this tradition, Žižek adamantly insists that "philosophy AS SUCH begins with Kant, with his transcendental turn," and that "the entire previous philosophy can be understood properly . . . only if read 'anachronistically,' from the standpoint opened up by Kant" (Žižek 2001c, 160). Kant's status as a pivotal linchpin in the history of philosophy is a central tenet of Žižek's oeuvre. Not only does he assert that all philosophy since Kant must conduct itself under the shadow of the critical-transcendental turn, but that the prior sequence of various philosophies doesn't become "Philosophy" per se until the advent of the Kantian "Copernican revolution." More specifically, Žižek, at various points in his work, explicitly acknowledges that Kant, instead of Descartes, is the true founder of the notion of the subject as split or divided against itself, a notion later brought to fruition by Lacan via his "barred S."[8] He clearly intends to align, as precisely parallel, Kant's distinction between noumenal and phenomenal subjectivity (i.e., the distinction between the "I" as an unknowable *an sich* kernel and the "I" as it appears to itself vis-à-vis various series of appearances and their qualities) and Lacan's separation of the *sujet* from the *moi*. What's more, in numerous places, Žižek argues that Lacan is deeply Kantian: Lacan, in contrast to his theoretical contemporaries, pursues a transcendental project involving a "critique of pure desire";[9] both the Kantian and Lacanian subjects are "empty," incapable of being collapsed back into the determinate empirical-phenomenal contents fleshing out this $ as a monstrous, faceless void;[10] the Lacanian distinction between the subjects of enunciation and utterance is ultimately a Kantian one;[11] Lacan's subject of the unconscious is nothing other than what Kant designates as the necessary failure of introspective reflection to establish any kind of stable, qualitative self-identity[12] . . . and so on. Similarly, when summarizing his own agenda apropos a philosophical theory of subjectivity, Žižek is quite clear about his intentions to redeploy the Kantian legacy:

> My work relies on the full acceptance of the notion of modern subjec-
> tivity elaborated by the great German Idealists from Kant to Hegel: for
> me, this tradition forms the unsurpassable horizon of our philosophical
> experience, and the core of my entire work is the endeavor to use Lacan
> as a privileged intellectual tool to reactualize German Idealism. (Žižek
> 1999c, ix)

Of course, this isn't to say that the "reactualization" of late-modern German philosophy effectuated via Lacanian psychoanalytic metapsychology
leaves the former in a pure, unaltered state after being passed through
the lens of the latter (nor the latter, for that matter, unchanged either).
As with any theoretically sophisticated and worthwhile combination of
seemingly disparate orientations, Žižek's orchestration of the confrontation of Kant *avec* Lacan is an encounter that transforms both sides involved. Despite placing a great deal of emphasis on the many surprising
similarities between Kant and Lacan, Žižek is nonetheless careful to take
stock of the important differences distinguishing these two thinkers. For
example, whereas Kant's transcendental idealism focuses on the category of the "subjectively objective" (i.e., the objectivity of external reality
as constituted through the synthesizing activities of the epistemological subject), Lacan's psychoanalytic concerns necessitate addressing the
obverse correlate of this category, namely, the "objectively subjective"[13]
(i.e., the core formations of the unconscious, particularly fantasies, as "in
the subject more than the subject itself" along the lines of the Lacanian
notion of the "extimate" as intimate-yet-alien structures inhabiting the
"inner space" of the psyche itself).[14]
    Žižek credits Kant with two significant theoretical contributions: one,
as already noted, Kant is the first to depict the subject as irreducibly split,
as rent by a constitutive, irresolvable antagonism in terms of its very structure; and two, Kant makes the notion of finitude absolutely foundational
in philosophical thought, placing it at the center of his account of the "I"
in all its various dimensions. Žižek's heterodox, psychoanalytic rereading
of Kant—nobody could plausibly argue that Žižek is simply a Kantian in
Lacanian clothing—is grounded upon the way in which he isolates distinct
senses of finitude within Kant's transcendental apparatus and its portrayal
of subjectivity. The most familiar type of finitude in Kantian thought is the
epistemological sort (as articulated primarily in the *Critique of Pure Reason*): due to the "limits of possible experience," all attainable knowledge
is necessarily and irremediably incomplete, since the presumed domain
of noumenal fullness beyond the scope of phenomenal awareness and
conscious cognizance forever withdraws itself from the subject's reflective
grasp. Kantian transcendental-epistemological finitude amounts to the

philosophical acceptance that knowledge is condemned to be (in Lacanian parlance) "not all," to be lacking and less than total (or as Lacan would put it, the big Other of the symbolic order is always barred). Žižek portrays Kantian subjectivity, in terms of its epistemological aspects, as endlessly chasing after an exhaustively complete system of knowledge (a futile quest Kant claims is uncompromisingly dictated by "the interest of reason"[15]) that interminably eludes the subject, always remaining beyond its reach as an inaccessible yet alluring vanishing point.[16] (Moreover, in this way, the subject of Kant's first *Critique* is governed, in its knowledge-assembling activities, by the dynamics of "desire" in the strict Lacanian sense.) From this, Žižek slides to the assertion that, apropos Kantian subjectivity, "what looks like an *epistemological limitation* of our capacity to grasp reality (the fact that we are forever perceiving reality from our finite temporal standpoint) is the positive *ontological condition* of reality itself" (Žižek 1999b, 158). On the Žižekian interpretation, Kant's theme of the finite subject isn't confined simply to the insubstantial, ephemeral sphere of an epistemology deprived of any ontological weight. He maintains that "the kernel of Kant's philosophical revolution" resides "in conceiving finitude as ontologically constitutive" (Žižek 2002a, 217). Furthermore, at this exact same textual point, Žižek admits that his version of Hegel is one in which Hegelian "absolute knowing"—a telltale sign of crude bastardizations of Hegel is when "absolute knowing" is erroneously referred to as "absolute knowledge"[17]—is nothing other than an ontologization of Kant's insight into the fundamental incompleteness of reality itself.[18] Generally speaking, Žižek's Hegel is an ontologized Kant, an ontologization essentially involving the acceptance of the "not all" of finite incompleteness as more than just an epistemological limitation.[19] The recurrent Žižekian motif of the subject as a "crack" in the very foundations of the ontological edifice (an insight first glimpsed by Descartes and unreservedly affirmed by Hegel) is indeed derived from the Kantian transcendental turn.[20] Thus, in this light, Kant's critical philosophy arguably entails an ontological sense of finitude as well as an epistemological one.

However, orthodox Kantian eyebrows will no doubt be raised in reaction to these sorts of assertions. How can one allege that, as far as Kant's philosophy is concerned, a link exists between epistemological-transcendental and ontological-material finitude? Isn't the entire point of the Kantian critical gesture to separate epistemology from ontology, to deny the former any positing power at the level of the latter (i.e., to prohibit "hypostatization" as the illegitimate constitutive employment of regulative/rational ideas)? More specifically, doesn't Kant's radicalization of the Cartesian cogito, in which Kant de-ontologizes Descartes' *res cogitans* in maintaining that the activity of the thinking "I" must not be substantialized as any sort of "*res*,"[21] move in precisely the opposite direction that Žižek wants to take it? These questions, and the answers that they call for, reveal the underlying philosophical agenda animating and tying together seemingly unrelated trajectories of the rapidly expanding Žižekian corpus: Žižek's work doggedly pursues the holy grail of a transcendental materialist theory of subjectivity. And although sometimes accused of being monotonously repetitive despite superficial variations of content—for instance, Terry Eagleton remarks that "the almost comic versatility of his interests masks a compulsive repetition of the same" (Eagleton 2001, 40) and that "the mercurial sparkle of his work is at odds with its bleak, mechanically recurrent content" (Eagleton 2001, 49)—this pursuit of a transcendental materialist theory of subjectivity exhibits a shifting, evolving dynamic (from a transcendentalist slant in the early writings to a dialectical materialist position advocated in more recent texts, including many variations and transitional developments in between). So, with the Žižekian Kant-Lacan hybrid as a point of departure, discovering and delineating the rapport (or perhaps non-rapport) between the epistemological and ontological facets of subjectivity, between the finite subject as defined on the basis of the limits of its possible (self-)knowledge and this same subject as defined on the basis of the limits imposed upon it by (its) material being, would represent a decisive step forward on the way toward formulating such a transcendental materialism.

Many of Žižek's engagements with post-Kantian figures evince this particular philosophical ambition. For instance, one could go so far as to contend that his writings devoted to Schelling, *The Indivisible Remainder* (1996) and "The Abyss of Freedom" (1997), mediate between his early proclamation that Lacan should be understood as a transcendental philosopher and his recent rejection of this early stance in favor of more historicist and materialist modes of analysis.[22] (A central feature of Schelling's work is his struggle to reconcile, among other things, transcendentalism and materialism.)[23] On several occasions, Žižek refers to Fichte's concept of the *Anstoss,* a term usually translated into English as "check." However, *Anstoss* conveys the double sense of both an "obstacle" or "hindrance" as well as an "impulse," "impetus," or "stimulus."[24] In a 1996 interview, when asked whether a book on Fichte might follow his then just-released study of Schelling, he replies with a "maybe."[25] Although he has yet to produce such a text, Žižek's brief, passing invocations of Fichte are revelatory as far as his own theoretical project is concerned.

A refrain repeated throughout the post-Kantian philosophical milieu

stems from F. H. Jacobi's famous remark to the effect that, without pre-
suming the existence of the thing-in-itself, one cannot enter into the
enclosure of the first *Critique,* but that, through this same presupposition
of the thing-in-itself, one always already violates the strict epistemological boundaries/limits of Kant's philosophy.[26] The *Ding an sich* evidently
involves a paradox, an unsustainable contradiction. So Fichte jettisons
the thing-in-itself in his development of transcendental philosophy, pre-
ferring an extreme form of idealism in which everything is grounded
upon the activities of an "absolute I." However, it should be noted that
this idealism isn't as extreme as it might appear at first glance.[27] Fichte
plausibly can be understood as making the more modest claim that the
foundational distinction between the "I" of subjectivity and the "not-I" of
objective/external reality is instituted exclusively by the "act" (*Tathand-
lung*) of the subject "positing" itself, thereby revealing the "not-I" to be
dependent upon the "I." Not only, as per Kant, does the subject shape all
of reality by being the unavoidable condition of possibility for the very
cognition of reality itself—but, as per Fichte, the distinction between
the "I" as agent of knowledge and the alterity of reality as what this agent
knows is instituted solely with the advent of this agent itself.[28] (Hegel
later captures the essence of this Fichtean position by insisting that the
distinction between thought and its objects is a distinction internal to
thought itself.)

Despite his adherence to a robust idealism in which the "I" is the
foundation of reality itself, Fichte nonetheless wishes to avoid falling
into an untenable solipsism—it is quite tempting to charge him with
being a die-hard solipsist—and the *Anstoss* crystallizes the attempt to advance a radical idealism without utterly eliminating the tension between
subjectivity and "something other." The transcendental idealist "I," in
the course of its various activities (both theoretical and practical), encounters impediments to its epistemological and volitional endeavors.
The "I" strives infinitely to assert itself as the Absolute, but it continually
bumps up against obstacles thwarting this ambition, throwing it back
upon itself as finite and limited.[29] Without the activity of the "I," such
checks wouldn't appear as such. The *Anstoss,* although opposed to the
subject, is still, given its strictly negative sense for Fichte, conditioned by
the active "I" and couldn't be said to have any distinct existence without
it.[30] And yet, while the *Anstoss* is only ever encountered and conceptu-
ally/discursively grasped through the mediation of subjective ideality,
it nonetheless marks, via its negations of and resistances to the ideal
subject's multiple efforts to posit itself as "All," those points at which the
solipsistic self-enclosure of transcendental idealist subjectivity collides
with an utterly asubjective Real.[31] Hence, Fichte is able simultaneously to

advance two seemingly contradictory theses: on the one hand, the self-positing "I" of idealist subjectivity is asserted to be the first principle, the axiomatic ground zero, of any viable philosophical system (this being Fichte's idealism); on the other hand, despite the fact that this "I" conditions everything "not-I" (and that this "not-I," as "not-I," is brought into existence in and through the being of the "I"), the negative alterity of the *Anstoss* with respect to subjectivity is indicative of a mysterious X subsisting apart from the subject[32] (this being what might be called Fichte's "materialism"). Žižek expresses this strange juxtaposition of standpoints as follows:

> The paradox of *Anstoss* resides in the fact that it is simultaneously "purely subjective" *and* not produced by the activity of the I. If *Anstoss* were not "purely subjective," if it were already the non-I, part of objectivity, we would fall back into "dogmatism," that is, *Anstoss* would effectively amount to no more than a shadowy remainder of the Kantian *Ding an sich* and would thus bear witness to Fichte's inconsequentiality (the commonplace reproach to Fichte); if *Anstoss* were simply subjective, it would present a case of the hollow playing of the subject with itself, and we would never reach the level of objective reality; that is, Fichte would be effectively a solipsist (another commonplace reproach to his philosophy). (Žižek 1997a, 45)

In his first book in English, *The Sublime Object of Ideology* (1989), Žižek deploys a distinction apropos the Lacanian register of the Real that perfectly mirrors the tension between solipsistic idealism and dogmatic materialism/realism involved in the notion of the *Anstoss*: the Real as "posed" (i.e., the Real is immanently produced, as an internally generated chimera, in and by the Symbolic) versus the Real as "presupposed" (i.e., the Real is wholly and completely external, as an anterior ground, in relation to the Symbolic).[33] Later, in *Tarrying with the Negative* (1993), he remarks that "a certain fundamental ambiguity pertains to the notion of the Real in Lacan: the Real designates a substantial hard kernel that precedes and resists symbolization and, simultaneously, it designates the left-over, which is posited or 'produced' by symbolization itself" (Žižek 1993, 36). Due to his cursory condemnation of Fichte as nothing more than the worst sort of solipsistic idealist à la Berkeley,[34] Lacan fails to utilize the resources of Fichtean philosophy in his own circumnavigations around the Real.

Fichtean materialism—Žižek hints that such a thing indeed exists—formulates itself vis-à-vis the deadlocks internal to radical transcendental idealism. On this account, materialism is philosophically tenable solely as the spectral inverse of idealism, accompanying it as the shadow cast by idealism's insurmountable incompleteness. In Lacanian terms, the Symbolic (as the incomplete "barred Other") is, at one and the same time, both the condition of possibility and the condition of impossibility for the subject's access to the Real. The Real-as-presupposed cannot be grasped or seized except through the mediation of Symbolic representation and its impasses, whereby the, so to speak, smudging fingerprints of the Symbolic always already transform the Real-as-presupposed into the Real-as-posed. The Symbolic unavoidably colors the Real in the very process of granting access to it, rendering it practically impossible to detach the "presupposed" part from the "posed" part. Hence, Žižek identifies Fichte's *Anstoss* with Lacan's *objet petit a,* since the latter stands for the loci at which the Real inheres within (and yet ceaselessly eludes) the representational matrix sustained by the Imaginary and the Symbolic. Furthermore, as Žižek also maintains, the Symbolic is, in a way, a response to or reaction against the Real, an attempted solution or answer to some sort of fundamental antagonism within the Real. Although the Symbolic arises from the Real, access to the Real is forever after hindered by that which it generated out of itself (again, Žižek relies heavily upon the later Schelling, especially the 1809 *Freiheitschrift* and the 1811–15 *Welt-alter* manuscripts, in explicating this relation between the Real and the Symbolic).[35]

The same structure that Žižek highlights as characteristic of the Kantian transcendental subject is discernible in Fichte's system. The only thing absolute about the Kantian-Fichtean subject is a striving to be absolute. The only thing infinite about this subject is an interminable pursuit of the infinite (propelled along toward an illusory epistemological completeness by the interest of reason [Kant] or compulsively driven by the catalytic inhibition of the *Anstoss* [Fichte]). Nothing can be intellectually or experientially encountered without the mediation of this transcendental subjectivity; and yet, at one and the same time, the concession is made that this subjectivity is finite, limited, and "not all." The unmediated is always known in a mediate fashion. That is to say, the subject confronts the asubjective in and through itself, within itself as the obscure but powerful feeling of an entirely alien limitation irreducible to the transparency of reflective self-consciousness. Žižek observes that the Lacanian notion of extimacy, as an intimate externality (i.e., an asubjective exteriority lying within the enclosed interiority of subjectivity), perfectly captures this situation: "*Anstoss* does not come from outside, it is *stricto sensu ex-timate:* a nonassimilable foreign body in the very kernel of the subject" (Žižek 1997a, 45). A particular Žižekian definition of materialism (one definition among several others) entails the somewhat counterintuitive consequence that Fichte, in terms of the conflict-laden relation between the idealist "I" and its own internally encountered check(s), is, contrary to familiar appearances, an authentic materialist: "True *materialism* does not consist in the simple operation of reducing inner psychic experience to an effect of the processes taking place in 'external reality'—what one should do, in addition, is to isolate a 'material' traumatic kernel/remainder at the very heart of 'psychic life' itself" (Žižek 2000b, 118). Given Žižek's combination of Kant and German idealism with Freudian-Lacanian psychoanalysis, what specific sort of "materiality" does he have in mind as constituting the inner core of subjectivity? What is the nature of the "hard kernel" subsisting within the structure of the seemingly immaterial subject, whether this is Kant's transcendental subject or Lacan's subject of the signifier? Does Žižek content himself, like Fichte, with leaving this notion in a quite abstract state, as an entirely indeterminate, enigmatic *je ne sais quoi* provoking yet defying any sort of conceptual concretization? These queries are best answered by returning to a focus upon Žižek's Lacan-influenced appropriation of Kant.

I or He or It, the Thing . . . That Dies: Death and the Euthanasia of Reason

As early as *The Sublime Object of Ideology,* Žižek employs the language of psychoanalytic psychopathology in "diagnosing" the shortcomings of the Kantian critical-transcendental framework. He repeatedly refers to Kant's thought as exhibiting features identical to patterns displayed by obsessional neurosis: "What is at stake in Kant's 'obsessional' economy is precisely the avoidance of the traumatic encounter of the Truth . . . it announces a desire to elude, at any price, an encounter with the Truth" (Žižek 1989, 190). Elsewhere, he states that "Kant, like a good compulsive neurotic . . . sets up the network of the conditions of possible experience in order to make sure that the actual experience of the real, the encounter with the Thing, will never take place, so that everything the subject will effectively encounter will be the already gentrified-domesticated reality of representations" (Žižek 1996b, 75). But what is this horrible, terrifying "Truth" that so frightens Kant as to push him into designing an incredibly sophisticated philosophical system as an elaborate defense mechanism for warding off a confrontation with it? What is the "traumatic encounter" that Kant allegedly struggles with all his intellectual might to avoid? According to Žižek, the noumenal-phenomenal distinction "conceals a foreboding that perhaps this Thing is itself nothing but a lack, an empty place" (Žižek 1989, 193). Along these same lines, Žižek speaks of "the monstrous noumenal Thing," an abyss or vacuum threatening to swallow up the subject that fails to maintain an appropriate degree of distance from it.[1]

In fact, this sort of descriptive language is regularly employed with regard to the theme of subjectivity as negativity: Žižek depicts Descartes' cogito as a "monster,"[2] and he repeatedly cites the young Hegel's macabre image of the subject as a dark and ominous night in which the body appears in a state of gruesome, butchered fragmentation.[3] Additionally, it should be observed, in the paragraph of the preface to the *Phenomenology of Spirit* from which Žižek extracts the phrase "tarrying with the negative," that Hegel associates this negativity with death, with "devastation" and "utter dismemberment."[4] Could this Hegelian connotation of negativity hold the key to illuminating Žižek's otherwise strange and perplexing characterizations of the Cartesian-Kantian subject (and by implication, the Lacanian $) as a horribly monstrous, spectral "creature from the abyss," as a traumatic lack or terrifying emptiness, the "thing from inner space"?[5] Could it be that the void skirted around by Kant is rendered disturbing by virtue of being, behind the concealing layers of philosophical-epistemological abstraction—Kant doesn't speak of the unimaginable subject-in-itself as anything more tangible than an ineffable, unknowable noumenon—an emblem or avatar of ontological finitude (specifically as the mortality inextricably intertwined with the individual's corporeal condition)? Is this the hidden link between epistemological and ontological finitude testified to by what Žižek psychoanalytically identifies as Kant's "obsessional neurotic" desperation to, as it were, avoid the void? Is this awful nothingness somehow related to the absence of annihilation? Speaking of the Hegelian "night of the world," Žižek claims that death itself stands for this "self-withdrawal, the absolute contraction of subjectivity, the severing of its links with 'reality'" (Žižek 1999b, 154). What if the inverse is (also) true? What if the negativity of Cartesian-Kantian-Hegelian subjectivity (as the monstrous cogito, the horrible void of the Thing, and the terrifying abyss of nocturnal dismemberment) is a symptomatic ideality-as-idealization derived from and conditioned by a contingent yet a priori material foundation (what, in psychoanalysis, would be designated as a violent "reaction-formation")?[6] Is the subject-as-negativity a response to its corporeal *Grund* (ground), to a primordially chaotic and discordant Real that produces its own negation immanently out of itself? Are Žižek's otherwise inexplicably odd choices of adjectives here indicative of such a link, of a thinly concealed umbilical cord tethering the (pseudo)immateriality of the modern subject to a dark base rendered obscure through a forceful disavowal/abjection?

Before attempting to answer these pressing questions, a few relevant observations ought to be put forward here. In his crucial metapsychological paper "On Narcissism: An Introduction" (1914), Freud draws a distinction between "ego-libido" (i.e., narcissistically invested libido) and "object-libido" (i.e., anaclitically invested libido), these two forms of libidinal cathexis being related to each other in a zero-sum balance.[7] According to Freud, the underlying barrier blocking the movement from ego-libido to object-libido, from narcissistic to anaclitic investment—neurotics are reluctant to surrender a quota of ego-libido to an extraneous love-object, whereas psychotics have withdrawn all of their libido from the reality of the external world and deposited it within themselves—is directly related to human beings' embodied condition. (Žižek likewise describes perversion, the avoidance of reproductively oriented heterosexual genital intercourse, as being a defense against "the Real of human finitude" à la the couple of death and sexuality.[8]) More specifically, what the individual is averse to in anaclitic sexual relations is the vague intimation of his or her finitude, of the mortality inherent in the condition of embodiment itself. As Lacan remarks, "The link between sex and death, sex and the death of the individual, is fundamental" (*SXI* 150). The individual rebels against being reduced to a mere "link in the chain," against being, as Freud (following August Weismann) puts it, a "mortal vehicle of a (possibly) immortal substance" (*SE* 14:78). (Contemporary biology continues to support the assertion of this connection between sexuality and death—rather than appearing simultaneously with the advent of life, the mortal individual organism doesn't come into being until the evolutionary advent of sexual reproduction.)[9]

Lacan furthers this Freudian line of thought through his portrayal of the libido in the myth of the lamella (a myth Žižek cites repeatedly). Sexuality is depicted as a frightening monster-parasite that aggressively grafts itself onto the being of the individual and drives him or her toward death.[10] In the same seminar in which the lamella is invoked (the eleventh seminar), Lacan also sketches a logic of two intersecting lacks, a Real lack (introduced by the fact of sexual reproduction) and a Symbolic lack (introduced by the subject's alienation via its mediated status within the defiles of the signifying big Other). The Real lack is nothing other than the individual's "loss" of immortality due to its sexual-material nature as a living being subjected to the cycles of generation and corruption, albeit as a loss of something never possessed except in primary narcissism and/or unconscious fantasy. Symbolic lack serves, in a way, as a defensive displacement of this more foundational lack in the Real.[11] Not only are psychoanalytic psychopathologies painful struggles with both of these lacks, but "it is this double lack that determines the ever-insistent gap between the real and the symbolico-imaginary, and thus the constitution of the subject" (Verhaeghe 2000, 147). One possible manifestation of the neurotic rebellion against this fundamental feature of the corporeal condition is a strong feeling of disgust in the face of all things fleshly, of everything whose palpable attraction and tangible yet fleeting beauty smacks of a transience evoking the inexorable inevitability of death (an attitude that Freud comments on in his short 1916 piece "On Transience").[12]

How can one not be struck by Žižek's recurrent expressions of just this sort of nausea? He confesses that "I always felt a deep sympathy for Monty Python, whose excessive humor also signals an underlying stance of profound disgust with life" (Žižek 1999c, viii). Time and again, in text after text, Žižek finds occasions for dwelling upon these powerful feelings of deep-seated revulsion, feelings that sustain an aesthetic omnipresent in his oeuvre: the Real (the Lacanian register with which Žižek is overwhelmingly concerned) is associated with an obscene mass of raw, palpitating slime.[13] Behind the calm, banal façade of reality (as the soothing, smoothing layers of idealizing Imaginary-Symbolic coating placed over a disturbing, unsettling materiality) lies "the horror of the Real" as "putrefied flesh," as "the disgusting substance of life"[14] and the "ugliness" of *jouissance*.[15] Human existence is tolerable only if a "proper distance," a "disidentification," is established by the subject in relation to this fleshly Real, a holding of the body at arm's length necessary for subjectivity to maintain itself as such.[16] Pursuing (sexual) pleasure too far must result, through a Hegelian/Moebius-like twisting around into the opposite, in anguished disgust, in pleasure becoming deeply unpleasurable through an excessive proximity to the object whose desirability is sustained solely at a safe distance.[17]

If Žižek is correct that Kant is, in a certain sense, an obsessional neurotic compulsively forestalling a confrontation with a *Ding an sich*, with a "Thing" that might very well be intimately related to the subject's ownmost mortality as the concrete expression of its embodied ontological finitude, then one could all too easily make the cliché remark that "it takes one to know one." In many instances, Žižek performs the very "pathologies" he diagnoses in others, effectively mirroring the explicit as well as implicit conceptual structures discerned in whatever material is at stake. In the present case under consideration, his ability to detect the traces of an "obsessional" dynamic (a dynamic so subtle as to be almost imperceptible, yet writ large once one "looks awry" in the appropriate fashion) at work within the very surface organization of Kant's incredibly abstract and ornate philosophical apparatus is perhaps tied to his awareness of this obsessional tendency in his own theoretical productions. However, isn't this strategy of reading Žižek's engagement with Kant (and with the modern philosophical vision of subjectivity in general) in danger of quickly degenerating into vulgar psychobiographical speculation, into, for instance, a crude ad hominem thesis that Žižek is driven to embrace this particular conception of the negativity of the subject by obsessional neurotic difficulties with fleshly finitude? Nothing of this sort is involved here.

The prominence, in Žižek's rhetoric, of a morbid fascination with the mortal Real-made-flesh is indicative of something more than just a personal, idiosyncratic fixation. Instead, this motif is directly revelatory at the impersonal, philosophical level. The family of affects, a set that includes disgust, horror, and revulsion, so frequently spoken of by Žižek (and which he imputes to, among others, Kant) is an index of the effective existence of subjectivity proper. One of Lacan's central claims, in his tenth seminar on anxiety (1962–63), is that "anxiety is not without its object"—and this contrary to the standard Freudian/Heideggerian distinction between fear and anxiety, according to which the latter lacks a definite point of referential attachment while the former is directly linked with some manner of determinate content.[18] A similar claim apropos subjectivity merits advancement: horrified revulsion is not without its subject. That is to say, if psychoanalysis is indeed correct to maintain that the subject ontogenetically emerges through and comes to constitute itself by a sort of radical, primordial gesture of negating rejection (whether as Freud's primal/primary repression as original *Verwerfung* or *Verneinung*, Lacan's "cut" of symbolic castration, or Julia Kristeva's abjection[19]), then feelings of revulsion toward the corporeal substratum of the mortal body essentially are indicative of the presence of a form of subjectivity resistant to being collapsed back into its material foundation.

But how does Kant fit into all of this? In his *Anthropology from a Pragmatic Point of View*, Kant observes, in the opening section "On the Cognitive Faculty," that the cognizing subject cannot actively cancel out or negate its own existence as subject. In other words, statements like "I am not" or "I do not exist" are manifest contradictions (here Kant merely spells out a further consequence of Descartes' central insight that the "I" as *res cogitans* is incapable of casting its own being into doubt at the moment in which it engages in the activity of doubting). And Kant mentions this impossibility while discussing the topic of death (a discussion later echoed by both Freud and Heidegger[20]). Identifying "life" as the necessary precondition for experience itself—this indication is not without its internally subversive significance for the critical-transcendental framework—he explains that:

> nobody can experience his own death (since it requires life in order to experience); he can only observe it in others. Whether death is painful cannot be judged from the rattling in the throat or the convulsions of the dying person, this seems rather to be a mere mechanical reaction of the vital power, and perhaps it is a gentle sensation of the gradual release from all suffering. The natural fear of death, entertained even by the most unhappy, or the most wise, is therefore not a fear of dying, but rather . . . a fear of having died (that is, of being dead). This is a thought the victim of death expects to entertain after dying, because he thinks of his corpse as himself, though it no longer is, and he thinks of it as lying in a dismal grave, or somewhere else. This deception cannot be removed because it is inherent in the nature of thinking as a way of speaking to oneself and of oneself. The thought, I am not, cannot exist at all; because if I am not, then it cannot occur to me that I am not. I may indeed

say that I am not well, and so forth, and negate similar predicates of
myself (as happens with all *verba*); but to negate the subject itself when
speaking in the first person (thereby destroying itself) is a contradiction.
(Kant 1978, 55–56)

As is common knowledge, the term *experience* has, for Kant, a precise
technical meaning, a meaning already operative in the pre-critical *Anthropology* (particularly in the section of the first book entitled "On Sen-
sibility in Contrast to the Understanding").[21] Experience is composed
of two "roots," namely, the passive, receptive faculty of perceiving (i.e.,
"intuition") and the active, organizing faculty of conceiving (i.e., "understanding").[22] Thus, the impossibility of experiencing one's own death
immediately can be rendered with greater specificity. In the preceding
passage, Kant is a little careless when he asserts that the thought of negating the presence of the first-person thinker "cannot exist at all." Rather,
although a speaker, for example, can proclaim that "I am not"—this can
be expressed as an articulated judgment, as a discursive statement—this
enunciation is incapable of taking on the slightest degree of experiential
sense, since no sensible intuition could ever furnish the enunciator with
a concrete, perceptual correlate of this peculiar idea. In short, in terms
of perceptual experience, nothing leads the cognizing subject to believe
in the possibility of its own nonexistence, of the removal of the seemingly
indelible stain of its own self-presence through the annihilating cancellation of its "being-in-the-world." Thus, one could conclude, subjectivity is
compelled, at the level of intuition, to (unconsciously) assert: "I am immortal" (or "I am non-mortal"). As Freud states, "in the unconscious every one of us is convinced of his own immortality" (*SE* 14:289). Similarly,
Žižek refers to the young Schelling's "Philosophical Letters on Dogmatism and Criticism" (1795), wherein Schelling emphasizes the irreducibility of the subject's *Dasein* as prohibiting its direct relation to its own
absence: "We can never get rid of our selves" (Schelling 1980, 181–82).

And yet, of course, human individuals are all too aware, in a very conscious manner, of their own mortality, of the fact that they could die at
any moment and that death is an unavoidable inevitability. Concerning
"Freud's notion that the unconscious knows of no death," Žižek asks,
"what if, at its most radical, 'consciousness' *is* the awareness of one's
finitude and mortality?" (Žižek 2000c, 256). If experience, as grounded
in intuition, fails to provide any credible evidence for the possibility of
the nonexistence of the "I"—although the Kantian faculty of intuition
might typically be viewed as being a predominantly conscious function,
in terms of mortal finitude, its implications remain somewhere below the
threshold of explicit cognitive thematization—the subject is left in the

position of entertaining an "intellectual acceptance of the repressed," of "I know full well that I am mortal, but nonetheless . . ."[23] Both Freud and Lacan directly address this phenomenon with reference to the elementary, stereotypical textbook syllogism: "All men are mortal. Socrates is a man. Therefore, Socrates is mortal." Speaking of this syllogism's major/universal premise, Freud observes that "no human being really grasps it" (*SE* 17:242). Lacan mentions this syllogism several times.[24] Žižek likewise asserts that psychoanalysis has an important qualification to add regarding "the most notorious case of universal judgment: 'All men are mortal' ":

> In its implicit libidinal-symbolic economy, such a judgment always excludes *me*—that is, the absolute singularity of the speaker *qua* subject of enunciation. It is easy to ascertain, from the observer's safe distance, that "everybody" is mortal; however, this very statement involves the exception of its subject of enunciation—as Lacan puts it, in the unconscious, nobody truly believes that *he* is mortal; this knowledge is disavowed, we are dealing with a fetishistic splitting: "I know very well that I am mortal, but still . . ." (Žižek 1994b, 164)

From a Lacanian perspective, the universal claim "All men are mortal" is akin to the proposition grounding masculine-phallic sexuation, namely, "All masculine subjects are 'castrated.' " For Lacan, the sexuated position of the masculine subject, as illuminated by Freud's myth of the primal horde in *Totem and Taboo,* is structured by both the universal "law of castration" ($\forall x \phi x$) governing "phallic *jouissance*" as well as the posited exception to this law, that is, the uncastrated "primal father" ($\exists x \neg \phi x$).[25] Interestingly enough, Freud, in *Inhibitions, Symptoms and Anxiety,* contends that the fear of death, due to its inability to take on an experiential referent, is ultimately derived, ontogenetically, from the fear of castration; for him, castration and mortality are tightly tangled together in the psyche.[26] Along related lines regarding the absence of *Vorstellungen* for material-temporal finitude, Lacan often identifies death as something Real:[27] death is the "quintessential unnameable";[28] the signifiers of the symbolic order have nothing to say about sexual reproduction and individual mortal finitude, silently leaving the subject in ignorance about these most pressing of concerns;[29] although language enables making reference to it, death remains essentially unrepresentable and unknowable;[30] death is an unthinkable impossibility[31] . . . and so on. Like Freud, Lacan contends that the phallus at stake in castration proper functions as a substitutive stand-in for a death with which one cannot have the slightest experiential acquaintance.[32]

So in what does the similarity of these two universals ("All men are mortal" and "All men are castrated") reside? "All men are mortal" is, for the subject condemned to first-person consciousness (Lacan also mentions this condemnation to the prison-house of conscious cognition[33]), a universal ($\forall x \phi x$) with a correlative exception ($\exists x \neg \phi x$), an internal exclusion puncturing the encompassing "All." This hole in the universal is the "I" as constitutively incapable of subsuming itself, except indirectly, under the jurisdiction of the mandatory law of "*le maître absolu.*" As Lacan puts it in "*L'étourdit,*" the subject's very existence itself, its ineliminable *Dasein,* is a "denial" of the universal proposition concerning human mortality, its universality suspended in remaining, for one exceptional case, an infinitely deferred possibility completely lacking the convincing heft of actuality.[34] In reality, all subjects are "symbolically castrated," deprived of access to a mythical "absolute enjoyment" beyond the Law; and yet, in fantasy, there always exists "the One" who is the exception to this rule, who enjoys an unfettered, immediate relation with the "Real Thing" of full, undiluted *jouissance.* Likewise, in reality, all individual human beings are mortal creatures, each destined to die in an indefinite future *à venir*; and yet, in fantasy, in an unconscious that is ignorant of both negation and time[35] (and hence of death, too), there always exists "the One" who is immortal, magically exempt from the cycles of generation and corruption. Further justification for drawing a connection between "All men are mortal" and "All men are castrated" is easily found in Lacan's teachings. Not only does the matrix of the big Other of the symbolic order generate and sustain a permanent non-rapport between living beings "sexuated" on the basis of its terms, but—Lacan himself hints at this link—the negativity of language (à la its ability to incarnate non-being through, for example, the future tense) also simultaneously introduces the *parlêtre* to its own mortality.[36]

Lacan notes that the sole means by which the individual grasps the intuitively unverifiable fact of his or her mortality is through the indirect mediation of the signifiers of the symbolic order.[37] Put differently, one's ownmost mortal finitude is, in Kant's terms, a regulative idea of pure reason devoid of constitutive sense. In "Sex and the Euthanasia of Reason," an essay which Žižek cites several times, Joan Copjec advances the thesis that the various antinomies delineated by Kant in his critical writings depict the antagonistic structure of sexuation as later delineated by Lacan in his twentieth seminar. Despite the absence of explicit references to such matters as sexuality or gender identity in Kant's critical writings, Copjec maintains that Kant initiates a groundbreaking exploration, albeit in a subliminatorily displaced way, into the "logic of sexuation," the deadlock of sexed being.[38] Especially as regards the first of Kant's four antino-

mies of pure reason from the *Critique of Pure Reason*, couldn't the same
move be made here apropos the topic of the individual's ontological-
material finitude? Shouldn't Copjec's essay be complemented by a piece
whose appropriate title would be "Death and the Euthanasia of Reason?"

In the first antinomy of pure reason (as a contradiction plaguing the
"cosmological idea"), reason, proceeding on the basis of the understanding's concepts of cause and effect, posits that the universe (as the "All"
of reality that Kant calls "the world") has a determinate spatiotemporal
point of origin (whether this is dubbed the Aristotelian "prime mover" or
the "big bang" of modern astrophysics). Despite the impossibility of the
finite epistemological agent ever achieving an experience of this origin
as such—the "pure forms of intuition" constrain the subject to cognize
all phenomena as themselves embedded within an open-ended spatiotemporal continuum—reason nonetheless confidently advances the thesis that "the world has a beginning in time, and is also limited as regards
space." Intuition, contrary to reason, is compelled to posit the antithesis
that "the world has no beginning, and no limits in space; it is infinite as
regards both time and space."[39] Why? For Kant, time and space, as pure
forms of intuition, are conditions of possibility for the occurrence of any
and every possible experience. Hence, one cannot intuit an originary
limit-point to the spatiotemporal universe, since such a hypothetical experience would involve intuiting a state prior to (i.e., outside time) or
external to (i.e., outside space) temporally and spatially mediated reality
(this also would apply to the notion of a cataclysmic end to the universe).
Such an intuition is, according to Kant, impossible, given the conclusion
of the "Transcendental Aesthetic" that time and space are necessary possibility conditions for the occurrence of any intuited experience whatsoever.[40] And yet, reason, in its compulsive extension of the concepts of the
understanding beyond the limits of possible experience, foists upon the
mind the conviction that the universe must, for instance, originate in the
moment of a primordial *Ur*-Cause. In extrapolating from the sequential
chains of causes and effects, reason is convinced that the universe of
reality must be finite, although intuition never allows for this finitude to
be grasped as either an actual or a potential experience. If the term *I* is
substituted for *world*, then couldn't it be proposed, from the perspective
of psychoanalysis, that at least one facet of Kant's first antinomy entails a
defensively projected working-through of the problem of subjective finitude? Doesn't Kant, in the *Anthropology*, concede that life is a contingent
yet a priori condition of possibility for experience? Isn't birth the concrete origin of idealist subjectivity's world, and death its final, concluding
moment? As André Green elegantly expresses it, "The origin of worlds,

of life, of man, emerges from a more personal mystery far behind: that of the origins of the questioner himself" (Green 2000a, 58).

As in a standard Kantian antinomy, the mortal psyche contains two diametrically opposed judgments: "My lived existence is finite" ("I was born at a certain point in datable time, and I will die at an indefinite yet inevitable time in the future—in short, my lived existence has a temporal beginning and is of limited duration") and "My lived existence is infinite" ("I cannot step outside of my own first-person experiential position, and therefore 'I' am incapable of nonexistence—in short, my lived existence neither has a temporal beginning nor is of limited duration"). Of course, the latter judgment appears ridiculous to sane, rational reflection. Nonetheless, given the status of finitude as articulated by, among others, Kant, Freud, and Lacan, such an antagonistic deadlock must be operative due to the gap that subsists between the faculties of reason and intuition. This is merely the logical extension of the implications of the third-person cosmological antinomy to what could be called the first-person "psychical antinomy." There is no strict difference in kind between the two; the same rift runs through the "I" as well as through the universe as a (non-)whole. The antinomy between finite limitation and the unlimited infinite is reflected within both the macrocosm and the microcosm.

The split within the structure of the subject that Žižek credits Kant with having discovered is that between the phenomenal and noumenal dimensions of subjectivity, namely, between the subject as it appears to itself in an experiential fashion (i.e., through conceptual and spatio-temporal mediation) and the subject as it exists/subsists "in itself."[41] The subject *an sich* that makes experience possible cannot itself fall, as a discrete experiential, representational element, within the frame of the field it opens up and sustains (a point already grasped by Descartes in his second meditation). Hence, Kant famously speaks of "this *I* or *he* or *it* (the thing) that thinks" (Kant 1965, 385 [A 346/B 404]). The noumenal subject is just as much of a permanently shrouded mystery as things-in-themselves.[42] The entire thrust of the first *Critique* (particularly the "Dialectic of Pure Reason") is to establish the epistemological grounds for forbidding any and every philosophical reference to the noumenal realm beyond the familiar limits of possible experience. The conclusion Kant draws from the antinomies is that the rational irreconcilability between theses and their parallel antitheses means that the ostensible external referents under irresolvable dispute (for instance, the [not-]All of the cosmos) cannot be objects of legitimate philosophical inquiry. Kant assumes that things as they really are in and of themselves must be devoid of contradiction, given the supposed self-consistency of the fabric of pure, unmediated, extra-ideational being. Since the attempt to assign ideas like that of a (finite or infinite?) universe an ontological status produces indissoluble contradictions, these ideas are devoid of any constitutive value; they are relegated to a mere auxiliary-regulative role, serving the interest of reason in achieving a unified, coherent epistemological systematicity. Hence, the grand whole of the cosmos must, in Kant's view, remain forever inaccessible, being yet another void in relation to necessarily limited human cognition.

As just seen, the psychical antinomy entails similar consequences at a microcosmic level. In addition to being unable phenomenally and introspectively to know itself as a "thinking thing," the subject also is unable reflectively to cognize itself as a finite being. Its ownmost ontological finitude, arising from the brute Real as both temporality and corporeality—there are justifications for viewing time itself, in its restless negativity, as belonging to the dimension of the Real in Lacanian theory[43] (see chapter 15)—can be encountered only as an antinomic deadlock. Consequently, such finitude also must be considered a noumenal, *an sich* feature of "this *I* or *he* or *it* (the thing) . . . that dies." The subject is inherently barred from any form of phenomenal self-acquaintance in which it would know itself as finite in the ontological-material sense. The nothingness fled from, the void that Kant allegedly labors so hard to avoid, is nothing other than the very absence of the subject itself, the negation of the insurmountable "transcendental illusion" of its apparent immortality.

4

Avoiding the Void: The Temporal Loop of the Fundamental Fantasy

According to Žižek's heterodox juxtaposition of Kant and Lacan, the psychoanalytic notion of fantasy has direct relevance to this splitting of subjectivity between, on the one hand, the noumenal subject of (unconscious) enunciation and, on the other hand, the phenomenal subject of utterances (as determinate signifier-predicates). Although, as Lacan might phrase it, the subject in the Real[1] (i.e., the *an sich Es*) is forever out of reach of introspective self-consciousness's grasp, the repeated attempts by reflective activity to "catch its own tail" generate a by-product, namely, fantasies as responses to this irreducible self-opacity:

> If . . . one bears in mind the fact that, according to Lacan, the ego is
> an *object*, a substantial "res," one can easily grasp the ultimate sense of
> Kant's transcendental turn: it desubstantializes the subject (which, with
> Descartes, still remained "*res* cogitans," i.e., a substantial "piece of real-
> ity")—*and it is this very desubstantialization which opens up the empty space
> (the "blank surface") onto which fantasies are projected, where monsters emerge.*
> To put it in Kantian terms: because of the inaccessibility of the Thing in
> itself, there is always a gaping hole in (constituted, phenomenal) reality,
> reality is never "all," its circle is never closed, and this void of the inacces-
> sible Thing is filled out with phantasmagorias through which the trans-
> phenomenal Thing enters the stage of phenomenal presence—in short,
> prior to the Kantian turn, there can be no black hulk at the background
> of the stage. (Žižek 1992a, 136)

Elsewhere Žižek draws out the consequences of this, maintaining that every mediated identity, all signifier-predicates appended to the original nothingness of subjectivity in its raw negativity, are "supplements" aiming to "fill out this void":

> Lacan's point here is that an unsurmountable gap forever separates
> what I am "in the real" from the symbolic mandate that procures my
> social identity: the primordial ontological fact is the void, the abyss on
> account of which I am inaccessible to myself in my capacity as a real sub-

stance—or, to quote Kant's unique formulation from his *Critique of Pure Reason*, on account of which I never get to know what I am as "I or he or it (the thing) which thinks [*Ich, oder Er, oder Es (das Ding), welches denkt*]." Every symbolic identity I acquire is ultimately nothing but a supplementary feature whose function is to fill out this void. This pure void of subjectivity, this empty form of "transcendental apperception," has to be distinguished from the Cartesian *Cogito* which remains a *res cogitans*, a little piece of substantial reality miraculously saved from the destructive force of universal doubt: it was only with Kant that the distinction was made between the empty form of "I think" and the thinking substance, the "thing which thinks." (Žižek 1994b, 144)

Thus, the entire range of significations and images proposed by the subject to itself in response to the question of self-identity ("Who or what am I?") falls under the heading of transcendental illusion. That is to say, these fantasmatic productions striving to seal this crack in reality are semblances. And yet they are the inevitable results of a structurally determined dynamic rooted in subjectivity's internal division: "The subject is this emergence which, just before, as subject, was nothing, but which, having scarcely appeared, solidifies into a signifier" (*SXI* 199).

What's more, Žižek, in *The Ticklish Subject*, provocatively suggests that the supposedly inaccessible dimension of subjectivity in Kant, that presumed *an sich* kernel (access to which is barred by phenomenal-reflective mediation), isn't the noumenal Real, but rather what psychoanalysis designates as the "fundamental fantasy."[2] In other words, the horrible abyss of the Thing that Kant seeks to avoid is precisely this fantasmatic core of the subject's very being as subject, the hidden nucleus of its identity structure. Furthermore, the fundamental fantasy, in analytic metapsychology, is directly related to the finite condition of the psyche. Consequently, Žižek's subsequent insinuation, also in *The Ticklish Subject*, regarding a link between the finitude of Kantian subjectivity and mortality is far from being a careless non sequitur.[3]

What is the fundamental fantasy? Perhaps the finest definition of its essence is to be found in the 1964 article "Fantasy and the Origins of Sexuality," written by two of Lacan's most prominent students, Jean Laplanche and Jean-Bertrand Pontalis. Therein, Laplanche and Pontalis maintain that the ultimate vanishing point on the horizon of all psychical fantasies is the enigma of "the origin of the subject himself."[4] In other words, fundamental fantasies, apart from whatever recurrent motifs are to be found in the particular fantasies of diverse individuals—Freud's tendency is to search for universal contents in his analysands' fantasies (i.e., the primal scene, castration, seduction, etc.)—share a lowest common structural/functional denominator. These fantasies invariably attempt to answer, through the fictions of personal myths, inquiries into matters of origins: Where do "I" come from? Why, and for what desires, am "I" here? What is the founding reason or purpose for sexuality? The obsession with origins is the defining feature of fundamental fantasies.[5] These troubling, burning enigmas can arise only for an essentially finite being, for a mortal creature born (or as Heidegger would say, "thrown") into a world not of its own making. And fantasies are the sole possible answers to these absolutely central origin-questions because finite subjectivity is intrinsically unable to construct, in the usual fashion, knowledge of its mortal finitude: "Fantasy is born there where knowledge is in default" (Green 2000a, 59). As Kant would express it, transcendental illusions are born there where the rift of a necessary incompleteness within the fabric of knowledge is encountered.

Similarly, Alenka Zupančič furnishes a rigorous definition of the Kantian transcendental illusion that clearly distinguishes it from any sort of contingent, empirical distortion (i.e., a falsifying depiction of some object "out there" in reality). Instead of being the misrepresentation of an underlying substratum,

> transcendental illusion is the name for something that appears where there should be nothing. It is not the illusion of something, it is not a false or distorted representation of a real object. Behind this illusion there is no real object; there is only nothing, the lack of an object. The illusion consists of "something" in the place of "nothing," it involves deception by the simple fact that it is, that it appears. (Zupančič 2002b, 69)

Or as she similarly phrases it, "this illusion is *an object in the place of the lack of an object*" (Zupančič 2000, 66; Zupančič 2002a, 68–69). The fantasy that fills the void visible in the fault line between thesis and antithesis in the psychical antinomy (see chapter 3) is a transcendental illusion in precisely this sense: the nothingness unavoidably entailed by the subject's finitude (i.e., the absence of subjectivity itself) is inevitably occluded by a fantasy as transcendental illusion wherein, literally, something appears "in the place of 'nothing.'" The stubbornly persistent presence of the fantasy gaze, of the subject as spectator witnessing the staged scene of his or her finitude, is itself the very illusion per se: "Transcendental illusion has to do not with the content of an 'image' but with its very existence— it deceives on the level of being" (Zupančič 2000, 67). In an earlier text, Zupančič explicitly couples this Kantian notion of illusion with the subject-gaze of the fundamental fantasy: "The anteriority of the gaze in relation to consciousness is seen as something that could be suspended and synchronized with this consciousness by means of *staging*—in the present or in the future, the hypothetical point of the successful encounter of the gaze and the consciousness—of their mutual recognition. It is apparent that the 'original fantasy' is always the fantasy of the origins" (Zupančič 1996, 47–48). She continues: "For what is at stake here is precisely their subjectivation, their emergence as pure subjects. It is the observer who could be said to be reduced to a 'mere object,' to the (impossible) pure gaze witnessing the subject's own coming into being" (Zupančič 1996, 48).

The fantasmatic illusion identified by Žižek and Zupančič relies, to a large extent, upon a manipulation of the categories of necessity and contingency. Apropos death, as Freud notes, the typical obsession with the always-specific causes of death—those witnessing the departures of others (this being the sole path of indirect phenomenal acquaintance with mortality) tend to fixate upon the accidental, circumstantial factors leading to demise—serves to deflect attention away from the ultimate inevitability of death.[6] Succinctly put, in confronting death, psychical defense mechanisms attempt to treat a necessity as if it were a contingency. Apropos birth, the inverse occurs: a contingency is treated as if it were a necessity. Once thrown into the condition of this particular human life and its attendant form(s) of subjectivity, the contingent occurrence of this particular "throw" thereafter becomes, for the being thus thrown, an enigmatic origin to which it can relate solely through the necessity of its own unsurpassable presence as subject, as, so to speak, an indelible "I." Georges Bataille eloquently describes the sense of contingency attached to the being of the "I":

> If I envisaged my coming into the world—linked to the birth then to the union of a man and a woman, and even, at the moment of their union . . . a single chance decided the possibility of this *self* which I am: in the end, the mad improbability of the sole being without whom, *for me,* nothing would be, becomes evident. Were there the smallest difference in the continuity of which I am the end point: instead of *me* eager to be me, there would be with respect *to me* only nothingness, as if I were dead. (Bataille 1988, 69)

Bataille continues: "This infinite improbability from which I come is beneath me like a void" (Bataille 1988, 69). This "improbability" is tied up with sexual reproduction. And, Jean-Claude Milner observes, sexuality indeed opens up a sublime plane of infinite contingency for beings whose very existence is intertwined with it.[7] However, as stipulated by Zupančič, the exclusively fantasmatic relation of the subject with its own contingent yet a priori causal ground partially forecloses this improbable point of origin as contingent per se. The necessary presence of the cogito-like subject-as-gaze, of the spectator there to witness in fantasy the moment of its own conception ex nihilo, tends to downplay or conceal the utterly contingent nature of the occurrence of this now-unknowable moment. That is to say, the necessary form of fantasy is at odds with the contingent content depicted within the diegetic reality of the materialized fantasy itself.

In a short essay with the curious title "Kant as a Theoretician of Vampirism," Žižek applies certain critical-epistemological distinctions to precisely such matters of life and death. He appeals to the difference between an "infinite judgment" and a "negative judgment." The former type of judgment merely denies the attribution of a predicate-term to a subject-term (leaving the nature of the subject infinitely/indeterminately open by declining to substitute a finite number of determinate predicates in place of the suspended predicate), whereas the latter type of judgment actively attributes a predicate-term (albeit a negative one) to a subject-term. In other words, an infinite judgment states that "S is not P," whereas a negative judgment states that "S is not-P" (or "S is non-P"). The crucial difference, from a Kantian perspective, is that the negative judgment assumes that the epistemic agent making the judgment does so on the basis of some sort of direct and immediate familiarity with the subject-term, a familiarity enabling the confident, positive assertion that this subject-term indeed possesses the predicate-term attributed to it. The infinite judgment avoids this assumption and thus refrains from offering itself as an assessment of the actually possessed attributes of the subject-term in question. According to Žižek, this is highly relevant to the topic of mortality:

> Herein lies . . . the difference between "is not mortal" and "is not-mortal"; what we have in the first case is a simple negation, whereas in the second case, *a nonpredicate is affirmed.* The only "legitimate" definition of the *noumenon* is that it is "not an object of our sensible intuition," i.e., a wholly negative definition which excludes it from the phenomenal domain; this judgment is "infinite" since it does not imply any conclusions as to where, in the infinite space of what remains outside the phenomenal domain, the *noumenon* is located. What Kant calls "transcendental illusion" ultimately consists in the very (mis)reading of infinite judgment as negative judgment. (Žižek 1994a, 27)

As Žižek reminds readers in this piece, Kant himself, in the section of the first *Critique* discussing his table of judgments, opts to illustrate this distinction between infinite and negative judgments using the subject-term "soul" and the predicate-term "mortal."[8] Like Lacan, Kant highlights an "undead" domain "between-two-deaths" (*entre-deux-morts*): "Kant was undoubtedly the first philosopher who, in his notion of 'transcendental illusion,' implicitly outlined a *theory* of the structural necessity of ghosts: 'ghosts' ('undead' entities in general) are apparitions which are constructed in order to fill in this gap between necessity and impossibility which is constitutive of the human condition" (Žižek 2000c, 235). As with the psychical antinomy, in trying to conceive of itself as either mortal or immortal, the subject instead encounters an indeterminate void gaping in the gap between two irreconcilably antithetical positions. In short, the necessity of ontological-material finitude is, on one level, an impossibility for the epistemologically finite subject; in the divide between this necessity and its impossibility, specters proliferate, undead ghosts, as transcendental illusions, uncontrollably multiply. The illusion of which Žižek speaks is the result of covering over the void by imagining that the phenomenal impossibility of consciously cognizing one's own absence is equivalent to an affirmation of one's eternal presence. In the terms of Lacan's matheme of the fantasy ($ \lozenge a$), the $ of "not mortal" is misleadingly made equivalent to the hypostatized a of immortal as "notmortal" (i.e., the unavoidable presence of the subject-as-gaze in fantasies regarding its own birth and/or death). Indeed, concerning the relation between $ and a, one of Žižek's several definitions of the Lacanian *objet petit a* is that it's the "phantasmatic 'stuff of the I'" filling out the empty frame of the *sujet barré*.[9] Stuart Schneiderman provides a succinct explanation of the error involved here: "Immortal simply means not mortal and 'not mortal' doesn't always mean living forever or eternally. Not mortal is also a characteristic of the dead. Only the living are mortal" (Schneiderman 1983, 76).

Lacan's scattered commentaries on the topic of mortal finitude refer to the structurally determined inevitability of just this sort of transcendental illusion, whereby the infinite judgment is treated as a negative one. In the third seminar, he notes in passing that "the question of death and the question of birth are as it happens the two ultimate questions that have precisely no solution in the signifier. This is what gives neurotics their existential value" (*SIII* 190). In this same seminar he introduces, in order to explain the genesis of psychosis, the concept of "foreclosure" (i.e., a "beyond" of repression—a signifier simply is missing from the unconscious, rather than being prohibited from entering consciousness).[10] With the psychoses, as resulting from foreclosure (more specifically, from the radical absence of *le Nom-du-Père*), that which is missing in the Symbolic returns in the Real (typically, for psychotics, in the form of delusions and hallucinations).[11] Lacan highlights a hole in the symbolic order regulating the subject's understanding of his or her ownmost mortal finitude; no signifiers respond to queries related to the individual's birth and death.[12] So, is this specific lack at the level of the Symbolic a catalyst for the emergence of undead specters as a fantasmatic "return in the Real"?

Several years later, in the sixth seminar, Lacan briefly alludes to a notion he refers to as "inverse foreclosure" (no further references to this notion are to be found in *le Séminaire*): "The one unbearable dimension of possible human experience is not the experience of one's own death, which no one has, but the experience of the death of another" (Lacan 1977, 37). Lacan continues:

> Where is the gap, the hole that results from this loss and that calls forth mourning on the part of the subject? It is a hole in the real, by means of which the subject enters into a relationship that is the inverse of what I have set forth in earlier seminars under the name of *Verwerfung* [repudiation, foreclosure].
>
> Just as what is rejected from the symbolic register reappears in the real, in the same way the hole in the real that results from loss, sets the signifier in motion. This hole provides the place for the projection of the missing signifier. (Lacan 1977, 37–38)

Lacan proceeds to describe the mourning rituals of cultural groups as manifestations of the manner in which the Symbolic big Other fabricates meaningful contents expressly for the purpose of plugging the "hole in the Real" opened up by death.[13] With inverse foreclosure, that which is missing in the Real returns in the Symbolic.[14] Much later, in the twenty-second seminar, Lacan declares that "it is strictly impossible, as regards the noumenon conceived in opposition to the phenomenon, not to make emerge . . . the metaphor of the hole" (*SXXII* 3/18/75). Lacan then immediately asserts that "the noumenon is nothing other than the hole" (*SXXII* 3/18/75). Thus, especially considering the prior Žižek-inspired articulation of the psychical antinomy plaguing Kantian-Lacanian subjectivity, one could argue that the same hole is at issue in both the third and sixth seminars (i.e., the hole as death) as well as the twenty-second seminar (i.e., the hole as noumenon). On this account, the enigma of mortal finitude, as part of the unknowable Real of subjectivity itself, functions like an abyssal vortex, generating a proliferation of significations to compensate for and conceal the eternal, irremediable absence of any firm signification whatsoever (akin to Freud's dream examples, wherein castration, as the absence of the phallus, is masked behind its opposite, namely, a thriving plethora of phallic symbols[15]). Elsewhere, in the thirteenth seminar, Lacan even claims that the subject itself is, ultimately and essentially, a "hole in the Real."[16]

Žižek maintains that one of the distinguishing features of consciousness, as distinct from the unconscious, is an awareness of the fact of mortality. However, although the unconscious is indeed ignorant of death (as a consequence of its ignorance of both time and negation[17]), this foreclosed finitude is not without its repercussions. Death, for example, cannot be repressed in the standard sense of the term. Since repression involves the barring of an ideational representation (a Freudian *Vorstellung*) from the sphere of conscious cognizance, one's own death, as utterly lacking any correlative psychical inscription due to its absolute exclusion from the ontogenetic history of the living individual, isn't "something" that could be subjected to defense mechanisms suited for use against *Vorstellungen*. This hole of nonexistence, as Lacan describes it, is, in a way, foreclosed rather than repressed. But whatever is dragged into associative proximity with this hole (for instance, sexuality or traumatic experiences) succumbs to vicissitudes such as repression. The repression of finitude occurs by proxy. Birth and death, as those emblems of mortality for which, Lacan alleges, there is "no solution in the signifier," are indicative of what could be dubbed a "fundamental foreclosure." Whereas foreclosure, according to its standard Lacanian definition, generally refers to a factor in the pathogenesis of the psychoses linked to the accidents and contingencies of the individual's personal history, adequate representational mediators for ontological-material finitude would be intrinsically missing/lacking in any and every unconscious. Therefore, this finitude would be fundamentally foreclosed as a necessary point of absence within any and every psyche. One of the symptoms (or, in a stronger Lacanian sense, *sinthomes*) of this constitutive void, the very void arguably avoided by the split Kantian subject, is the fundamental fantasy.

The important contributions of Otto Rank to an understanding of the place of mortality in psychical life are quite useful in the present context. Due to Freud's withering criticisms of his 1924 book *The Trauma of Birth*,[18] Rank has fallen undeservedly into relative obscurity. One of his suggestions is that the Oedipus complex should be viewed as a symptom of the underlying tension that Freud discerns between ego-libido and object-libido. This complex is centered on the child's fantasies of usurping the place of the paternal figure and thereby securing amorous fusion with the maternal figure. Rank interprets this as expressing the individual's desire to attain an impossible *causa sui* status (with both Norman O. Brown and Ernest Becker fruitfully developing these connections between the fantasies of a "*causa sui* project," the Oedipal family drama, and the individual struggle against mortality[19]). That is to say, by replacing the father as progenitor, the child, in coupling with the mother, seeks to beget him/herself, to be his/her own progenitor. (This also helps to explain the asymmetry of the Oedipus complex as regards both genders—girls are just as much committed to the *causa sui* project as boys, and hence are likewise just as interested in coupling with the mother.[20]) Rank points to the biblical myth of Eve being created from Adam's rib as expressing the same theme: instead of accepting the finite condition of being created creatures ("born of woman"), human beings reverse the natural order of things. More specifically, the woman-mother (Eve) doesn't give birth to the self (Adam); rather, the self is portrayed as the origin-source of the woman-mother.[21] Not only does Rank insightfully perceive the Oedipus complex as involving problems concerning mortal finitude as well as sexuality, but he also uncovers a retroactive temporality structuring Oedipal fantasies, a temporality upon which Žižek lays great emphasis.

Žižek repeatedly returns to the topic of the fundamental fantasy. He dwells mainly on the odd sort of temporality exhibited by such fantasies. Typical fundamental fantasies stage scenarios in which the fantasizing individual is (ostensibly) absent from the fantasized scene. The epitome of a "fantasy of origins" (as discussed by Laplanche, Pontalis, and Green, among others) would be, of course, an individual's imaginings about his or her own conception and birth:

> The basic paradox of the psychoanalytic notion of fantasy consists in a kind of time loop—the "original fantasy" is always the fantasy of the origins—that is to say, the elementary skeleton of the fantasy-scene is for the subject to be present as a pure gaze before its own conception or, more precisely, at the very act of its own conception. The Lacanian formula of fantasy ($ \diamond a$) denotes such a paradoxical conjunction of the subject and the object *qua* this impossible gaze: the "object" of fantasy is not the fantasy-scene itself, its content (the parental coitus, for example), but the impossible gaze witnessing it. (Žižek 2002a, 197)

Žižek adds: "The basic temporal paradox of the fantasy consists precisely in this 'nonsensical' temporal short circuit whereby the subject *qua* pure gaze so to speak *precedes itself* and witnesses its own origin" (Žižek 2002a, 197). Later he characterizes "the elementary matrix of fantasy" as "a pure gaze present at the act of his own conception" (Žižek 1994b, 120). This "elementary matrix" is then identified as an answer to "the enigma of the Other's desire" (for instance, to the question, "What am I for my parents, for their desire?").[22]

In fantasmatically witnessing the necessarily mythical moment of conception, the individual covers over his/her nonexistence, retroactively inserting him/herself (as subject-as-gaze) into this gap, this point of creation ex nihilo, in the narrative organization of ontogenetic experience. Žižek treats the other pole of finitude, death, in an identical fashion:

> When one indulges in fantasies about one's own death, one always imagines oneself as miraculously surviving it and being present at one's own funeral in the guise of a pure gaze which observes the universe from which one is already absent, relishing the imagined pathetic reactions of relatives, and so on. We are thereby again at the fundamental time-loop of the fantasy. (Žižek 1996b, 22)

Žižek contends that the fantasy-phenomenon of "seeing oneself looking," of reducing one's subjectivity to this disembodied "pure gaze," is a representational stand-in for death.[23] Socrates, in the *Phaedo* dialogue, insists that death is nothing more than the moment at which the ethereal, indestructible soul finally achieves a complete separation from the corruptible matter of the body (assuming, of course, that the soul in question has led a philosophical life, ignoring the demands of the flesh by living "in a state as close to death as possible").[24] In Žižekian terms, death, insofar as it forms an object of (unconscious) fantasy, would be nothing more than the complete separation of the gaze from the body. Furthermore, Žižek pinpoints this juncture wherein gaze and body are severed as a paradigmatic manifestation of the cogito itself:

> *Cogito* designates this very point at which the "I" loses its support in the symbolic network . . . and thus, in a sense which is far from metaphorical, ceases to exist. And the crucial point is that this pure *cogito* corresponds perfectly to the fantasy-gaze: in it, I found myself reduced to a nonexistent gaze, i.e., after losing all my effective predicates, I am nothing but a gaze paradoxically entitled to observe the world in which I do not exist (like, say, the fantasy of parental coitus where I am reduced to a gaze which observes my own conception, prior to my actual existence, or the fantasy of witnessing my own funeral). (Žižek 1993, 64)

As Žižek subsequently argues, "the temporal loop which defines the structure of a fantasy" is the phenomenon whereby "prior to his very being, the subject is miraculously present as a pure gaze observing his own nonexistence" (Žižek 1996b, 19). The irreducible presence of this "pure gaze" in those fundamental fantasies veiling the void stretching out beyond birth and death (as the two ends of finite being) is thus to be identified with the cogito (a conception of subjectivity, in Žižek's account, "raised to its Notion" by Kant). Whereas Descartes conjures up a maliciously deceptive deity in order to achieve this separation by casting the body's being into radical doubt (thereby reducing the indubitable "I" to the activity of a mental "gaze"), Žižek elegantly demonstrates that such extreme hypothetical/fictitious devices aren't required to achieve this distinction between the gaze of *res cogitans* and the inert, innerworldly being of *res extensa*. The fundamental fantasies uncovered by psychoanalysis, in which the spectator-subject persists despite its supposed absence within the reality framed by the fantasy, directly depict this cogito, this disembodied yet seemingly ineliminable presence divorced from any and every determinate, substantial attribute or incarnation.

Is this also to suggest that such subjectivity is fantasmatic? Does this entail that the cogito is something symptomatic in the strict analytic sense, namely, an essentially defensive device whose emergence is prompted by an underlying conflict or antagonism? Certain remarks made by Žižek hint at an affirmative answer to these questions:

> The ultimate gap that gives rise to suture is ontological, a crack that cuts through reality itself: the "whole" of reality cannot be perceived/accepted as reality, so the price we have to pay for "normally" situating ourselves within reality is that something should be foreclosed from it: this void of primordial repression has to be filled in—"sutured"—by the spectral fantasy. (Žižek 2001b, 71)

As is now quite clear, this crack, this necessary lack of full closure haunting the domain of manifest, concrete reality, is, for Žižek, nothing other than the subject itself. Furthermore, what makes such subjectivity finite is not only the epistemological dimension of its limitations—as per Kant, its experiential reality is always incomplete, and this incompleteness is illusorily eclipsed by the regulative ideas of pure reason[25]—but, at the same time, its ownmost ontological-material condition (a condition directly related to its epistemological limitations). A facet of epistemological finitude, as the unknowable limits beyond all possible experience marked off by birth and death, mirrors ontological-material finitude itself. This is precisely what Heidegger is driving at when, in division 2, section 1 of *Being and Time* ("Dasein's Possibility of Being-a-Whole, and Being-Towards-Death"), he maintains that the impossibility of *Dasein* reflectively seizing itself as a complete and self-sufficient object (i.e., as a whole) isn't due merely to "any imperfection of our *cognitive powers*."[26] Instead, this epistemological deadlock is an epiphenomenal manifestation of the fundamental fact of death; in death, as the ever-so-transitory moment at which *Dasein* becomes a whole, this being loses the "there" (*Da*) of its very being (*Sein*), its possibility for grasping itself in the fullness of its completely exhausted presence.[27] Žižek's delineations of the relation between fantasy and finitude add two further Freudian-Lacanian points here: first, these gaps/voids in the fabric of reality are akin to black holes, exerting a powerful force of attraction;[28] and second, the pure gaze of the cogito-like subject is precisely what gets drawn into these vortices, effectively serving to plug them up and thereby establish a false sense of reality's unsurpassable, unruffled plentitude (a feeling of plentitude isolated by Freud, in the first chapter of *Civilization and Its Discontents*, during his discussion of the "oceanic feeling" as a person's sense of not being able to "fall out of this world"[29]). If and when this fantasy-frame collapses—one way of understanding what Lacan means by the "subjective destitution" that results from "traversing the fantasy," given Žižek's elaborations, is as the sudden failure of subjectivity-as-gaze to seal adequately the rifts in reality arising from its finitude—the subject is confronted with "the raw Real of the life-substance: life becomes disgusting when the fantasy that mediates our access to it disintegrates, so that we are directly confronted with the Real" (Žižek 2001b, 169). As Freud and Lacan themselves indicate, when the subject's being is tinged with traces of vital mortality, the neurotic reaction is to recoil in horror from this "life-substance," to flee from this Real into a subjectivity whose very status is shaped by the trajectory of this flight itself.

Hence, the cogito simultaneously serves two defensive functions: it establishes a distance from sexuality (à la Descartes' notorious detachment of the "I" from its body) as well as mortality (for the modern subject, its own nonexistence is, strictly speaking, foreclosed as an unthinkable impossibility). This isn't to say, following the dominant anti-Cartesianism of today, that this sort of subjectivity doesn't really exist, that it's an untenable denial of a deeper mind-body unity. Rather, the essential idea here is that subjectivity, in its effective existence, is the most profound symptom of the human condition (the *sinthome* par excellence), a violent reaction-formation precipitated by and setting itself up against the corporeal condition. Along these lines, as Silvana Dalto notes regarding a psychoanalytic account of the material emergence of modern subjectivity, "there is no *cogito* as a transcendent, but an immanent *cogito*, completely implicated in the body that it was produced in order to exclude" (Dalto 2002, 223). And Zupančič's motif of "the Real of an illusion"[30] is especially apt in the present context: from a certain sort of strict materialist standpoint, the fleeting negativity of the subject might well be treated as an illusory epiphenomenon in relation to the hard base of a substantial foundation. And yet this illusion itself, once generated out of the Real, becomes something efficacious, operating as a *proton pseudos* (a "lie" that becomes a quite tangible, self-fulfilling prophecy) inscribing its apparently ephemeral existence into this same bedrock of the Real and generating perturbations therein. In this light, the infamous division between *res cogitans* and *res extensa* is symptomatic of a prior split, an underlying antagonistic discordance, within the material substratum of (libidinal) being itself.

5

Against Embodiment: The Material Ground of the More-than-Material Subject

According to Freud, one feature of neurosis is a problematization of sexual life triggered by its associations with mortal finitude. He also mentions, during the course of the Rat Man's case history, that obsessional neurotics in particular have a tendency to latch onto topics enabling them to indulge themselves in their favorite mental-affective state, namely, the uncertainty of doubt (an uncertainty sustaining a ceaseless activity of thinking—if "I think, therefore I am," then "if I do not think, then I am not"). Two of these topics listed by Freud are "length of life" and "life and death."[1] Likewise, indications of a profound relation between obsessional neurosis and mortality are scattered throughout Lacanian and post-Lacanian psychoanalytic literature. The standard interpretation here is that the obsessional, through the rigidity of repetitive ritual, attempts indefinitely to stave off death through the strange strategy of turning him/herself into a living corpse.[2] Serge Leclaire evocatively speaks of a "spatialization of time" that terminates in the "freezing of becoming."[3] André Green widens the scope of this, characterizing symptomatic repetition in general (in melancholia and compulsiveness as well as obsessional neurosis) as bound up with the matter of death.[4] Picking up on this line of thought, Žižek discerns a paradox within the obsessional strategy of rigidifying self-cadaverization: the very effort to avoid death leads to a de-vitalizing mortification.[5] In fact, regarding this specific dimension of neurosis (the pathology whose structure Žižek claims to discern in Kant), Žižek asserts that a Hegelian dialectical oscillation, an unstable reversal of opposites into each other, takes place between the terms *life* and *death*.[6]

Expanding on his notion of the space between two deaths, a notion first proposed toward the end of the seventh seminar in connection with a reading of Sophocles's *Antigone*,[7] Lacan, in the eighth seminar on transference, further specifies the difference between these two sorts of death. The "first death" is, simply enough, mere physical demise, the cessation of vital functions in the organism. The "second death," by contrast, is essentially linked to the registers of the Imaginary and the Symbolic, having more to do with the annihilating yet eternalizing effects of subjective alienation in the spheres of both the image as well as the signifier:

> This boundary . . . of the second death . . . one can define it under its most general formulation in saying that man aspires to annihilate himself there in order to inscribe himself there in the terms of being. The hidden contradiction . . . is that man aspires to destroy himself in eternalizing himself. (*SVIII* 122)

The "hidden contradiction" of this second dimension of death is that the barred subject, as a finite power of unrepresentable negativity, achieves its illusory eternalization exclusively through, so to speak, destroying itself by exporting its very (non-)being to the domain of external representational mediators. Lacan refers to the Symbolic axis of this dynamic as "corpsification," as the "cadaverizing" effects of the signifiers of the big Other on the living being that thereby becomes a *parlêtre*.[8] In Lacanese, the subject of enunciation (i.e., the unsuturable void of $) secures its fantasmatic transcendence of finitude only via the mortification of alienating meditation vis-à-vis the subject of the utterance. At stake in this second death is, rather than the biological body of the individual, the subject as signification, as routed through the circuitous networks of images and signifiers. Here, as both Lacan and Žižek observe, mortality and immortality cross over into each other. The paradoxes of this dialectical convergence of opposites are vital to the framing of a transcendental materialist theory of the subject, a theory arising, in part, from this heterodox endeavor to couple, with the help of Žižek, Kant *avec* Lacan.

This oscillation between mortality and immortality exhibits itself in both the Imaginary, with the ego, and the Symbolic, with the subject. Regarding the former aspect of this dialectic as exhibited in the mirror stage, Žižek states:

> At the level of the Imaginary, Lacan—as is well known—locates the emergence of the ego in the gesture of the precipitous identification with the external, alienated mirror-image which provides the idealized unity of the Self as opposed to the child's actual helplessness and lack of coordination. The feature to be emphasized here is that we are dealing with a kind of "freeze of time": the flow of life is suspended, the Real of the dynamic living process is replaced by a "dead," immobilized image—Lacan himself uses the metaphor of cinema projection, and compares the ego to the fixed image which the spectator perceives when the reel gets jammed. (Žižek 1997c, 94)

Dolar offers a similar analysis of the Lacanian ego:

> The shadow and the mirror image are the obvious analogs of the body, its immaterial doubles, and are thus the best means to represent the soul. They survive the body due to their immateriality—reflections constitute our essential selves. The image is more fundamental than its owner, it institutes his substance, his essential being, his "soul," it is his most valuable part, it makes him a human being. It is his immortal part, his protection against death. (Dolar 1996, 137)

Lacan's declarations concerning the imago-gestalt forming the genetic nucleus of the ego emphasize, among other features of this *moi*, its temporal (or, more precisely, anti-temporal) character. In particular, Lacan underscores the fact that this reflected image supports a feeling of "permanence," lending to the Imaginary "me" a sense of stable, enduring self-sameness over time[9] (hence Dolar's perspicacious observation of the link between the soul and one's self-image). He sees in images a resistance to the perpetual motion of time itself: "There is in the image something which transcends movement, the mutability of life, in the sense that the image survives the living being" (*SVIII* 413). Or, as Moustapha Safouan puts it: "The body image eternalises the subject, and the love that binds the subject to this image . . . is, in its essence, love of eternity, of its own eternity" (Safouan 1983, 60). This imago serves as an identificatory anchor, a constant point of reference; the volatile, ever-changing "lived body" of the infant, mired in the anxiety-provoking state of its primordial, corporeal helplessness (*Hilflosigkeit*), is tamed and domesticated by the placid surface-image of this same body. As Lacan has it, the ego is always an ideal ego, namely, the ego is not so much reflective of a present, achieved psychical actuality as a continual anticipation of a forever *à venir* transcendence of the weighty burden of embodied materiality.[10] Succinctly stated, this Imaginary freezing of the visceral "flow of life" establishes a sense of enduring permanence, of a trans-temporal self. (Richard Boothby, among others, describes the Imaginary as associated with a certain stagnant "inertia.")[11] Hence, a kind of (pseudo-)immortalization is brought about via the image encountered in the mirror stage.

And yet Lacan also contends that the mirror stage is a requisite condition for the individual becoming cognizant of his or her mortality. In "On a Question Prior to Any Possible Treatment of Psychosis," he explains:

> Indeed, it is by means of the gap in the imaginary opened up by this prematurity, and in which the effects of the mirror stage proliferate, that the human animal is *capable* of imagining himself mortal—which does

not mean that he could do so without his symbiosis with the symbolic, but rather that, without the gap that alienates him from his own image, this symbiosis with the symbolic, in which he constitutes himself as subject to death, could not have occurred. (Lacan 2006j, 461)

Lacan's reasoning here is quite straightforward, and can be broken down into a simple syllogism. First, one's ownmost mortality is unimaginable (i.e., the individual cannot have any direct experiential acquaintance with his or her nonexistence). Second, mortality is capable of being imagined or experienced exclusively in a secondhand fashion (i.e., by witnessing the demise of others as a spectator). Therefore, once one becomes, as it were, other-to-oneself—the mirror stage results in the "alienation" of the individual, the mediation of selfhood through the external domain of the reflected image—one is able to apprehend oneself as an object-spectacle.[12] As with the fundamental fantasy, the individual now can imagine him/herself as nonexistent by playing the part of the ineffaceably existent witness-gaze at, for example, his or her own funeral (already in the mirror stage, a split arises between the static, objectified body image and the elusive gaze that relates to but nonetheless exceeds this objectification). Thus, the moment of Imaginary identification founding the ego, although erecting a seemingly immortalized image of the self, also involves the introduction of this living being, however indirectly, to the inevitability of its own eventual dissolution. In the second seminar, Lacan comments upon this paradox: "To the extent that the being's identification with its pure and simple image takes effect, there isn't any room for change either, that is to say death" (*SII* 238). But, Lacan goes on to note, such a being, by virtue of its Imaginary alienation, is "both dead and incapable of dying, immortal."[13]

However, this immortalizing yet mortifying investment in the imago-gestalt of the Imaginary *moi* is quickly found to be faulty. The imago is a reflection of the actual physical body, the physique subjected to the ravages of time, and, as such, it eventually comes to display its lack of real permanence. In the 1949 version of the mirror stage essay (the extant version published in the *Écrits*), Lacan foreshadows the distinction between Imaginary ego and Symbolic subject.[14] (From an ontogenetic point of view, the former precedes the latter—the linguistic "I" is overlaid on top of the imagistic "me"—although Lacan subsequently revises and complicates this somewhat simplistic developmental picture.) Later, in 1955, he clarifies the dynamic catalyzing the shift from Imaginary to Symbolic identification precisely in terms of temporality:

The *percipi* of man can only be sustained within a zone of nomination. It is through nomination that man makes objects subsist with a certain consistence. If objects had only a narcissistic relation with the subject, they would only ever be perceived in a momentary fashion. The word, the word which names, is the identical. The word doesn't answer to the spatial distinctiveness of the object, which is always ready to be dissolved in an identification with the subject, but to its temporal dimension. The object, at one instant constituted as a semblance of the human subject, a double of himself, nonetheless has a certain permanence of appearance over time, which however does not endure indefinitely, since all objects are perishable. This appearance which lasts a certain length of time is strictly only recognisable through the intermediary of the name. The name is the time of the object. (*SII* 169)

The Hegelian ring to this passage—in the *Phenomenology of Spirit,* the dialectical ball gets rolling right at the very moment when the immediacy of "sensuous experience" exiles itself to the mediated realm of conceptual articulation—is far from accidental. Prior to the start of *le Séminaire,* in a 1953 lecture entitled "*Le symbolique, l'imaginaire et le réel,*" Lacan makes similar remarks concerning the rapport between perceptual objects (including the ego as imago, as the "semblance of the human subject"), names (as signifiers, symbols, words, etc.), and temporality. And in so doing, he cites Hegel[15] (likewise, the Kojèvian one-liner, "the word is the murder of the thing," aims at evoking this same rapport[16]). Furthermore, in this early lecture, Lacan explicitly links the permanence of the interminably iterable symbol-signifier (i.e., the basis of the Symbolic *je*) to death as well as time in general:

The symbol of the object is precisely "the object there." When it is no longer "there," it is the object incarnated in its duration, separated from itself and which, via the "there" itself, can always be present to you in some way, always "there," always at your disposal. We rediscover here the relation between the symbol and the fact that everything that is human is symbolically conserved. The more it is human, the more it is preserved from the shifts and decompositions of natural processes. Man makes everything that endures as human, above all himself, live on in a certain permanence. (Lacan 2005b, 42)

The distinctly human attains a degree of separation from nature, as that unstable and transient materiality accessible to the senses, through the register of the Symbolic. In other words, in "murdering the thing" (to put it in Kojève's terms), the word as symbol-signifier establishes a trans-perceptual object-referent capable of being addressed by the *parlêtre* regardless of whether or not the entity in question is perceptually present in an empirical here and now (all of this, of course, makes its way into the first seminar[17]). This plane of permanence, standing above the fray of the natural cycles of generation and corruption, is the domain in which humanity as humanity proper dwells. What's more, in the seventh seminar, the "second death" is defined as "the point at which the very cycles of the transformations of nature are annihilated."[18] Hence, human beings are fully human insofar as they "ex-sist" in this deathly state, in a sort of suspended animation halfway between immortalizing permanence and cadaverizing alienation.

Lacan, in his 1953 lecture, even invokes memorials to the dead as fitting representations of the human being's general relation to the signifiers of the symbolic order (including his or her proper name). He continues:

> We find an example. If I had wanted to approach this from the other side of the question of the symbol, rather than starting with the word, with speech or the little seed, I would have started with the burial mound that rests atop the tomb of a chieftain or whoever else. It is this that precisely characterizes the human species: to surround a cadaver with something that constitutes a grave, to maintain the fact that "this endured." The burial mound or whatever other sign of a burial place merits very exactly the name of "symbol." It is something humanizing. I call "symbol" everything of which I have tried to show the phenomenology. (Lacan 2005b, 42–43)

In a way, the burial marker is an ideal metaphor for the signifiers that simultaneously immortalize and cadaverize the subject, situating subjectivity outside the material flux of transient, tangible being by condensing its essential identity into a different "material" register altogether (i.e., into elements of a symbolic order that both precedes the individual's existence and persists after his or her vanishing).[19] Whereas the Imaginary *moi* itself is, at least initially, exposed to the negativity of time in its reliance upon the reflection of the "body in pieces" (*corps morcelé*), the taking up of this image into the "defiles of the signifier" (i.e., the Symbolic coding of the *moi* as *je*) lends the "I" (whether as Emile Benveniste's shifter or Saul Kripke's rigid designator—see chapter 14) a degree of permanence over and above that of the perceived body.[20] However, this permanence comes at a price: "Lacan's barred subject writes the subject, yet as long as it is already dead" (Miller 2001b, 24).

In this alienating mortification by the signifier, the subject of the Symbolic is, at one and the same time, "murdered" by its name(s) as well as endowed with a life beyond death through this same process of nomination. This subject is inscribed in the records of the trans-individual symbolic order. Furthermore, concerning this aspect of the signifier in relation to subjectivity, the two registers of the Symbolic and the Real begin to overlap. Freud, with his penchant for biological models, portrays the tension between ego-libido and object-libido as arising specifically from the brute physical facts of sexual reproduction: the individual rebels against being reduced to "a mere link in a chain," that is, to the mortal vessel of a seemingly immortal genetic material. The psychical subject is ill at ease with the "selfish gene" (as Richard Dawkins characterizes these biological replicators). If, as Lacan provocatively indicates in passing, strands of DNA are to be taken as signifiers,[21] then they are signifiers in the Real (or perhaps "letters" in the strict Lacanian sense, as signifiers in their pure, nonsensical materiality). And yet, isn't something precisely analogous operative in the process of properly Symbolic alienation? The thus-alienated subject, instead of being used by the dictates of the selfish gene, becomes the plaything of the signifier in the Symbolic (akin to another of Dawkins's notions, the "meme")—this theme is, obviously, writ large across the entire span of Lacan's corpus. The subject is hence doubly subjected, facing, on the one side, exploitation by signifiers in the Real (condemning him or her to mortal finitude), and, on the other side, cadaverization by signifiers in the Symbolic (winning "immortality" through, oddly enough, annihilating mediation).

Žižek adds a further twist to these reflections. He describes Symbolic alienation as being "dead while alive." The correlative inverse of this, he argues, is being "alive while dead":

> For a human being to be "dead while alive" is to be colonized by the "dead" symbolic order; to be "alive while dead" is to give body to the remainder of Life-Substance which has escaped the symbolic colonization ("lamella"). What we are dealing with here is thus the split between . . . the "dead" symbolic order which mortifies the body and the non-symbolic Life-Substance of *jouissance*. (Žižek 1997c, 89)

He continues:

> These two notions in Freud and Lacan are not what they are in our everyday or standard scientific discourse: in psychoanalysis, they both designate a properly monstrous dimension. Life is the horrible palpitation of the "lamella," of the non-subjective ("acephalous") "undead" drive which persists beyond ordinary death; death is the symbolic order itself, the structure which, as a parasite, colonizes the living entity . . . The

> basic opposition between Life and Death is thus supplemented by the
> parasitical symbolic machine (language as a dead entity which "behaves
> as if it possesses a life of its own") and its counterpoint, the "living dead"
> (the monstrous Life-Substance which persists in the Real outside the
> Symbolic). (Žižek 1997c, 89)

These two monstrosities, being "dead while alive" and "alive while dead,"
are each incarnations of what Žižek, borrowing from the fictional genre
of horror, names "the undead"—neither biologically dead nor naturally
alive, the subject is stranded in a no-man's-land between two deaths. In
a psychical economy constitutively ignorant of mortality, these two poles
(paraphrasing Laplanche, "life and death in Lacanian psychoanalysis")
both stand for "the way *immortality* appears within psychoanalysis."[22] The
individual experiences the embodied domain of the drives, incarnated
in the myth of the lamella as the undead excess of *jouissance*, as something frightful and repugnant, a threat to be avoided at all costs. This
Lacan-inspired Žižekian theme is a consequent extension of Freud's
contention that the drives are perceived as "internal aggressors," as dan-
gerous and potentially overwhelming forces whose compulsive *Drang*
continually must be tamped down and fended off in order for status quo
reality to remain intact.[23] Especially for the infant "still trapped in his
motor impotence and nursling dependence,"[24] these powerful libidinal
impulses emanating from its agitating and agitated body are particularly
disturbing. And, as Lacan indicates, the jubilant embracing of the imago,
establishing the *moi* and paving the way for the advent of the *je*, is an outcome conditioned by the desperate struggle to tame and cope with this
monstrous, palpitating *corps morcelé*. The ontogenetic catalyst forcing the
subject to "choose" alienating *corpsification* in images and words is thus to
be found at the level of the body itself.

So what does this have to do with a transcendental materialist theory
of subjectivity? Is there a connection between, on the one hand, Žižek's
musings concerning the nature of life and death and, on the other hand,
his multifaceted engagement with modernity's subject-as-negativity? In
many ways, psychoanalysis and phenomenology occupy overlapping
explanatory terrain. And one might, at this juncture, be left with the
misleading impression that the preceding Lacanian-Žižekian reflections
on finitude are quite consonant with existential phenomenological descriptions of, for instance, being-towards-death. However, despite many
superficial similarities, psychoanalysis and phenomenology are fundamentally at loggerheads as regards the theorization of the (non-)rapport
between subjectivity and the ontological finitude of its corporeal condition. As Žižek observes, one of the most scandalous features of Lacan's

thought, from a contemporary standpoint, is his continued recourse to the Cartesian cogito.

Phenomenology, particularly embodiment theory as inspired by Merleau-Ponty, is frequently an enthusiastic participant in today's endlessly repeated burials of Descartes. Like other anti-Cartesians, embodiment theorists generally tend to replace the dichotomy between thinking substance and extended substance with a more Aristotelian symbiotic fusion between mind and body involving the soul of the so-called "lived body." In the wake of supposedly having destroyed the disembodied transcendental subject, this "I" pretentiously pretending to be irreducible to its corporeal ground, they gleefully and rapturously celebrate the happy cohabitation of the soul with its proper substance. Dancing on Descartes' grave is a mandatory public ritual in such theoretical circles. But this approach is in danger of throwing out the proverbial baby with the bathwater. On a Žižekian reading (a reading shaped by the later Schelling[25]), the crucial dimension of subjectivity brought out by both Descartes and Kant involves not so much the denigration of the body as it does the internally divided, tension-laden structure of the subject. Utterly dispensing with the Cartesian-Kantian cogito by overemphasizing the blissful union of "self" and "stuff" risks resulting in a conflict-free model of subjectivity. Embodiment theory threatens unjustifiably to downplay the various ways in which the body becomes a burdensome problem, something violently dis-identified with by the "I." In psychoanalysis, the body frequently presents itself as a disturbing source of trouble to be evaded through negations and rejections. Furthermore, for Lacanian theory in particular, the very notion of "embodied subjectivity" is an oxymoron.

Lacan doesn't start drawing out explicit equivalences between Descartes' cogito and the subject of the Freudian unconscious until the mid-1960s. And at first glance, the early Lacan might appear to be in favor of an anti-Cartesian stance. The concluding sentence of the opening paragraph of his essay on the mirror stage proclaims an analytic opposition to "*toute philosophie issue directement du* Cogito."[26] Doesn't the mirror stage demonstrate that the supposed locus of subjective agency, the ego as the immediately lived sense of self, is in fact an inert object, that is, a stagnant, objectified representation of the body? Doesn't Lacan here accomplish the psychoanalytic de-subjectification of the traditional subject? To complicate matters further, how can this declared opposition circa 1949 be reconciled with a 1946 call by Lacan, in "Presentation on Psychical Causality," for a "return to Descartes"?[27] Lacan objects to grounding a theoretical system upon the cogito as an underived, axiomatic foundation or a metaphysical first principle. However, this isn't because he thinks that there's no such thing as this sort of subjectivity;

rather, Lacan views the subject as an outcome, product, or result instead of as a zero-level point of departure.

In two recent pieces on the status of the body in Lacanian thought, Jacques-Alain Miller (the interpreter of Lacan most influential for Žižek) clarifies the crucial discrepancies between the lived body of phenomenology and the *corps* at issue in psychoanalysis. As early as his 1893 study of the distinction between organic and psychosomatic motor paralyses, Freud distinguishes between the actual physiological body per se and the visual-imaginary body image (the latter governing the anatomical distribution of hysterical conversion symptoms).[28] Similarly, the appearance of the Imaginary imago signals the beginning of a progressive process of alienation. A rift opens up between the organism and its image, a rift that subsequently becomes the site for the inscription of the symbolic order's signifiers: "The mirror stage entails an essential difference between the biological organism and the visual body, a difference that one can qualify as gap, which Lacan did by showing the subject divided between its organic sensations and its perception of formal totality" (Miller 2001b, 35). Miller continues: "It's as if this visual totality, staggered by the relationship to the being there (*l'être là*) of its organism, was not a vital image but an already anticipated cadaver" (Miller 2001b, 35). This "anticipated" cadaverization is nothing other than the entry into the realm of that second death sustained in and by the symbolic order.

Although the distinction between the physiological/organic body and the visualized/imagined body is far from objectionable for phenomenological embodiment theory, the Lacanian handling of this division involves more than the facile thesis that embodied experience is mediated by images. Near the end of the eighth seminar, Lacan attempts to correct what he perceives as a set of untenable suggestions latent within the original presentation of the mirror stage, suggestions that encourage misunderstandings. Instead of a linear developmental sequence running from an imagistic, intrapsychical Imaginary enclosed upon itself to a sociolinguistic Symbolic transcending the solipsistic narcissism of the neonate, the very moment of Imaginary recognition is itself an overdetermined by-product of the prior intervention of the symbolic order, more specifically, of the familial big Other. Lacan observes that the child typically comes to identify with its reflection in the mirror precisely because it's prompted to do so by its parents (in many cases, the mother holds the child up to the mirror herself, using gestures and speech to encourage the process of identification). The supposedly elementary, gestalt-like images of the specular *moi* are not, in actuality, purely Imaginary constituents forming the archaic foundation of the ego. These images are determined by the Other; they are awash in a universe of meanings and significations circulating within the preexistent symbolic order.[29] The ego as body image isn't just the site of an anticipated future colonization of the body by signifiers. Rather, this site is a space opened up by the intrusion of the Symbolic big Other. From the very beginning, the phenomenal image isn't simply an image—the lived body, once severed from the physical organism, is always already entangled in structuring chains of signifiers. These signifiers are, as it turns out, responsible for this moment of separation between body and body image, acting as catalysts triggering an alienating *méconnaissance*. As Lacan insists throughout the closing sessions of the eighth seminar, the underlying support for the imagistic ego is the "unary trait" (Lacan renders the Freudian *ein einziger Zug* as "*le trait unaire*"), namely, an iterable Symbolic mark.[30] Thus, the Symbolic is both the origin and telos of the Imaginary, the cause of the emergence of the specular *moi* as well as the linguistic *je* that eventually results from the encoding effects of signifiers.

Miller productively employs Lacan's distinction between "being" and "having" (originally developed apropos the role of the phallus) in order to explain why Lacan continues to cling to the terribly passé cogito. The reflective externalization of the body in images and words turns it into something possessed:

> "Having a body" is significant in its difference from "being a body." We can justify the identification of being and body in the animal, but not in man, because no matter how corporeal he is, corporified, he is also made a subject by the signifier, that is to say, he is made lack-in-being. This lack in being as effect of the signifier divides being and body, reducing the body to the status of having it. (Miller 2001b, 21)

Or as Miller puts it elsewhere:

> The subject, from the moment in which it is subject of the signifier, cannot identify itself as its body, and it is precisely from there that its affection for the image of its body proceeds. The enormous narcissistic bombast, characteristic of the species, proceeds from this lack of subjective identification with the body . . . Lacan constantly critiques, implicitly or explicitly, the phenomenology of Merleau-Ponty who tries to restore the co-naturalness of man to his world, who centers on the corporeal presence, who studies presence in the world in, by, and through a body. This presence is also evident in Heidegger's philosophy of the *Dasein*, where it is displaced in accordance with what it has circumvented. The presupposition, as Lacan says, for Merleau-Ponty, is that there is somewhere a place of unity, which is the identification of the being and body,

> and which has as result the effacement of the subject . . . Psychoanalysis
> makes its space in the lack of this identification between being and body,
> in maintaining that the subject has a relationship of having with the
> body. (Miller 2001a, 16)

The subject subjected to the signifier (a subjection whose way is paved by
Imaginary *méconnaissance*) is incapable of harmoniously and unproblematically being at one with its body, of letting its very being remain fused
with this corporeality.[31] In fact, Freud is first led toward his discovery of
the unconscious by hysterical conversion symptoms as instances where,
as Lacan puts it, "thought is in disharmony with the soul" (Lacan 1990a,
6)—that is, unconscious thoughts as networks of ideational representations provoke the emergence of troubling, painful difficulties at the level
of the physical body, a body whose soul-like functional/organic unity is
disrupted by the symptoms of these thoughts. According to Lacan, without the signifier, there is no *sujet;* signifiers engender subjectivity. Furthermore, given that Lacan tends to endorse an "ontological dualism" in
which the symbolic order and the organic body are situated in separate
domains,[32] he feels a greater affinity for Descartes than for those (like
certain existential phenomenologists) who seek to collapse the subject
back into an embodied state. In Lacanian theory, a subject "reunited"
with its body is no longer a subject.

However, Lacan is far from uncritical of Descartes. The Lacanian recasting of the cogito, like the one previously effectuated by Kant, introduces some significant modifications (Žižek and the Slovenian school
have gone furthest in the delineation of this recasting). What's more, a
proper understanding of these modifications reveals that Lacan formulates a position allowing for the justifiable rejection of a false dilemma
tacitly governing many contemporary discussions: the choice between,
on the one hand, a crude mind-body dualism (attributed to Descartes)
and, on the other hand, a reduction of subjectivity to corporeal substance (whether this substance be the organic body of the natural sciences or the lived body of phenomenology).

In the fifteenth seminar, Lacan describes the Cartesian eclipse of the
body as a rejection (*Verwerfung*) in the Freudian sense: "The rejection
of the body outside of thinking is the great *Verwerfung* of Descartes. It
is signed with its effect that it reappears in the *Real,* that is to say, in the
impossible" (*SXV* 1/10/68). Lacan's allusion here to his own concept
of foreclosure is obvious: at least with Descartes, the body is foreclosed
from the sphere of thought (with "thought," for Lacan, being a Symbolic
category, something intimately bound up with signifiers). Nonetheless,
this exclusion is never total, since the excluded element, as the Lacan-

ian formula of foreclosure has it, always returns/reappears. Quite a few of the sticking points in recent debates wherein Descartes features as a whipping boy hinge, perhaps, on another false dilemma: either the mind and the body are utterly unrelated (as, supposedly, in Cartesian dualism) or the mind and the body are positively related (i.e., harmonized, integrated, fused, etc.). The missing third option here, as explored by Lacanian theory, is the one in which the mind and the body are, so to speak, negatively related—oppositional discord is, obviously, a form of relation. Psychoanalysis advances a (Schellingian) model wherein, although subjectivity arises out of corporeality through a process of immanent genesis, it nonetheless subsequently comes to posit itself in antagonistic opposition to this primordial material *Grund*. Through a series of founding rejections and disavowals (or in Kristeva's terms, abjections) the ontogenetically emergent cogito of Freudian-Lacanian psychoanalytic metapsychology comes to establish itself in its ostensibly sovereign negativity. In the negative relation between corporeality and cognition, the latter comes into being through its splitting off from the former, while the former comes into full thematic view as an object or problem after the fact of this very gesture of splitting.[33] The body participates in giving birth to the subject, after which the subject interminably struggles to sever this umbilical cord tethering it, however tenuously, to the material foundation of its embodied origin.

Lacan, particularly in the eleventh seminar, develops a notion of causality ideally suited to depict the (non-)rapport between body and subject: cause as "*tuché*." In the tenth seminar, the 1964 discussion of the *tuché-automaton* couple is foreshadowed when Lacan mentions a psychoanalytic sense of causation as anterior to the phenomena studied by phenomenology (i.e., what Kant would call "objects of experience").[34] Imaginary-Symbolic reality, as the structured, ordered space within which phenomenal objects (including the *moi*-self's ego as grounded upon the gestalt of the body image) present themselves as governed by certain law-like regularities, is set in motion by causes that, as originary and foundational, cannot themselves appear within this same frame.[35] Lacan situates these necessarily foreclosed causes at the level of the Real, given their inaccessible, eclipsed nature. The automatic run of things (i.e., the effect of *automaton*) is sparked into existence by the violent "trauma" of a founding moment (i.e., the cause of *tuché*). However, *tuché* cannot thereafter (re)appear within the field subsequently shaped by the *automaton* it creates. Once situated within the domain of Imaginary-Symbolic reality, the subject is condemned to relate to its own corporeal cause as a "lost cause,"[36] as a structurally excluded origin. (One manifestation of this loss of a direct, unmediated relation to the causal-bodily

Real, as Lacan has it in the eleventh seminar, is that underlying somatic impulses are accessible to the subject of psychoanalysis only insofar as they are always already dissolved into the Imaginary-Symbolic mediating matrix of ideational representations, of *Vorstellungen*.[37]) Furthermore, how can one avoid concluding that the subject's ownmost finitude qualifies as just this sort of Real, as a "tychic"[38] point generating deadlocks and antinomies? As claimed by Žižek, Laplanche, and others, all fantasies are, at root, organized around the central void created in the psyche by the enigmas of finitude. One's own birth is a Lacanian "lost cause," just as one's own death is an unimaginable end. These two holes in the fabric of subjective reality are filled in and covered over by the fantasmatic formations of the unconscious, with the gaze of the cogito-subject itself being precisely what sutures the wounds inflicted upon the skin of lived experience by vital mortality.

In the course of examining the relation between the *tuché-automaton* dichotomy and a possible Lacanian understanding of embodiment, Paul Verhaeghe arrives at a few observations echoing some of those made by Žižek. The horror that Žižek so frequently speaks about (especially apropos Kant's "obsessional neurosis") is addressed, by Verhaeghe, as indicative of a vehement resistance against the "depersonalization" of being reduced to "the real of the flesh":

> The real body shows itself only in exceptional cases: for example, when depersonalization occurs, which always amounts to some sort of desymbolization. In such a case, a part of the body becomes unrecognisable because the signifier has been withdrawn from it. As a consequence, the subject is confronted with the real of the flesh, with something anxiety provoking and uncanny. The very same process can be recognised in hysterical revulsion: if the body (my own or another's) loses its erotic investment (Freud), or its signifier (Lacan), then the hysterical subject reacts with disgust to this emergence of the real of the flesh. (Verhaeghe 2001b, 69)

Perhaps one of the best artistic instances of just this sort of anxiety effect is Gustave Courbet's *The Origin of the World,* a painting owned by Lacan that graphically depicts a vagina. Its message is simple: "This is the fleshly ex nihilo from whence you came! This is the dark, dank hole beyond which you are nothing!" While commenting on Freud's famous Irma dream, Lacan describes the dream-spectacle of the woman's gaping, wounded throat as provoking, by virtue of functioning as a slightly distorted depiction of the "origin of the world," the same thoughts and feelings as those aroused by Courbet's piece:[39]

> There's a horrendous discovery here, that of the flesh one never sees,
> the foundation of things . . . the flesh from which everything exudes,
> at the very heart of the mystery, the flesh in as much as it is suffering, is
> formless, in as much as its form is something which provokes anxiety.
> Spectre of anxiety, identification of anxiety, the final revelation of *you are
> this—You are this, which is so far from you, this which is the ultimate formless-
> ness.* (*SII* 154–55)

The subject's anxiety in the face of anything that threatens to strip it of
its seemingly transcendent, immaterial status through a reduction to its
brute corporeal condition isn't a mysterious, inexplicable phenomenon.
Only a form of subjectivity that constitutes itself as inherently incompatible with its own finitude experiences the prospect of being plunged back
into its fleshly materiality, the inevitably occluded ground of its mortal
being, as a horrible danger to be avoided no matter what.

Similarly, the ultimate point of dialectical convergence for the opposition between life and death is to be located precisely at the level of that
state which Žižek describes as being "alive while dead." Žižek associates
this notion with life in all of its raw, pulsating, and disgusting transient
vitality. The excessive, overwhelming, and unrelenting push of *jouissance,* of the drives in their brutal disregard for homeostatic balance and
harmonious well-being, arouses anxiety in the being subjected to these
inescapable demands of the libidinal economy. For psychoanalysis, the
clamoring of *Trieb* (drive), as the imperative of a monstrous *jouissance*—
in his later seminars, Lacan refers to a superegoistic dimension of *jouissance*[40]—is synonymous with the untamed essence of vital being itself.[41]
From the very beginning, the living human creature, initially stranded in
a prolonged state of pre-maturational helplessness, is left vulnerable to
the dictates of the drives. In *Inhibitions, Symptoms and Anxiety,* Freud speculates that primary repression (in Lacanian terms, a sort of radical foreclosure), rather than resulting from an internalized set of sociocultural
norms encoded in the form of the superego, might be brought about
in connection with "the earliest outbreaks of anxiety," outbreaks "which
are of a very intense kind" and which "occur before the super-ego has become differentiated" (*SE* 20:94). Freud goes on to posit that "it is highly
probable that the immediate precipitating causes of primal repressions
are quantitative factors such as an excessive degree of excitation and the
breaking through of the protective shield against stimuli" (*SE* 20:94).
A few years earlier, in *Beyond the Pleasure Principle,* Freud notes that this
"protective shield against stimuli," as a two-sided surface entity, is doubly
exposed, facing internal as well as external forces. Additionally, whereas
the organism can remove itself from sources of excitation and/or pain

in its *Umwelt,* it's unable to escape from those sources stemming from the *Innenwelt* (hence the prominent role of projection as a psychical defense mechanism).[42] Consequently, the thriving, fleshly id-body of the drives is precisely what falls under the shadow of primal repression and thus becomes irreversibly eclipsed. On the psychoanalytic account (an account inextricably tied to an ontogenetic perspective), the gesture of violently foreclosing/abjecting this libidinal *Grund* of existence is a precondition for the emergence of any subjectivity whatsoever. If and when, after this primordial act of negation, fragments of this banished Real threaten to return within the tame, domesticated frame of the subject's Imaginary-Symbolic reality, the invariable affective repercussions of this are anxiety, disgust, horror, and the like. But why, as Žižek himself so adamantly insists time and again, does this dimension of excessive vitality provoke such overwhelming nausea? What makes bodily *aphanasis* such a terrible prospect, and what links it with death?

The drives of the libidinal economy, as representing the demands of life, are avatars of death too. The helpless neonate, incapable of caring for itself, faces the danger of perishing if its basic bodily needs go unmet. The ravenous drive-sources and their accompanying pressure, as a deathly dimension of embodied being evoked by Freud's *Todestrieb,* batter the child's body, tirelessly pressing for discharge and gratification at all costs. The body, right from the start, is a source of distress (and therefore, experiences bringing the subject back into too excessive a proximity with his or her body generate an alarm associated with this distressing drive-body). Later, after the advent of genital sexuality, these urges of the flesh unambiguously point toward the dissolution of the individual as their ultimate terminus. Through the lens of certain cognitive-developmental achievements, the libidinally charged body is retro-actively identified, by the backward glance of a subject "having" (rather than "being") this body, as the culprit insofar as the inevitability of a despised demise is concerned. Although the death preordained by the living body cannot succumb to the vicissitudes of repression—repression operates upon ideational representations, and one's own death is unrepresentable—the Imaginary-Symbolic objects latched onto by the undead drives indeed can be defended against by a form of subjectivity whose very integrity is predicated upon its repulsion of corpo-reality, its keeping bodily being at bay. The representational/signifying mediators of the foreclosed body, a body embodying both life and death (or, as Žižek has it, a living death), are substitutive stand-ins bearing the brunt of the subject's struggle with its own extimate, libidinal-corporeal Real (its corpo-Real)—hence sexuality's thematic prominence at the level of repressed unconscious content.

As already noted, Žižek credits Kant with discovering, through a radicalization of Descartes, the split subject. Due to an inherent division
internal to the very structure of subjectivity, an introspective, reflective
self-acquaintance, a reflexive grasping of one's ontological essence in
and of itself, is impossible. The *an sich* being of the Kantian noumenal
subject can only ever appear, within the boundaries of phenomenal experience, as an absence, lack, or void, as an always-withdrawn substantiality. For Žižek, one of the major accomplishments of the first *Critique*
is its development of the insight into the relation between subjectivity
and negativity. However, unlike the static model of critical philosophy,
the genetic dimension of psychoanalysis entails the assertion that the
transcendent(al) subject delineated by Kant immanently arises out of
the ontological domain against which, after emerging, it subsequently
distinguishes itself in an oppositional fashion. As Žižek has it, the Kantian
distinction between the noumenal and the phenomenal is a distinction
internal to the phenomenal itself.[43] Žižek's transcendental materialism
is nothing other than the attempt to narrate the dynamic of this immanent genesis of the transcendent (the narration of which compels him
to turn to Schelling and Hegel in addition to Kant). The Real generates
ruptures with itself out of itself. Transcendental materialism posits, in
short, a self-sundering material *Grund* internally producing what (subsequently) transcends it. After this immanently produced break, there's no
going back—the "one-way street" of this (onto)genesis thwarts the arrival
of any sort of eventual dialectical reunion, resolution, or reconciliation
with the thus-self-shattered Real.

One crucial feature of the Žižekian engagement with Kant's split subject is the tracing of much more precise and specific contours around
the edge of the void that Kant christens the "I or he or it," the empty, insubstantial "subject = x." This crack in the texture of reality is essentially
related to the Real of the subject's ontological finitude. The psychical
antinomy plaguing the epistemologically finite subject is a symptomatic manifestation of its problematic (non-)rapport with the foreclosed
ground of its ontological-material finitude, with the unimaginable nothingness out of which it emerged and to which it is destined to return. Succinctly put, direct experiential self-acquaintance with oneself as finite is
exactly what remains forever barred. That is to say, the eternally elusive
X of the subject-in-itself is simply the phenomenal subject of first-person
consciousness as absent, as nonexistent prior to birth and/or vanished
after death. From the Žižekian perspective, the void that Kant's "obsessional neurosis" is designed to avoid is the nonexistence of the "I" as implied by its fully finite status. However, isn't this to remain within the horizon of Kant's total and complete de-ontologization of subjectivity? Isn't

a sharp separation maintained here between the subject in the finitude of its being and the subject as that which knows or doesn't know about this finitude? Again, is it possible, even after taking into account Žižek's modifications of Kant, to speak, in the context of the present discussion, of a transcendental materialism in which epistemological-transcendental finitude and ontological-material finitude maintain some manner of relation with each other? A deliberately perverse misappropriation of Badiou's terminology—Badiou rails against Kant and the entire thematic of the finite subject (including the topic of the mortal individual's "being-toward-death")[44] and also refuses to equivocate between the notions of subject and void[45]—enables the strange link between these two finitudes that Žižek discerns in Kant to be further elucidated.

The (presupposed) being of the Kantian noumenal subject can only ever appear, within the frame of phenomenal (self-)experience, as a void. And this void marks the point where the subject's own ontological-material finitude (dis)appears, being veiled by the pure gaze indelibly present within the unusual temporality of the fundamental fantasy. According to Badiou, "being qua being" (*l'être en tant qu'être*) is, like Kant's *Ding an sich*, inaccessible to experience and the forms of knowledge it licenses (although this resemblance to Kant is only superficial). In Badiou's vocabulary, the pure, inconsistent multiplicity of being qua being is incapable of inscription as either a presentation or representation within the structure of a situation and/or this situation's metastructural state. Presentation within a situation requires a consistency made possible by the synthesis of a "counting-for-one" (*compter-pour-un*).[46] To risk retranslating this back into familiar Kantian parlance, the Badiouian division between inconsistency (the oneless infinities-without-end of *l'être en tant qu'être*) and consistency (the one-ified sphere of counted, constituted entities) roughly corresponds to the distinction between noumenality and phenomenality respectively. As such, the ontological domain appears in the epistemological domain as, at least in part, a void (hence Badiou's assertion that the mark of the empty set is the "proper name of being").[47]

However, Badiou insists that no situation is without its relation to withdrawn, inconsistent being. In fact, he asserts that the void invariably subsisting within any given presentational situation and its representational state is precisely what sutures the epistemologically accessible plane of consistency to the inconsistency of being internally excluded within it: "At the heart of every situation, as the foundation of its being, there is a 'situated' void, around which is organized the plentitude (or the stable multitudes) of the situation in question" (Badiou 2001, 68). Or, as he puts it elsewhere, "the void . . . is the matheme of the suture of any discourse to the Being by which it is sustained" (Badiou 2006, 116). Being qua being, although refusing situational integration through the consistency-rendering one-ification of the structuring count, nonetheless "impresents" itself as (at least potentially) a delineable void capable of being located within the site of a situation: "I term *void* of a situation this suture to its being. Moreover, I state that every structured presentation unpresents 'its' void, in the mode of this non-one which is merely the subtractive face of the count" (Badiou 2005a, 55). Consequently, the situated void isn't just symptomatic of a negative, valueless shortcoming or failure on the part of the powers of presentation and representation. Rather, this void marks a coordinate within a situation where that situation retains a link with its foreclosed ontological underside.[48] Or, in Lacanian terms, those places where the established order of Imaginary-Symbolic reality breaks down and becomes inconsistent signal points where this reality is disrupted by the intrusion of the impossible Real; reality remains tied to the Real through its own internal gaps and inconsistencies.[49]

In an analogous way, the subject of the signifier, broken off from the being of its body, only ever encounters this corpo-Real either as something that disturbs the signifying structures in which this subject circulates (i.e., the *jouissance* of the drives) or as the void of an unrepresentable absence (i.e., as the origin of birth and the end of death). However, especially as regards the latter, this failure internal to the epistemological dimension of subjectivity and the effects that this negative limitation generate are precisely what signal the ominously silent presence of an indissoluble bond to an ontological dimension: the raw materiality of mortal flesh stripped of its reflective mediators and fantasmatic embellishments. The transcendental materialist subject is the epistemologically finite subject of transcendental philosophy as invisibly anchored to (and, in an often traumatic, "tychic" fashion, continually buffeted by) the eclipsed ground of its ontological-material finitude. The voids that fundamental fantasies rush to fill in demarcate those spots where quasi-dematerialized subjectivity is unavoidably impacted by the *tuché*, the vanishing cause, of the transient vital body that it never entirely succeeds in transcending. In this sense, the Žižekian refrain about the relation between the subject and its necessary lack of self-acquaintance takes on a much more exact sense: subjectivity, associated with the pure gaze of the cogito-like subject that Žižek discerns as brought out in stark relief by the fundamental fantasy, is coextensive with its ignorance regarding its own finite being.

In the *Critique of Practical Reason,* Kant describes what would happen if the subject could somehow overcome the split within itself by bridging the gap between noumenality and phenomenality in such a fashion that the former is made to appear in its naked, unmediated presence within the frame of the latter. In other words, what would it be like if the nature of the subject-in-itself became directly accessible to a reflective, experiential self-consciousness? The passage in which Kant describes this hypothetical scenario (found near the conclusion of the "Dialectic of Pure Practical Reason") is one frequently referred to by Žižek. Kant imagines that "God and eternity in their awful majesty would stand unceasingly before our eyes . . . The conduct of man . . . would be changed into mere mechanism, where, as in a puppet show, everything would gesticulate well but no life would be found in the figures" (Kant 1993a, 154). Kant's remarks have a powerful contemporary resonance. Now more than ever, this is an age in which the scientific view of human nature seemingly threatens to collapse the subject into the body, to transform human beings into just such overdetermined mechanisms of the material world, gesticulating at the sole behest of a genetic-evolutionary puppeteer.

In *Tarrying with the Negative,* Žižek, commenting upon this passage from Kant's second *Critique,* takes the opportunity to underscore the thesis that "self-consciousness . . . *is possible only against the background of its own impossibility*" and that "I retain my capacity of a spontaneous-autonomous agent precisely and only insofar as I am not accessible to myself as a Thing" (Žižek 1993, 15). Dolar provides a similar gloss on this matter: "The subject of the Enlightenment is, for Kant, a split subject and can remain free only so long as it accepts this split. The enduring split is the place of freedom, not an obstacle" (Dolar 1994b, 17). Subsequently, in *The Ticklish Subject,* this same Kantian theme of the close connection between subjectivity and ignorance receives a slightly different treatment, and the discrepancy between Žižek's 1993 and 1999 remarks on this matter are revelatory of his own internal shift away from Kant and toward post-Kantian German idealism. Kant's imaginary scenario of the subject confronting itself as *das Ding* tacitly endorses, according to Žižek, the problematic assumption that the Real is utterly homogeneous and internally consistent.[50] Advancing a thesis developed through a psychoanalytic-metapsychological appropriation of Schelling and Hegel, Žižek maintains that "the only way to account effectively for the status of (self-)consciousness is to assert *the ontological incompleteness of 'reality' itself*" (Žižek 1999b, 60).

If the material Real were wholly and completely at one with itself in harmonious self-integration, as a natural-cosmic automaton secretly controlling everything that exists, then there would be nothing but a stifling ontological closure precluding anything resembling subjectivity. The most vulgar determinism would indeed be correct. However, in his recent writings Žižek isn't willing merely to maintain, in a quasi-Kantian manner, that deliberately cultivating ignorance about the essence of humanity's physical being by, for example, arbitrarily prohibiting certain sorts of scientific inquiries is the way to save human freedom (as he observes, this reduces to the absurd strategy of supposedly salvaging freedom by restricting it).[51] He claims that Kant doesn't go far enough, remaining content to assume that the inconsistencies and antinomies he isolates are restricted to the de-ontologized enclosure of mind as opposed to matter, of the subject as opposed to the body. Psychoanalytic metapsychology, by contrast, locates inconsistent heterogeneity within the corporeal condition itself. For Freud, the very foundation of the libidinal economy is plagued by strife between incompatible tendencies and discrepancies inherent to physically predetermined levels of psychical functioning (for example, the inharmonious disjunction between, on the one hand, the perception-consciousness system with the organizations of mnemic traces to which it gives rise and, on the other hand, the somatic cycles striving for expression through this more-than-somatic perceptual-mnemic medium). And, as Lacan likewise asserts, the human body is a *corps morcelé*, an uncoordinated, tension-ridden burden that propels the perturbed child into forms of subjectivity taking whatever distance is possible from this set of volatile corporeal forces. Hence, what both German idealism and psychoanalysis point to is, as developed by Žižek, a more radical solution to the problems masterfully uncovered (but nonetheless left unresolved) by Kant: the material Real of "nature" (especially human nature) isn't smoothly integrated and free of internal conflicts, but rather is torn apart from within by inner antagonisms.

This absolutely axiomatic Freudian-Lacanian notion of (human) nature as, from the start, a heterogeneous, unintegrated field, instead of as an organically unified set of elements and functions (with this organic unity allegedly being broken up solely by virtue of external intrusions impinging upon its inner workings), ought to be recognized as a register complementary to Lacan's "barred" big Other (i.e., the symbolic order as permanently containing, within its own organizational constellations, contradictions, deadlocks, incompleteness, lack, etc.). More specifically, the Lacanian Real, viewed in the context of the preceding analyses, is a barred Real—not only the symbolic order, but the very substance of being is inconsistent and often divided against itself. Furthermore, the theory of subjectivity sketched above (through the focused examination of the relations between corporeality, temporality, and representational mediation), according to which the subject is formed via the immanent material genesis of a more-than-material transcendence, requires positing this barred Real, namely, stipulating that the Real-being (or, one could say, the corpo-Real) of the individual is ontologically structured in such way as to sustain spaces, spaces located at the fault lines of conflicts embedded within this "natural" materiality, out of which emerges that which subsequently breaks with this level of being.[52] Through a Lacanian-Žižekian lens, it can be seen that existent forms of (transcendent) subjectivity struggling to stand against embodiment are, paradoxically enough, engendered by this same embodied condition while nonetheless remaining irreducible to it.

Part 2

Driven to Freedom: The Barring of the Real

(Schelling–Žižek)

6

Groundless Logos: From the Transcendental to the Meta-Transcendental

The German idealist philosopher F. W. J. Schelling, long obscured behind the shadow cast by his contemporary Hegel, plays an absolutely pivotal role in the overall structure of the Žižekian theoretical matrix. Žižek's 1996 book *The Indivisible Remainder* and his 1997 essay "The Abyss of Freedom" not only make great strides toward reviving interest in Schelling through demonstrating his philosophical innovativeness and direct relevance for contemporary debates—Žižek endeavors to show that Schellingian thought courageously confronts the difficulty of thinking through the conflict between idealist transcendentalism and materialist historicism—but his engagement with Schelling also functions as a crucial conceptual crossroads, a significant switch-point, dividing yet conjoining two seemingly separate sequences in Žižek's still-unfolding intellectual itinerary. The "early Žižek" (à la such texts as *The Sublime Object of Ideology* [1989] and *Tarrying with the Negative* [1993]) sometimes comes across as rather Kantian in terms of his underlying philosophical orientation. Even Žižek's Hegelianism is, both at this stage as well as quite recently, a sort of ontologized Kantianism, with Hegel depicted as merely "radicalizing" Kant.[1] In his 2004 study of Gilles Deleuze, *Organs Without Bodies,* he again reaffirms that "philosophy as such is Kantian" and that "it is only with Kant (with his notion of the transcendental) that true philosophy begins" (Žižek 2004c, 44–45).

However, the "late Žižek" (especially in *The Ticklish Subject* [1999][2] and the set of interviews collected in the volume *Conversations with Žižek* [2004][3]) frequently expresses ambivalence about Kant in terms of a marked discomfort with transcendentalism (particularly with readings of Lacan as a transcendental thinker, readings for which he himself is partly responsible). In his most current writings, Žižek, almost certainly due to his fears of the pessimistic quietism it risks encouraging and legitimating, repeatedly hesitates to endorse a transcendentalization of the theory of subjectivity resulting from the interface between Kant and post-Kantian German idealism with Freudian-Lacanian psychoanalytic metapsychology. (At least from a standpoint influenced by specific socio-political concerns, it generally feels safer to insist upon the contingent historical status of the foundations underpinning the subject, since this appears to be necessary in order to safeguard the possibility for radical change in relation to the status quo.) In Žižekian terms, Schelling functions as a vanishing mediator—Žižek uses this very phrase in reference to Schelling,[4] particularly insofar as the latter is situated between "absolute Idealism and post-Idealist historicism"[5]—between the early and the late Žižek, representing the potential resolution of the apparent discord between these two phases of Žižek's work. More specifically, it is through his Lacan-inspired appropriation of Schelling that Žižek comes closest to the detailed formulation of a theory of the subject productively combining transcendentalism and materialism (while nonetheless preserving the tension between these two philosophical poles).

As early as his 1988 book *Le plus sublime des hystériques*, Žižek describes aspects of Schelling's philosophy as involving a "radicalization of Kant"[6] (albeit a radicalization somewhat different from the one effectuated by Hegel). Much later, he identifies the key post-Kantian theoretical contribution of Schelling as the asking and answering of the question regarding what, exactly, underlies the structural scaffolding of fully formed transcendental subjectivity as it is portrayed in Kant's critical apparatus[7] (although he also claims that Schelling's solution to this enigma remains somewhat unsatisfactory[8]). Whereas Kant's transcendental system implicitly treats the subject, embedded in experiential reality and its world of constituted objects, as always already existent and operative, Schelling seeks to account for the very emergence of such subjectivity, for the origins of this agent-function. That is to say, Schelling, especially in his texts from 1809 and after, attempts to sketch the (transcendental) subject's (ontogenetic) pre/proto-history[9] (a task largely neglected by Kant, although an examination of the connections between the pre-critical *Anthropology from a Pragmatic Point of View* and the *Critique of Pure Reason* reveals an awareness on Kant's part of this problematic matter[10]). Žižek refers to Schelling's relation to the Kantian legacy as the "materialist problematic of 'real genesis' as the obverse of the transcendental genesis."[11] Or, as he phrases it in Deleuzian parlance, "the problem of materialism from Lucretius through Schelling's *Weltalter* and the Marxist notion of commodity fetishism to Deleuze's 'logic of sense' is . . . *the genesis of the semblance itself:* how does the reality of bodies generate out of itself the fantasmatic surface, the 'incorporeal' sense event?" (Žižek 1997a, 58). And Andrew Bowie aptly observes that Schelling identifies a "fundamental problem that goes to the heart of the Kantian project: how does one explain the genesis of transcendental subjectivity itself?" (Bowie 1993, 34).

Generally speaking, Schelling seeks to delineate the process wherein more-than-material subjectivity (as a spiritual transcendence or transcendental ideality) immanently emerges out of a substantial material base (as the real ground [*Grund*] of "productive" nature). And yet, although Schelling maintains that subject arises from substance, he nonetheless insists that, following this movement of genetic emergence, the subject thus produced remains thereafter irreducible to the materiality of its (now-occluded) source(s).[12] This search for the first-order genetic conditions of possibility for the transcendental subject (a subjectivity which operates as a set of second-order possibility conditions for experiential reality once this subjectivity itself is formed) is tantamount to the quest for a meta-transcendental account of the subject, for, so to speak, the genetic possibility conditions underlying those static possibility conditions outlined in the Kantian critical system. But before delving into an examination of the Schellingian notions most central to Žižek's theoretical agenda, a little more needs to be said about Schelling's relationship to Kant.

In his 1797 "Treatise Explicatory of the Idealism in the *Science of Knowledge*," the young Schelling poses what is perhaps the defining question obsessing him throughout the rest of his philosophical labors: "What, then, is ultimately the reality that inheres in our representations?" (Schelling 1994b, 69). Shortly after formulating this query, he contrasts "the real" with "reality" (*die Wirklichkeit*), and indicates that the latter refers to experience as given to the subject (i.e., "reality" in the Kantian sense, as the realm of experiential objects), while the former designates something more fundamental, a tangible, solid ontological foundation that remains resistant to being accounted for by any purely idealistic emphasis on the subject's self-enclosure within the confines of reality as experience. (Lacan distinguishes between the Real and reality along strikingly similar lines,[13] although Schelling isn't mentioned once during the twenty-seven years of *le Séminaire*.) Even at this early point in his development, Schelling expresses philosophical ambitions pronounced impermissible by his immediate idealist predecessors. He insists that the very raising of an inquiry into what is "real" within the subject's representations demands a striving "towards the real" (*zum Realen*), that is to say, a struggle to step outside the closed circle of the finite, limited reality of consciousness. This amounts to a reintroduction of questions forbidden by the spirit of critical philosophy: What is the ontological status of the objects of experience? How do things-in-themselves (as a noumenal Real), through what Schelling designates as the subject's "receptivity for the real," become registered as part of reality (i.e., as phenomenal objects of experience)?

Schelling's choice of words (as quoted immediately above) already, even at this preliminary stage in 1797, hints at his eventual solution as offered in his later "post-idealist" works. He speaks of something that "inheres" in the subject's representations. Instead of positing a link between thing and object as two external entities otherwise opposed to each other, Schelling, deviating from the standard Kantian notion of *das Ding an sich* being a transcendent exteriority beyond or behind the experienced object, insinuates that the Real, ontological level of the *an sich* is itself immanently embedded within the reality of the subject's experiential field (as Žižek puts it, the Schellingian Real is the obfuscated originary/primordial underbelly of reality that nonetheless repeatedly "insists" within the fragile, framed field of experience, an unruly proto-materiality constantly threatening to irrupt within the domain of mundane reality—the "existence" of reality is to be opposed to the "insistence" of the Real[14]). Several paragraphs after announcing the urgency of an investigation into "the reality that inheres in our representations," Schelling turns his attention to Kant:

> Kant proceeded from *intuition* as the *first* element in our cognition. This soon led to the claim that intuition was the *lowest form of cognition*. Yet is the highest in the human spirit, that from which all further cognition derives its validity and reality. Furthermore, Kant said that intuition had to be preceded by an affection of our sensible faculty [*Sinnlichkeit*], although he left the question concerning the origin of this faculty altogether undecided. Here, he deliberately left behind something that was to emerge later as the ultimate and supreme problem of reason <never to be resolved>. (Schelling 1994b, 70)

Almost certainly, Schelling is alluding to B 145 in the *Critique of Pure Reason,* the disturbing passage (from section 21 of the B version of the "Transcendental Deduction") where Kant concedes that "the manifold to be intuited" must be given prior to the synthetic activity of the understanding (despite Kant's insistence throughout the first *Critique* that the understanding is "prior to" or "precedes" any particular given instances of intuition).[15] As Schelling correctly observes, Kant himself never provides the solution to this difficulty.

For Schelling, the Kantian prioritization of the formal, conceptual understanding over the concrete, sensible intuitions of actual experience inverts the genuine precedence that the latter has over the former. Additionally, he asserts that Kant's failure to account for the genesis of experience (through, for instance, an explanation of how the Real affects the subject so as to produce the known objects of reality) threatens to rob transcendental philosophy of its foundational status: "The crucial move, which Schelling carries out, is the demonstration that a system of reason cannot finally explain the fact of its own existence" (Bowie 1993, 162). In other words, if Kant simply takes the givenness of experience as an inexplicable, silently presumed "fact," then his whole system rests on what appears to be an unexplained empirical contingency; Kantian rational Logos is in danger of being left in a state of opaque, irrational groundlessness. Lacking an explicit theoretical narrative addressing the emergence of experience itself (its subject as well as its objects), the critical apparatus must be demoted from its self-proclaimed position as an ultimate foundation for philosophy. In a footnote to his lecture on Kant's position in the history of modern philosophy, Schelling says precisely this:

> If the question is whether philosophy itself and as a whole is an *a priori* or an *a posteriori* science, then Kant . . . did not really make up his mind. For if it has, for instance, been his opinion that philosophy consisted in the *Critique of Pure Reason* which he established, then it is clear that he obtained the content of this critique just from observation and experience, and correspondingly declared philosophy itself in the last instance to be a science of experience. Kant fights against empiricism only insofar as he, in opposition to Locke and above all to David Hume, demonstrates an *a priori* element for the understanding in the empirical representations themselves—but how he himself arrives or arrived at this assertion he basically does not explain, or does so only tacitly by only beginning with experience in the founding of this assertion, namely the experience of the observed generality and necessity of those concepts. (Schelling 1994a, 104)

As is well known, Kant turns the tables on Hume by showing how one cannot be a consistent empiricist: even if one succeeds in establishing that all knowledge is derived from "impressions," one is still left with the problem that the capacity for actually having impressions, as well as the impressions' invariant formal features, must be explained in a non-empirical fashion. Schelling attempts a similar turning of the tables with respect to Kant: he proposes that the only way for one to be a consistent transcendental philosopher as a practitioner of philosophy as an a priori science is to go beyond the explanatory framework of Kantian transcendental idealism by furnishing its prior genetic *Grund* (as sensation, nature, and so on). Otherwise, as he puts it regarding critical philosophy, "This system requires no refutation. To propound it is to overturn it from the bottom up" (Schelling 1988, 26). Schelling accuses a Kantianism bereft of such a basis as being, in the end, just as empiricist as the Humean epistemology it supposedly surpasses.

Nonetheless, Schelling is far from denying the validity of Kant's insights regarding epistemology and subjectivity. However, he maintains that the Kantian system must be placed on the firmer foundations of a precise philosophical articulation of the anterior ground conditioning the genesis of the experiential field from which Kant's critical analyses depart.[16] (For example, in the years around 1800, Schelling envisions his *Naturphilosophie* playing the role of the ontological basis for subsidiary epistemological investigations.) In fact, Rolf-Peter Horstmann observes that the need to confront the incompleteness of the Kantian critical system is one of the most important impulses propelling the young Schelling into the study of philosophy: "There is no doubt that his basic motives for becoming involved in philosophy at all were rooted mainly in his being drawn into the discussions about the shortcomings of Kant's philosophical theory and the possible ways of overcoming them" (Horstmann 2000, 129). As Schelling states, apropos Kant, in *Ideas for a Philosophy of Nature* (1797/1803): "How it happens that things come to be represented at all, about that there is the deepest silence" (Schelling 1988, 26). The Schellingian task, spurred on by this silence, is to formulate a genetic transcendentalism, a system in which the gradual emergence of the transcendent(al), along with its corresponding modes of experience, is grasped as a philosophically explicable process immanent to a monistic ontological register. (This is a task that Žižek, too, can be seen to take up via his combined use of German idealism and psychoanalysis in the effort to forge a transcendental materialist theory of the subject according to which, to put it in Schellingian language, the seemingly transcendent ideality of subjectivity is a rupture in the fabric of being immanently produced within and by the inconsistent, unstable [proto-]materiality of the Real-as-ground.) In his 1936 lecture course on Schelling, Heidegger, speaking of this same issue, alleges that "the critique as critique was itself not founded" (Heidegger 1985, 41). Schelling sees himself as the thinker who rectifies this shortcoming.

And yet, despite the fundamentally Kantian inspiration driving much of Schelling's work, there are significant differences between the two philosophers that cannot be overlooked. In *The Indivisible Remainder*, Žižek provides a concise description of a particular gap separating Schelling from Kant:

> Here Schelling is the exact opposite of Kant: Reason is originally "ecstatic," outside itself; it never begins in itself; its activity is never founded in itself, but always triggered by . . . some collision which provides the

impulse to the thought—this collision, this encounter with the real, distinguishes an actual experience from the mere possibility of experience. On the contrary, Kant . . . proceeds in the opposite direction: he sets up the network of the conditions of possible experience in order to make sure that the actual experience of the real, the encounter with the Thing, will never take place, so that everything that the subject will effectively encounter will be the already gentrified-domesticated reality of representations. (Žižek 1996b, 74–75)

For Kant, reason, in the broader, nontechnical sense of conceptual Logos, is the ultimate foundation grounding reality itself. The basic gist of his Copernican revolution amounts to re-centering the experiential real upon the activities of the cognizing intellect, instead of on any kind of ontological edifice beyond the boundaries of epistemological subjectivity. Schelling, on the other hand, insists that this revolution must itself be overturned, although not in the sense of simply reverting to pre-Kantian forms of philosophy. He contends that Kant's results require a supplementation that Kant himself would exclude as illegitimate. Rather than being the ground of experience, reason is parasitic in relation to its encounter with something outside its own self-enclosed confines. And Žižek emphasizes that this archaic *Grund* beneath reason, giving rise to the rational and yet excluded from it, is to be conceived of as a whirling abyss of pre-symbolic drives in conflict with each other.[17] That is to say, instead of focusing on Schelling's attempted solutions to the troubling Kantian problematic of the (non-)rapport between noumenal thing and phenomenal object, Žižek turns his attention to the deeper difficulty of how, according to Schelling, something like this split between the noumenal and the phenomenal could have arisen in the first place (with such a split assuming the genesis of a subject broken off from what is presupposed as an inaccessible *an sich* Real).

Furthermore, Žižek's assessment of the Kant-Schelling-Hegel triad better enables one to appreciate the philosophical uniqueness of Schelling's position. Thought (i.e., the Ideal) and being (i.e., the Real) are neither antithetical or mutually exclusive (as per stereotypical Kantianism) nor wholly and completely identical (as per the commonly understood final result of the Hegelian dialectic). In his genetic account, Schelling postulates that Ideal-thought (I) emerges from Real-being (R). But, as becomes clear in Schelling's later texts (in particular, with the models of causality deployed in the 1809 *Philosophical Inquiries into the Nature of Human Freedom* and the 1813–15 drafts of *The Ages of the World*), although I emerges from R, and although the Ideal medium of the epistemological subject's experiential reality harbors within its own heart a primordial kernel of the Real (the existence of experience reflects both levels simultaneously as I/R), this kernel is nonetheless lost in terms of its direct accessibility for the subject (in the style of Schelling's 1809 notations, experiential reality as I/R, although having arisen out of the *Grund* of R, is nevertheless irreducible to R—that is, $I/R \neq R$).[18] Unlike Kant, the Real is not external to the Ideal. The ontological *an sich* is internal to the subject as the immediacy of brute, raw sensation unprocessed by formal, ideational mediation. Correlatively, unlike simplified versions of Hegel, the Ideal never manages to succeed fully in incorporating and conceptually digesting the Real (being remains, to a large extent, the inexplicable ground of thought, that for which no rational system can account, despite its dependence on this ground).[19] In this light, Žižek has recourse to a distinction from Schelling's later works: "ground" versus "existence." The latter rcfcrs, in the context of the present discussion, to experience as it's given to an already constituted subject (i.e., "experience" as the point of departure that Schelling accuses Kant of taking for granted in the construction of the first *Critique*); the former is the primordial, archaic origin of the existence of experience (involving, on the Žižekian reading, the "rotary motion of drives"[20]).

Although he makes sure to underscore certain differences of detail between Kant and Schelling, Žižek paints a larger picture of a Schelling who, in the course of his criticisms of critical philosophy, remains perversely faithful to Kant (or, one could say, forces Kantian philosophy to confront some of its disavowed consequences and implications). *Grund*, rather than being the hard, ontological substance behind the ephemeral façade of experience (as it's been characterized here thus far), is, in fact, "pre-ontological": "The enigma resides in the fact that Ground is ontologically non-accomplished, 'less' than Existence, but it is precisely as such that it corrodes the consistency of the ontological edifice of Existence from within" (Žižek 1996b, 62; Žižek 1997a, 7). In "The Abyss of Freedom," Žižek proclaims that "the Ground is in itself ontologically hindered, hampered, its status is in a radical sense *preontological*—it only 'is' *sous rature*, in the mode of its own withdrawal" (Žižek 1997a, 6). And in *The Plague of Fantasies,* he utilizes this interpretation of the Schellingian Real as pre-ontological (instead of it being the ontological per se) to identify Schelling as a thinker who completes Kant's insight into the "ontological incompleteness of reality":

> German Idealism outlined the precise contours of this pre-ontological
> dimension which precedes and eludes the ontological constitution of
> reality (in contrast to the standard commonplace according to which
> German Idealists pleaded the "panlogicist" reduction of all reality to

the product of the Notion's self-mediation). Kant was the first to detect this crack in the ontological edifice of reality: if (what we experience as) "objective reality" is not simply given "out there," waiting to be perceived by the subject, but an artificial composite constituted through the subject's active participation—that is, through the act of transcendental synthesis—then the question crops up sooner or later: what is the status of the uncanny X which *precedes* transcendentally constituted reality? It was Schelling, of course, who gave the most detailed account of this X in his notion of the Ground of Existence . . . the pre-logical Real which remains forever the elusive Ground of Reason which can never be grasped "as such," merely glimpsed in the very gesture of its withdrawal. (Žižek 1997c, 208)

According to this reading, Schelling basically agrees with Kant that attributing a notion such as "existence" to the noumenal ground underlying reality is erroneously to apply a concept forged within the boundaries of already constituted experience to the pre-experiential foundation of this same experiential field (in short, it amounts to a category mistake). Like Kant, Schelling forbids using discursive concepts to analyze and characterize the Real. However, unlike Kant, Schelling refuses to conclude that the question as to the origin of experience (for instance, the enigma of how a thing affects the receptivity of the senses so as to become an object) is therefore meaningless and not worth asking. (As Žižek points out, even after the Kantian critique, "the question" concerning the ground of experience "crops up sooner or later"—B 145 is evidence that Kant himself acknowledges the stubborn persistence of this problem despite his burning desire to have done with the whole mess.)

Additionally, it's worth noting that the lengthy passage quoted in the paragraph immediately above also offers a hint as to what, exactly, Žižek identifies as the nature of Schelling's peculiar radicalization of Kant (a radicalization crucial to allowing for the possibility of forging a transcendental materialist account of subjectivity). Žižek alludes to the idea that both Kant and Schelling uncover (although the former, in restricting himself to an epistemological investigation, fails to appreciate the true significance of this discovery/insight) the fact that being itself is shot through with antagonisms and tensions, riddled with cracks, fissures, and gaps (rather than being something homogeneous and harmonious, an ontological plane placidly consistent with itself). What one could call this "barring" of the Real is absolutely essential to Žižek's philosophical project, a project centered on deploying and defending, in the midst of a prevailing postmodern *doxa* hostile to the very notion of subjectivity, a robust theory of the subject.

In *Organs Without Bodies*, Žižek insists, while discussing Kant, that free-dom (in the form of autonomous subjectivity) is possible only if being, construed as whatever serves as an ultimate grounding ontological reg-ister, is inherently incomplete and internally inconsistent[21] (and, in the opening pages of the first chapter of *The Indivisible Remainder*, he declares that "Schelling was first and foremost a philosopher of freedom" [Žižek 1996b, 15], a declaration with significant consequences for the Žižekian interpretive appropriation of Schellingian thought). He goes on bluntly to assert that "either subjectivity is an illusion or reality is *in itself* (not only epistemologically) not-All" (Žižek 2004c, 115). If being is entirely at one with itself, if material nature is a perfectly functioning machine in which each and every cog and component is organically coordinated into the single, massive whole of an uninterrupted "One-All," then no space remains, no clearing is held open, for the emergence of something capable of (at least from time to time) transcending or breaking with this stifling ontological closure. Being must be originally and primordially unbalanced in order for the subject as a (trans-)ontological excess to become operative.[22] As Schelling himself succinctly states, "Were the first nature in harmony with itself, it would remain so. It would be constantly One and would never become Two" (Schelling 2000, 12). Those points and moments where being becomes dysfunctional (i.e., when, to put it loosely, "the run of things" breaks down) signal the possibility for the genesis of subjectivity as that which cannot be reduced to a mere circuit in the machinery of a base material substratum in which everything is exhaustively integrated with everything else. In "The Abyss of Freedom," Žižek makes the move of identifying the Schellingian-Lacanian subject with this inconsistency internal to the ontological edifice itself: "Sub-ject designates the 'imperfection' of Substance, the inherent gap, self-deferral, distance-from-itself, which forever prevents Substance from fully realizing itself, from becoming 'fully itself'" (Žižek 1997a, 7).

So how does Žižek conceive of the Schellingian notion of *Grund*? And what does he mean when he insists upon its "pre-ontological" status? Žižek's slightly shifting uses of the term *ground* in his reading of Schelling are in danger of giving rise to certain misunderstandings. He relies prin-cipally on Schelling's three drafts of the *Weltalter* manuscripts, in which, arguably, there are two meanings of the term *Grund*. (Also, one should be aware that the theosophical bent of this Schellingian text, its explicit thematic focus on God, is treated in Žižek's psychoanalytically influenced borrowings from it as allegorical/metaphorical, as a cosmic, grand-scale narrative of the ontogenesis of subjectivity:[23] "Schelling's *Weltalter* is to be read as a *metapsychological* work in the strict Freudian sense of the term" [Žižek 1996b, 9].) Žižek often describes the Schellingian ground as consisting of a clashing jumble of primordial drives, as a violent, whirling maelstrom of archaic, untamed passions.[24] Similarly, he frequently associates this notion with images of a raw, formless proto-substance as an amorphous materiality underlying the clearly drawn contours of reality (i.e., with a version of the Real). Žižek speaks here of "the pre-ontological proto-reality, the Real of the unformed ghastly matter."[25]

However, isn't this originary substantiality the ontological par excellence, instead of being "pre-ontological"? Isn't this barred Real of passionate drives fiercely at war with each other the hard, tangible foundation (i.e., the corpo-Real) beneath the delicate, virtual surface of experiential reality as mediated by a (transcendental) subject establishing itself over and against this unruly ground? Perhaps things can be clarified by mentioning the other sense of *Grund* sometimes invoked by Žižek: ground as "the abyss of freedom" preceding the vortex of *Trieb*, as the nothingness/negativity situated beneath or prior to this "unformed ghastly matter" (this abyss seems to be the appropriate referent for the concept of the pre-ontological). Hence, at least for the sake of greater precision, one could say that a distinction ought to be drawn here between ground (*Grund*) and primal ground (*Urgrund*)[26]—the former refers to the rotary motion of the drives, while the latter refers to the state of nothingness allegedly underlying or coming before these same drives. In fact, in his 1809 *Freiheitschrift*, Schelling speaks of "a being *before* all basis and before all existence" as a "primal ground" that he associates with the notion of "the 'groundless.' "[27] But the manner in which *Grund* and *Urgrund* relate to each other has yet to be specified (this specification will require an exploration of Schelling's discussions of temporality, autonomy, and acts).

At this juncture, Logos, as the disembodied ideality of the transcendental subject and its conceptually mediated reality, can be deemed "groundless" for two reasons: first, the sphere of the rational Ideal arises from and rests atop an irrational Real (i.e., reason is not self-grounding, but rather is covertly dependent upon its disavowed/abjected other[s]); and second, this irrational Real is itself not an ultimate basis, but an arbitrary contingency suspended over a void (i.e., the true Beginning "is" an abyssal absence of any foundation whatsoever, the lack of any firmly grounding ground). Although this pre-ontological groundlessness is always already past—the *Grund* and the *Urgrund* are aspects of, so to speak, a time before time that cannot be accessed directly in their unmediated forms within the here and now of experiential reality—it nonetheless occasionally resurfaces within the confines of mundane existence through exceptional circumstances. More than anything else, human freedom (and not mere irruptions of blind, driven *jouissance*) is, perhaps, the principle avatar or manifestation of such Schellingian "returns of the Real."

Substance Against Itself: The Disturbing Vortex of *Trieb*

In line with his descriptions of the Cartesian cogito, the Kantian nou-menal *Ding an sich,* and the Hegelian "night of the world" (all of which he describes as terrifying monstrosities—see chapter 3), Žižek likewise characterizes the Schellingian ground as something awful and disturbing: "The gap between the ethereal image and the raw fact of the—inert, dense—Real is precisely the gap between Existence (ethereal form) and its impenetrable Ground, on account of which, as Schelling puts it, the ultimate base of reality is the Horrible" (Žižek 1997a, 23–24). He is alluding here to a passage from Schelling's *Weltalter* that proclaims, "But were they capable of penetrating the exterior surface of things, they would see that the true prime matter of all life and existence is precisely what is horrifying" (Schelling 2000, 104). Whereas neither Descartes nor Kant, for example, paint pictures of their central concepts in these shades and tones employed by Žižek, Schelling explicitly does so in his later texts. In a similar vein, in *The Fragile Absolute,* Žižek's discussions of Schelling refer to the "ultimate *monstrosity* of the truth" and its reliance upon "a pre-ontological obscene idiosyncratic scenario."[1] These characterizations refer to the Schellingian ground more in the sense of *Grund* than of *Urgrund.* The material substratum beneath ideationally mediated experiential reality and its ephemeral structures is something horribly formless, a repulsive, fleshly mass (Žižek identifies this substratum as "the bodily depth of the Real"[2]).

As already seen (see chapter 3), a possible explanation for Žižek's seemingly strange choice of adjectives like *horrible, monstrous,* and so on with respect to particular modern philosophical notions has to do with the finitude of embodied being, with the mortal destiny of "the way of all flesh" (i.e., the corpo-Real as the thriving id-body of drives, with all drives being, to a certain extent, death drives[3]). Along precisely these lines, Schelling, in his *Clara* dialogue, speaks of the "horror of nature,"[4] claiming that "within nature there was something nameless and frightful" (Schelling 2002, 21). He then points to the "hideous" necessity of nature's transient nature.[5] In *The Ages of the World,* he maintains that intuiting the "inner life" lying beneath the "peaceful" façade of reality's appearances is liable to provoke "terror."[6] This Schellingian theme, which comes to the fore in those later texts heavily favored by Žižek's interpretive agenda (especially the *Freiheitschrift*, the "Stuttgart Seminars," the *Clara* dialogue, and the *Weltalter* manuscripts), is incredibly important for a metapsychologically informed transcendental materialist theory of subjectivity insofar as it tacitly advances two axiomatic theses crucial for such a theory: first, the underlying ontogenetic base of the subject consists of the materiality of a certain Real, more specifically, of an internally conflicted libidinal economy at odds with itself from the very beginning (i.e., the Schellingian-Žižekian "vortex of *Trieb*" as the volatility of, as it were, substance against itself); and second, the subject is genetically produced as a consequence of the fact that the disturbing discontent of this initial state—the originally dysfunctional libidinal economy is plagued by unsettling antagonisms—prompts efforts at taming and domesticating this corpo-Real, efforts that come to constitute and define the fundamental contours of subjectivity itself (à la a subject-position characterized by a partial transcendence of embodied materiality). Žižek zeros in on the *Weltalter* manuscripts as containing the keys to extracting this philosophical-metapsychological account of subjectivity from Schelling's quasi-religious musings on God and the creation of the world.

Various passages in Schelling's 1809 essay on human freedom foreshadow the subsequent theosophical narrative sketched in *The Ages of the World*. For instance, Schelling declares therein that:

> following the eternal act of self-revelation, the world as we now behold it, is all rule, order and form; but the unruly lies ever in the depths as though it might again break through, and order and form nowhere appear to have been original, but it seems as though what had initially been unruly had been brought to order. This is the incomprehensible basis of reality in things, the irreducible remainder which cannot be resolved into reason by the greatest exertion but always remains in the depths. Out of this which is unreasonable, reason in the true sense is born. Without this preceding gloom, creation would have no reality; darkness is its necessary heritage. (Schelling 1936, 34)

An occluded yet insistent underbelly, an anarchic base, lies just beneath the calm, smooth surfaces of rationally governed, formally structured reality (surfaces that arose out of this same foundation—even though, after having arisen, a sustained tension is generated between surface and depth, the Ideal and the Real). At least as far as human existence is concerned, Schelling here seems to be positing a law of reverse entropy: chaos comes first, and any established order is necessarily preceded by this same chaos that it emerges out of and subsequently excludes (with this exclusion condemning the unruly ground to the status of "irreducible remainder," that is, Žižek's "indivisible remainder" as "that which STICKS OUT from the organic whole, the excess which cannot be incorporated/integrated into the socio-historical Totality"[7]). Schelling continues:

> All birth is a birth out of darkness into light: the seed must be buried in the earth and die in darkness in order that the lovelier creature of light should rise and unfold itself in the rays of the sun. Man is formed in his mother's womb; and only out of the darkness of unreason (out of feeling, out of longing, the sublime mother of understanding) grow clear thoughts. We must imagine the primal longing in this way—turning towards reason, indeed, though not yet recognizing it, just as we longingly desire unknown, nameless excellence. This primal longing moves in anticipation like a surging, billowing sea, similar to the "matter" of Plato, following some dark, uncertain law, incapable in itself of forming anything that can endure. (Schelling 1936, 35)

Starting at least as early as 1809 (if not earlier), Schelling consistently maintains that the Real is necessarily prior to the Ideal,[8] namely, that the palpitations of an archaic, shadowy (proto-)materiality precede and condition the subsequent blossoming forth of the luminous flower of a more evanescent, spiritualized dimension of existence rooted, nonetheless, in this dense, heavy soil.[9] However, the crucial caveat he attaches to the delineation of this basic dynamic is that "dependence does not determine the nature of the dependent, and merely declares that the dependent entity, whatever else it may be, can only be as a consequence of that upon which it is dependent; it does not declare what this dependent entity is or is not" (Schelling 1936, 18). In other words, acknowledging that the Ideal is (ontogenetically) conditioned by the Real isn't tantamount to a reductionistic assertion to the effect that the Ideal is merely epiphenomenal in relation to the Real (i.e., that the [quasi-]immateriality of the Ideal is, in the final analysis, reducible to the materiality of the Real). Here, in conformity with a general tenet of dialectical thought, (Ideal) effects can outgrow their (Real) causes, a tenet reflected, for instance, in Lacan's *tuché-automaton* model of causality as presented in the eleventh seminar (see chapter 5). This allows for the possibility that the ground of the material Real can internally/immanently give rise to a process of "de-materialization" eventually resulting in the emergence of a more-than-material form of subjectivity, a subject that enjoys a relative degree of autonomy in relation to the *Grund* from which it splits itself off in the process of being created and/or creating itself. Schelling himself underscores the anti-Platonic thrust of this thus-delineated dynamic: to Plato's movement of descent from the static, preexistent heights of *eidos* to the lowliness of mundane material reality, Schelling opposes this creative, generative movement of ascent out of murky, opaque depths.[10]

Furthermore, Schelling's invocation of the notion of a "primal longing" in the quotation above refers to an aspect of his later works that is of great importance to Žižek: the proposition that such forces as drives, desires, passions, and so on play an absolutely foundational role in the constitution of reality (a proposition central to any psychoanalytic explanation of the human condition). In the 1810 "Stuttgart Seminars," Schelling proclaims that "desire" (*Begierde*) is the primordial manifestation of spiritual ideality:

> What we call *spirit* exists *by virtue of itself*, a flame that fuels itself. However, because as something existing, it is opposed by Being, the spirit is consequently nothing but an addiction to such Being, just as the flame is addicted to matter. The most base form of the spirit is therefore an addiction, a desire, something ethereal. Whoever wishes to grasp the concept of the spirit at its most profound roots must therefore become fully acquainted with the nature of *desire*. (Schelling 1994c, 230)

He subsequently characterizes desire in similar terms, describing it as "an unremitting striving" and "an eternally insatiable obsession"[11] (one cannot help but think of the Lacanian conception of desire as sustained through the infinite deferral of satisfaction, a libidinal restlessness incapable of alighting upon an adequate provider of gratification). This desirous, passionate spirit (*Geist*) both "fuels itself" and "is addicted to matter"—that is to say, Ideal spirituality, initially incarnated in desire, is simultaneously independent of and dependent upon Real materiality (or, as Schelling puts it in *The Ages of the World*, coveting, situated halfway between nothingness and being, is a non-being that, nonetheless, isn't a mere nothing;[12] again, Lacanian theory resonates with Schellingian philosophy, given Lacan's linking of desire as "*manque-à-être*" to absence, lack, negativity, non-being, nothingness, etc.). Isn't this an untenable contradiction?

This puzzling paradox becomes comprehensible once one understands that, according to Schelling, a contradictory antagonism/tension always already perturbs being from the heart of its inner core (in Lacanian locution, there is something in being more than being itself). As he tirelessly asserts again and again, the Real of natural being contains within itself (as, perhaps, something "extimate") the Ideal of spiritual negativity as that which comes to break away from and transcend this ground. The world bears within it something foreign to it[13]—more specifically, the sensuous harbors the spiritual.[14] Schelling's treatment of desire here is an outgrowth of his general tendency to chart the immanent genesis of the transcendent in its various forms and modes. He claims that "nature . . . liberates itself from the inside out" (Schelling 2000, 58). Apropos desire as the original embodiment of the spiritual dimension, this means that a passionate longing proper to the Real of natural being (rather than its collision with the otherness of a preexistent external agency or force) internally generates the momentum needed for that which is eternally "in being more than being itself" to break out of the ontological closure of what Schelling portrays as the sterile cycles of expansion and contraction. The momentum behind the "escape velocity" from the prison-house of the vortex of *Trieb* comes from within the confines of this same prison. The *Weltalter* manuscripts are quite explicit regarding this matter. Primal life is haunted by "the wish to escape from the involuntary movement and from the distress of pining," by an "obsession" or "yearning" to attain freedom from the rotary motion of the drives[15] (with this rotary motion, this circulating movement, being identified as the "first nature"[16]). Moreover, this primordial state involves, as part of its very essence, the imbalance of contradiction:

> The first existence is the contradiction itself and, inversely . . . the first actuality can only persist in contradiction. All life must pass through the fire of contradiction. Contradiction is the power mechanism and what is innermost of life . . . Were there only unity and everything were in peace, then, forsooth, nothing would want to stir itself and everything would sink into listlessness. (Schelling 2000, 90)

Schelling adds:

> Matter, as if posited in a self-lacerating rage, shatters into individual and independent centers . . . Everything that becomes can only become in discontent. And just as anxiety is the fundamental sensation of every living creature, so, too, everything that lives is only conceived and born in violent struggle. (Schelling 2000, 91)

The "fire of contradiction" as the "discontent" of a "self-lacerating rage" immanent to the materiality of being catalyzes/prompts the emergence of and striving toward a "higher" plane of existence standing above the roiling, seething cauldron of driven matter. If by "desire" Schelling is referring to this basic impulse within the material Real, then it should now be clear why desire, as the basis of Ideal spirituality, is simultaneously independent of and dependent upon the Real materiality of being: being gives birth to the not-being of a desire that, although owing its existence to being, seeks to achieve a relative autonomy with respect to it.

However, Žižek's Lacan-inspired reading of Schelling cautions against too quickly equivocating between *Begierde* and *Trieb*, between desire and drive.[17] (Although one also must be careful not to telescope retroactively a subsequent metapsychological conceptual distinction back into Schellingian philosophy—it's difficult to tell whether Schelling recognizes any sharp distinctions between the words *desire, drive, obsession, passion, yearning*, etc., either within a given text or across the span of his writings from the post-1809 period.) Near the end of his 1997 essay on Schelling, "The Abyss of Freedom," Žižek discusses the Lacanian dichotomy between desire and drive: desire is "historical and subjectivized," whereas drive is repetitive and asubjective.[18] And yet, in, for example, Schelling's *Clara* dialogue, the suggestion is made that "the seat of desire and passion within us may belong to us but it isn't we ourselves" (Schelling 2002, 54); that is, Schellingian desire is an extimate foreign entity akin to the Lacanian-Žižekian drive. This hints that Schelling doesn't maintain a clear conceptual line of demarcation between the terms *desire* and *drive* parallel to the one operative in Lacanian theory—unless, of course, one were to distinguish between "the seat of desire and passion" (identifying this seat itself as the extimate *Trieb*-Thing) and "desire and passion" (*Begierde* and *Leidenschaft* as subjectified versions of this extimate entity distinct from *Trieb* proper). However, the more productive way to redeem the Žižekian invocation of the drive-versus-desire opposition in the context of his engagement with Schelling is to turn to the latter's delineation of the tripartite body-soul-spirit structure and the related notion of "spiritual corporeality" (*geistige Körperlichkeit*).

In the "Stuttgart Seminars," Schelling briefly mentions what he dubs "the demonic," defined as "the corporeal aspect of the spirit and the spiritual aspect of the body."[19] But it is in the *Clara* dialogue that he provides the most sustained articulation of spiritual corporeality. Therein, Schelling distinguishes between the body (as the material Real of the organic being), the spirit (as the immaterial Ideal of subjective mind), and the soul (as something situated between and connecting these two facets of the individual)—the "whole person" is the unity of these three dimensions.[20] In fact, Schelling's description of the relations between body, spirit, and soul sounds akin to a structure obsessing the late Lacan, namely, the Borromean knot (tying together the Real, the Symbolic, and the Imaginary). The Schellingian "whole person" could be conceived of as just such a knot-structure whose three rings (i.e., body, spirit, and soul) are linked together in a specific manner so that if one ring is broken or missing, then the entire knot comes undone and ceases to exist (in other words, only the combination of these three codependent elements makes for a "whole person"[21]). Schelling speaks of this Borromean-like codependency as a "living rotation"[22] (in *The Ages of the World*, he likewise posits a movement of "circulation" between the bodily Real and the spiritual Ideal[23]). He then proceeds to propose that both body and spirit are double in nature, each internally split into a bodily (Real) and a spiritual (Ideal) side:[24] the body contains a bodily body (BB) and a spiritual body (SB), and the spirit contains a bodily spirit (BS) and a spiritual spirit (SS).[25] One might think of the Schellingian soul as the junction of overlap between SB and BS, namely, a spiritual body and/or bodily spirit (a similar, earlier version of this conception of the soul is sketched by Schelling in two 1802 pieces: the *Bruno* dialogue and his lectures *On University Studies*[26]). And, (onto)genetically speaking, one might stipulate that the spiritual body as spiritual corporeality (as the desire within the materiality of nature to exceed this materiality) gives rise to or prompts the emergence of the bodily spirit as corporeal spirituality (as the desire actually exceeding the materiality of nature).

Žižek declares that the crucial upshot of this line of Schellingian speculation is the assertion that "there is no *Geist* without *Geisterwelt*, no pure spirituality of *Logos* without the obscene spectral 'spiritual corporeality' of the living dead" (Žižek 1996b, 3–4). Consequently, the insistence on the theoretical necessity of positing the paradoxical existence of the soul as *geistige Körperlichkeit* renders problematic simplistic philosophical distinctions between materialism and idealism[27] (and, reflecting upon his early endeavor to formulate a systematic *Naturphilosophie*, Schelling, in his lectures on modern philosophy from the 1830s, describes the difficulty of trying to fit his own philosophy into allegedly outmoded oppositions such as that between materialist and idealist positions[28]). Insofar as Schelling maintains that the body inherently contains within it that which comes to transcend purely physical being, his matter (as spiritual corporeality) is not the stuff of a reductionistic, mechanistic materialism; additionally, insofar as he simultaneously maintains that the spirit cannot exist without incarnating itself in the supporting medium of some sort of strange quasi-materiality (as corporeal spirituality), Schellingian subjectivity is not the disembodied mind of modern philosophical idealism in its more traditional guises. Although not material in the sense of being an epiphenomenal residue of organic matter, the (pseudo-)immateriality of subjective ideality relies upon the existence of an external matrix of mediation, an ethereal "substance" providing it with a support for its peculiar sort of (non-)being. In short, the immaterial subject is not so immaterial after all. Hence, Žižek hails Schelling as the forefather of subsequent materialist critiques of idealism.[29]

So, given that this detour into an exploration of the Schellingian soul as a sort of spiritual corporeality and/or corporeal spirituality was motivated by the problem of how to situate Schelling in relation to Žižek's Lacanian distinction between drive and desire, how does Žižek translate *geistige Körperlichkeit* into Lacan's language? He claims that "from the Lacanian perspective, it is easy to identify this 'spiritual corporeality' as materialized *jouissance,* '*jouissance* that turned into flesh'" (Žižek 1997a, 47; Žižek 2001b, 102). He then proceeds to propose that:

> there is no symbolic order without the fantasmatic space, no ideal order of *logos* without the pseudomaterial, "virtual," Other Scene where the fantasmatic apparitions can emerge, or, as Schelling put it, there is no Spirit without Spirits, no pure spiritual universe of Ideas without the obscene, ethereal, fantasmatic corporeality of "spirits" (undead, ghosts, vampires . . .). Therein, in this assertion of the unavoidable pseudomaterial fantasmatic support of Ideas, resides the crucial insight of true ("dialectical") materialism. (Žižek 1997a, 60–61)

One of the most philosophically subversive features of psychoanalytic metapsychology, an implication that contemporary thought is still struggling to grasp and digest adequately, is its unique fashion of undermining the distinction between an ephemeral, intangible *Innenwelt* (as, for instance, the ideal realm of subjective mind, replete with its mental activities and insubstantial representational contents) and a tangible, weighty *Umwelt* (as, primarily, the "raw matter" making up everything that simultaneously opposes yet complements immaterial mind and its representations). Lacan could be said to propose that the signifier has, so to speak, its own body, that it possesses a special kind of corporeality (albeit an embodied materiality irreducible to either pole of the standard dichotomy between *res cogitans* and *res extensa*): "Language is not immaterial. It is a subtle body, but body it is" (Lacan 2006f, 248). Or, as Lacan later alludes to this absolutely central thesis, "There is, in a way, a structural substance . . . this is not a metaphor" (*SXIV* 2/1/67). On several occasions, he goes out of his way to emphasize that this special use of the term *material* isn't to be construed as merely metaphorical.[30]

In the very first year of his annual seminar, Lacan, speaking of Freud's *Traumdeutung,* argues that the "sole aim" of this foundational psychoanalytic text "is the demonstration, in the function of the dream, of the superposed significations of a material signifier" (*SI* 244). In the second seminar, Lacan describes language as "something material."[31] In the third seminar, Lacan declares that "the signifier is to be taken in the sense of the material of language" (*SIII* 32). Elsewhere, in "The Direction of the Treatment and the Principles of Its Power," Lacan, when stipulating what a practice of analytic interpretation based on the axiom that "the unconscious is structured like a language" entails, once again employs the word *material:* "Interpretation is . . . grounded . . . in the fact that the unconscious has the radical structure of language and that a material operates in the unconscious according to certain laws" (Lacan 2006k, 496). During this inaugural period of his teaching (in the 1950s, before the ostensible "materialist turn" circa 1960), Lacan makes it abundantly clear that, as a psychoanalyst, he's interested in materiality rather than meaning. He later summarizes this position thus:

> If you open a book of Freud, and particularly those books which are properly about the unconscious, you can be absolutely sure—it is not a probability but a certitude—to fall on a page where it is not only a question of words—naturally in a book there are always words, many printed words—but words which are the object through which one seeks for a way to handle the unconscious. Not even the meaning of the words, but words in their flesh, in their material aspect. (Lacan 1970, 187)

Throughout his later work, Lacan continues to insist that language isn't clearly immaterial in terms of the lightness of conceptual transparency.[32] The signifier is, indeed, a special sort of matter, an incarnate form of material being.[33]

In *Clara*, Schelling, foreshadowing Lacan in a striking way, proclaims that "even language contains a spiritual essence and a corporeal element" (Schelling 2002, 72). Similarly, the Lacanian signifier, in its various guises and instantiations across the span of Lacan's corpus, is, for those embroiled in philosophical competitions pitting materialism against idealism, a paradoxical point of convergence or juxtaposition. The Lacanian signifier is nothing other than that which psychoanalysis demands to be conceptualized as an ideational materiality, as the very "stuff" of mental life, the asubjective "thingliness" of thinking situated within the interiority of the psyche as a foreign embodied presence. Jacques Derrida's well-known essay "*Le facteur de la vérité*," in which he argues that the so-called materiality invoked by Lacan thinly veils what essentially amounts to an "ideality of the signifier"[34]—Lacan is accused of deceptively baptizing his idealism as a form of materialism—neglects this strange status of the Lacanian signifier as part of an ideational materiality, as something neither wholly ideational nor material in any ordinary sense. For someone usually so eager to problematize binary distinctions as inadequate and untenable, Derrida ironically mobilizes a quite standard version of the opposition between ideality and materiality in attacking Lacan: since Lacan's "Seminar on 'The Purloined Letter'" qualifies the signifier as letter as "indivisible," and since physical matter (what Derrida refers to as "empirical materiality") is capable of (phenomenologically speaking) seemingly infinite decomposition, Derrida concludes that "*this 'materiality' deduced from an indivisibility found nowhere, in fact corresponds to an idealization*" (Derrida 1987, 464). Must the acoustic and/or graphic substances constituting ideational traces exhibit the exact same properties as other bits of matter (for instance, the attribute of divisibility)? Would Derrida really force a choice between empirical materiality (in terms of a naïve conception of matter as simple physical stuff, as perceived objects "out there" in the world) and ideality? More intriguingly still, what might be the nature of the implicit yet unmentioned "non-empirical materiality" here?

To return to the main thread of the discussion, Žižek's contention appears to be that the Schellingian notion of spiritual corporeality presages this Lacanian thematic of the materiality of the signifier (the "materialized *jouissance*" mentioned by Žižek above as the Lacanian equivalent of Schellingian *geistige Körperlichkeit* being nothing other than the "letter," that is, *joui-sens* [enjoy-meant] as the structural crystallization of *jouissance* in and through signifiers reduced to their nonsensical, "fleshly" materiality[35]). In line with Schelling's claims about the spiritual domain involving both a spiritual spirit (*SS*) and a bodily spirit (*BS*), Lacan views language (construed in the broad sense of Symbolic structures) as split between significance (the ephemeral, ethereal side of language [*SS*]) and substance (the opaque, weighty side of language [*BS*]). And, like Schelling, he vehemently insists that one cannot have the former without the latter (as Žižek puts it, "no Spirit without Spirits")—namely, one is unable directly and immediately to access the lucid transparency of language as conveyor of meaning without passing through the dark, dense (interfering) medium of language as meaningless matter. (This materiality often, as psychoanalysis reveals, derails the purely conscious-ideal intention to signify, generating unwanted excesses/surpluses in relation to the intended meaning attached to the bodily spirit of signifiers deployed in the process of articulation.[36]) What's more, given Lacan's linkage of subjectivity to the mediation of signifiers, the negativity/non-being of the Schellingian-Lacanian subject is indeed somehow buttressed by a special variety of corporeal spirituality—this spirit as subject cannot exist without spirits as signifiers (although, of course, Lacan would object simply to equating subjectivity with this corporeal spirituality as the support of its [non-]being). In the terms of the Žižekian Schelling, the agitating, conflict-ridden whirlpool of drives (as a spiritual corporeality) produces the violent rupture resulting in the genesis of a split between being and non-being, substance and subject—desire, subsisting within the realm of spiritual corporeality, is what remains after this hemorrhaging, simultaneously conjoining and disjoining this spiritual non-being to bodily being (a formulation akin to Lacan's equation according to which desire is the remainder left over after the subtraction of need from demand[37]).

Having set the stage in this manner, it's now possible to examine productively Schelling's *Weltalter* and Žižek's employment of it (more specifically, the thematic of *Trieb*). As seen, Žižek reads this text as a story of the (onto)genesis of psychical subjectivity, a tale of the emergence of conscious existence out of a non-conscious ground, told in theosophical terms. Schelling himself offers an explanation for why he feels forced to resort to allegories and metaphors that might seem less clear and unambiguous than the discourse of late modern philosophy employed in his earlier writings. The three drafts of the *Weltalter* manuscript represent an unfinished project, a project aiming to treat the three temporal epochs of the past, present, and future. The three extant abortive versions of this project deal exclusively with the past. And by "past," Schelling means the eternally past, namely, a time before (linear) time that precedes the present temporal period (as a chronologically structured succession of now-points): "The primordial state of the contradiction, that wild fire, that life of obsession and craving, is posited as the past. But, because the Godhead, having been from eternity, can never come to have being, that primordial state is posited as an eternal past, as a past that did not first become past, but which was the past from the primordial beginning and since all eternity" (Schelling 2000, 38–39).

However, the philosopher has no choice but to struggle to conceptualize this eternal past, a past differing radically from the present, from within the confines and constraints of the era of the present: "Should everything in this presentation not be utterly intelligible, then one might want to consider that the state described here is a past state, utterly distinct from the present state that one has involuntarily placed as the basis of reflection. The past state is not comprehensible from the present state. Rather, the past state lies at the basis of the present state" (Schelling 2000, 100). The epistemological problem here is similar to what motivates Lacan to refer to his register of the Real as "the impossible." (Imaginary-Symbolic reality is predicated upon the exclusion/subtraction of the Real, so adequately comprehending and describing the Real from within the framework of reality cannot be accomplished directly—only once the Real is "past" can there be both reality and subjectivity.) Additionally, Žižek identifies this Schellingian eternal past as nothing other than the vortex of *Trieb:* "The rotary motion of drives *is in itself past:* it was not once present and now past but *is past from the beginning of time*" (Žižek 1997a, 30). Schelling's "primordial antagonism of drives" is part of a "timeless past."[38] Given his manner of contrasting drive and desire, Žižek views *Trieb* as intrinsically atemporal or anti-temporal due to its functioning as a "rotary movement" in a "repetitive loop"[39] (although this conception of drive as timeless is not without its significant problems[40]).

During Schelling's "Stuttgart Seminars," there are moments when preliminary outlines of the *Weltalter* endeavor are quite visible. Therein, he explicitly asserts that there is a definite parallel between, on the one hand, the genetic dynamics involved in the formation of individual subjectivity and, on the other hand, the process of God's creation of the existent natural world through the elevation of himself above the murky fray of his own drive-laden being.[41] With both the singular subject and the divine creator, a "coming-to-consciousness" proceeds out of a prior "preconscious state (*Bewusstlosigkeit*)" (one could also translate this as "non-conscious") devoid of "any consciousness of division and distinction (*Scheidung und Unterscheidung*)" (Schelling 1994c, 206). What's more, in this same text, Schelling maintains that consciousness itself requires separation, discord, conflict, antagonism, and so on—in short, "division and distinction."[42] To a psychoanalytically inclined ear, an immediately audible resonance with Freud's descriptions of the ego's ontogenesis (especially in the second topography and the metapsychological essays paving the way for this post-1920 shift) can be heard: a discrete conscious "self" arises through a rupture with a preceding state of undifferentiated indistinction. The structured psychical apparatus is built upon sharply drawn lines of demarcation, lines supposedly absent during the earliest phases of the individual's ontogenetic life history.[43]

In *The Ages of the World,* Schelling's theosophical narrative refers to a primordial condition (as the "preconscious state" mentioned in the "Stuttgart Seminars") characterized by a sterile pulsation, a recurrent oscillation, between the opposed forces of expansion and contraction[44] (with Žižek reading this as the repetitive rotary circulation of archaic drives). He even alludes to the notion that this condition, marked by this opposition of forces, entails being trapped in the closure of a vicious circle.[45] So what finally breaks this deadlock? If this pulsation/oscillation between expansion and contraction were in perfect balance, involving a strict complementarity, then this initial state would persist indefinitely. However, Schelling surmises that some sort of disturbing imbalance, an unsettling tension disrupting the cyclical movement of drives, intervenes so as to prompt this originary condition to sunder itself, to give rise to something other: "Contradiction . . . is alone what drives, nay, what co-erces, action. Therefore, without the contradiction, there would be no movement, no life, and no progress. There would only be eternal stop-page, a deathly slumber of all of the forces" (Schelling 2000, 12). He continues:

> A transition from unity to contradiction is incomprehensible. For how should what is in itself one, whole and perfect, be tempted, charmed, and enticed to emerge out of this peace? The transition from contradic-tion to unity, on the other hand, is natural, for contradiction is insuffer-able to everything and everything that finds itself in it will not repose until it has found the unity that reconciles or overcomes it. (Schelling 2000, 12)

Thus, one must ask: Is the non-conscious condition, supposedly subsist-ing in the eternal past as a time before time, really just a philosophical-theoretical fiction as retroactive construction? Is this Real of rotating drives, of the push-and-pull between expansion and contraction, a myth-ical idea associated with and tied to aspects of the present existence of reality (rather than genuinely being an ontological ground preceding this existence)? The reason for asking such questions is that Schelling himself seems to suggest here that a primordial state of balanced equilib-rium between diametrically opposed tendencies never was to begin with, not even in the eternal past (Žižek himself admits as much[46]). If, in the beginning, such equilibrium had been in place, then, strictly speaking, there wouldn't ever have been a beginning as the start of a trajectory of movement (capable of) departing from and leaving behind this point of origin. Schelling unambiguously maintains that, in the beginning, there is "contradiction" (i.e., antagonism, imbalance, strife, tension, etc.).

Consequently, the *Grund* of the drives isn't a solid, cohesive, unified ontological foundation of harmoniously integrated natural energies and impulses, a homogeneous, monolithic mass of dense corporeality at one with itself, but, rather, a fragmented and perturbed juxtaposition of con-flicting elements lacking overall symmetrical measure, proportion, or ratio. In order to account for the (hypothesized) transition from the Real of ground (past) to the reality of existence (present), this past must be presumed to be (in Lacanian parlance) a barred Real (i.e., a Real that is always already out of joint with itself). One must assume that, as it were, the ground fails to ground, that *Grund* is *Ungrund,* an abyssal groundlessness.

8

Acting in Time: Temporality and the *Ent-Scheidung*

In the *Weltalter* narrative, the unbalanced *Grund* as *Ungrund,* due to its dissatisfying instability and desire-provoking contradictions, prompts the sudden event of a gesture of negation (with ground's internal inconsistency being a vital condition of possibility allowing for this gesture's very occurrence—the cracks within the foundation of *Grund* are the open spaces, the clearing, within and out of which can burst forth something other than this ground's own drives). According to Schelling, this exit from (via immanent negation of) the inconsistent ground of the barred Real is the true moment of beginning (rather than the eternal past of the vortex of *Trieb* qualifying as a proper beginning). He asserts that the beginning of any movement whatsoever is predicated on a negation, a negation of a point that becomes a starting point through this very negation (i.e., the starting point is a locus of beginning only insofar as it's overcome or surpassed).[1] In combined theosophical and psychoanalytic terms, God must "abject" his unconscious, quasi-material side in order to become himself as a fully constituted subject; in fact, it is through this expulsive act of abjection, this violent taking of distance from the drives, that God comes to (be) himself.[2] Once again, Freud comes to mind: in the concluding paragraphs of his 1925 essay "Negation" ("*Die Verneinung*"), he proposes that such foundational distinctions as inner versus outer, self versus other, and so on are produced by the mechanism of negation broadly construed (the earliest ontogenetic version of this being the movement of casting out, forcefully rejecting, or turning away from that which is unpleasurable).[3]

From a Lacanian perspective, an especially interesting feature of Schelling's theosophy here is his employment of a distinction between "being" and "having" (see chapter 5). Immediately after asserting that non-being is far from mere nothingness (i.e., specific sorts of negativity enjoy a certain ontological status), Schelling states, "For that which is in each thing the actual Being cannot . . . ever be one and the same with that which has being" (Schelling 2000, 14). Therefore, it follows that whatever "has" being is something other than this being itself; whatever has being must, as other than being, be a sort of non-being/negativity (just as the Lacanian subject-as-$ "has" a body, but, as itself a lack of be-ing, isn't reducible to this corporeality). Schelling proceeds to align be-ing with the drives and, hence, to maintain that the drives don't "have" being—they just "are." The transition from the being of the drives (the Real as *Grund*) to the having of this being (a possessing made possible through the negating of this ontological ground) is brought about by what Schelling names the "cision" (*die Scheidung*—a divorce, parting, or separation).[4]

For the Žižekian interpretation, the event of rupture with the bog of the drives is of special interest. As early as *Les plus sublime des hystériques* (1988), Žižek's attention is drawn to this crucial moment. He emphasizes that the Schellingian act (as a decision [*Entscheidung*] to divorce, part, or separate [*scheiden*][5]), like aspects of the Lacanian Real, is an occurrence that has never taken place within the field of established reality (as the domain of existence opposed to that of ground), but that, nonetheless, must be presupposed as having happened, as always already past, in or-der to account for the status quo of the present.[6] As Jean-Marie Vaysse puts it in his examination of Schelling's role as an intellectual predeces-sor of psychoanalysis, "The pre-historic is that advent of the origin which has never taken place, which has the force of fate and never comes to the odyssey of consciousness that it nonetheless governs" (Vaysse 1999, 281). Insofar as historicity is coextensive with the chronological temporality of present reality (as opposed to the immobile eternity of the forever-past Real), this founding intervention (i.e., the act as *Ent-Scheidung*) is "out-side of history" (*hors l'histoire*).[7] Žižek opens the first chapter of his book on Schelling, *The Indivisible Remainder,* with a discussion of this issue of the beginning (this analysis appears verbatim early on in "The Abyss of Freedom"[8]):

> How, then, should one begin an essay on Schelling? Perhaps the most appropriate way is by focusing on the *problem of Beginning itself,* the cru-cial problem of German Idealism . . . Schelling's "materialist" contribu-tion is best epitomized by his fundamental thesis according to which, to put it bluntly, *the true Beginning is not at the beginning:* there is something that precedes the Beginning itself—a rotary motion whose vicious cycle is broken, in a gesture analogous to the cutting of the Gordian knot, by the Beginning proper, that is, the primordial act of decision. The begin-ning of all beginnings, the beginning *kat' exohen*—"the mother of all beginnings," as one would say today—is, of course, the "*In the beginning was the Word*" from the Gospel according to St John: prior to it, there was nothing, that is, the void of divine eternity. According to Schelling, how-ever, "eternity" is not a nondescript mass—a lot of things take place in it.

Prior to the Word there is the chaotic-psychotic universe of blind drives, their rotary motion, their undifferentiated pulsating; and the Beginning occurs when the Word is pronounced which "represses," rejects into the eternal Past, this self-enclosed circuit of drives. In short, *at the Beginning proper stands a resolution, an act of decision which, by differentiating between past and present, resolves the preceding unbearable tension of the rotary motion of drives:* the true Beginning is the passage from the "closed" rotary motion to "open" progress, from drive to desire—or, in Lacanian terms, from the Real to the Symbolic. (Žižek 1996b, 13)

In *Les plus sublime des hystériques* as well as his later texts, Žižek associates the act of decision-separation with the shift toward the mediation of Symbolic structures, with the move into the realm of the word-signifier. His 1988 reading of Schelling compares this act with the Lacanian notion of the "master-signifier" (S_1):[9] the *Ent-Scheidung* is tantamount to the utterly contingent, groundless gesture of raising an arbitrary Symbolic element to a foundational status (as an inexplicable "truth" [*vérité*]), thereby enabling the ensuing construction of a whole series of derivative substructures (S_2 as the chain of signifiers, as "knowledge" [*savoir*], constructed on the basis of S_1).[10] In *The Ages of the World,* Schelling indeed refers to the pacifying effects of the "word."[11] And, as seen, Žižek's Lacanian embellishments on this aspect of Schelling's philosophy stress the movement from the drive of the Real to the desire of the Symbolic. But, more importantly, he utilizes this facet of his Lacan-influenced exegetical appropriation of Schelling to rethink, with the combined resources of philosophy and psychoanalysis, the rapport between temporality and autonomy (the topic of freedom will be given detailed treatment in chapter 9).

In the "Stuttgart Seminars," Schelling bluntly asserts that the event of the *Ent-Scheidung* isn't to be thought of as an act that occurs at some point within the flow of chronological-linear time. He maintains that this intervention is itself atemporal: "Is this act of self-differentiation temporal? Does it take place against the background of an infinite or a determinate time? Answer: Neither of these is true. It bears no relation to time, and is by definition eternal" (Schelling 1994c, 205). He goes on to note that "the Universe . . . does have a beginning . . . but it does not have a beginning *in time;* all time inheres *in* the universe, and no time is outside of it" (Schelling 1994c, 205). One key effect of the *Ent-Scheidung* is to give rise to chronological temporality, to initiate the linear movement of time. This decision-separation is not "*in* the universe" (and thus, in time), but, rather, it creates the universe (and thus, time). Although treated as archaic and primordial (albeit not archaic and primordial in the sense of a now-past-but-once-present moment), the rotary motion of the drives is not to be mistaken for the "true beginning" per se. That is to say, only with the cancellation/negation of this vortex of *Trieb* through the gesture of the *Ent-Scheidung* is a genuine beginning possible, an initiation of a (temporal) movement of change and flux (instead of cyclical repetition) flowing away from its thereafter-surpassed past point of origin.[12] As with Lacan's Real cause as *tuché* or Derrida's description of the founding of the law and its apparatuses,[13] Schelling's act of breaking away from the Real of ground cannot itself be included within the parameters of the reality of existence that it generates as an outcome (here, one encounters the logic according to which a certain type of cause is necessarily obfuscated by its effects—the domain of the cause's effects is structurally unable to accommodate or integrate its own "lost cause"). Time begins with the *Ent-Scheidung*. But this decision-separation cannot be included within or contained by the temporal frame that it erects.

Žižek highlights the ground-versus-existence distinction as absolutely central to the later Schelling's post-idealist philosophy (or, more accurately, philosophies). However, this distinction evidently entails an even more fundamental dichotomy between the closure of eternity (i.e., the permanently-past iterative looping of the drives—the Real of ground) and the openness of temporality (i.e., the present epoch of historical time—the reality of existence). He explains:

> Schelling's "materialism" is . . . encapsulated in his persistent claim that one should presuppose an eternally past moment when God himself was at the mercy of the antagonism of matter, without any guarantee that A—the spiritual principle of Light—would eventually prevail over B—the obscure principle of Ground. Since there is nothing outside God, this "crazy God"—the antagonistic rotary motion of contracted matter—has to beget out of himself a Son, that is, the Word that will resolve the unbearable tension. The undifferentiated pulsation of drives is thus supplanted by the stable network of differences that sustains the self-identity of the differentiated entities: in its most elementary dimension, Word is the medium of differentiation. We encounter here what is perhaps the fundamental conceptual opposition of Schelling's entire philosophical edifice: the opposition between the atemporal "closed" rotary motion of drives and the "open" linear progression of time. The act of "primordial repression" by means of which God ejects the rotary motion of drives into the eternal past and thereby "creates time," that is, opens up the difference between past and present, is *his first deed as a free Subject:* in accomplishing it, he suspends the crippling alternative of the subjectless abyss of Freedom and the Subject who is unfree, caught in the vicious cycle of rotary motion. (Žižek 1997a, 30–31)

The conceptual pivot here is the Freudian notion of "primal repression" (a few pages later, Žižek makes an explicit reference to Freud on this matter[14]). As Freud defines it, primal repression (itself a speculative notion referring to something that cannot directly be observed or analytically recovered as a kind of long-lost memory of a specific episode) occurs once a drive is first attached to a drive-representative, after the ideational-mnemic traces composing a distinct object are inscribed within a specific sector of the libidinal economy. Following the defensive stigmatization of this libidinally charged representation, the cathexis of this *Ur*-object creates, in a manner of speaking, a psychical black hole, a point of powerful attraction dragging everything that subsequently enters its orbit into the oblivion of repression. In more straightforward language, Freud stipulates that the original object-representative of a drive undergoes primal repression, and that all other repressions subsequent to this (i.e., "secondary repressions") are a result of other representational elements in the psyche having entered into associational connection with the mass of previously repressed materials (the accumulation of this mass being, at root, catalyzed in the first instance by primal repression).[15] It's worth noting that Žižek's invocation of this Freudian notion falls prey to a common misreading of Freud on this topic. According to Freud, primal repression occurs after a drive-representative already has been established in the psyche's libidinal economy (in Schellingian language, after Logos or the Word has been introduced into the vortex of *Trieb*). However, Žižek speaks of the very introduction of this representational mediation into the domain of the drives as itself the moment of primal repression (rather than this moment being, as it appears to be in Freud's metapsychological system, a prerequisite for primal repression—perhaps this moment, the one erroneously spoken of by Žižek as primal repression, might more productively be conceptualized as akin to a sort of Lacanian fundamental foreclosure [see chapter 4]). In Žižek's hands, Schelling makes a crucial contribution to Freudian theory not in terms of providing a clarification concerning the nature of primal repression, but rather at the level of shedding light on the relationship between, on the one hand, the unconscious dimension of psychical subjectivity and, on the other hand, the initiation and execution of decisions and deeds.

Here and there, Freud occasionally mentions what he puzzlingly designates as the "choice of neurosis."[16] What does it mean to say that an individual "chooses" his or her psychopathological character structure, especially for a model of mind based upon the axiom that an unconscious beyond conscious control (and, hence, presumably outside the parameters of any decision-making agency capable of choice) overdetermines mental life? Don't psychopathologies, at least according to psychoanalysis, befall individuals, instead of being opted for through some sort of strange decision-making process? In certain ways, the Lacanian "subject of the unconscious" exhibits a similar perplexing oddness: isn't the unconscious fundamentally asubjective, that which escapes or exceeds the domain of subjectivity? Through his reading of Schelling, Žižek provides a depiction of the unconscious allowing for a resolution of this apparent Freudian-Lacanian paradox, a resolution that hinges on positing the category of "unconscious acts" (some might view this as replacing one paradox with another). In the lengthy passage quoted in the paragraph above, Žižek links subjectification (i.e., the dynamic of becoming a subject, of subjectivity emerging out of the morass of the libidinal economy as a substance divided against itself, as a barred Real) with primal repression as the representational *Aufhebung* of the vortex of *Trieb*. For Schellingian philosophy as well as Freudian-Lacanian metapsychology, prior to the advent of repression (itself conditioned by a prior establishment of the rudiments of Symbolic-structural mediation), there is no distinction to be made between that which is conscious and that which is unconscious; neither psychical system exists yet per se. Through a certain "cut" (the Schellingian *Ent-Scheidung* as the moment of Lacanian "symbolic castration"[17]), two new strata are created simultaneously: the unconscious and the subject. The advent of representational mediation permits subjectivity (i.e., the *parlêtre* as $) to arise as what detaches itself from and transcends the turbulent immediacy of the drives, with this immediacy having correlatively become what forever after must be permanently repressed (i.e., unconscious). The Žižekian fusion of Schelling and psychoanalysis seems to propose that the unconscious and the subject are co-emergent, owing their existence to the same ontogenetic factors. Thus, Lacan's phrase "subject of the unconscious" might be interpreted as, in one sense, signaling the claim that the process of subjectification is conditioned by or dependent upon the movements and mechanisms generating the unconscious. In other words, no subject(ification) is possible without the creation of an unconscious. At least for traditional versions of the modern philosophical subject, this contention is quite subversive: the lucid transparency of the cogito is merely one side of a coin whose other side, its necessary obverse, is an opaque impenetrability—the one entails the other.

In *The Ages of the World*, Schelling describes a deed that cannot ever be brought before conscious awareness. More specifically, he identifies the mythical moment when an individual "decides" upon the nature of his or her essential character (strikingly akin to Freud's idea that someone "chooses" his or her neurosis) as precisely such a deed:

> There is a law in humanity: there is an incessant primordial deed that
> precedes each and every single action and through which one is actually

Oneself. Yet this primordial deed sinks down into unfathomable depths with respect to the consciousness that elevates itself above it. Thereby, this primordial deed becomes a beginning that can never be sublimated, a root of reality that cannot be reached through anything . . . The decision that would make any kind of act into a true beginning may not be brought before consciousness. (Schelling 2000, 85)

This Schellingian thematic concerning a decisive founding/grounding act opening up (and yet thereafter excluded from) the space of conscious experience is a theoretical object of fascination for Žižek, beginning with his earliest texts. His glosses on it establish clear linkages between the eternal past, the primal repression of the *Ent-Scheidung*, and the genesis of autonomous subjectivity: "The basic character of every human being—good or evil—is the result of an original, eternal, eternally past, a priori, transcendental choice—that is, a choice which was *always already made*, although it never took place in temporal, everyday reality" (Žižek 1989, 168). This remark by Žižek raises two important questions. First, are the drives and their rotary motion the distinctive, exclusive content of the temporal epoch of the eternal past (as Žižek repeatedly claims elsewhere), or, alternatively, does this eternal past also contain the act-decision that breaks with these same drives (as he maintains here)? Second, although this "choice" might be a priori or transcendental in relation to fully constituted experiential reality (as opposed to its Real ground), what are the (meta-transcendental) conditions of possibility for the occurrence of this decisive moment itself, that is to say, what clears the ground for the irruption of the *Ent-Scheidung*? As will become evident (see chapter 9), these two questions are bound up with each other. Moreover, the ensuing effort to answer them promises to reveal both the strengths and the limitations of Žižek's philosophically significant interpretation and employment of Schelling.

Later on, in two texts from 2001 (*On Belief* and *The Fright of Real Tears*), Žižek notes: "At the apogee of German Idealism, F. W. J. Schelling deployed the notion of the primordial decision-differentiation (*Ent-Scheidung*), the unconscious atemporal deed by means of which the subject chooses his/her eternal character which, afterwards, within his/her conscious-temporal life, is experienced as the inexorable necessity, as 'the way s/he always was'" (Žižek 2001c, 147; Žižek 2001b, 151). Again, a tangled knot of complexities is embedded in a brief passage. The most pressing problem concerns the status of the subject here. Is subjectivity an outcome/result of this "unconscious atemporal deed"? Or instead, is subjectivity that which performs this deed rather than that which is produced by this deed? Does Žižek rigorously distinguish between the subject and this subject's "character" (perhaps along the lines of Lacan's *sujet-moi* distinction)? If not, then how can subjectivity be both that which is generated by the deed of the *Ent-Scheidung* as well as that which decides upon this same deed? How can the subject give birth to itself? Simply baptizing a vicious circle a "temporal loop" of ex nihilo auto-engendering doesn't get around the problem. It provides only a specious pseudo-solution by renaming the difficulty without thereby resolving it.

So why is it that the Schellingian deed, as viewed through the lens of Freud's "choice of neurosis" or Lacan's act, must necessarily be unconscious? Why can't the *Ent-Scheidung* be brought back before the subject's consciousness? The complementary inverse of the Hegelian effect that exceeds its cause is operative here, namely, the Kantian cause that exceeds (or recedes behind) its effect. The transcendental act/deed founding consciousness cannot be (re)introduced into the circumscribed reality of the experiential field to which it gives rise. In other words, as Kant maintains, the conditions of possibility for experience cannot be experienced directly in and of themselves, since they always already underlie any and every possible experience as a priori enabling mechanisms. (A Schellingian version of this is the insistence that the "moment" founding [linear] time cannot itself be considered as having occurred in time; or, as Freud similarly notes, primal repression leaves no traces behind that could even potentially be accessed by a reflective introspection in search of a discrete memory-episode.) Likewise, the microcosmic version of Kant's macrocosmic cosmological antinomy (i.e., the psychical antinomy—see chapter 3) also prohibits the transcendental ground of the subject from being fully subjectified. Terry Eagleton alludes to a comparable logic in the opening lines of his review of Badiou's *Ethics*. Eagleton comments that "if a transformation is deep-seated enough, it might also transform the very criteria by which we could identify it, thus making it unintelligible to us. But if it is intelligible, it might be because the transformation was not radical enough" (Eagleton 2003, 246). Perhaps the Schellingian-Žižekian act-decision is precisely the sort of "deep-seated transformation" mentioned in the first of the two alternatives proposed by Eagleton, that is, an alteration so radical that the criteria for its representation and recognition aren't available—and this because such criteria (as well as any representations and recognitions) depend upon it for their very existence.

In certain places, Žižek uses Schelling to argue that the unconscious isn't to be identified merely as the vortex of *Trieb* (in orthodox Freudian terms, the unconscious isn't simply the id). Instead, what remains unconscious in the constituted subject is, above all else, the cutting, disruptive gesture of the act/deed as *Ent-Scheidung* founding subjectivity itself in its (attempted) jettisoning of the drives. Subjectivity's ownmost origin is the most foreign and inaccessible thing for it:

> This primordial act of "repression" which opens up the dimension of temporality *is itself "eternal," atemporal*, in strict analogy with the primordial act of decision by means of which man chooses his eternal character. That is to say: apropos of Schelling's claim that man's consciousness arises from the primordial act which separates present-actual consciousness from the spectral, shadowy realm of the unconscious, one has to ask a seemingly naïve but crucial question: what, precisely, is the unconscious here? Schelling's answer is unambiguous: the "unconscious" is not primarily the rotary motion of drives ejected into the eternal past; rather, the "unconscious" is the very act of *Ent-Scheidung* by means of which drives were ejected into the past. Or—to put it in slightly different terms—what is truly "unconscious" in man is not the immediate opposite of consciousness, the obscure and confused "irrational" vortex of drives, but the very founding gesture of consciousness, the act of decision by means of which I "choose myself"—that is, combine this multitude of drives into the unity of my Self. The "unconscious" is not the passive stuff of inert drives to be used by the creative "synthetic" activity of the conscious Ego; the "unconscious" in its most radical dimension is, rather, *the highest Deed of my self-positing.* (Žižek 1996b, 33–34)

Based on this passage, one must conclude that, from the Žižekian perspective, the Schellingian temporal category of the eternal past contains both the vortex of *Trieb* as well as the act of the *Ent-Scheidung* (i.e., the drives as well as their primal repression). The unconscious is not "primarily" the thriving id-body of the drives, although they too are part of it. Perhaps this qualification introduced by Žižek here ("primarily") can be understood as signaling an implicit line of argumentation: prior to the "cision" of the act-decision generating the subject through a splitting-off from the Real of its own *Grund*, there is no distinction whatsoever between the unconscious and consciousness (meaning that neither of them yet exists as such). Hence the unconscious, along with consciousness, is created by the *Ent-Scheidung*, and the latter itself is almost instantaneously absorbed into one of the products of its very own intervention (i.e., the act-decision creates the unconscious, and is then swallowed up by this same unconscious which it produced, devoured by its own progeny). As Schelling himself puts it: "Man must first develop and grow even to get to freedom; and even freedom rises up in this world from necessity's obscurity, bursting forth only in its last appearance as inexplicable, divine, as a flash of eternity that splits up the darkness of this world, but that is also immediately devoured by its very own effect" (Schelling 2002, 28). In and of themselves, in their (hypothetical) existence prior to the event of the subject's genesis, the drives are neither conscious nor unconscious, since these two sectors of the divided psyche have yet to congeal out of an archaic, undifferentiated ground. Thus, in relation to the unconscious, the primal repression of the *Ent-Scheidung* is "primary," with the drives as unconscious being "secondary" insofar as their unconscious status is conferred upon them only after the occurrence of this act-decision.

This recasting of the unconscious leads Žižek to contend that the unconscious, concealed behind the veils of repression, isn't to be understood (merely) as an aggregate of overdetermining forces and factors compromising or impeding the individual's autonomous capacities as a free agent (this being a crude yet common depiction of the psychoanalytic unconscious). Rather, repression frequently conceals the opposite, namely, what Žižek dubs the Schellingian "abyss of freedom," a radical indeterminacy and groundlessness covered over by various psychical layers seeking to avoid this void. Confronting the unconscious, instead of involving a realization that one is a puppet dancing on the end of personal-historical strings held firmly in the grasp of a libidinal puppet-master, might very well amount to coming face-to-face with an abyssal autonomy, an anonymous groundlessness situated as the extimate kernel of one's subjective existence. Paraphrasing Freud ("the normal man is not only far more immoral than he believes but also far more moral than he knows" [*SE* 19:52]), one could say that the normal man is not only far more determined than he believes but also far freer than he knows.[18]

9

The Terror of Freedom: The Forever Missing Mandate of Nature

One might think that human freedom, an apparent autonomy seen nowhere else in the natural world, is something individuals prize as singu-
larly emblematic of their humanity, as a quasi-divine gift forming the
core of a sense of dignity and worth. One of Schelling's post-Kantian
innovations is his reversal of this impression as regards freedom. Already
in Kant's practical philosophy, the status of human autonomy, itself an
innate property of beings endowed with reason, is somewhat ambiguous.
Although deserving of esteem, this autonomy is, at least phenomenologically speaking, experienced by those to whom it is bequeathed as, more
often than not, a painful burden, a guilt-inducing voice commanding
obedience and demanding the sacrifice of the comfortable pursuit of
pleasure-oriented inclinations.[1] Schelling goes much further: the true
extent of human freedom is such that encountering it is liable to provoke horror or terror. In the *Clara* dialogue, Clara herself observes that
"the sight of freedom—not the freedom that is usually so-called, but the
true and real one—would have to be unbearable to man, even though
people talk about it continually and praise it at every instant" (Schelling
2002, 28). The *Weltalter* manuscripts echo Clara's remark: "Most people
are frightened precisely by this abyssal freedom . . . where they see a flash
of freedom, they turn away from it as if from an utterly injurious flash
of lightning and they feel prostrated by freedom as an appearance that
comes from the ineffable, from eternal freedom, from where there is no
ground whatsoever" (Schelling 2000, 78). As Žižek puts it, "in German
idealism it was Kant, and especially Schelling, who said that the most horrible thing to encounter for a human being is this abyss of free will; when
somebody simply acts out of free will. And that's very traumatic to accept" (Žižek and Daly 2004, 166). Elsewhere, he characterizes Schellingian freedom as the unsettling "explosion" of an "abyss," as the violent,
intrusive return of the archaic *Urgrund* within the restricted realm of
experiential reality.[2]

Psychoanalytically speaking, this would suggest that "abyssal freedom"—Žižek stresses that the Schellingian act as *Ent-Scheidung* is ground-
less/self-grounded, being an utterly contingent gesture with nothing

preestablished above or beneath it[3]—isn't "unconscious" simply in the sense of being structurally incompatible with consciousness. (The preceding analyses of the primal repression effectuated by the "cision" of the act/deed suggest that an inherent, necessary barrier bars consciousness from reflectively grasping the "primal scene" of its own point of originary auto-engendering.) Rather, the specter of this freedom is barred from consciousness—in a perturbing, upsetting "flash," it occasionally irrupts into the sphere from which it normally remains excluded—more for defensive than for structural reasons. In other words, autonomy is repressed (and hence unconscious) not just because the groundless founding act generating consciousness cannot itself become conscious; this autonomy is repressed/unconscious also because it's disturbing, even, in some cases, terrifying (or, as Žižek claims, "traumatic"). In several texts following the publication of his two studies centered on Schelling (*The Indivisible Remainder* and "The Abyss of Freedom"), Žižek increasingly highlights this abyssal freedom ("this horrifying abyss of Will"[4]) and its defensive occlusion.

Already in *Les plus sublime des hystériques*, Žižek touches upon the Schellingian theme concerning the frightening nature of freedom. At this early point, he identifies Schelling's meditations on evil as prompting this particular, peculiar characterization of human autonomy.[5] In the *Critique of Practical Reason* and *The Metaphysics of Morals*, Kant risks implicitly asserting that the exercise of freedom invariably results in opting for the Good, for what is ethically or morally right (although his *Religion Within the Limits of Reason Alone* nuances matters with its well-known account of "radical evil"[6]). If an agent "chooses" evil, he does so not on the basis of utilizing his transcendental freedom, possessed as part of a rational-noumenal subjectivity, but, rather, due to heteronomous, irrational forces (i.e., instincts, passions, etc.) overriding his agency itself. In short, one cannot freely choose evil, since such a "choice" is prompted by the very abdication of one's position as an autonomous subject capable of the act of choosing. (Apropos this Kantian difficulty, Henry Allison attempts to circumvent the problem by arguing, via his "incorporation thesis," that the exercise of freedom occurs at the level of the agent choosing to abdicate his or her agency—thus, one can indeed freely opt for evil by voluntarily annulling one's freedom in favor of one's "pathological inclinations.")[7] Schelling's 1809 *Freiheitschrift* intends, in part, to address directly this apparent shortcoming in Kant's practical philosophy.

Schelling asserts that human autonomy is a freedom for evil as well as good, that individuals contain an a priori propensity for the diabolical as well as the angelic.[8] Given that Schellingian freedom is, in essence, groundless, there is no transcendent law, no higher, normative principle of practical reason, governing its employment (as Lacan would put it, "there is no Other of the Other," or "the big Other does not exist"). The "good" side of this freedom (i.e., the one explored at length by Kant) is frequently a source of pain insofar as it obliges individuals, in the name of a moral rule, to do what doesn't feel pleasurable. But the "evil" side of this freedom is also painful, albeit for a different reason. Schelling's treatment of this topic suggests that individuals, if they truly stopped to ponder what they're capable of thanks to the void of abyssal freedom situated at the groundless core of their very being, would realize that they possess the capacity to engage in the most monstrous of atrocities: "It would be desirable if the rottenness in man could only go so far as animality; but unfortunately man can only stand above or beneath animals" (Schelling 1936, 49). One aspect of autonomy rendering it disturbing is the fact that there's no guarantee whatsoever that those endowed with it will act "properly," in ways respectful of others (or even of themselves—one must keep in mind that Žižek repeatedly links the autonomous subject with the Freudian-Lacanian death drive;[9] and the death drive involves masochistic self-destructiveness, the human capacity to deviate from the paths laid down by natural or rational self-interest).

In his 2000 book *The Fragile Absolute*, Žižek deploys an implicit revision of his own previous interpretive glosses on the Schellingian notion of *Grund* (as with his later critiques of the reading of Lacan as a quasi-Kantian transcendental thinker, this shift of perspective in relation to Schelling involves Žižek reacting against his own earlier exegetical positions). The whole thematic of the vortex of *Trieb* seems to entail that the horrible, terrifying nature of the ground as Real has to do with it being a disgusting mass of palpitating, raw flesh, of formless, roiling matter (or, at a minimum, the fully constituted subject can encounter or experience it only in this shocking form). As seen, Žižek dwells extensively on such imagery (and not just during his discussions of Schelling). However, in *The Fragile Absolute* he moves in a different direction:

> What we encounter here is . . . the logic of the "vanishing mediator": of the founding gesture of differentiation which must sink into invisibility once the difference between the "irrational" vortex of drives and the universe of *logos* is in place. Schelling's fundamental move is thus not simply to ground the ontologically structured universe of *logos* in the horrible vortex of the Real; if we read him carefully, there is a premonition in his work that this terrifying vortex of the pre-ontological Real itself is (accessible to us only in the guise of) a fantasmatic narrative, a lure destined to distract us from the true traumatic cut, that of the abyssal act of *Ent-Scheidung*. And today this lesson is more relevant than ever:

> when we are confronted with an image of that deep horror which under-
> lies our well-ordered surface, we should never forget that the images of
> this horrible vortex are ultimately a lure, a trap to make us forget where
> the true horror lies. (Žižek 2000f, 73)

What is "the true horror"? Žižek replies with a rhetorical question: "And
what if *this* is . . . the ultimate lesson of Schelling: that the horror of the
ultimate *Grund,* this monstrous apparition with hundreds of hands, this
vortex that threatens to swallow everything, is a lure, a defense against
the abyss of the pure *act?*" (Žižek 2000f, 78). The genuine horror of
the Real isn't, at root, that a thriving, pulsating materiality lies beneath
the smooth, polished surfaces of Imaginary-Symbolic reality; rather, this
horror of bodily depths is actually superficial, a misleading, defensive
distraction, in relation to the truly terrifying "abyss of freedom," the faceless void of (in)human autonomy, the (as Vaysse describes it) inhuman
part of human freedom[10] (which is akin to the monstrous visage of the
Cartesian-Kantian-Hegelian subject, this "night of the world" as a contractive black hole—see chapters 1 and 13).

   This shift in emphasis from *Grund* (as the rotary motion of the drives,
the fleshly id-body) to *Urgrund* (as abyssal freedom, the ultimate, groundless nothingness out of which everything springs ex nihilo) corresponds
to a more overarching change in Žižek's recent work, a change involving
a reassessment of the register of the Real. Along these lines, in *The Puppet and the Dwarf* (2003), he asks whether, "with reference to the notion
of the Thing as the ultimate traumatic unbearable Referent that we are
unable to confront directly, since its direct presence is too blinding: what
if this very notion that delusive everyday reality is a veil concealing the
Horror of the unbearable Thing is false, what if the ultimate veil concealing the Real is the very notion of the horrible Thing behind the veil?"
(Žižek 2003b, 67). How should one handle this apparent shift of exegetical weight between, on the one hand, the earlier Žižekian interpretation
of Schelling centered on the material Real (i.e., *Grund* as the vortex of
Trieb) and, on the other hand, the later Žižekian focus on what could be
called an "immaterial" Real (i.e., *Urgrund* as the abyss of freedom)?

   Much of the preceding analysis has been quietly and steadily building
to the following assertion: the opposition between *Grund* and *Urgrund,*
between the vortex of *Trieb* and the abyss of freedom, is a false dichotomy.
The domain of the drives is itself the domain underpinning human autonomy. *Trieb* is freedom—or, at a minimum, it is the contingent material
condition of possibility for the emergence of full-fledged autonomy.[11]
In Schellingian parlance, *Grund* is *Ungrund;* the ground is incapable of
functioning in a grounding capacity insofar as it is antagonistically and

unstably divided against itself. The ground is not a ground as something grounded or grounding (Heidegger declares that from Schelling's standpoint, "the nature of man is grounded in freedom" [Heidegger 1985, 9], which would now, in this present context, require being interpreted as saying that the ground of humanity's distinctly human essence is the very lack of a grounding essence or nature). Before reconnecting this assertion with Schelling himself, a brief detour through some of Žižek's recent remarks concerning new trajectories for his research promises to be productive. In his interviews with Glyn Daly as well as his study centered on Deleuze, Žižek offers a thumbnail sketch of these trajectories. In both contexts, he somewhat paradoxically asserts that genuine materialism (as opposed to a materialism that would cede explanatory terrain to idealist systems or an idealism masquerading as materialism) has to base itself on the notion of "the disappearance of matter."[12] (One might call to mind here the example of quantum physics, in which the ultimate constituents of material reality are unimaginable, ephemeral pseudo-entities devoid of dense, earthy weight, entities that can be descriptively captured only through pure, "immaterial" mathematical formalizations; with quantum physics, the substantiality of substance is, so to speak, desubstantialized—see chapter 13.) Referring to Kant, he declares that "the only consistent materialist position is that the world does not exist—in the Kantian sense of the term, as a self-enclosed whole" (Žižek and Daly 2004, 97). In the Žižekian view, an authentic materialist paradigm must be based upon the axiomatic contention that material being itself (whether as body, nature, world, etc.) is internally inconsistent, shot through with antagonisms, fissures, gaps, and tensions. For a (Žižekian) materialist, the foundations of the ontological edifice must contain cracks. In other words, the materiality of the Real is not homogeneous and harmoniously at one with itself; the Real is barred. Why is this thesis so crucial? Why is it, as Žižek alleges, essential for advancing a materialist theory of the subject that is not vulnerable to relapses into idealist models?

Succinctly stated, if one maintains that the Real of material being isn't barred (i.e., that body, nature, and world are organically integrated substances in which the functions of their various constituent elements are coordinated and operate in tandem), then one must either deny the existence of subjectivity (at a minimum, dismissing it as an epiphenomenal residue of physical reality) or regress back into crude versions of the Real-versus-Ideal dichotomy. Given its stifling ontological closure, the materiality of vulgar materialism cannot give rise to a non-epiphenomenal subjectivity. Thus, if one wishes to assert the materialist thesis concerning the primacy of the material Real while simultaneously positing the effective existence of a non-epiphenomenal subjectivity, either one immediately betrays materialism by endorsing the idealist contention that an entirely separate domain "above" material being "exists" on its own, or, alternatively, one struggles to find a means of delineating the material genesis of the more-than-material subject. Žižek explains his current materialist philosophical program by contrasting it with Badiou's thought. Whereas Badiou allegedly insists upon a strict separation between the ontological level of being and the non/trans-ontological dimension of event[13] (a dimension on whose plane subjects are constituted), Žižek is in search of a theory that demonstrates how, to put it in Badiouian terms, the event can emerge from being (i.e., how what breaks with and transcends being could be generated out of being itself). This, he says, is "the ultimate materialist problem . . . How does being explode into event? . . . That is to say, how does the order of being have to be structured so that something like event is possible?" (Žižek and Daly 2004, 137). Put somewhat differently, what are the meta-transcendental conditions (here, the very structure of being making possible the emergence of something other than being) for the transcendental subject (i.e., a subjectivity that, once produced, is thereafter decisive for the shaping of its mediated reality)? Žižek's answer is clear and unambiguous: the material Real of being must be "not all," that is, it must contain splits within itself, splits within whose crack-like clearings is held open the possibility for the self-sundering of this same substance. This sundering is a vital part of what produces the subject.

Žižek's current dabbling in the area of cognitive science is motivated by the same set of concerns stemming from his Schelling-inspired reassessment of materialism (see also chapter 13). He insists on the need to engage cognitivism, on the urgency of a philosophically informed psychoanalytic encounter with the challenges posed by this competing explanatory paradigm.[14] What does he anticipate emerging from this engagement? Žižek, loosely employing the biologistic language usually favored by cognitive science, indicates that he's interested in developing the theme of human self-reflexive consciousness as the "by-product" of a glitch in the evolutionary program of nature, "a kind of snag in the biological weave."[15] As he articulates it just a few pages later, "Something goes terribly wrong in nature: nature produces an unnatural monstrosity . . . This would be my fundamental model. It is this primordial dimension, this transcendental condition, which interests me" (Žižek and Daly 2004, 65). So the "transcendental condition" (in this case, a sort of contingent-material a priori) making possible the production of "an unnatural monstrosity" (i.e., Žižek's Lacanian version of the subject of modern philosophy) is a "snag in the biological weave" (i.e., the fractured inconsistency of the fabric of nature as the "not all" of being's materiality).

Right after mentioning what might be involved in a philosophical-psychoanalytic appropriation of select features of cognitivism ("In cognitivism we encounter a dysfunctional paradox: that awareness and the human mind presuppose a certain non-economic gesture, a certain failure. So you get the contours of a certain fundamental malfunction which cannot be explained in terms of cognitivist evolutionism" [Žižek and Daly 2004, 61]), Žižek announces, on the same page of this text, that his theoretical apparatus is ultimately grounded on its establishment of an equivalence between the German idealist depiction of the subject and the Freudian-Lacanian notion of the *Todestrieb* (see also chapter 13). In this context, Žižek vacillates between identifying the death drive either with the gap in the order of being (i.e., the [meta-]transcendental condition for the genesis of subjectivity) or with the subject itself (i.e., the product of this very same gap).[16] Regardless, at this point, one can see quite easily why Schelling, given what Žižek here proclaims to be the "basic thesis" of "the big obsession of my entire work," is so absolutely indispensable for the Žižekian theoretical matrix: for Schelling (at least the later, post-1809 Schelling as portrayed by Žižek), the ideality of subjectivity arises from the Real of a fractured, conflicted being as a means of overcoming, surmounting, or transcending this tortured, writhing mass of drive-disturbed matter. Žižek attributes to Schelling the formulation of "the materialist concept of subject . . . as the point at which nature 'runs amok' and goes off the rails."[17]

From the beginning of his work onwards, Žižek repeatedly underscores that the register of the Real exhibits various quasi-Hegelian properties. In it, one can discern certain convergences of opposites. For instance, Žižek declares that the Lacanian Real is simultaneously the positive plentitude of material, bodily being as well as the negative void of absence evading incarnation and defying representation; it both overflows and withdraws from the register of the Symbolic, being a surplus and a deficit all at once.[18] This move would seem to allow for treating the Schellingian Real in a similar manner—more specifically, to treat this primordial ground, the (pre-)ontological foundation of reality, as simultaneously the "plentitude" or "surplus" of the vortex of *Trieb* and the "void" or "deficit" of the abyss of freedom, with these two dimensions being combined together in the notion of *Grund* as *Un/Urgrund*. And yet, there is evidence that Žižek maintains a non-dialectical distinction between *Grund* and *Un/Urgrund* in his reading of Schelling:

> Schelling has to venture into speculations on the *Ungrund* of the Absolute *qua* primordial Freedom. His fundamental problem is human freedom, its possibility: without the abyss of primordial Freedom which

precedes the vortex of the Real, it would be impossible to account for the emergence of human freedom in the heart of the realm of natural necessity. The chain of natural necessity can be torn asunder, the Light of freedom can break out of the vicious cycle of natural drives and illuminate the obscure Ground of being, only if natural necessity itself is not the original fact but results from the contraction of the primordial abyss of Freedom, of a Willing which wills nothing—that is to say, only if this primordial Freedom which, by means of its contraction, gets entrapped into the vicious cycle of its own self-imposed chains, in man blows these chains asunder and regains itself. In other words: human freedom is actual, not just an illusion due to our ignorance of the necessity that effectively governs our lives, only if man is not a mere epiphenomenon of the universe but a "being of the Centre," a being in whom the abyss of the primordial Freedom breaks through in the midst of the created universe. (Žižek 1996b, 53–54)

Later he states that "what, according to Schelling, precedes the material-temporal process is not an eternal ideal order, and so on, but the pure void/abyss [*Ungrund*] of Freedom" (Žižek 1996b, 72). Why separate these two levels? What if, instead of a chronological sequence running from nothing (*Un/Urgrund*) to being (*Grund*)—sequencing itself should be highly problematic here, since linear temporality supposedly doesn't exist in the mythical Schellingian epoch of the eternal past—this void (as the abyss of freedom) is embedded in the materiality of being as the fissures and inconsistencies subsisting within the latter?

One way to interpret Heidegger's remarks, in his 1936 seminar on Schelling's 1809 *Freiheitschrift,* apropos the Schellingian "spiritualization of nature"[19] is along these precise lines: "Nature" as the ontological ground of material being isn't to be opposed to "Spirit" as the pre- or trans-ontological groundlessness of immaterial autonomy; rather, the "spiritualization of nature" signifies that the *Ungrund* of autonomy inheres within the *Grund* of material being. Translated into psychoanalytic terms—recall that Žižek reads Schelling as a metapsychological thinker—the libidinal economy (as the ontogenetic ground out of which full-fledged subjectivity emerges) is linked to the embodied existence of the individual. And yet, at the same time, this ground is riddled with antagonisms and tensions right from the beginning—as conflicts within each and every drive, between different drives, and between drives and their *Umwelt.* Žižek's psychoanalytic appropriation of Schelling enables one to argue that the inner inconsistency of the libidinal ground of the individual's being is a condition of possibility for the subsequent genesis of a subject linked to, but distinguishing itself from, this same ground.

Moreover, this emergent subjectivity possesses a degree of freedom insofar as its drive-ridden "nature" bequeaths to it the absence of a natural
program, namely, the absence of a deterministic agenda automatically
oriented around the coordinated pursuit of a set configuration of closely
related means and ends. This could be described as a gift of lack. This
missing mandate of nature, its original lack in relation to the conflicted
libidinal being of human beings, is a (pre)condition for the coming-to-
be of the "unnatural" subject of freedom. In terms of its clinical dimension, psychoanalysis tends to associate conflict with psychopathological
difficulties that rob the individual of autonomy (such as, for example, intrapsychical conflicts prompting repressions that result in neurotic rigidity). However, in terms of the broader implications of Freudian-Lacanian
metapsychology for philosophical theories of human freedom, conflict
is a double-edged sword, since it also serves as a fundamental possibility
condition for this freedom.

In his thorough examination of Badiou's oeuvre, Peter Hallward
contrasts Kant and Badiou in terms of their treatment of subjective autonomy. Whereas the Kantian notion of transcendental freedom entails
that autonomous subjectivity is an abiding, underlying constant (even in
instances when it doesn't intervene and thereby manifest its presence),
Badiouian autonomous subjectivity, as "evental" (i.e., as conditioned
by and contingent upon events), is "exceptional" and "rare." As Sylvain
Lazarus articulates this conception of evental subjectivity, "The subjective is not continuous. It arises suddenly, then ceases to be" (Lazarus
1996, 59). In other words, apropos the topics under discussion here,
the freedom of the subject is not part of an invariant noumenal bedrock, but rather is an evanescent occurrence that fleetingly flashes into
existence only occasionally.[20] What's being proposed here is, in a sense,
a transient transcendence, a momentary break, from time to time, with
the natural or cultural run of things (on one occasion Badiou, when
designating events as disruptions of given regimes of reality ["the event
is a deregulation of the logic of the world"], suggestively speaks of a
"transcendental dysfunction"[21]). In Lacanian terms, one could say that
the freedom of autonomous subjectivity is provided the chance briefly
to emerge at those junctures where the Real or the Symbolic become
(temporarily) barred—more specifically, in this context, when the libidinal economy or the big Other becomes internally inconsistent, unable
solidly to dictate a course to be followed; when neither *Trieb* nor *Umwelt*
move with clear, directed authority due to the interference of conflictual
disharmonies between or within themselves. (It should be noted that, on
the basis of the explanations formulated in this discussion, one ought
to question Hallward's Badiouian step of straightforwardly opposing,

along the lines of Badiou's overarching dichotomy between being and event, the drive as asubjective and the domain of evental truth promising the possibility of subjectification.)[22] As Schelling articulates it in his "Stuttgart Seminars," human beings are free insofar as they stand "at the point of indifference" between nature (i.e., the Real) and God (i.e., the Symbolic), thereby remaining partially undetermined by either of these two orders.[23]

Using an example familiar to Lacanians, Sophocles's *Antigone* nicely illustrates this point/position. Antigone is forced to be free insofar as she confronts a deadlock in her surrounding symbolic order (i.e., in the big Other). Caught between two competing obligations (the familial-religious duty to bury the dead and the civic-political duty to obey the laws of the state), Antigone, unable immediately to invoke an overarching third principle that would unproblematically adjudicate between these two competing duties (duties forced into competition by unusual circumstances), subjectifies herself by responding to the event of this rupture (her brother's death followed by Creon's edict) with a resolute decision whose consequences she is compelled to assume, consequences that carry her far beyond the "pleasure principle" (whether as Kantian pathological inclination or Freudian libidinal satisfaction). This deadlock in the big Other (i.e., the fact that contradictions can and do arise between its various injunctions, that it doesn't always speak with one voice) interpellates Antigone (or Antigone allows herself to be interpellated by it in a certain way) so as to transform her, transubstantiating a mere human individual into an almost inhuman subject. To be more precise, one could think of this as the exact inverse of Althusserian interpellation. Whereas, for Althusser, "interpellation" designates a process wherein the positive, functional dimensions of "ideological state apparatuses" (i.e., facets of Lacan's big Other as the symbolic order) imprint/impress themselves upon the individual and thereby subjugate him or her—subjectivity here amounts to subjection, to anything but autonomy[24]—this analysis now underway points to a similar yet different process, the process of "inverse interpellation," wherein the negative, dysfunctional dimensions of the big Other as the symbolic order (i.e., the necessary structural incompleteness and inconsistency of this Other/order, denoted by its "barring") sometimes, due to various factors, "hail" the individual and thereby force him or her to become (temporarily) an autonomous subject, to be jarred out of the comfortable non-conscious habits of the automaton of quotidian individuality and plunged into an abyss of freedom devoid of the solid ground of unproblematic, taken-for-granted socio-normative directives and guarantees. (In his *Nicomachean Ethics*, Aristotle already discerns this intimate link between structural breakdown and the void of autonomy insofar as he stipulates that reflective deliberation tends to occur only in instances when the predictable yet unthematized circuits connecting the second nature of acquired habits and this nature's normal environment break down, ceasing to function as usual.)[25] When not disrupted by snags in the threads of its fabric, the symbolic order forms an implicit backdrop, a sort of second nature, quietly yet effectively governing the flow of the individual's life in socially and linguistically mediated reality; it tacitly steers both cognition and comportment. But in becoming temporarily dysfunctional thanks to loopholes in its programs (i.e., inconsistencies subsisting within the structures of the symbolic order), the barred big Other's inherent incompleteness, when activated by crises or unforeseen occurrences, offers the opening/opportunity for a transient transcendence as a momentary, transitory break with this Other's deterministic nexus:

> Far from signaling any kind of closure which constrains the scope of the subject's intervention in advance, the bar of the Real is Lacan's way of asserting the terrifying abyss of the subject's ultimate and radical *freedom*, the freedom whose space is sustained by the Other's inconsistency and lack . . . "The moment of decision is the moment of madness" precisely in so far as there is no big Other to provide the ultimate guarantee, the ontological cover for the subject's decision. (Žižek 2000c, 258)

The example of Antigone highlights the link between the barring of the Symbolic and autonomous subjectivity. However, these cracks and gaps in the big Other, as the barring of the Symbolic, can be exploited as openings/opportunities for the exercise of a transcendent freedom only by an entity pre-configured with a constitution that itself is barred, namely, an entity lacking a homogeneous, unified nature whose program would be activated automatically in instances when the big Other's determining function falters (i.e., a natural fallback position that guarantees a certain default steering direction for individual action when clear socionormative mandates are inoperative). What's required is again a barred Real: "human nature" as an inconsistent and conflict-saturated corpo-Real, a libidinal economy intrinsically lacking in balanced cohesiveness and coordination. The transient transcendence of freedom is sparked into being when the cracks and gaps of the Real overlap with those subsisting within the Symbolic. This explosive combination of antagonisms ignites the bursting forth of exceptional subjectivity out of mundane individuality.

Before proceeding further, another crucial difference with Kant merits marking. Whereas Kant's practical philosophy maintains that autonomy is an attribute or property possessed by rational beings at the level of their inalienable noumenal essence,[26] the analysis offered here treats autonomy as an insubstantial phenomenon bound up with the faltering or failure of this essence. In other words, freedom doesn't arise from a special faculty with an innate capacity for autonomy hard-wired into the individual's constitution; instead, the capacity for autonomy is a consequence of the deficient and incomplete harmonization of the various faculties forming the individual's constitution. This represents a "negative" account of human freedom, namely, an account based on the absence, rather than the presence, of certain attributes and properties (by contrast, Kant could be said to pursue a "positive" account in which a noumenal faculty for subjective autonomy is added to the otherwise overdetermined phenomenal individual). The surplus of autonomy is made possible by the deficit of heteronomy. Freedom emerges from the dysfunctioning of determinism.

Through a startling reversal running contrary to the vulgar perspective that views psychoanalysis as a fatalistic discourse of determinism, the notion of *Trieb* must be reconceived as precisely that which promises to yield a substantial theoretical conceptualization of human freedom. Rather than being the final psychoanalytic barrier to positing the potential of liberation from the deterministic nexus of (physical or psychical) nature, the Freudian drive is, in and of itself, the very possibility condition for what comes to present itself as a transcendent form of freedom. The psychoanalytic drive is the dysfunctional instinct of human nature, destining this nature for denaturalization. As Joan Copjec accurately articulates it, "the notion of drive . . . implies not an overriding so much as a redefinition of nature . . . The question one must ask is: how does drive determine human embodiment as both a freedom from nature and a part of it?" (Copjec 2004, 180).

In his seminar on Schelling, Heidegger discusses the fundamental implications of the Schellingian dissolution of the traditional dichotomy between "system" (more specifically, nature as the exhaustive theoretical model of the necessary relations between phenomenal appearances and entities) and freedom (as an unconditioned agency incapable of reduction to the causal chains of naturally determined necessity). In Schelling's eyes, overcoming the standard conceptual antagonism between these two spheres is the most pressing and important task facing philosophy.[27] His rhetoric concerning the mutually reinforcing efforts to "naturalize" freedom and, correlatively, "liberate" nature implies that the very foundations of philosophy in general (above and beyond practical philosophy alone) are at stake here. Following this line, Heidegger notes that Schelling's reassessment of freedom has consequences going far beyond treating it either as a mere subcomponent of ethical philosophy or as a simple empirical feature of human beings. Fundamental onto-logical issues hinge upon the German idealist vision of an always already "spiritualized" natural ground out of which springs everything that is, in-cluding autonomous subjectivity. No doubt, Heidegger sees in Schelling a precursor of his own notion of *Dasein,* a notion declaring the essence of human being to reside in an open "clearing" of temporally structured possibilities.[28] One could say, regarding the Heideggerian conception of human being, that temporality and possibility are not qualities or attributes of the subject, but, inversely, that subjectivity is a residual, particular determination occurring within the overarching domains of being and time. Similarly, Heidegger alleges that Schelling's naturaliza-tion of human freedom entails that the subject is itself an outgrowth of an unconditioned *Urgrund,* an abyssal openness within which empirical human nature gradually constructs and constrains itself. Echoing these Schellingian-Heideggerian lines of thought, Giorgio Agamben remarks, "Insofar as he has neither essence nor specific vocation, *Homo* is consti-tutively nonhuman; he can receive all natures and all faces" (Agamben 2004, 30), and "The humanist discovery of man is the discovery that he lacks himself" (Agamben 2004, 30).

Freudian-Lacanian psychoanalysis, despite the usual conclusions drawn from it, must be situated properly within this Schellingian lineage. Freud concretizes Schelling's speculations about "natural freedom" through his basic, foundational concept of *Trieb.* In the 1905 *Three Essays on the Theory of Sexuality,* which is Freud's first sustained treatment of the drives, the crucial thesis of the book (a thesis absolutely central to the theoretical edifice of psychoanalysis) is that human beings do not have constitutionally predetermined instincts that are invariantly correlated with fixed types of natural objects. By insisting on the need "to loosen the bond that exists in our thoughts between instinct and object,"[29] Freud problematizes, in a decisive fashion, standard conceptualizations of hu-man nature. For psychoanalysis, humans are naturally unnatural.

Individuals are capable of achieving the ideality of a freedom tran-scending material determination precisely because their drives are con-stitutionally divorced from a strict anchoring to the innerworldly do-main of natural objects (and this "loosening" of the ties to objects is only the most basic feature of *Trieb* involved in engendering autonomous subjectivity—as indicated, the multiple axes of conflict dwelling within the psychical ground of the libidinal economy are vital factors here too). Instead of hindering the development of a theory of human freedom, this conceptualization of the initial, primordial *Urgrund* of the drives (as formulated specifically by psychoanalytic metapsychology) is what makes

possible an account of the autonomous subject that is capable of acknowledging the emergent, genetic essence of subjectivity in relation to an
underlying heteronomous, material origin. Psychoanalysis brings to full
theoretical fruition Schelling's obscure theosophical ruminations, moving from abstract, poetic speculations about God and *Grund* to a richly
elaborated vision of the tension-permeated rapport between the Real and
the Ideal as manifest in the lives of flesh-and-blood human beings.

10

Temporalized Eternity: The Ahistorical Motor of Historicity

According to Žižek, the Schellingian *Urgrund* is the abyss of freedom subsisting at the very bottom of the depths of the atemporal past, the time before time. The reappearance of this archaic autonomy within the framework of the reality of existence (as the temporalized present) amounts to an irruption of the timeless within the temporal: "Freedom is atemporal: a flash of eternity in time" (Žižek 1997a, 33). By itself, this abyssal autonomy is not the possession of a constituted subject, the attribute or ability of an agent-entity. As Heidegger phrases it in his discussion of Schelling, "Freedom is here, not the property of man, but the other way around: Man is at best the property of freedom" (Heidegger 1985, 9). To speak in a Heideggerian fashion, the ontological clearing of the *Urgrund,* as a groundless ground, is the enveloping space within which *Dasein* takes shape. This antagonism-plagued foundation-space produces subjectivity out of itself.

Žižek goes on to distinguish between this sort of freedom (i.e., the asubjective *Urgrund* as an anonymous abyss) and the more familiar kind (i.e., freedom as a property of human subjectivity)—the intervention of the *Ent-Scheidung* is necessary for the passage from the former to the latter. Although the *Ent-Scheidung* is a contingent, gratuitous act/deed, it nonetheless functions as the condition of possibility, as a necessarily presupposed and always already past occurrence, for the effective existence of a free subject. In short, it's a non-necessary event necessary for autonomous subjectivity. Žižek explains:

> Freedom can become the predicate of a Subject only insofar as this Subject accomplishes the act of self-differentiation by means of which it posits itself as grounded in and simultaneously different from its contracted Substance: a free Subject has to have a Ground that is not itself; it has first to contract this Ground and then to assume a free distance toward it via the act of primordial decision that opens up time. (Žižek 1997a, 33)

On its own, the asubjective abyss of freedom isn't human autonomy per se, that is, freedom as something exercised by an autonomous subject.

The conflict-ridden vortex of *Trieb* is the ground of subjective autonomy, but only after a subject has been constituted via the moment of "cision" in which a separation from this vortex has been effectuated. The imbalanced inconsistency of the *Grund* as *Ungrund* is what allows for this rupture to occur from out of itself as a sort of immanent self-sundering. Žižek proceeds to establish a connection with the topic of historicity:

> Contrary to the commonplace according to which Schelling outlined the consequences of the thorough historicization of the Absolute, Schelling's greatest achievement was to *confine* the domain of history, to trace a line of separation between history (the domain of the Word, *logos*) and the nonhistorical (the rotary motion of drives). Therein resides Schelling's relevance for today's debate on historicism: his notion of the primordial act of decision/differentiation (*Ent-Scheidung*) aims at the gesture that opens up the gap between the inertia of the prehistoric Real and the domain of historicity, of multiple and shifting narrativizations; this act is thus a quasi-transcendental unhistorical condition of possibility and, simultaneously, a condition of the impossibility of historicization. Every "historicization," every symbolization, has to "reenact" this gap, this passage from the Real to history. (Žižek 1997a, 37)

History begins when the Real is broken with by a "quasi-transcendental" gesture, a kind of act-as-*tuché*, that cannot itself be absorbed into the historical dynamic it sets in motion. Along related lines, the structure delineated here is quite similar to the one spelled out by Žižek during his defense of the continued validity of the Cartesian depiction of subjectivity: the historicized play of multiple, shifting identity-positions unfolds within the empty space of the non-historicizable, cogito-like subject (see chapter 2). Simply put, this temporalized content presupposes an atemporal form. (Žižek proceeds to invoke Freud again, comparing this distinction between "the prehistoric Real and the domain of historicity" with the difference between primary and secondary repression—the vicissitudes of particular historicized repressed contents are shaped by the ahistorical form of the unconscious as constituted through the interaction between primary and secondary repression.)[1] Additionally, in the quotation above, he emphasizes that historicity is made possible by something that can't itself be historicized.

In a different context, Žižek draws a distinction between "historicism" and "historicity." In fact, he goes so far as to assert that extreme forms of historicism are, contrary to appearances, inextricably and unavoidably tied to an ahistorical formalism:

> Kantian formalism and radical historicism are not really opposites, but two sides of the same coin: every version of historicism relies on a minimal "ahistorical" formal framework defining the terrain within which the open and endless game of contingent inclusions/exclusions, substitutions, renegotiations, displacements, and so on, takes place. The truly radical assertion of historical contingency has to include the dialectical tension between the domain of historical change itself and its traumatic "ahistorical" kernel *qua* its condition of (im)possibility. Here we have the difference between historicity proper and historicism: *historicism* deals with the endless play of substitutions within the same fundamental field of (im)possibility, while *historicity* proper makes thematic different structural principles of this very (im)possibility. (Žižek 2000b, 111–12)

Radical historicism, in Žižek's view, is simply self-defeating.[2] Historicism, as a philosophical-theoretical paradigm, must either posit itself as an ahistorical invariant (thus generating within itself an intractable contradiction which it cannot resolve with its own resources) or treat itself as yet another contingent-finite construction (in which case, it cannot fiercely oppose ahistorical theories on a theoretical level, since historicism's reflexive auto-historicization would prevent it from assuming the position of a general paradigm capable of competing with other ostensibly general paradigms situating themselves on a trans-historical conceptual terrain). Žižek sees historicism as tending to succumb to the fate whereby, in its attempts to combat ahistorical transcendental formalism, it ends up becoming that which it fights against (it elevates situated contingency into the unsurpassable condition of possibility for any and every phenomenon). By contrast with historicism, Žižekian historicity entails rejecting the very opposition between radical historicism and ahistorical transcendental formalism, diagnosing this as a false dilemma. As an alternative third option, historicity involves the assertion that there is an ahistorical motor to historicity and, moreover, that the manner in which the ahistorical (as the Real) affects and is dealt with by the historical (as Imaginary-Symbolic reality) is itself a relationship that undergoes shifts and transformations over time. The movement of history, as a flux of ever-changing particularities, is driven along by something that cannot be reduced to a particular moment of this same flux. Succinctly stated, Žižek asserts that the Real, understood specifically as the ineliminable internal inconsistency of the Symbolic as big Other, is this driving factor. The field of the historical remains historical (i.e., stays in perpetual flux) precisely because it never arrives at a final, satisfying point of closure, a moment when it achieves a harmonious state capable of enduring thereafter without change (i.e., a Hegelian-style "end of history"). The symbolic order continually undergoes a historical series of alterations and reconfigurations insofar as it is internally plagued by an immanent negativity, a negativity that can take on varying incarnations depending on the specific historical configurations in which it is contextually inscribed, but that cannot ever be eliminated (or reduced to the status of a historical contingency) through the symbolic order attaining a perfectly coordinated, organic self-integration.[3]

How does this relate to Schelling and the topic of freedom? On Žižek's reading, Schellingian autonomy, as embodied in a subject's act, is a resurgence of the primordial, forever-past *Un/Urgrund* within the confines of present existence. In other words, an autonomous act involves the momentary, sudden return of the abyss of freedom, namely, the resurfacing of the archaic void within the realm of the here and now. The distinction between the Real and history (with historicism ineffectively ignoring the Real while historicity attempts to think the conjunction between the Real and history) parallels the previously mentioned contrast between Schelling's temporal epochs of the past and the present (i.e., the eternal past is Real, and the chronological-linear temporality of the present corresponds to history, broadly speaking). As seen, Žižek characterizes Schellingian freedom as the fleeting manifestation of (ahistorical) eternity in the medium of (historical) time. The unprecedented novelty of a genuine act of freedom interrupts the chronological-linear flow of historical temporality, introducing something there that cannot be accounted for in historical terms as an outgrowth of what came before: "The moments of the emergence of the New are precisely the moments of Eternity in time" (Žižek 2004c, 11). There is something timeless about acts (or, for that matter, Badiouian events) to the extent that they are out of joint with their surrounding historical-temporal environs. They have no prearranged place there where they take place. Moreover, from the Schellingian perspective, such unconditioned deeds are intrusions into time of something coming from outside of this time (i.e., returns of the pre-historical abyss of freedom within the movement of history).

In his 1991 book *For They Know Not What They Do,* Žižek treats autonomy as something never actually possessed and exercised in the present. Instead, freedom is always glimpsed retroactively by a backward glance cast over a prior historical field in which points of indeterminacy and openness are discerned only after the fact of having passed by the individual unnoticed during the course of his or her lived experience:

> The *act of freedom* . . . is never fully "present," the subjects are never
> fully aware that what they are doing "now" is the foundation of a new

symbolic order—it is only afterwards that they take note of the true dimension of what they have already done. The common wisdom about how history *in actu* is experienced as the domain of freedom, whereas retroactively we are able to perceive its causal determination, is therefore idiotic after all and should be reversed: when we are caught in the flow of events, we act "automatically," as if under the impression that it is not possible to do otherwise, that there is really no choice; whereas the retrospective view displays how the events could have taken a radically different turn—how what we perceived as necessity was actually a free decision of ours . . . we never *are* free, it is only afterwards that we discover how we *have been* free. (Žižek 2002a, 222)

One might object to a hasty generalization here. Although there are ample instances confirming the reversal of received wisdom proposed by Žižek in this passage, aren't there also many other instances in which subjects believe themselves to be acting freely in the immediate here and now? In fact, four basic permutations are possible: the subject experiences itself as free in the present and free retroactively; the subject experiences itself as determined in the present and determined retroactively; the subject experiences itself as free in the present but determined retroactively; and the subject experiences itself as determined in the present but free retroactively. And in his subsequent work (influenced by earlier readings of Schelling), Žižek appears to back away from the insistence that freedom only exists *après-coup*, when it's too late for it to be deployed deliberately by a subject actively intervening in the flux of history (this backing away has a lot to do with his sociopolitical concerns). In Schelling's language, although the abyss of freedom is always already past, the returns of this void of autonomy via human consciousness can and do sometimes transpire, however briefly, in the lived immediacy of the present.

The Schellingian-Žižekian subject, as free, inhabits the intersection between the transcendental and the historical. More precisely, autonomous subjectivity, according to this account, operates in the space of the division between, on the one hand, the *Un/Urgrund* (as the anonymous abyss of freedom) and, on the other hand, the chains of natural or historical determination (as the reality of existence). The effective employment of freedom amounts to the localizing inscription of the ahistorical void of faceless autonomy (here functioning as a transcendental Real) within the register of empirical-material history. In *Organs Without Bodies*, Žižek observes that "the Kantian transcendental is irreducibly rooted in the empirical/temporal/finite—it is the transphenomenal *as it appears within the finite horizon of temporality*" (Žižek 2004c, 44). Likewise, the Real of Schellingian-Žižekian subjective autonomy, manifesting itself through acts as exceptional deeds that cannot be accounted for through explanatory recourse to prior determining historical grounds, is the way in which the ahistorical *Un/Urgrund* (as the ultimate transcendental possibility condition for a free subject) appears within the temporal frame of historicity. Schelling maintains that "all existence must be conditioned in order that it may be actual, that is, personal, existence" (Schelling 1936, 79). Similarly, autonomy must be conditioned—the impersonal abyss of groundlessness must incarnate itself in the form of a subject embedded in a determinate historical-social-temporal site—in order that it may be actual(ized) autonomy. Without the forever-past *Un/Urgrund*, subjectivity wouldn't ever have a chance to exist. And yet, without the concrete existence of situated subjectivity, the abyssal freedom harbored by this groundless ground would be nothing, an insubstantial potentiality without actuality. The nothingness of the cracks and gaps in the barred Real (as well as those in the barred Other of the Symbolic) becomes something solely through the subject's reflexive gesture of putting to work the negativity that gave birth to it, harnessing this indeterminacy built into the structures of both being and its symbolizations so as to attain a transcendence of these same structures, however fleeting and transitory this transcendence might be. Although often incredibly brief when measured according to the temporal standards of chronological-linear time, these moments of transient transcendence are points where time stands still, where blinks of eternity punctuate the movement of history.

Part 3

The Semblance of Substance and the Substance of Semblance: The Thing and Its Shadow

(Hegel–Žižek)

11

The Immanence of Transcendence: From Kant to Hegel

At the end of an interview conducted in September 2003, Žižek declares that "ultimately if I am to choose just one thinker, it's Hegel. He's the one for me" (Žižek 2003a). Elsewhere, he concedes that "even when I try at times to be critical of Hegel, I remain Hegelian" (Žižek and Daly 2004, 63). There are about as many references to Hegel scattered throughout Žižek's corpus as there are to Lacan. As already noted, Žižek insists again and again that the core of his project consists in the redeployment of a German idealist theory of subjectivity revised in being passed through the lens of Freudian-Lacanian psychoanalytic metapsychology. However, the majority of extant commentaries on his work either ignore the foundational role of late modern philosophy therein—in Astra Taylor's documentary film on him (*Žižek! The Movie* [2005], produced by the Documentary Campaign), Žižek complains, "That part of the message doesn't get through" because his audience prefers to dwell primarily on the cultural and political dimensions of his writings—or else, if the philosophical component of the Žižekian oeuvre is addressed, it's almost always Hegel who is the center of exegetical attention. That is to say, for whatever reasons, Kant and Schelling, two of Hegel's contemporaneous principal interlocutors as well as sources of abundant theoretical inspiration for Žižek himself, tend to be passed over in relative silence.

Adequately understanding Žižek's relation to Hegel (and consequently the Žižekian project *tout court*) is simply impossible in the absence of a thorough delineation of the multiple ménage à trois scenarios that transpire in his texts between three hybrid entities: Kant-Žižek, Schelling-Žižek, and Hegel-Žižek (with Lacan as a floating fourth circulating among these three). In fact, at the very moment in the same 2003 interview when he proclaims his fidelity to Hegel as absolutely central to his endeavors, Žižek makes three other points worth highlighting:

> If you were to ask me at gunpoint, like Hollywood producers who are too stupid to read books and say, "give me the punchline," and were to demand, "Three sentences. *What* are you really trying to do?" I would say, Screw ideology. Screw movie analyses. What really interests me is the

following insight: if you look at the very core of psychoanalytic theory, of
which even Freud was not aware, it's properly read *death drive*—this idea
of beyond the pleasure principle, self-sabotaging, etc.—the only way to
read this properly is to read it against the background of the notion of
subjectivity as self-relating negativity in German Idealism. That is to say,
I take literally Lacan's indication that the subject of psychoanalysis is the
Cartesian cogito—of course, I would add, as reread by Kant, Schelling,
and Hegel. I am here very old fashioned. I still think that basically this—
the problematic of radical evil and so on—is philosophy, and all the rest
is a footnote. (Žižek 2003a)

After briefly summarizing his interpretation of the conceptual move-
ment connecting Kant, Schelling, and Hegel (as well as noting that
"Hegel didn't know what he was doing. You have to interpret him"),
Žižek continues:

I'm trying to do what Deleuze forgot to do—to bugger Hegel, with
Lacan . . . so that you get monstrous Hegel . . . It's a very technical, modest project, but I believe in it. All other things are negotiable. I don't
care about them. You can take movies from me, you can take everything.
You cannot take *this* from me . . . What really interests me is philosophy,
and for me, psychoanalysis is ultimately a tool to reactualize, to render
actual for today's time, the legacy of German Idealism. (Žižek 2003a)

First, Žižek unambiguously maintains that the cultural and political features of his corpus are of less interest to him in comparison with the
utilization of psychoanalysis as a device for updating German idealism.
Second, it's evident from these remarks (as from many others of a similar
sort) that Hegel is handled by Žižek as part of a sequence involving Kant
and Schelling, a sequence tied together through Lacan's analytic appropriation of the depiction of subjectivity first delineated by Descartes.
Third—this point, as will be seen, is linked to the previous one—Žižek
states that his philosophical project hinges on successfully equating the
German idealist subject and the psychoanalytic death drive.

On numerous occasions, Žižek indicates that his interest in "buggering" Hegel with Lacan so as to engender a "monstrous Hegel" is a result
of his desire to demonstrate the equivalence between the subject of German idealism and the Freudian-Lacanian *Todestrieb*[1] (the significance and
stakes of this equivalence won't become clear here until much later—see
chapter 13). Apart from playing this role, Hegel also is identified as incredibly important insofar as he, to put it one way, enables a trajectory to
be outlined wherein notional necessity arises out of material contingency

(and not vice versa). Against the cartoon version of Hegel's philosophy according to which the invisible hand of Hegelian *Geist* pulls the strings of history as a hidden puppet-master, Žižek asserts that the appearance of a governing spiritual structure is an *après-coup* effect, an image that arises retroactively from sequences of aleatory events.[2] In other words, as with Freud's "Wo Es war, soll Ich werden" (Where it was, there must I come to be) as well as Lacan's cybernetic-style formal model of unfolding chains of randomly determined pluses and minuses (from both the second seminar and the "Seminar on 'The Purloined Letter' "[3]), a series of seemingly unrelated contingent occurrences internally generates out of itself, in a bottom-up manner, a perspective according to which these contingencies are no longer able to appear as contingent. The opposites of contingency and necessity converge: for whatever given present moment serving as the temporal context from which the subject surveys its past, this present is itself contingent to the extent that it is the conditioned outcome of past contingencies (i.e., things could have been otherwise, could have turned out differently)—although, at the same time, this present's past sequence of conditioning contingencies is necessary for this particular present to be what it is (i.e., this particular present has no choice but to conceive of its own past as necessary in relation to itself and to view itself as a determined moment in a structured dynamic).

Žižek emphasizes the centrality of contingency in Hegelian thought, contending that Hegel's basic position on the relationship between contingency and necessity can be formulated as a thesis according to which historical necessity itself (embodied in the metaphor of *Geist*) is grounded upon a series of utterly undetermined contingencies (as shifting circumstances and happenings initially free of any deep, underlying, rule-bound order corresponding to some sort of preexistent spiritual substance[4]): "The acme of the dialectic of necessity and contingency arrives in the assertion of the contingent character of necessity as such" (Žižek 1994b, 36). As he summarizes it later, "The ultimate mystery of what Hegel calls 'positing the presuppositions' is the mystery of how contingency *retroactively* 'sublates' itself into necessity . . . in short, the mystery of how . . . order emerges out of chaos" (Žižek 2000c, 227). It's not that there is a synchronic order (i.e., the necessity of the spiritual Notion) timelessly preceding a merely illusory chaos (i.e., the contingency of historical-temporal experience) as the diachronic actualization of this order. Instead, chaos comes first, and its ordering is an after-the-fact process that tends to conceal the primacy of this chaos. Žižek goes so far as to assert that Hegel is the philosopher of contingency par excellence.[5] Precisely at this point, the question of who Žižek's Hegel is becomes crucial.

As mentioned, Hegel typically is portrayed, particularly in the various currents of postwar French thought forming an integral part of the theoretical background against which Žižek writes, as the philosopher of "absolute knowledge," a thinker who treats the contingent vicissitudes of human history as epiphenomenal manifestations of a necessary conceptual movement (i.e., experientially accessible reality amounts to the temporal-material unfolding of a set of atemporal-immaterial structures). Along related lines, Hegel is often seen as thumbing his nose at Kant by ignoring any supposed "limits of possible experience" and shamelessly indulging in a regressive return to a pre-critical speculative metaphysics of the worst dogmatic kind. Žižek does nothing less than turn this widely accepted caricature of Hegel on its head.

The best starting point for an assessment of the place of Hegel in Žižekian philosophy is the issue of how Hegel relates to Kant (at least according to Žižek). Žižek's "monstrosity," his heterodox Hegel, is the figure who accomplishes the fulfillment of Kant's "Copernican revolution" à la the critical-transcendental turn[6] (bringing to fruition that which is "in Kant more than Kant himself"—as Žižek puts it in one discussion, Hegel is the "for itself" in relation to Kant as the "in itself,"[7] that is, the full realization of the nascent yet unrealized potentials within Kantian thought). As such, Hegel is anything but the cheerleader for an omniscient philosophical self-consciousness, for a complete and exhaustive encyclopedic knowledge from whose firm grasp nothing whatsoever escapes.

As is well known, Kant's *Critique of Pure Reason* seeks, among other things, to reveal the futile, pointless intractability of a variety of (pseudo-) problems in philosophy which are fabricated as a result of the assumption that decisive claims can be made about an objective reality existing in and of itself in a state independent of the subject's reflections upon that reality. Kant demonstrates both how these intractable problems spontaneously arise from the interaction between the various faculties of the mind (i.e., intuition, understanding, and reason) as well as how they cease to be genuine problems once philosophers agree to remain within the limits of possible experience, as defined by the framework of transcendental idealism, while philosophizing. (Similarly, Žižek remarks that a standard Hegelian procedure, a procedure indebted to the tactics of Kantian critique, is to resolve a philosophical problem not so much by directly responding in a straightforward manner to the question it poses, but rather by shifting perspective so that the problem is displaced, sometimes even reappearing as its own solution within the new perspective;[8] that is to say, Kant and Hegel often arrive at answers to specific theoretical enigmas in simply "looking awry" at these mysteries.) Hence, Žižek regularly observes that the theme of finitude sits at the center of Kant's theoretical apparatus. In other words, Kant proposes that transcendental idealist subjectivity is ensconced within a reality (i.e., the world as circumscribed by the limits of this subject's finite field of experience) riddled with aporias and impasses due to this subjectivity's finitude, a reality in which knowledge is always and necessarily "not all."

Kant's first *Critique* tries to restrict itself to the elaboration of a specific epistemology. The stipulation that nothing concrete is to be said about the noumenal realm of things-in-themselves lying beyond the boundaries of subjectively accessible experience can be construed as a prohibition bearing upon metaphysical attempts to develop a detailed ontology. The finite subject of transcendental idealism knows objects solely as they appear to the conjoined faculties of intuition and the understanding; direct access to the being of these objects as Things is impossible, and attempts to force this access throw subjectivity back into itself burdened with a series of irresolvable contradictions (as shown in "The Dialectic of Pure Reason"). In demarcating a division between epistemology and ontology as well as arguing for a distinction between phenomenal objects-as-appearances and noumenal things-in-themselves, Kant assumes—he simply takes it for granted—that contradictions dwell within the confines of subjective cognition alone. According to this presupposition, only thinking can harbor antinomies and antagonisms; substantial being must be internally at one with itself and without contradiction. Žižek, departing from Hegel's observation that Kant's assumption regarding the contradiction-free nature of Real being is just an article of dogmatic faith,[9] frequently portrays Hegel as taking the small but enormously significant step of transforming Kant's epistemology into ontology. (In fact, Hegelian dialectics is both an epistemology and an ontology, namely, a mobile, dynamic knowledge-process that, in its functioning [and, more importantly, malfunctioning], simultaneously reveals the very configuration of being itself.)[10] Through this move, being becomes something incomplete and inconsistent, a sphere penetrated by divisions and ruptures. (As seen, Žižek's engagement with the later Schelling also aims at sketching the contours of this ontological vision of the Real of being as involving inherent deadlocks and gaps; only in this way, Žižek indicates, is it possible to develop a materialist theory of the subject that effectively bridges the chasm between transcendental idealism and dialectical materialism by accounting for the subject's rapport with the substance of being without reducing such subjectivity to a negligible epiphenomenal status—see part 2.)

Žižek presents the transition from Kantian epistemology to Hegelian ontology in various ways, extracting several different consequences from

this. *The Ticklish Subject* contains one of the most lucid instances of the
general manner in which he outlines the basic import of the shift from
Kant to Hegel:

> All Hegel does is, in a way, to supplement Kant's well-known motto of
> the transcendental constitution of reality ("the conditions of possibil-
> ity of our knowledge are at the same time the conditions of possibility
> of the object of our knowledge") by its negative—the limitation of our
> knowledge (its failure to grasp the Whole of Being, the way our knowl-
> edge gets inexorably entangled in contradictions and inconsistencies) is
> simultaneously the limitation of the very object of our knowledge, that
> is, the gaps and voids in our knowledge of reality are simultaneously the
> gaps and voids in the "real" ontological edifice itself. (Žižek 1999b, 55)

A few pages later, he describes this gesture as "Hegel's breathtaking
achievement":

> Far from regressing from Kant's criticism to pre-critical metaphysics
> expressing the rational structure of the cosmos, Hegel fully accepts (and
> draws the consequences from) the result of Kantian cosmological antin-
> omies—there *is* no "cosmos," the very notion of cosmos as the ontologi-
> cally fully constituted positive totality is inconsistent. (Žižek 1999b, 60)

Interestingly, Žižek chooses to italicize "is" (rather than "no") when he
proclaims that, with Hegel's ontologization of Kant (specifically, the projection of the rational contradictions delineated in Kant's "Dialectic of
Pure Reason" into being itself[11]), "there *is* no cosmos." This is no accident,
since Žižekian ontology (as elaborated via Kant, Schelling, Hegel, and
Lacan) portrays the Real of being as a groundless ground shot through
with tensions and scissions. Being "*is*" this very acosmos, this unstable
absence of a cohesive, unifying One-All.

　　As Žižek sees it, Hegel's notorious "absolute knowledge" (*das absolute
Wissen*) amounts to nothing more than the acceptance of the irreducible
incompleteness not only of the subjective human understanding of the
world (as per Kantian epistemology), but also of the reality of being in
and of itself.[12] Žižek describes *das absolute Wissen* as involving an experience of "radical loss," rather than an intoxicating ascension into omni-
science.[13] In fact, as regards its significance in the 1807 *Phenomenology of
Spirit,* "*das absolute Wissen*" might better be translated as "absolute knowing," insofar as this concluding moment of the dialectic arguably involves
an insight into the interminability of the restless dialectical movement
("-ing"), instead of marking a point at which a stable body of knowledge

is consolidated once and for all (in the final section of the *Phenomenology*, Hegel describes Spirit's arrival at the stage of absolute knowing in exactly these terms[14]—see also chapter 15). Žižek states:

> Hegel knows very well that every attempt at rational totalization ulti-
> mately fails, this failure is the very impetus of the "dialectical progress";
> his "wager" is located on another level—it concerns, so to speak, the
> "squared totalization": the possibility of "making a system" out of the
> very series of *failed* totalizations, to enchain them in a rational way, to
> discern the strange "logic" that regulates the process by means of which
> the breakdown of a totalization itself begets another totalization. What
> is *Phenomenology of Spirit* ultimately if not the presentation of a series of
> aborted attempts by the subject to define the Absolute and thus arrive
> at the longed-for synchronism of subject and object? This is why its final
> outcome ("absolute knowledge") does not bring about a finally found
> harmony but rather entails a kind of reflective inversion: it confronts the
> subject with the fact that *the true Absolute is nothing but the logical disposition
> of its previous failed attempts to conceive the Absolute*—that is, with the vertigi-
> nous experience that Truth itself coincides with the path towards Truth.
> (Žižek 2002a, 99–100)

In the eyes of Žižek's Hegel, Kant didn't follow his Copernican revolution through to the very end. Kant thereby failed to formulate the
most far-reaching consequences of his own breakthrough. If anything,
Žižek claims, Kant, rather than Hegel, is the one who still remains wed-
ded to pre-critical metaphysics.[15] In separating ontology from epistemology along the fault line of the split between the fields of the noumenal
(i.e., the ontological Real of things-in-themselves) and the phenomenal
(i.e., the deontologized enclosure of the subjective theater of appearances), respectively, Kant clings to the assumption that, beyond the
contradiction-ridden confines of the experiential reality in which the
subject is imprisoned, there subsists an inaccessible substratum of being
unperturbed by these contradictions:

> We fail to grasp the Absolute *precisely in so far as we continue to presuppose
> that, above and beyond the domain of our finite reflected reasoning, there is an
> Absolute to be grasped*—we actually overcome the limitation of external
> reflection by simply becoming aware of how this external reflection is
> inherent to the Absolute itself. *This* is Hegel's fundamental criticism of
> Kant: not that Kant fails to overcome the external reflection of Under-
> standing, but that he still thinks there is some Beyond which eludes its
> grasp. What Kant does not see is that his *Critique of Pure Reason*, as the

critical "prolegomena" to a future metaphysics, *already is* the only possible metaphysics. (Žižek 1999b, 84–85)

According to Žižekian Hegelianism, the Absolute is the absolutely finite. Reaching the vantage point of the Absolute amounts to realizing
that there's no seamless transcendent Elsewhere in which the snags and
tears in the fabric of experiential reality are magically mended. In other
words, once the specter of a radical Outside is exorcized, the phenomenal realm itself becomes the Absolute, since there is nothing else opposing itself to this realm as a greater constraining limitation (such as a
noumenal Beyond).

In the passage quoted above, Žižek uses the term "Understanding."
Both Kant and Hegel each have their versions of a distinction between
understanding (*Verstand*) and reason (*Vernunft*). Loosely speaking, the
understanding is responsible for superimposing a conceptual grid on
the flux of sensuous experience. It organizes the temporal flow of intuited phenomena by carving up this flow along lines of division drawn
by its categories and oppositions. In this sense (a sense pinpointed by
Hegel), understanding could be said to inflict a certain amount of violence on the fluid, fleshly surface of phenomenal intuition, leaving a
nagging feeling that a gap remains to be bridged between intuition
and understanding, between sensory-perceptual experiences and their
conceptual-ideational codifications. Reason attempts to bridge this gap
by going beyond the understanding, by reflecting upon the inadequacies and shortcomings of the understanding's concepts and distinctions
(usually through demonstrating how the categorical divisions of the understanding are too black-and-white in relation to experience's subtle
shades of gray, or how the oppositions of the understanding readily can
be problematized, reversed, or deconstructed).

However, what Hegel emphasizes is that allowing reason's critical reflections on the limitations of the understanding's schemas to prompt
an abandonment of these schemas in the hope of bypassing such ideational interference so as directly to seize experience as experience results in the loss of any meaningful access to experiential reality whatsoever.[16] Like Kant, he too has a "critique of pure reason." Hegel insists
that the violence of conceptual abstraction, its apparently brutal cadaverization and dissection of reality, is an integral and unavoidable aspect
of a reality always already saturated through and through by spiritual-
notional mediation.[17] Moreover, Žižek suggests that the ultimate upshot
of Hegel's version of the distinction between *Verstand* and *Vernunft* is the
destruction of the myth of an unstructured, vital fullness of being that
is disclosed through the flux of lived experience.[18] The understanding

must come to accept a "loss of loss," an acknowledgment that what was supposedly lost (i.e., unstructured, vital fullness) never really existed in the first place and, hence, cannot be recovered through reason as an ostensibly higher power. Succinctly stated, the finite subject is faced with a forced choice between either the flawed, partial access to the being of phenomena offered by the understanding or the sterile dead-end of no access at all. If one refuses to carve reality at the joints violently and imperfectly using always-inadequate conceptual oppositions, then there simply is no reality (at least for the knowing subject): "If you take away the distorting perspective, you lose the thing itself" (Žižek and Daly 2004, 96). Hegelian reason (*Vernunft*), as Žižek explains, is the understanding (*Verstand*) once it has relinquished the fantasy of its own Beyond (à la a rational power surmounting the limitations internal to the workings of the understanding) and accepted its own absolute status insofar as it has no superior, quasi-divine Other compensating for its finitude.[19]

And yet, even if this image of a homogeneous, conflict-free noumenal Beyond haunting the Kantian critical-transcendental system is an illusion, it is nonetheless a persistent and pervasive illusion (in Kantian parlance, perhaps this is even a necessary illusion). So how does Hegel (or Žižek) account for the emergence and endurance of this notion to which Kant gives precise philosophical expression in the form of his noumenal-versus-phenomenal dichotomy? Answering this question requires revisiting Hegel's criticisms of the Kantian distinction between things-in-themselves and objects-as-appearances. Grasping what is at stake in these criticisms is also essential for appreciating the evolving role of the Lacanian register of the Real in Žižek's oeuvre.

All of the major representatives of German idealism (Fichte, Schelling, and Hegel) share in common a rejection of what they understand to be Kant's presentation of the distinction between noumenal Thing (*Ding*) and phenomenal object (*Objekt*)—especially since Kant's *Critique of Pure Reason* stubbornly refuses to explain how things-in-themselves give rise to objects-as-appearances (for Kant, such an "explanation" necessarily would violate the critical prohibition against applying concepts of the understanding, such as causality, to anything other than what is intuited in [possible] experience). In his 1794 *Science of Knowledge*, Fichte maintains that the thing-in-itself isn't, as it seems to be in the *Critique of Pure Reason,* an utterly unconditioned, self-subsistent entity unrelated to the structure of subjective cognition, an inaccessible substance completely separate from the mind. Fichte's argument is that, at a minimum, for this Thing to emerge as an X entirely opposed to the subject, the subject itself must first come into existence. The positing of the "I" creates the foundational distinction between the "I" and the "not-I" (with the latter being, in Kant's system, the noumenal domain of things-in-themselves—although, of course, it's worth remembering here that a noumenal dimension subsists within the heart of the Kantian "I"). Hence, rather than being unconditioned by the mind, the thing-in-itself is a conditioned by-product of dynamics and processes bound up with subjectivity. If nothing else, *das Ding an sich* is, according to Fichte, an index of the subject's experience of an extreme passivity, of an encounter with a point of stubborn resistance to its Ideal/ideational activities (and the registration of such resistance requires the prior existence of an active subjectivity whose activity is checked—hence the priority of the positing "I" in Fichtean idealism).[20] Consequently, Fichte concludes that the thing-in-itself is a product of thought, instead of, as per Kant, being that which is wholly and completely alien to subjective cognition.[21] Without the thinking subject, there is no thing-in-itself. Simply put, in Fichtean idealism, the distinction between self and non-self is a distinction internal to the self itself.

Schelling similarly portrays *das Ding an sich* as a product of the activity of consciousness, as an immanently generated consequence of the operations characteristic of the thinking subject. Speaking of the subject's relation to noumena, the early Schelling, in his 1800 *System of Transcendental Idealism*, explains:

> The thing-in-itself arises for it through an action; the outcome remains behind, but not the action that gave rise to it. Thus the self is originally ignorant of the fact that this opposite is its own product, and must remain in the same ignorance so long as it stays enclosed in the magic circle which self-consciousness describes about the self; only the philosopher, in breaking out of the circle, can penetrate behind the illusion. (Schelling 1978, 68)

The illusion spoken of by Schelling here is the Kantian notion that things-in-themselves are atemporal beings preexisting and standing outside the sphere of a self-enclosed subjectivity, independent of and untouched by this "I." Instead, *das Ding an sich* is produced through the activity of the self, even though the latter often fails to discern the traces of its fingerprints on this thus-constituted ideational Thing. Much later (but still in a similar vein), in his 1830s lectures on modern philosophy, Schelling rapidly enumerates three interrelated criticisms of Kant's thing-in-itself: first, the thing-in-itself only becomes a thing through being thought (i.e., insofar as it's a thing, it's a thing of thought);[22] second, given that the thing-in-itself is an abstraction arrived at through the gesture of stripping objects-as-appearances of all their determinate attributes and properties, this thing is nothing (i.e., an empty abstraction, a void hollowed out by an abstracting act of subjective cognition);[23] and third, the thing-in-itself involves an irresolvable contradiction, since things as things are at least partially dependent on the "I" in order to be posited/constituted as things, and therefore these things aren't purely "in themselves" (i.e., apropos *das Ding an sich,* as a thing, it's not in itself, and, as in itself, it's not a thing).[24]

Hegel's objections to the Kantian thing-in-itself are the best known of the German idealist criticisms of this notion, especially since today, whether justifiably or not, Hegel towers over the other post-Kantian idealists. However, in the 1812 *Science of Logic,* Hegel, without naming names, credits his fellow idealists (presumably thinkers such as Fichte and Schelling) with having discerned the vacuity involved in Kantian transcendental idealism's conception of noumena.[25] Like them, he too consistently maintains that *das Ding an sich* is a residual "lump" remaining from an intellectual process of voiding phenomena of their phenomenal features.[26] This Thing is portrayed as a mere object of thought ("thought-thing"),[27] a fabricated idea ultimately amounting to nothing more than "a formless abstraction, an empty beyond."[28] Early on in his body of work, Žižek remarks upon this Hegelian recasting of the thing-in-itself as a "pure 'Thing-of-Thought' [*Gedankending*]."[29] This assertion is important in the subsequent unfolding of Žižek's project insofar as it clearly implies that inconsistent and incomplete phenomena come first, with the subject's (unconscious) labor of, so to speak, hollowing out noumenal holes in the terrain of experienced appearances being an activity that follows after the initial givenness of a not-whole world: "*Limitation precedes transcendence:* all that 'actually exists' is the field of phenomena and its limitation" (Žižek 1993, 37).

In his 1801 text *The Difference Between Fichte's and Schelling's System of Philosophy,* Hegel, still writing under the influence of the young Schelling's identity philosophy, claims that Kant's critical philosophy simply cannot reduce everything to the status of being mere appearances for consciousness, since the concepts of both "appearance" and "consciousness" themselves unavoidably require positing things opposed to them (such as the ontological "what" that does the appearing before the conscious mind).[30] In other words, as Hegel later puts it long after his break with Schelling, to know the limits of possible experience as limits, one must already have overstepped these limits via the requisite apprehension of the Beyond thus separated and demarcated by these same limits (as limits with respect to the internal confines of phenomenal experience):

> No one knows, or even feels, that anything is a limit or defect, until he
> is at the same time above and beyond it . . . A very little consideration
> might show that to call a thing finite or limited proves by implication the

very presence of the infinite and the unlimited, and that our knowledge
of a limit can only be when the unlimited is *on this side* in consciousness.
(Hegel 1975, 91–92 [§60])

This line of argumentation regarding the inconsistent, self-subverting
character of the Kantian figure of limit is a regularly recurring refrain in
Hegel's texts: "With respect to the form of the *limitation* . . . great stress is
laid on the limitations of thought, of reason, and so on, and it is asserted
that the limitation *cannot* be transcended. To make such an assertion is
to be unaware that the very fact that something is determined as a limitation implies that the limitation is already transcended" (Hegel 1969,
134), and, "For any limit or lack is only recognized through comparison
with the idea of the whole and the complete" (Hegel 1990, 65 [§34]). In
his 1802 *Faith and Knowledge,* Hegel contends that Kant himself already
oversteps the critical limit of possible experience in that the first *Critique*
deems the thing-in-itself "thinkable" (although not "knowable" as capable of being experienced).[31] Noumena somehow can be cognized, and
consequently aren't entirely "in themselves."[32]

The *Phenomenology of Spirit* further nuances Hegel's line of criticism
contra the thing-in-itself, particularly in its discussions of the "inverted
world" and the stance of relating to "appearances as appearances" (in
the section entitled "Force and the Understanding: Appearance and the
Supersensible World"). Without the time here to do adequate exegetical
justice to the complexity of this Hegelian text, it can be said that Hegel's
fundamental contention in 1807 with respect to the Kantian noumenal
Thing is that this supposedly supersensible *an sich,* rather than being an
isolated, independent level of existence unconditioned by the subject
and its cognizing activities, is a by-product of consciousness's own epistemological gesture of treating phenomena as if they are appearances.[33]
And, as Hegel rightly maintains, the notion of appearance automatically
implies a veiled presence, something lurking behind the accessible façade (as he articulates this in another text, "only if the essence of nature
is determined as interior, does one know the outer shell" [Hegel 1990, 93
(§89)]). Interestingly, this also hints at a reversal of the standard understanding of the chronological hierarchy between perception and apperception (i.e., perceiving and perceiving that one is perceiving). It's usually assumed that perception developmentally precedes apperception,
that the individual begins with immediately perceiving appearances,
and then, subsequently, through higher-order self-reflection, perceives
that he is perceiving (and hence, that his perceptions are appearances
for him). Hegel's remarks about the logic of appearance suggest that

apperception comes first. In other words, subjectivity begins by self-reflexively apperceiving itself as perceiving (i.e., as a subject relating to objects through the interface of perception), and, as a result, after doing so phenomena appear to be perceptions as appearances (i.e., phenomena are transformed into masks concealing an inner ontological depth, rather than simply being the naked revelation of being). Succinctly stated, perception (as perception) is the product of apperception, and not vice versa. As Žižek phrases this train of thought quite recently, "Things do not simply appear, they *appear to appear* . . . once things (start to) appear, they not only appear as what they are not, creating an illusion; they can also appear to just appear, concealing the fact that they are what they appear to be" (Žižek 2006, 29–30). Here's how Hegel elaborates this:

> The inner world, or supersensible beyond, has, however, *come into being:* it *comes from* the world of appearance which has mediated it; in other words, appearance is its essence and, in fact, its filling. The supersensible is the sensuous and the perceived posited as it is *in truth;* but the *truth* of the sensuous and the perceived is to be *appearance.* The supersensible is therefore *appearance qua appearance.* (Hegel 1977c, 89 [§147])

Hegel identifies the supersensible (which would include the Kantian conception of a noumenal realm of things-in-themselves) as "*appearance qua appearance.*" This signifies that, for Hegel, the supersensible is a result of treating phenomena as appearances, namely, of the subject opting to view phenomena as superficial experiential surfaces veiling a deeper, hidden Real that remains inaccessible. Instead of noumena independently preceding the limited knowledge of phenomenal objects to which Kant condemns consciousness, Hegel argues that these apparently *an sich* entities are genetic outcomes brought into existence solely through their being posited by the knowing subject. In essence, the subject hypostatizes its own activity/attitude with respect to phenomena, thereby generating the illusion of a "supersensible beyond."

In the *Science of Logic,* Hegel observes that Kant makes the thing-in-itself unknowable through the way in which he defines this entity. By stripping away every determinate characteristic from objects of experience—objects are known through the fashions in which they appear, through their particular discernible features—Kant produces a void, an abstract nothingness about which little can be said or known:

> Things are called "in themselves" in so far as abstraction is made from all being-for-other, which means simply, in so far as they are thought devoid

138

of all determination, as nothings. In this sense, it is of course impossible to know *what* the *thing-in-itself* is. For the question: *what?* demands that *determinations* be assigned; but since the things of which they are to be assigned are at the same time supposed to be *things-in-themselves,* which means, in effect, to be without any determination, the question is thoughtlessly made impossible to answer, or else only an absurd answer is given. (Hegel 1969, 121)

However, in the *Encyclopedia Logic* Hegel takes a different critical approach, arguing that the question "What is the thing-in-itself?" rather than being unanswerable, is a quite easily answered question:

The Thing-in-itself (and under "thing" is embraced even Mind and God) expresses the object when we leave out of sight all that consciousness makes of it, all its emotional aspects, and all specific thoughts of it. It is easy to see what is left—utter abstraction, total emptiness, only described still as an "other-world"—the negative of every image, feeling, and definite thought. Nor does it require much penetration to see that this *caput mortuum* is still only a product of thought, such as accrues when thought is carried on to abstraction unalloyed: that it is the work of the empty "Ego," which makes an object out of this empty self-identity of its own . . . Hence one can only read with surprise the perpetual remark that we do not know the Thing-in-itself. On the contrary, there is nothing we can know so easily. (Hegel 1975, 72 [§44])

According to Hegel, *das Ding an sich* is entirely knowable because, instead of being a fully subtracted alterity dwelling within a foreign "other world" (i.e., the supersensible Elsewhere of noumena situated outside the limits of possible experience), this "thing" is the subject itself, the positing activity of the "I." What subjectivity discovers behind the curtain of appearances is not the hard kernel of the Real Thing, but rather its own gesture of going beyond the immediacy of present phenomena:[34] "Beyond the veil of the phenomena . . . consciousness only finds what it itself has put there" (Žižek 2004d, 260). There is nothing behind this curtain of appearances.

As Žižek is fond of emphasizing, this nothing is the subject as such in its ceaseless, insatiable negativity, its irreducibility to and exceeding of all presentations and representations:[35] "Hegel radicalized Kant by conceiving the void of the Thing (its inaccessibility) as equivalent to the very negativity that defines the subject" (Žižek 1992a, 137). Or, as he phrases it in *The Sublime Object of Ideology* (departing from a reference to the Hegelian supersensible as appearance qua appearance):

> The appearance implies that there is something behind it which appears through it; it conceals a truth and by the same gesture gives a foreboding thereof; it simultaneously hides and reveals the essence behind its curtain. But what is hidden behind the phenomenal appearance? Precisely the fact that there is nothing to hide. What is concealed is that the very act of concealing conceals nothing. (Žižek 1989, 193)

Žižek continues:

> To "unmask the illusion" does not mean that "there is nothing to see behind it": what we must be able to see is precisely this *nothing as such*—beyond the phenomena, there is nothing *but this nothing itself, "nothing" which is the subject.* To conceive the appearance as "mere appearance" the subject effectively has to go beyond it, to "pass over" it, but what he finds there is his own act of passage. (Žižek 1989, 195)

In the first of these two quoted passages, it sounds as though Žižek is using Hegel to underscore a Lacanian line of thought. In the eleventh seminar, for instance, Lacan recounts a story about two artists (Zeuxis and Parrhasios) competing to paint the most convincing trompe l'oeil painting. Zeuxis paints a picture in which grapes are depicted so realistically that birds fly down from the sky to peck at them. Zeuxis, satisfied with his artistic feat, then turns to Parrhasios and asks him to pull down the veil covering what he, Parrhasios, has painted—failing to realize that the veil itself is Parrhasios's trompe l'oeil painting, that it is a lifelike painting of a cloth cover.[36] Like Hegel's appearance qua appearance, the surface of Parrhasios's painting deceives not by concealing something else behind it, but instead by generating the illusion that there is a concealed depth behind it waiting to be revealed. Žižek, addressing Lacan's distinction between *das Ding* and *objet petit a,* claims that object *a* deceives in exactly this way: "*a* qua semblance deceives in a Lacanian way: not because it is a deceitful substitute of the Real, but precisely because it invokes the impression of some substantial Real behind it; it deceives by posing as a shadow of the underlying Real" (Žižek 1993, 36–37). Or, in broader terms proposed in his 1988 work *Le plus sublime des hystériques,* "We are . . . thrust into the thing by that which appears to obscure it, that which suggests that 'the thing itself' is hidden, constituted around some lack" (Žižek 2005c, 39). (In relation to Lacan's trompe l'oeil example, the covering that appears to block visual access to the supposedly underlying painting-thing is already the painting-thing itself.)

However, in the second of the two passages from *The Sublime Object of Ideology* quoted above, Žižek takes an additional step, a step he deems

to be quintessentially Hegelian: he asserts that this no-thing is not nothing—that is to say, this void(ing) internally situated within the phenomenal world of appearances is subjectivity itself in its restless negativity.
For Žižek, the passage from Kant to Hegel is the transition from an
epistemological void to an ontological one, from the inaccessible Thing
beyond the subject's reach to the subject itself as the Thing incapable of
ever being reduced to the phenomena amongst which it is nonetheless
condemned to circulate (i.e., the Lacanian $).[37] And, when proposing
this equivalence between the Beyond of phenomena and the activity
of going beyond phenomena (an activity remaining immanent to the
world of appearances that it's constantly exceeding), Hegel claims that
the thing-in-itself is really subjectivity insofar as the latter is an X utterly
undetermined by any particular empirical contents, something out of
joint with the objects of experience.[38] As such, this subjectivity is freedom per se[39] (and this is also crucial for Žižek's project of rethinking the
concept of autonomy at the intersection of German idealism, a Marxist
theory of ideology, and the psychoanalytic conception of the unconscious).

Hegel's reflections on the Kantian thing-in-itself lead him to conclude
that the supersensible world of noumena supposedly hidden behind
phenomena is a spectral, virtual fantasy-construct consisting of posited
false essences. It's not that *das Ding an sich* is the genuine, solid essence
invisibly grounding the ephemeral, fragile façade of the inessential
object-as-appearance. Instead, Hegel repeatedly asserts that it's the essence of essence to appear.[40] To be more precise, once one fully accepts
the ontological consequences of Kant's Copernican revolution—this
world here is the Absolute because there is no Outside, no supersensible
world external to it—appearances are nothing other than essences since
there are no essences beyond appearances (save for the subject's own
activity of exceeding the givenness of the here and now). In the *Encyclopedia Logic*, Hegel maintains that "the things of which we have direct
consciousness are mere phenomena, not for us only, but in their own
nature" (Hegel 1975, 73 [§45]). Similarly, in the outline of his philosophical system, he proposes that "essence . . . is not behind or beyond
appearance, but rather, precisely because it is the essence which exists,
the existence is appearance" (Hegel 1990, 89 [§81]).

Žižek accurately describes the Hegelian dialectical subversion of the
Kantian essence-versus-appearance (as Thing-versus-object, noumenon-
versus-phenomenon) hierarchy as an inversion of presumed subject and
predicate positions.[41] In the section of the *Science of Logic* entitled "The
Thing and Its Properties," Hegel observes that what would here be the
supposed subject-term (i.e., the noumenal thing-in-itself) is actually just

a predicate-term of what was previously presumed to be this Thing's subsidiary predicate-term (i.e., the phenomenal object-as-appearance).[42]
That is to say, the Thing is what it is (i.e., a determinate "this," a specific
being/entity) thanks to its individuating properties as its apparent attributes. Hence, these properties are what is essential, and the invisible
supersensible ground ostensibly grounding these properties is really a
mere epiphenomenal property of the sensible; instead of the Thing being the subject and its properties being the predicate, the opposite is the
case. Tucked away in a footnote to a postface, Žižek offers an important
clarifying qualification to this: Hegel isn't saying that there's some internal necessity driving the essence to manifest itself as appearance—no-
tice that wording things this way would surreptitiously reintroduce the
suspect notion of there being essences prior to appearances—but rather
that "essence is *nothing but* the appearance of essence" (Žižek 2000h,
181), that is, essence-as-noumenon is an illusory image arising from phenomena. In *The Parallax View*, Žižek further clarifies the Hegelian dialectic between appearance and essence:

> We should always bear in mind that, in Hegel's dialectic of appearance
> and essence, it is appearance which is the asymmetrical encompassing
> term: the difference between essence and appearance is internal to ap-
> pearance, *not* to essence. When Hegel says that essence *has* to appear,
> that it is only as deep as it appears, this does not mean that essence is
> a self-mediating power which externalizes itself in its appearing and
> then "sublates" its otherness, positing it as a moment of its own self-
> movement. On the contrary, "essence appears" means that, with regard
> to the opposition essence/appearance, immediate "reality" is on the
> side of appearance: the gap between appearance and reality means that
> reality itself (what is immediately given to us "out there") appears as an
> expression of inner essence, that we no longer take reality at its "face
> value," that we suspect that there is in reality "more than meets the eye,"
> that is to say, that an essence appears to subsist somewhere within reality,
> as its hidden core. This dialectical shift in the meaning of appearance is
> crucial: first, immediate reality is reduced to a "mere appearance" of an
> inner essence; then, this essence itself is posited as something that ap-
> pears in reality as a specter of its hidden core. (Žižek 2006, 106)

Žižek insists here upon a reversal of yet another bit of popular interpretive *doxa* regarding Hegel. Just as he upends the perceived hierarchy
between contingency and necessity in Hegelian thought (as explained,
Žižek unconventionally argues that contingency has the upper hand in
Hegel's philosophy), so too does he invert the superficial perspective ac-

cording to which, for Hegel, experiential appearance is an epiphenomenal residue of an underlying conceptual essence.

However, before proceeding further, a previously posed question still
remains to be answered: what prompts the emergence of the supersensible "other world" (as the noumenal domain of things-in-themselves) out
of the plane of phenomena? Kant already hints at an answer to this query:
pure reason makes metaphysical appeals to an ultimate Real beyond, beneath, or behind the disclosed surfaces of experience (as constituted on
the basis of the interaction between intuition and the understanding)
in its ambitious striving to overcome the limited, "not all" nature of the
experienced world, in its drive to surmount its own finitude. Hegel says
something similar: "The thing in itself, which has become so famous in
the philosophy of Kant, shows itself here in its genesis, namely, as the
abstract reflection into self which is clung to at the exclusion of different determinations as the empty basis for them" (Hegel 1990, 87 [§75]).
These "different determinations," as a kaleidoscopic multitude, prompt
and provoke a "clinging" to a transcendent X as a means of taming and
domesticating this thriving chaos. Put differently (and perhaps a little
too simply), the world of appearances presents the subject with a dizzying
plurality of phenomena, a disorienting flux of ever-changing fragments
of experience. Confronted with this apparent disorder, subjectivity lends
it a degree of cohesive stability by grounding it via the invocation of an
underlying non-phenomenal foundation (i.e., the supersensible world).
Such posited essences are testimony, according to Žižek, to the fragmentary and unstable nature of the phenomenal field of appearances. And
for this reason, he defines "essence" as the "self-fissure"/"self-rupture" of
appearance.[43] In other words, "The multiple perspectival inconsistencies
between phenomena are not an effect of the impact of the transcendent
Thing—on the contrary, this Thing is nothing but the ontologization of
the inconsistency between phenomena" (Žižek 2003b, 66).

On several occasions Žižek notes that, for Hegel, limitation precedes
transcendence, that the latter is sparked into arising by confrontations
with a world of appearances riddled with antagonisms and deadlocks.[44]
And a 1994 essay contains the proposition that "the Thing-in-itself is *the
limitation of the phenomena as such*" (Žižek 1999f, 278). *Das Ding an sich*
is the avatar/representative of the fact that phenomenal appearances
can't be taken together to form a uniform whole, an organic cosmos, a
being at one with itself.[45] The supersensible world à la Kant's noumenal
sphere is the symptom of a struggle; more specifically, it's an outgrowth
of the subject's failed attempts to harmonize the cacophony of a disharmonious phenomenal immanence. More recently, *Organs Without Bodies*
summarizes things thus:

> For Hegel, the gap between phenomena and their transcendent Ground is a secondary effect of the *absolutely immanent* gap of/in the phenomena themselves. "Transcendence" is the illusory reflection of the fact that the immanence of phenomena is ruptured, broken, inconsistent. To put it in somewhat simplified terms, it is not that phenomena are broken, that we have multiple partial perspectives, because the transcendent Thing eludes our grasp; on the contrary, the specter of this Thing is the "reified" *effect* of the inconsistency of the phenomena . . . immanence generates the specter of transcendence because it is already inconsistent in itself. (Žižek 2004c, 60–61)

A few pages later, Žižek adds that "the tension between immanence and transcendence is . . . secondary with regard to the gap within immanence itself: 'transcendence' is a kind of perspective illusion, the way we (mis)perceive the gap/discord that inheres to immanence itself" (Žižek 2004c, 65). So the immanence of phenomenal reality isn't "not all" because of the withdrawal of a transcendent noumenal being; on the contrary, a transcendent noumenal being is posited precisely because the immanence of phenomenal reality is "not all." In Žižek's view, a core component of his own philosophical materialism is this inversion of idealism's prioritization of transcendence over immanence. He insists that phenomenal immanence is the zero-level point of departure out of which is generated (the mirage of) noumenal transcendence (one might even detect a slight Heideggerian inflection here—in particular, an affirmation of the subject's "thrownness" into the world,[46] its insurmountable immersion within the field of phenomena). For Žižek, the transition from Kant to Hegel amounts to the "shift . . . from the tension between immanence and transcendence to the minimal difference/gap in immanence itself."[47]

From a Žižekian standpoint, the being of phenomenal immanence splits into itself and (the appearance/illusion of) noumenal transcendence due to what could be described as a sort of insufficiency or lack within immanence itself. In other words, some of Žižek's musings on Hegel seem to suggest that appearances (i.e., phenomenal immanence) prompt subjective reflection's positing of essences (i.e., noumenal transcendence) because the former are inherently incomplete, aspiring toward a stable harmony of which they are constitutively deprived (a movement akin to Schelling's theosophical tale of God's self-transcendence of his own drive-ridden being as told in the *Weltalter* manuscripts). At this level, subjective reflection, instead of (as with Kantian transcendental idealism) being an externally imposed disruption of the otherwise harmonious wholeness of being *an sich*, is a reflecting process entirely embedded within the ontological plane it reflects upon, a process which lends this plane a certain sort of cohesive consistency. (Žižek mentions several times how subjective reflection upon things is part of the very essence of these same things, rather than being external to them.)[48] One could say that, according to Žižek's Hegelian-Lacanian ontology, being achieves whatever partial degree of always-incomplete unity it's capable of achieving specifically through one of its particular moments—more precisely, through the subject as an immanent rupture, a point of singularity "in being more than being itself."

Substance as Subject:
The Self-Sundering of Being

In his 1974 televised interview, Lacan describes (Imaginary-Symbolic) reality as "a grimace of the real."[1] Žižek reverses this description: the Real is a grimace of reality.[2] He implies that Lacan's 1974 formulation remains too Kantian: it hints that there is an inaccessible dimension (i.e., the noumenal Real) which can only ever be approached asymptotically through the distorting mediation of superficial appearances (i.e., phenomenal Imaginary-Symbolic reality). From the very beginning, Žižek's work has concerned itself with explicating Lacanian theory vis-à-vis German idealism and vice versa. In particular, his elucidations of Lacan's register of the Real are inextricably intertwined with his interpretations of the previously mentioned controversies traversing the philosophies of Kant, Fichte, Schelling, and Hegel. For the past few years, the self-critical story Žižek tells in narrating the development of his theorizing involves the claim that early texts such as *The Sublime Object of Ideology* too closely link the Lacanian Real with the problematic Kantian thing-in-itself. He characterizes his changes of mind regarding the Real as amounting to his own traversal of the path leading from Kant to Hegel in the way sketched above (even though, as has been argued already, Žižek is often more Schellingian than Hegelian; additionally, as will be argued, Žižek's subtler depictions of the Real also bring him into proximity with, somewhat surprisingly, Fichte). Accordingly, in, for instance, both his *Welcome to the Desert of the Real!* (2002) and *The Puppet and the Dwarf* (2003), he calls for an abandonment of the conceptualization of the Real as a substantial excess lying outside the boundaries of Imaginary-Symbolic reality.[3] However, through his successive (re-)elaborations of the fashions in which Kant and post-Kantian German idealism clarify the status of various aspects of Lacanian psychoanalysis, Žižek manages to raise serious doubts in the mind of the attentive reader as to whether his specifications concerning the Real are fundamentally consistent, and, if so, whether they're consistent in the manner he consciously believes them to be as per his self-reflexive narration of his own theoretical "progress" from a Kantian to a Hegelian Real. Many problems are the result of his somewhat haphazardly alternating between and conflating static versus genetic analyses of the Real (i.e., the Real as it is in relation to the already constituted subject situated in Imaginary-Symbolic reality versus the Real as it is in relation to the formative genesis of both the subject and reality).

To begin with, one could claim that, as regards the ontology of the Real, Žižek consistently has oscillated between Kantian and Hegelian positions starting with some of his earliest texts. As ought to be crystal clear by now, he tends to align Lacan's distinction between the Real and reality—the latter is constituted on the basis of the registers of the Imaginary and the Symbolic—with the Kantian dichotomy between the noumenal and the phenomenal respectively (if only to undermine this alignment in the course of revealing the Hegelian dialectical subtlety of Lacanian thought). Here, the Kantian version of the Real would entail presupposing the existence of some substantial thing-in-itself enjoying an ontological status entirely independent of Imaginary-Symbolic reality and its world of re/presentations. Correlatively, the Hegelian version of the Real would amount to asserting that this X defying representation and eluding symbolization is always posited from within the framework of Imaginary-Symbolic reality. So—this is the fundamental question regarding philosophical idealism—is the Real transcendent or immanent with respect to reality? Although Žižek usually sounds quite decisive when answering this basic query—during the past several years, he has come to insist upon the immanence of the Real to reality—the details of his various expositions of the relations between late modern philosophy and Lacan's doctrine of the three registers betray a certain indecisiveness, an indecisiveness that deserves to be highlighted, thematized, and preserved (and not quickly resolved in favor of either a Kantian or Hegelian depiction of the Real). Žižek's ontology of the Real is neither Kantian nor Hegelian, although significantly influenced by both thinkers (as observed, if anything, it's closer to Fichte and Schelling, the two intermediary figures between Kant and Hegel).

Beginning with his first publications, Žižek characterizes the Lacanian Real, with reference to Hegel, as exhibiting a dialectical coincidence of opposites, as being a point of condensing convergence for a series of mutually exclusive dimensions (it should be noted that Žižek's story according to which he progresses from his early Kantian version of the Real to his later Hegelian one is inaccurate and misleading). Along these lines, Žižek distinguishes between the (Kantian) Real-as-presupposed (*présupposé*) and the (Hegelian) Real-as-posed (*posé*).[4] On the one hand, the Real-as-presupposed is a sort of substantial fullness preceding the advent of Imaginary-Symbolic reality; for instance, in terms of the ontogenetic model of subject formation espoused by psychoanalysis, this Real would be, first and foremost, the mysterious state of existence prior to the acquisition of language. On the other hand, the Real-as-posed is an empty void situated entirely within the strictures of Imaginary-Symbolic reality; in relation to the Real-as-presupposed, the idea here would be that any such pre-linguistic state of being is rendered permanently inaccessible by entry into the symbolic order and, moreover, that the Real as inassimilable to the representational realm of reality can be reached only through the breakdowns and impasses internal to this realm. Additionally, the Real-as-presupposed appears exclusively as presupposed, that is, as a retroactive reconstruction posited from within the enclosure of Imaginary-Symbolic reality, as an always-after-the-fact rendition covered with the smudging traces of reality's words and images.

The Real-as-presupposed is associated with the recurrent motifs in Lacan's texts evoking the plentitude of the pre-Symbolic flesh, the brute, raw immediacy of the body prior to its being colonized and overwritten by the signifiers of the big Other. The Real-as-posed, by contrast, is associated with an insubstantial, ephemeral nothingness, a fleeting non-presence haunting the constituted field of reality and rendering it "not whole":

> The Real is the fullness of the inert presence, positivity; nothing is lacking in the Real—that is, the lack is introduced only by the symbolization; it is a signifier which introduces a void, an absence in the Real. But at the same time the Real is in itself a hole, a gap, an opening in the middle of the symbolic order—it is the lack around which the symbolic order is structured. The Real as a starting point, as a basis, is a positive fullness without lack; as a product, a leftover of symbolization, it is, in contrast, the void, the emptiness created, encircled by the symbolic structure. (Žižek 1989, 170)

Immediately after tracing the contours of this complex convergence of opposites, it sounds as though Žižek endorses one sense over the other. He apparently comes out in favor of treating the Real primarily as posed, namely, as a void entirely immanent to the representational fabric of reality (rather than as presupposed, as a pre-representational transcendence—a depiction of the Real he identifies as Kantian):

> Lacan's whole point is that the Real is *nothing but* this impossibility of its inscription: the Real is not a transcendent positive entity, persisting somewhere beyond the symbolic order like a hard kernel inaccessible to it, some kind of Kantian "Thing-in-itself"—in itself it is nothing at all, just a void, an emptiness in a symbolic structure marking some central impossibility. (Žižek 1989, 173)

Here, appearances are at risk of being deceptive. Despite what seems to be an endorsement of reading the Real as fully posed (i.e., as absolutely internal to the symbolic order)—this would entail that the Real-as-presupposed is wholly and completely fantasmatic, nothing but an *après-coup* fiction fabricated by the *parlêtre*—Žižek's reference to "some central impossibility" indexed by the deadlocks of the big Other hints that there is indeed an X that isn't entirely immanent to Imaginary-Symbolic reality. Žižek forbids conceiving of this X as akin to Kant's *Ding an sich*, as a dense, heavy presence/substance. However, taking into account the preceding delineation of the shift from Kantian epistemology to Hegelian ontology, this "central impossibility" need not be thought of as purely logical-structural (i.e., as something devoid of the heft of ontological weight). For both Schelling and Hegel, the Real is, in fact, "barred." As explained above, Kant assumes that the noumenal Real is a positive ontological plentitude unperturbed by the antagonisms and contradictions plaguing human reason, whereas Hegel projects the Kantian antinomies into the order of being itself. Hence, impossibilities aren't necessarily ideational constructs internal to subjective cognition, that is, knots subsisting simply within Imaginary-Symbolic reality. These knots are (also) part of the very nature of being.

As will become increasingly apparent here, for Žižek, those nodes within reality where reality itself becomes dysfunctional (i.e., the Real-as-posed) are the nodes where reality (re)connects with a dysfunctionality inherent to the Real of being *an sich* (i.e., the Real as something other than a construct internally generated in and by the symbolic order). Given Žižek's brand of Hegelianism, he's committed to the idea that speaking subjectivity "touches the Real" (i.e., comes into contact with something other than objects constituted in and through linguistic-representational mediation) precisely at those points where the Imaginary-Symbolic matrix disrupts and subverts itself (as Lacan puts it, the Real is reached through "an impasse of formalization"[5]): "Far from signaling the failure of our thought to grasp reality, the inherent inconsistency of our notional apparatus is the ultimate proof that our thought is not merely a logical game we play, but is able to reach reality itself, expressing its inherent structuring principle" (Žižek 1999b, 99).

Certain articulations make clear that Žižek properly appreciates the aporetic essence of the Real, rather than viewing this as a confusion awaiting eventual theoretical resolution: "A certain fundamental ambiguity pertains to the notion of the Real in Lacan: the Real designates a substantial hard kernel that precedes and resists symbolization and, simultaneously, it designates the left-over, which is posited or 'produced' by symbolization itself" (Žižek 1993, 36). Broadly speaking, one needn't feel forced to choose between naïve realism and equally naïve idealism.

(In Žižek's Hegel-influenced interpretation, Kant arguably and regrettably chooses both, simultaneously insisting on the existence of an unmediated bedrock of asubjective being [i.e., naïve realism] as well as on the subject's condemnation to the enclosed confines of its own cognition [i.e., naïve idealism].) And yet, despite these instances where he affirms the existence of a facet of the Real as more than just a by-product/leftover produced by the Symbolic, Žižek frequently lapses into a sort of (for want of a better phrase) radical idealism of the Symbolic (especially at times when he seems excessively intoxicated by Hegelian-style dialectical flights of thought).

On a number of occasions, Žižek, using Hegel's language, maintains that the division between the notional (as the Symbolic) and the extra/non-notional (as the Real) is a division internal to the notional itself. The border between the Symbolic and the Real is a border situated within the territory of the Symbolic: "*Every tension between Notion and reality, every relationship of the Notion to what appears as its irreducible Other encountered in the sensible, extra-notional experience, already is an intra-notional tension, i.e., already implies a minimal notional determination of this 'otherness'*" (Žižek 1993, 20). What's more, Žižek sometimes claims that the extra/non-notional Real comes into being solely as a result of the notional Symbolic malfunctioning and short-circuiting itself: "The real emerges from the impasses of formalization . . . the Real is not a hard external kernel which resists symbolization, but the *product* of a deadlock in the process of symbolization" (Žižek 1996b, 110), and "nonconceptual reality is something that emerges when notional self-development gets caught in an inconsistency, and becomes nontransparent to itself" (Žižek 2003b, 66). Connecting this to Hegel, he states:

> The standard notion of reality is that of a hard kernel which resists the conceptual grasp; what Hegel does is simply to take this notion of reality more literally: non-conceptual reality is something which emerges when notional self-development gets caught in an inconsistency, and becomes non-transparent to itself. In short, the limit is transposed from exterior to interior: there is Reality because, and in so far as, the Notion is inconsistent, does not coincide with itself . . . In short, the multiple perspectival inconsistencies between phenomena are not an effect of the impact of the transcendent Thing—on the contrary, the Thing is nothing but the ontologization of the inconsistency between phenomena. (Žižek 2002a, xxix–xxx)

As just seen, in certain contexts, Žižek indicates that the Real isn't utterly reducible to a mediated feature of the Symbolic. But in the passage quoted immediately above, "reality" as "hard kernel," as an extra/non-ideational X, is apparently reduced to the status of a residual after-effect of the operations of conceptual/notional mediation. And one of his invocations of the distinction between the linguistic and extra/non-linguistic indeed gestures in the direction of an idealism of the Symbolic: he claims that the distinction between the Symbolic as linguistic and the Real as extra/non-linguistic is a distinction internal to the linguistic Symbolic itself.[6] So, at this point, the obvious question arises: is Žižek simply being philosophically sloppy, carelessly contradicting himself with no effort whatsoever to avoid incompatible formulations concerning the Real?

In a 1993 interview, Žižek explicitly expresses the tension between these two versions of the Real. He designates this as a "paradox" that must be accepted and embraced: "The real does not refer to some substantial, positive entity beyond the symbolic, resisting symbolization . . . what Lacan calls 'the real' is nothing beyond the symbolic, it's merely *the inherent inconsistency of the symbolic order itself*" (Žižek and Salecl 1996, 41). He goes on to stipulate: "Still, not everything is cultural, that's the paradox. Although you cannot pinpoint a moment which is pure nature, which is not yet mediated by culture, in spite of this you must not draw the conclusion that everything is culture. Otherwise you fall into 'discursive idealism'" (Žižek and Salecl 1996, 41).

The same year as this interview, in *Tarrying with the Negative,* he indeed accepts and embraces this paradox, maintaining there, through recourse to the nature-culture opposition (handled as structurally identical to the Hegelian opposition between the notional and the extra/non-notional), that although the distinction between nature and culture is a distinction internal to culture itself, this doesn't mean that there's no such thing as nature existing apart from culture's mediation.[7] In other words, although the distinction between the Real and reality is a distinction internal to reality itself, this doesn't mean that there's no such thing as the Real existing apart from reality's mediation—just because it's impossibly inaccessible doesn't mean it isn't there. But isn't Žižek himself repeatedly at risk of being guilty of promulgating, under the banner of a Hegelianized Lacan, precisely the type of "discursive idealism" he dismisses in the above quotation? It would be easy to stop here and simply chide Žižek for failing to integrate his reflections on the Real (while not allowing for the cheap excuse that the Real thwarts any and every effort to treat it in a consistent fashion—an excuse often used by theoreticians borrowing from Lacan to license sheer intellectual laziness, to turn the necessity of their incapacity to be conceptually systematic and logically consequent into a supposed sophisticated virtue). However, the more

productive path forward from this crossroads is to examine how bringing
Fichte and Schelling (the two key figures situated, both chronologically
and, in various ways, philosophically, between Kant and Hegel) to bear
on these superficially contradictory formulations regarding the Real reveals that these contradictions aren't what they appear to be to a casual
initial glance.

As already mentioned, Žižek proposes that Fichte, the supposed arch-
idealist of the post-Kantian period, should be read as a certain sort of
(proto-)materialist (or at a minimum, he need not be construed as a
Berkeley-style solipsist denying the reality of anything unconditioned by
the mediation of subjectivity and its attendant ideational structures—see
chapter 2). In hybrid German idealist and Lacanian terms, Fichte need
not be understood as contending that there is no objective Real apart
from the fantasmatic specter of this supersensible bedrock constructed
from within the framework of the subjective Ideal as the Imaginary-
Symbolic reality of the *parlêtre* (i.e., in Žižekian terms, that the Real is
purely posed in and by reality). Instead, as is the case for Lacan too, the
Fichtean Real (embodied in the *Anstoss*) is something impossible yet indispensable for the subjective Ideal. What does this mean?

Starting at least as early as Aristotle's account of perception, a persistent notion in the history of philosophy is that the surest indication of
the conceiving and perceiving individual having contact with something
beyond him or her, bumping up against a radical Outside-Otherness,
resides in experiences involving constraint, passivity, and a general lack
of freedom. For instance, perceptions seem "real" (i.e., reflections of
an unconditioned objective reality) whenever the perceiver is powerless
to alter the contents of these perceptions at will, to change what reveals
itself based on mere whim and fancy. By contrast, perceptions seem "unreal" (i.e., artificial fabrications of the human imagination) whenever
the perceiver possesses the power to alter the contents of these perceptions at will. Likewise, Freud claims that the psychical apparatus of the
young, nascent subject-to-be is forced to acknowledge the existence of
a reality greater than it, external to its narcissistic fantasmatic kingdom,
exclusively through colliding with moments when its wants and wishes
are thwarted. It's only when hallucinatory auto-erotic satisfaction and/or
imagined omnipotent control of desired objects fails to quell the clamoring of the drives of the archaic libidinal economy that the fledgling
psyche is compelled to constitute notions of an outer alterity (as both
material and social reality).[8] Psychoanalytically speaking, reality announces itself with a slap to the face.

In this general vein, Fichte essentially argues that Ideal subjectivity

encounters Real objectivity through an indirect rather than a direct approach. The subject touches the Real only at those points where, from
within itself and its spontaneous activity, it runs up against inhibitions or
resistances, where it faces barriers or obstacles internal to its sphere of
operations.[9] The asubjective Real registers its (non-)presence solely in
relation to the subjective Ideal—which means that the existence of the
positing subject as active spontaneity is a precondition for the manifestation of that which exceeds manifestation, for the Beyond of appearance (i.e., the noumenal *an sich* dimension) appearing in the form of
a check/impediment internal to the subjective sphere.[10] This helps further clarify what Lacan means when he insists that the Real is reached
only through the impasses in symbolization. It's not that there is no Real
that isn't immanent to the Symbolic. Instead, the non-immanent Real is
accessible exclusively through the deadlocks and inconsistencies immanent to the Symbolic. And, apropos the distinction between the Real-as-
presupposed versus the Real-as-posed, this brief Fichtean aside permits
finessing the apparent contradictions at play in Žižek's depictions of the
Real without losing the subtle nuances conveyed by these same troubling
logical-conceptual tensions. The Real-as-presupposed actually exists "for
us" only insofar as it indirectly shines through the cracks in the façade of
Imaginary-Symbolic reality, insofar as it is asymptotically approached by
the *parlêtre* along the fault lines of this reality's inner conflicts. (In fact,
given the Hegelian treatment of Kant's noumenal-versus-phenomenal opposition endorsed by Žižek, it could be said that the presupposed proto-
reality of the Real is posed/posited by the subject in response to reality's
inner conflicts.)

Like Fichte (but in a different manner), the young Schelling (and
not just the later Schelling focused on by Žižek) permits formulating a
more sophisticated understanding of the underlying systematicity of the
Žižekian ontology of the Real. However, when reading what follows, one
should keep in mind that, as Hegel once put it, Schelling is a thinker who
is guilty of conducting his private philosophical education on the public
stage—that is, Schelling repeatedly changes his mind about various matters, rapidly jumping from system to system with the publication of each
new text. Hence, especially as concerns his reading of Kant, Schelling's
lines of thought presented below do not necessarily harmonize with his
remarks cited above apropos the Kantian thing-in-itself (and, of course,
the purpose here is to analyze critically Žižek's Hegelian-Lacanian
treatment of the Real, rather than to construct a satisfying exegetical-
historical account of Schellingian thinking in its various guises).

The interesting and unique features of the Schellingian reassessment
of the status of *das Ding an sich* are to be found, as indicated earlier, in

some of Schelling's 1797 remarks on Kant (see chapter 6). In the "Treatise Explicatory of the Idealism in the *Science of Knowledge*," he clarifies that Kant's thought should not be interpreted as a form of strict idealism, namely, as a doctrine that condemns the individual subject to live out its experiential existence in a solipsistic prison populated by empty, spectral semblances devoid of genuine existence.[11] In a footnote to this caveat regarding the sense in which Kant should be understood, Schelling adds:

> Kant denied that the representations are copies of things in themselves. At the same time, however, he ascribed reality to the representations. Hence—this was a necessary conclusion—there could not exist any things in themselves whatsoever and, for our representation, no *original* [*"x"*] *outside* of it. Otherwise the two claims could not be reconciled. (Schelling 1994b, 75)

Schelling equates "reality" with "existence," and thus argues that, if Kant is not to be caught up in a blatant contradiction, the thing-in-itself, as excluded from the only known reality as representational experience, must be deemed nonexistent. Although it appears that he's denying outright the existence of anything akin to Kant's *an sich* noumenon, Schelling seems to be, at this stage, merely maintaining that the notion of the thing-in-itself as lying "beyond" or "outside" the subject is untenable. Later in the same essay, complications arise due to an additional comment made regarding *das Ding an sich:*

> Kant *symbolized* this supersensible ground of all sensibility with his expression of *things in themselves*—an expression that, like all symbolic expressions, contains a *contradiction* because it aims at presenting the unconditioned [*das Unbedingte*] by means of something conditional [*ein Bedingtes*]. Yet such contradictory (inconsistent) expressions are the only ones by means of which we are able to present *ideas* at all. (Schelling 1994b, 106)

Surprisingly, the contradiction plaguing the thing-in-itself, instead of being a fatal liability warranting the dismissal of critical philosophy, is a virtue of Kantian thought. Schelling's position here with regard to Kant foreshadows the full-blown version of the identity philosophy articulated in the years immediately following, a philosophy in which the "absolute ground" of both nature and subjectivity is supposedly approached by knowledge solely through a focus on the antagonistic, contradictory interstices that simultaneously separate and unite all conceptual oppositions. This vision of the Absolute is expressed in a catchphrase shared by

Schelling and the young Hegel in the years after 1800 as a first principle for philosophy: "the identity of identity and difference."[12] The "Idea" in the identity philosophy is that which mediates between all conceivably possible oppositional levels: the Ideal and the Real, the infinite and the finite, the universal and the particular, the soul and the body, and so on. In 1797, Schelling already introduces this portrayal of the Idea as mediator between conceptually incompatible dimensions vis-à-vis the ostensibly contradictory nature of Kant's thing-in-itself.

The fact that this *Ding an sich* leads to aporias for rational cognition signifies, for Schelling, the surest indication that, instead of being an empty, nonsensical abstraction, this Kantian "idea" hits upon a genuine, true Real. To be more precise, given Schelling's later assertions (as presented, for instance, in the 1802 dialogue *Bruno*) that only the Idea as the "point of indifference" between conceptual-cognitive opposites is "really real,"[13] he insinuates that, since the thing-in-itself entails a contradiction between *das Unbedingte* (i.e., the unconditioned as the Real ground of the Thing in terms of it being an ontological *Stoffe* independent of the subject's conscious representations) and *ein Bedingtes* (i.e., the conditioned as the Ideal existence of the object in terms of it being an experiential entity couched within the parameters of the subject's power for re/presentation), Kant's formulation inadvertently succeeds in subverting the standard opposition between "in itself" (i.e., the unconditioned Real) and "for another" (i.e., the conditioned Ideal). The Kantian idea of the thing-in-itself thereby, according to a logic already seen here in Fichte, Hegel, Lacan, and Žižek, opens out the horizon onto the absolute *Grund* through an internal impasse generated within the mediating structures of understanding and reason. Due to the constraints imposed by language—truths must be articulated in a language that is itself not fully up to this task, since, as Schelling observes, language borrows its expressive powers from the finite, limited understanding[14]—the truth of the Absolute Idea can only ever be tangentially glanced off of by means of aporias woven into the conceptual fabric of language. The monistic One can be accessed solely via the antagonistic, contradictory Two.

From the perspective of the epistemological subject, including the consciousness of the philosopher, the noumenal Real and the phenomenal Ideal necessarily appear to be separate and incompatible domains. But for Schelling this separation is, in and of itself, the appearance to be overcome, the inherent perspectival distortion (or, in Kantian parlance, the transcendental illusion) to be dissolved by a philosophical approach that recognizes the subjectively conditioned nature of this very opposition.[15] With Kant, the object alone is the appearance, strictly speaking; with the subsequent German idealist tradition (Fichte, Schelling, and

Hegel), the dichotomy between object and Thing is itself the fundamental appearance generated by the subject.[16] As will soon become evident, one of Žižek's central concerns in his deployment of Hegelian philosophy is the vexing question of how the very split between the noumenal Real and the phenomenal Ideal emerges in the first place—of how a presumably monistic ontological sphere internally splits itself into a series of incommensurable "parallaxes," of how being auto-affectively refracts itself into sets of antinomic, incompatible strata.

Returning to the thread of argumentation in Schelling's 1797 essay, after having ruled out the notion of a supersensible ontological realm outside the closed circle of consciousness, Schelling proceeds to claim that thinking already presupposes a precognitive reality. The cognizing subject always already assumes, whether it admits so or not, that a world exists independently of its reasoning and willing.[17] Although this sounds quite consistent with his earlier insistence in the same essay on the sterility and vacuity of any kind of extreme idealism, isn't there a tension here between, on the one hand, the apparently dogmatic assertion of the existence of a precognitive reality and, on the other hand, the allegation that *das Ding an sich* cannot meaningfully be understood if it's assumed to be a supersensible entity subsisting behind/beyond the subject's experiences? Oddly enough, for Schelling, no incompatibility hampers these two positions. He rejects the version of the thing-in-itself as a separate ontological X because, in his view, completely divorcing the ontological Thing from the epistemological object results in the destruction of epistemology by leading it into the dead-end trap of solipsistic idealism (or, as Hegel points out, this divorce in Kant leads to the absurd implication that the subject has true knowledge of false entities; paradoxically, the subject has a legitimate understanding based on references to superficial appearances veiling a more essential domain of authentic being[18]). Instead, Schelling proposes that philosophy should depart from a firmer foundation by accepting that, at least originally, the substantial Thing and the appearing object are one.

Immediately after affirming the existence of a precognitive reality, Schelling reminds readers that a question perennially plaguing philosophy is the enigma of how it is that an external entity becomes an "internally" grasped object of knowledge, of how matter and mind interact. Of course, a defining gesture of Kant's Copernican revolution is to evade this traditional problem by inverting its standard form. Instead of asking how the subject's internal cognition comes to be in conformity with external entities, one asks, rather, how external entities (i.e., things-in-themselves) come to be in conformity with the subject's internal cognition (i.e., the ensemble of possibility conditions for a Thing becoming an object of experience).[19] But this inversion still fails to get rid of the problem (Schelling says as much in his 1830s discussion of Kant[20]). It simply declares the question of how Things affect the subject's sensibilities, so as to register themselves as experienced objects, to be an illegitimate extension of a concept of the understanding (i.e., causality) beyond its proper jurisdiction of application, namely, the field of already given phenomenal experience. In short, Kant tries to banish the problem, to forbid anyone from asking this troubling question.

However, because of Kant tying his own hands in this manner, Schelling is convinced that the Kantian critical edifice lacks an adequate account of its genuine ontological foundation. Furthermore, he maintains that this lack is critical philosophy's fatal flaw, since Kant must nonetheless presuppose, if his system is indeed to be distinguished from Berkeley-esque solipsism, that Things do somehow manage to affect the senses so as to generate the appearance of objects. In his 1797 "Treatise" Schelling maintains:

> The question now arises how it should be possible for something external and strictly heterogeneous from the soul to cohere with our interiority in so immediate a manner . . . Nothing is more crucial than to think this question through in a rigorous manner and to ensure that this rigor not be compromised by our desire to arrive at some answer. (Schelling 1994b, 85)

He continues:

> For all the failed attempts to answer this [question] share the mistake of attempting to explain conceptually what effectively precedes all concepts; they all betray the same incapacity of the spirit to transcend discursive thinking and to ascend to the immediacy that exists within itself. (Schelling 1994b, 85)

Schelling begins by reasserting, contra the Kantian critical gesture, the urgency of rigorously addressing the enigma of the relation between the external and the internal, between, in the parlance of the identity philosophy, the Real and the Ideal. However, in diagnosing the past failures to answer this question as stemming from an attempt "to explain conceptually what effectively precedes all concepts," he echoes Kant's insistence that the concept of causality cannot be applied legitimately to the speculated rapport linking Thing to object. Taking into account what was established above concerning Schelling's criticisms of *das Ding an sich* in conjunction with his remarks in this present passage, one is left with two core claims: first, the thing-in-itself is not some supersensible X lying beyond/outside a self-enclosed consciousness; and second, the "Real Thing" preceding cognitive knowledge transcends the subject's concepts. Therefore, the Schellingian thing-in-itself (as opposed to the object-for-the-subject as mediated by a formal-conceptual matrix) is an ontological excess, a brute givenness of being, situated immanently within the domain of conscious experience itself (i.e., Schelling's Thing is "extimate" in the strict Lacanian sense). This is precisely the signifi- cance of the perplexing reference above to "the immediacy that exists within itself," that is, the unmediated presence of Things inhering within the very structure of subjectivity. In the *Bruno* dialogue, Schelling, speak- ing through the voice of the dialogue's namesake, proclaims that "sensa- tion is the real element of intuition" (Schelling 1984, 188).

Thus, one aspect of Schelling's solution to the Kantian conundrum as articulated in B 145 (in the *Critique of Pure Reason*) is to identify a pre- conceptual immediacy (i.e., "sensation") as "internally" subsisting within the experiential field accessible to the subject.[21] In other words, for the young Schelling, there is something "in experience more than experi- ence itself"—there is a primordial identity between Thing and object (an identity existing in the immediate oneness of entity and appearance at the level of raw sensation *an sich*) that becomes inaccessible with the gradual emergence of a cognizing subject whose epistemological gaze disrupts and divides this identity/unity through the refraction of experi- ence resulting from the lenses of its concepts and notions.[22] Schelling here solves Kant's problem of the relation of priority between intuition and the understanding by inverting the standard Kantian portrayal of the in-itself status of noumena: for the subject, what exists "in itself" is not a supersensible realm, but, on the contrary, is precisely the immediately sensible in and of itself, prior to being mediated by concepts. Schelling insists that the assumption of "everyday consciousness" regarding the in- separable identity of perceived object and Real Thing contains a kernel of truth that must be defended against the tendencies of the "formal phi- losopher" to drive a permanent wedge "between appearances and things in themselves."[23] He goes on to posit a "primordial identity of the pure and the empirical in us," arguing that "primordially, there exists in us no distinction between the Real and the Ideal" (Schelling 1994b, 120).

What makes this lengthy detour back through Schelling relevant to appreciating the intricacies of Žižek's (Lacanian) Hegelianism? Surpris- ingly, yet another rapid detour, a momentary return to Freud, is useful for driving home the upshot of this particular Schellingian recasting of the Kantian Thing. As is well known, in his landmark 1900 work *The Inter- pretation of Dreams*, Freud refers to a point encountered in certain dreams where analytic interpretation breaks down, where the labor of decoding the concealed, disguised meaning of the latent dream-thoughts underpinning the manifest dream-text runs aground.[24] He dubs this point the dream's "navel," defined as "the spot where it reaches down into the unknown."[25] Now, one might be tempted to translate this hastily into the terms of a Kantianized version of the Lacanian Real by claiming that this navel is the locus within the dream-text wherein the dreaming subject bumps up against a Real incapable of being presented or represented. In other words, on this reading, the navel would mark the absence of an impossible Thing that withdraws from or recedes behind psychical reality.

However, Freud hints at something different. Immediately after he introduces and explains the notion of the dream's navel, he notes, "The dream-thoughts to which we are led by interpretation cannot, from the nature of things, have any definite endings; they are bound to branch out in every direction into the intricate network of our world of thought" (*SE* 5:525). If one chooses to treat the dream being interpreted as a set of (experiential) presentations (akin to Kant's faculty of intuition) and the interpretation of the dream as a set of (conceptual) representations (akin to Kant's faculty of the understanding), then one can say Freud is suggesting that representation in the form of interpretation-concepts is thwarted by the excessive full disclosure of the dream's presentation à la the manifest dream-text's experiential superabundance (instead of the representational process of interpreting being blocked because a key kernel of deep meaning has somehow subtracted itself from the field of the interpretable). That is to say, the Freudian navel is, at least in some instances, a Schellingian rather than a Kantian "Real Thing." In this case, one is confronted with the precise inverse of a structure outlined through a specific interpretive rule of thumb proposed by Freud: with reference to, for example, the multiple snakes covering the head of Medusa, Freud contends that the thriving plethora of phallic symbols (i.e., the vital, writhing mass of numerous snakes) conceals the opposite, namely, castration as the absence of any phallus whatsoever—behind the façade of many lurks the specter of none.[26] By contrast, in light of how Schelling and Hegel recast Kant's *Ding an sich*, this Thing is an apparent zero (i.e., the void of the transcendent noumenal Real) that obfuscates a prior, underlying multitude (i.e., the wild, untamed chaos of the immanent phenomenal plane of being-as-appearances)—behind the façade of none lurks the specter of many.

Through overwhelming the interpreting analyst with too much potential significance, the navel, as a point of signifying hyperdensity in which a dizzying multitude of associative linkages are condensed (like the tightly packed matter constituting a black hole), hollows out a void in the representational fabric of the analyst's interpretations. The analyst is made to suffer from the proverbial "poverty of riches," being flooded by an incalculable number of implied interconnecting threads trailing off in all directions from the dream's navel. The "too much" of this hyper-dense point of condensation results in a "not enough" of interpretation due to the "too muchness" overloading (and thereby short-circuiting) the representational operations of the analyst. In Lacanian parlance, if the analyst's dream-interpretations are a form of Symbolic knowledge (designated by the matheme S_2), then the Freudian navel would be a Real generated by and internal to Imaginary-Symbolic reality (as, in the example under discussion, the manifest dream-text, a text which drowns the analyst as [supposed] agent of knowledge with too many proliferat-ing Ss: S_3, S_4 . . .). Or, alternatively, the navel, like the character of the minister in Poe's "The Purloined Letter," conceals an X not by tucking it away in some dark, obscure corner, but rather by openly displaying it as such, blinding the vision of the interpretive seeker with a brilliant abundance of potentially significant representations.

In fact, using the example of Freud's dream-navel, one could argue that, in both the operation of interpreting a dream involving a navel and (more generally) the ontogenetic emergence of fully constituted subjec-tivity, the movement is from the overwhelming surplus of the Schelling-ian Real (as the excess of experiential presentation over conceptual representation) to the withdrawn deficit of the Kantian Real (as the stabilizing voiding via conceptual representation prompted by this dis-orienting excess of experiential presentation)—and it is Hegel, with his critical analysis of Kant's noumenal-phenomenal distinction (in particu-lar, his discussions of the "supersensible world" and "appearance qua ap-pearance" as summarized earlier), who enables the very dynamic of this transition from the Schellingian to the Kantian Real to be explained.

Once again, Žižek's depiction of the Real as reflecting a Hegelian-style convergence of opposites is helpful: the Real is both an excessive surplus (à la Schelling) and a recessive deficit (à la Kant). Žižek remarks that "the paradox of Kant's *Ding an sich* is that it is at the same time the excess of receptivity over intellect (the unknowable external source of our passive sensible perceptions) *and* the purely intelligible content-less construct of an X without any support in our senses" (Žižek 2006, 389). However, the "paradox" here arises from this potentially misleading "at the same time": although the Real is simultaneously both a surplus-excess and a deficit-void in the synchronic conceptual universe of philosophical the-ory, these two faces of the Thing (as overwhelming presence versus with-drawn absence) appear at different ontogenetic stages in the unfolding of subjectivity's structure, with the balance between which side predomi-

nates alternating according to the context of actualization. Thanks to
a Hegelianized psychoanalytic account of subject formation, these two
faces of the Real don't amount to a simple muddle-headed contradiction:
the voiding of phenomena is a subsequent result produced out of and
in reaction to an initial excessiveness of phenomena. The supersensible
world is fabricated in an effort to tame and domesticate the instability
of the sensible world. Thereafter, the sensible world always involves the
mediation of a supersensible dimension, a mediation whose advent turns
things upside-down (as Hegel's "inverted world") by coming to render
the pure sensible *an sich* an inaccessible extimacy "in experience more
than experience itself" (as per the young Schelling circa 1797).

How does this resolve the apparent contradictions that seem to plague
Žižek's various ways of talking about his distinction between the Real-
as-presupposed and the Real-as-posed? Maybe the Real-as-presupposed
should be subdivided into, for lack of less awkward phrases, the Real-as-
"pre" versus the Real-as-(presup)posed. The former is the Real as prior
to Imaginary-Symbolic reality (as, for instance, the ontogenetic period
preceding the acquisition of language and/or an order of being absolutely external to the thinking subject), whereas the latter (the Real-as-
[presup]posed) is this same Real (i.e., the "pre" Real unconditioned
by the positing activity of subjectivity, preceding this activity) as posed
from within Imaginary-Symbolic reality on the basis of the contradictions and inconsistencies within this reality itself. What Žižek calls the
Real-as-presupposed is, ultimately, just the "pre" Real as posed, namely,
a reconstruction from within reality of whatever is prior to or outside
of reality (hence, a reconstructed Real covered with the fingerprints of
Imaginary-Symbolic reality—that is, a mediated Real). The Real-as-"pre"
is impossible—recall that Lacan frequently qualifies the Real as (the)
impossible—in the strong sense, as something wholly and completely
inaccessible in and of itself for the subject. In other Lacanian terms, this
pre-reality is foreclosed without a trace by the cut of primal repression
instituted with the entry into socio-symbolic reality.

Nonetheless, subjectivity, although totally immersed in Imaginary-
Symbolic reality, is later grazed by the impossibility of this lost Real-as-
"pre" through another sort of impossibility, more specifically, the irresolvable impasses and paradoxes in which the foreclosed Real indirectly
returns thanks to the occasional yet inevitable malfunctions and short
circuits of the big Other. Additionally, given the reading of Schelling
presented immediately above, this foreclosed Real is always ready to return since it is extimate as internally excluded in relation to reality (and
not, as per traditional Kantian transcendental idealism, simply exterior
as transcendently beyond). This Real exerts an insistent pressure that's

kept at bay by the structure of subjectivity as sustained by the operative symbolic order (just as, in traditional Freudian metapsychology, one of the basic purposes of consciousness, of the selective attention of secondary process cognition, isn't to be open to the world, to take in the incalculable richness of revealed reality, but, instead, to filter out this intense "too much" deluge of sensory-perceptual excitations bombarding the receptive surface of the perception-consciousness system—psychoanalytically speaking, consciousness entails a narrowing down rather than, as is commonly assumed, an opening up). But when this structuring order of the big Other temporarily breaks down, that which is in reality more than reality itself has a chance fleetingly to shine through. However, the Fichtean caveat here, a caveat Žižek would likely insist upon, is that this Real which shines through can do so only due to the tension already established between it and reality. As Fichte puts it, the subjective can know the asubjective only as a feeling of resistance felt by subjectivity—minus the subject's registration of resistance, asubjective objectivity is nothing (for it). Without the bordering edge between subjective reality and the holes within this reality (as those points of breakdown in which the Real shines through), the Real would be nothing "for us" (and, thus, for all theoretical intents and purposes, nothing at all).

As is now glaringly apparent, one of the common thematic threads binding Fichte, Schelling, and Hegel into the unity of a single orientation (i.e., "German idealism") is their shared insistence on the genetically produced nature of the Kantian dichotomy between noumena and phenomena, between things-in-themselves and objects-as-appearances. However, whereas Fichte focuses on the Thing as an *Anstoss* internally posited within subjectivity as an inner resisting obstacle to its spontaneous autonomous activity—in short, for Fichtean thought, the distinction between subject and Other is a distinction internal to the subject itself— Schelling and Hegel indicate that this series of dichotomous oppositions generated from the perspective of the Kantian critical apparatus is an effect or outcome in relation to a prior monistic ontological register. In the preceding chapter (chapter 11), the Schellingian-Hegelian "geneticization" of Kant's noumenal-phenomenal dehiscence was somewhat inaccurately and misleadingly described as the process wherein the illusion of the unifying, underlying void of the transcendent noumenal Thing arises from the fragmentary, kaleidoscopic immanence of the plane of ever-multiplying phenomena—that is, the noumenal arises from the phenomenal. To be more accurate, the Kantian phenomenal, for Hegel, refers to what emerges when the givenness of that-which-is-disclosed appears to appear, when phenomena are presented as phenomenal appearances behind which something (i.e., the noumenal Thing) mysteriously appears (at the same time, in so doing, this Thing also appears to hide the kernel of its true ontological essence). So, to be as precise as possible, it's not that noumena emerge from phenomena. Instead, both noumena and phenomena emerge from something else, an ontological X that is neither strictly noumenal nor phenomenal per se.

At one point, in a footnote in *Tarrying with the Negative*, Žižek seemingly explains Hegel's post-Kantian gesture apropos noumena-versus-phenomena in a manner exactly opposite the one outlined earlier (the one according to which noumena arise from phenomena): "The truly Hegelian problem is not to penetrate from the phenomenal surface into Things-in-themselves, but to explain how, within Things, something akin to phenomena could have emerged" (Žižek 1993, 241). The way to reconcile this additional inflection/twist with what has already been said above is to insist upon a difference in this sentence between the first "Things-in-themselves" (as the emergent correlate of treating phenomena as "appearances qua appearances") and the second "Things" (as the ground of being out of which is generated the bifurcation between phenomenal objects-as-appearances and noumenal things-in-themselves). Further support for this reconciliation is to be found in the roughly contemporaneous text *Enjoy Your Symptom!* in which Žižek maintains that Hegel's move in relation to Kant is to transpose the split between noumena and phenomena onto things themselves.[27] In other words, this rupture, rather than marking a barrier or limitation to the subject's ability to make contact with an asubjective Real(ity), is a rupture forming an intrinsic part of being in and of itself (or, as Hegel puts it, "the thing-in-itself essentially possesses this external reflection within itself" [Hegel 1969, 490]).

Consequently, there is an ontological register enjoying a certain priority with respect to (using a turn of phrase featuring prominently in Žižek's current work) its parallax refractions. And a juncture has now been reached at which what would otherwise come across as abstruseness verging on incomprehensibility can be rendered perfectly understandable. For instance, in *The Puppet and the Dwarf*, Žižek puzzlingly proclaims:

> The Real is . . . *simultaneously* the Thing to which direct access is not possible and the obstacle that prevents this direct access; the Thing that eludes our grasp and the distorting screen that makes us miss the Thing. More precisely, the Real is ultimately the very shift of perspective from the first standpoint to the second. (Žižek 2003b, 77)

The first (previously delineated) ontogenetic shift—this isn't the shift spoken of by Žižek here—is the transition from the Schellingian Real (i.e., the excessive surplus of presentation over representation) to the Kantian Real (i.e., the withdrawn deficit of the un[re]presentable), a transition prompted by the struggle to stabilize the overwhelming flux of being (as per Hegel's account of the genesis of the idea of the thing-in-itself). This first shift produces the Kantian critical standpoint according to which epistemology is to be rigidly separated from ontology along the boundary line of the limits of possible experience; Things divide into their knowable-yet-deontologized phenomenal manifestations and their unknowable-yet-ontologized noumenal cores. However, with Hegelian philosophy, there is a second shift, the shift spoken of by Žižek in the quotation above: through ontologizing Kant's foundational antinomic distinctions (thereby, in a way, mending the rift between epistemology and ontology), Hegel transitions from the Kantian transcendental idealist standpoint to a perspective that sees the Real of being *an sich* as internally self-splitting, as auto-dividing. Hence, the very gap between noumena and phenomena is immanent to being itself, an inherent feature inscribed into the ontological Real per se. Or, with recourse to the Schellingian theoretical resources developed here, being "eludes our grasp" (i.e., recedes from the cognizing subject's powers of ideation in the manner of the inaccessible void of *das Ding an sich*) precisely through the "screen" of its superabundant presentation in the form of too many disclosed experiential facets. The proper dialectical gesture here is to combine these sides of the Real as codependent recto and verso faces, namely, to assert that the Real appears to withdraw as a transcendent alterity specifically through exceeding subjectivity's capacities to digest (via representation at the level of Imaginary-Symbolic reality) the "too much-ness" of its direct revelation. In the paragraph immediately following the one just quoted, Žižek remarks, "What prevents us from accessing the Thing directly is the Thing itself" (Žižek 2003b, 77). Reformulated with a little more technical precision, the subject cannot "access" the Real Thing, in terms of subjective access at the level of the representational matrix of mediated reality, because of the potential hyper-representability presented by the disclosed, naked "Thing itself" (a hyper-representability akin to a power surge overwhelming and, thus, short-circuiting the machinery of reality through whose channels such power flows). But the question still remains: how and why does being sunder itself, dividing into these various dichotomous parallaxes?

Žižek's most recent work puts this exact question at the top of the contemporary theoretical agenda. In *The Parallax View* (2006) he asks:

> The fundamental lesson of Hegel is that the key ontological problem is not that of reality, but that of appearance: not "Are we condemned to

the interminable play of appearances, or can we penetrate their veil to the underlying true reality?," but "How could—in the middle of the flat, stupid reality which just is there—something like appearance emerge?" (Žižek 2006, 29)

Relating this to Lacan, Žižek elaborates:

> Lacan's thought moves from the "internal externality"—the famous "ex-timacy"—of the Real *qua* Thing to the Symbolic (the Real as the inaccessible traumatic core around which symbolic formations circulate like flies around the light which burns them if they approach it too closely) to the absolute inherence of Real to Symbolic (the Real has no subsistence, no ontological consistency of its own, it is *nothing but* the inherent inconsistency, gap, of the Symbolic). This, however, does not solve the key *materialist* question: if the Real has not subsistence of its own, if it is inherent to the Symbolic, how, then, are we to think the emergence-explosion of the Symbolic out of the presymbolic X? Is the only alternative to naïve realism really a kind of "methodological idealism" according to which "the limits of our language are the limits of our world," so that what is beyond the Symbolic is strictly unthinkable? (Žižek 2006, 390)

Undoubtedly, Žižek refuses to rest content with such idealism, to allow for relapsing into and accepting as philosophically satisfactory a stance along the lines of the overly cautious critical epistemology of Kantian transcendental idealism (i.e., nothing can be said about the presymbolic Real due to the fact that the linguistic network of the symbolic order necessarily mediates the reality of subjective experience). A few years earlier, Žižek, with reference to Badiou's foundational distinction between being and event (the latter designating that which is more or other than being, irreducible to the given ontological order), announces that his guiding project now involves figuring out a materialist account of how the trans-ontological level of the event (including subjectivity as something more than being breaking out of being itself) emerges from the ontological plane of being:

> What the Lacanian notion of drive tries to account for—and this I think is maybe the ultimate materialist problem—is, to put it very simply, how an event can emerge from the order of being. How does being explode into event? Although he would reject this insinuation, I think that on this question even Badiou remains stuck in some kind of Kantian opposition between being, which is simply a deposited order of being, and the magical moment of the event of truth. The materialist problem is

rather how to think the unity of being and event. That is to say, how does the order of being have to be structured so that something like event is possible? (Žižek and Daly 2004, 137)

In short (postponing until later an examination of the role of drive mentioned here), the central enigma for a materialist theory of subjectivity to tackle is the mystery of how the ontological material of being becomes the trans-ontological event of the subject. Žižek wants to explain, without recourse to the rationalist-idealist insistence on an always already established separation of planes (such as Plato's visible versus intelligible realms), the conditions of possibility at the level of a fundamental ontology for this dynamic of genesis. And in striving to formulate such an explanation, he relies heavily on Hegel.

One of the most regularly recurring philosophemes in Žižek's oeuvre (and a thematic never far removed therein from references to Kant, Schelling, and Hegel) is the notion that being as such is "not all." He repeatedly insists upon the incomplete and discordant nature of whatever constitutes the foundational substance of ontology.[28] Žižek describes the Hegelian Absolute (i.e., the monistic One enjoying priority over its dichotomous Twos) not as a calm, serene, universal All peacefully at one with itself but, on the contrary, as at war with itself, as internally rent asunder by antagonisms and unrest.[29] Gaps inhere within the Real of the ground-zero ontological register; a crack runs through being. Žižek identifies this crack as the subject: "The Hegelian 'subject' is ultimately nothing but a name for the externality of the Substance to itself, for the 'crack' by way of which the Substance becomes 'alien' to itself, (mis)perceiving itself through human eyes as the inaccessible reified Otherness" (Žižek 1993, 30).

In the preface to the *Phenomenology of Spirit*, Hegel declares that "everything turns on grasping and expressing the True, not only as *Substance*, but equally as *Subject*" (Hegel 1977c, 10 [§17]). In the paragraph that follows this declaration, he goes on to note that "this Substance is, as Subject, pure, *simple negativity*, and is for this very reason the bifurcation of the simple; it is the doubling which sets up opposition, and then again the negation of this indifferent diversity and of its anti-thesis [the immediate simplicity]" (Hegel 1977c, 10 [§18]). What does this mean for Žižek? It's appropriate once again to recall the significance of the shift from Kant to Hegel accomplished through the latter's ontological radicalization of the former's epistemology (a periodic reminder helps because it's so difficult consistently to remain in a Hegelian philosophical mind-set without backsliding into pre-Hegelian metaphysical outlooks better approximating quotidian, spontaneous, and vulgar views of real-

ity). One of the implications of this shift is that what appears as external
reflection (i.e., the gaze of the subject upon substance) is not confined
merely to an epistemological field separated off from the reflected-upon
reality of being. Rather than being external, this reflection is inscribed
within the reality of being upon which it reflects as an internal inflection,
an immanent folding-back of substance upon itself; the gaze of the subject upon substance is substance-as-not-all gazing upon itself. According
to Žižek, the fact that the substance of being generates this "bifurcation"
and "doubling" from within itself (these are the exact terms used by
Hegel) testifies to a restlessness dwelling within the very heart of this same
being-substance: "The external gaze of the Subject upon the inscrutable
Substance is from the very beginning included in the Substance itself as
an index of its disparity with itself" (Žižek 2002a, 106). Žižek adds that
"this is what escapes the position of 'external reflection' (the position
which perceives the Substance as an unattainable Thing-in-itself): how
its externality to the Substance is a self-alienation of this Substance itself;
the way Substance is external to itself" (Žižek 2002a, 106). Or, as he words
it later elsewhere, "Hegel's motto 'one should conceive the Absolute not
only as Substance, but also as Subject' means: 'subject' is the name for a
crack in the edifice of Being" (Žižek 2004c, 45).

So, through a reading of Hegel, Žižek claims that subjectivity is an
inner perturbation within substance, something (to resort to a now-
familiar formulation) in being more than being itself. The Hegelian-
Žižekian subject could be described as a sort of "transubstantiation" of
substance.[30] However, before proceeding further, a crucial terminological clarification is necessary here in order to avoid certain possible misunderstandings: Žižek carefully distinguishes between subject(ivity) and
subjectification. For Žižek, the subject is not the "I" of the "self"; it isn't
consciousness or self-consciousness (he takes Lacan to task for making
a straw man out of Hegel by erroneously depicting Hegelian subjectivity
as amounting to conscious transparency[31]—more generally, he contends
that Lacan is an unconscious Hegelian insofar as Lacan fails to realize at
which points he's in proximity to Hegel[32]). Instead, the subject is defined
by Žižek as a pure negativity—his list of terms for this negativity includes
the Cartesian cogito, the Kantian subject-as-Thing, the Hegelian night of
the world, the Freudian-Lacanian death drive, and the Lacanian barred
S ($)$, among other names—bursting forth from the substantial dimension of being and, thereafter, permanently resisting any and every attempt to absorb the void of this negative rupture back within the positive
order of the ontological plane from which it broke. Subjectification, on
the other hand, is defined as the series of interminable efforts, of vain
attempts structurally doomed to partial success at best (and, no matter

what, always upset by an inexpugnable margin of dissatisfying failure), to reinscribe the subject-as-$ within the gentrified domain of actualized re/presentations.[33] This renders Žižek's equation of substance-as-not-all (i.e., the self-sundering One of the Hegelian Absolute, being as cracked and fissured, etc.) with subject a little more intuitively comprehensible. No longer associated with the mental processes of a self-conscious agent or even with the gradual sedimentation of determinate psychical content occurring through subjectification, the term *subject* is now free to designate the immanent openness within the ontological Real of substance itself made possible by the inherent incompleteness of this not-whole being.

Near the conclusion of *The Sublime Object of Ideology,* Žižek observes that substance becoming subject entails the self-subjectification of substance, that is, substance reflectively treating itself as the givenness of inert appearance. He explains:

> We could say, paradoxically, that the subject is *substance precisely in so far as it experiences itself as substance* (as some alien, given, external, positive Entity, existing in itself): "subject" is nothing but the name for this inner distance of "substance" towards itself, the name for this empty place from which the substance can perceive itself as something "alien." Without this self-fissure of the essence, there can be no place distinguished from essence in which essence can *appear* as distinct from itself—that is, as "mere appearance": essence can appear only in so far as it is already external to itself. (Žižek 1989, 226)

However, the same old question keeps stubbornly insisting on being both asked and answered: Why and/or how is ontological substance prompted into taking an "inner distance" from itself? What sparks the coming to light of $ as, so to speak, a black hole ensconced within the galaxy of being? These queries inquire into the absolutely fundamental conditions of possibility for the very emergence of the subject (and subjectification too) out of the foundations of being. The responses given to these questions will constitute a sort of meta/ultra-transcendentalism, a delineation of what, at an ontological level, makes possible the advent of both the subject-as-$ (immanently arising out of substance) as well as the procedures of subjectification associated with this void. There are two inter-linked reasons for why substance subjectifies itself, for why it splits from within itself and then sets to work endlessly struggling to heal this self-inflicted wound.

The first step of this two-part explanation, a step outlined in the answers to questions posed by Glyn Daly during the series of interviews col-

lected in the volume *Conversations with Žižek,* brings Žižek back into the
company of Heidegger. In the context of a discussion involving the topic
of cognitive science (as tied up with evolutionary psychology), Žižek begins by admitting that he's tempted to return to the early Heidegger's
recasting of subjectivity as *Dasein,* more specifically, of human being as
distinctive insofar as this being's own being is a question for it[34] (as per
Being and Time, in which "Dasein is an entity which does not just occur
among other entities. Rather it is ontically distinguished by the fact that,
in its very Being, that Being is an *issue* for it" [Heidegger 1962, 32]). He
then proceeds briefly to discuss the function of consciousness, characterizing it as an accidental, gratuitous "by-product" of natural-material
evolutionary processes:

> What I am currently engaged with is the paradoxical idea that, from a
> strict evolutionary standpoint, consciousness is a kind of mistake—a mal-
> function of evolution—and that out of this mistake a miracle emerged.
> That is to say, consciousness developed as an unintended by-product
> that acquired a kind of second-degree survivalist function. Basically, con-
> sciousness is not something which enables us to function better. On the
> contrary, I am more and more convinced that consciousness originates
> with something going terribly wrong—even at a most personal level. For
> example, when do we become aware of something, fully aware? Precisely
> at the point where something no longer functions properly or not in the
> expected way. (Žižek and Daly 2004, 59)

This thesis is quickly translated into Lacanese:

> Consciousness is originally linked to this moment when "something is
> wrong," or, to put it in Lacanian terms, an experience of the Real, of an
> impossible limit. Original awareness is impelled by a certain experience
> of failure and mortality—a kind of snag in the biological weave. And all
> the metaphysical dimensions concerning humanity, philosophical self-
> reflection, progress and so on emerge ultimately because of this basic
> traumatic fissure. (Žižek and Daly 2004, 59)

Apart from the debatable features of this line of speculation at the phylogenetic level—the historical genesis of conscious (self-)awareness likely
brought with it startling evolutionary advantages for human beings as
well as the disadvantages alluded to above (like many things, it is prob-
ably a double-edged sword)—it hits upon something pivotal for an ontogenetic account of subject formation formulated through a combination of philosophy and psychoanalysis. Žižek maintains that although

this subjectifying dynamic arose from the materiality of evolutionary forces and pressures, it nonetheless, after the fact of its genesis, cannot be accounted for by a cognitivist approach relying exclusively on a discourse privileging genetically dictated biological survival imperatives as ultimate determining factors.[35]

The parallels between Žižek's ruminations here and Heidegger's famous distinction between "ready-to-hand" (*zuhanden*) and "present-at-hand" (*vorhanden*) are too obvious to ignore (especially since Žižek opens this stretch of conversation by confessing to his renewed interest in Heidegger). In *Being and Time,* this distinction offers a concrete phenomenological illustration of how metaphysical and ontological questions are prompted into being posed by *Dasein*—*Dasein* truly becomes authentic, genuine *Dasein* to the extent that it's hurled into an abyssal vortex of existential questioning of its own being—by, to put it in Žižekian terms, something going wrong, by a malfunction jamming up the otherwise smooth flow of the mundane run of things in the context of the extant, established life-world. As is well known, Heidegger uses the example of the human relationship to tools to exemplify the difference between ready-to-hand and present-at-hand. Normally, in the functional, quotidian life-world context of *Dasein* as it goes about its daily ontic business, tools (as whatever enable or facilitate contextually determined tasks to be accomplished) are merely ready-to-hand, namely, "there" to *Dasein* in a non-thematized way, overlooked in their bare existent particularity (as objectified entities) insofar as they're caught up in the movement of goal-oriented activity. Such ready-to-hand objects become present-at-hand beings when they suddenly stand out against their environmental background by virtue of failing to function properly, by posing an obstacle rather than, as when usually functional, facilitating the seamless transition from task to task. This naked objectivity as present-at-hand (i.e., the thing no longer as a non-obstructive link in a contextual chain, but as an obstructive, protruding presence) thereby ignites a sequence of questions ultimately leading to the foundations of epistemology, ontology, and metaphysics (hence, philosophical consciousness arises out of disruptions encountered by everyday consciousness). When a ready-to-hand piece of equipment ceases to work properly and thereby becomes a present-at-hand being, both the entity itself as well as the life-world context of concern-driven tasks with which it's bound up move from the status of being aspects of a non-thematized surrounding subconscious environment to being explicitly thematized facets of *Dasein*'s phenomenal experience of "being-in-the-world."[36]

However, another quite non-Heideggerian example not only resonates with the preceding notion that substance subjectifies itself thanks to moments when "something goes wrong" (à la an accident, break, failure, malfunction, mistake, rupture, snag, trauma, etc.), but also points toward the second half of the explanation for why this subjectification of substance occurs. Broadly speaking, one could say that natural evolution, in producing out of itself the human species, gave rise to organic beings so complex that they achieved a relative autonomy in relation to nature as their material ground (and this by, largely unwittingly, playing off elements of their nature against each other). More specifically, some of the very developments that endowed human beings with a potent advantage in the evolutionary struggle for survival (such as sapience above and beyond mere sentience), especially when such complex evolutionary developments were condensed into the nature of a single type of being, likely entailed double-edged-sword effects (i.e., disadvantages attached to advantageous capacities, new problems going hand in hand with solutions to old problems). In fact, at the most general of levels, it's obviously true that both the probability and number of possible "bugs" or short circuits in a system increase in tandem with the increased degree of complexity of that system. This holds for both material systems (such as the barred Real of human nature—see part 2) and symbolic systems (such as the barred Other of the never-wholly-internally-consistent symbolic order).

For instance, take the United States federal tax code as an example of a symbolic system. This code is a body of technical legal stipulations so massive that no single person, not even the most knowledgeable tax expert, has a complete understanding of the entire network of laws and how these laws fit together with one another. Moreover, year after year, successive legislative sessions of Congress change the code, adding, subtracting, and modifying laws. Of course, this means that the creation of ever-more loopholes in the tax code is a foregone conclusion, since those altering this body of laws cannot know in advance what unforeseen possibilities will arise from the structural interactions between the already less-than-fully-understood prior set of existing laws and the changes (as additions, subtractions, and modifications) made to these laws. Firms dealing with accounting and tax advice make their money by discovering and exploiting the loopholes in the body of laws forming the entirety of the U.S. federal tax code. Analogously, using this particular illustration of Lacan's barred big Other as an internally inconsistent symbolic system, one could think of the material system of evolving nature along similar lines: the more complex the products of evolving nature, the more likely the creation of certain sorts of "loopholes" that might come to disrupt this material system from within, immanently interrupting the predictable ontological-substantial run of things. (Antonio Damasio alludes to this possibility apropos the human brain by suggesting that this evolved neurological "system is so complex and multilayered that it operates with some degree of freedom.")[37]

These loopholes in the ontological-substantial run of things—these are the moments when the Real becomes (if only temporarily) barred, when certain dysfunctions surface within it—forestall material nature achieving an internal balance as a cohesive, harmonious, and integrated One-All, as a stable organic unity (see part 2). Instead, especially as regards human nature, these (as Žižek puts it) "snags in the biological weave" permit and prompt singular elements of this nature to assert themselves as dominant structuring forces exerting an organizing authority over the entire field of this conflicted, inconsistent nature to which these same elements are attached: "Hegel was well aware that the constitutive gesture of subjectivity is a violent reversal of the preceding 'natural' substantial balance—the 'subject' is some subordinated moment of the presupposed substantial totality that retroactively 'posits its own presuppositions' (i.e., elevates itself into the Master of its own Ground)" (Žižek 1998c, 248). Consequently, in some cases, these out-of-nature "master elements" radically alter the very essence of the natural field thus restructured. How does this relate to Žižek's Lacanian engagement with Hegel? And what evidence is there for this alleged denaturalization of (human) nature transpiring immanently out of this nature itself?

Žižek contends that the subject, for Hegel, is nothing other than an inner perturbation within substance, a disturbing, disruptive crack or gap in the order of being. Moreover, Žižek insists, substance is subject only insofar as the former is "not all," torn apart from within by a series of antagonistic splits:

> the key point is to read Hegel's proposition "Substance is Subject" not as a direct assertion of identity, but as an example (perhaps *the* example) of "infinite judgment," like "the Spirit is a bone." The point is not that the Substance (the ultimate foundation of all entities, the Absolute) is not a pre-subjective Ground but a Subject, an agent of self-differentiation, which posits its otherness and then reappropriates it, and so on: "Subject" stands for the non-substantial agency of phenomenalization, appearance, "illusion," split, finitude, Understanding, and so on, and to conceive Substance as Subject means precisely that split, phenomenalization, and so forth, are inherent to the life of the Absolute itself. There is no "absolute Subject"—subject "as such" is relative, caught in self-division, and it is *as such* that the Subject is inherent to the Substance. (Žižek 1999b, 88–89)

He immediately adds:

> In contrast to this *speculative* identity of Substance and Subject, the
> notion of their *direct* identity thus involves the redoubling of subjects,
> which again reduces subjectivity proper to an accident ("vehicle") of the
> substantial Absolute, of an Other who speaks "through" finite human
> subjects. This also opens up the false, pseudo-Hegelian notion of a dia-
> lectical process in which its Subject ("cosmic spirit") posits its external-
> ity, alienates itself from itself, in order to regain its integrity on a higher
> level: the misleading presupposition at work here is that the Subject of
> the process is somehow given from the outset, not engendered by the
> very process of the Substance's splitting. (Žižek 1999b, 89)

Yet again, one must keep in mind that with Hegel's ontological radicalization of Kant's philosophy of epistemological finitude, there is no
transcendent Other-Beyond of the One-that-is. This means that the substance of being cannot relate to itself as a totality, since substance being
able to do so would necessarily entail substance's capacity to step above
and outside of itself through some sort of meta-level reflection on itself
as a given whole to be reflected upon. There is no external point of reflection; such self-objectification is always immanent. Therefore, Žižek
dismisses as illegitimate the reading of Hegel's substance-as-subject as
an absolute subjectivity surmounting the limitations of finitude (limitations stressed by, most notably, Kant). The finite subject is absolute not
because it mystically transcends its limitations by somehow managing to
plug into the ethereal hyper-reality of an infinite and eternal spiritual
Other secretly orchestrating the temporal dance of empirical-historical
contents. Rather, the finite subject is absolute because the Absolute itself,
like subjectivity, is permeated by contradiction and strife. The Absolute
too is "not all," less than internally consistent or sufficiently self-enclosed.
Ultimately, the Hegelian-Žižekian subject-as-$ is the very "not-all-ness" of
the Absolute.[38] And without this "not-all-ness," there would be no subject
at all. In other words, the incompleteness and inconsistency of being is,
in Žižek's elaboration of a theory of subjectivity integrated with a fundamental ontology, a condition of possibility for the coming-to-be of any
subject whatsoever.

Now, the material fundaments of human nature (crystallized in the
workings of the libidinal economy as conceived in psychoanalysis) are
components of substance. And this subsector of substance, as with substance in general (as per Hegel-Žižek), is shot through with conflicts creating cracks along their fault lines (see part 2). These cracks, these negative spaces subsisting within the groundless ground of human nature, are

the subject per se ($) as what holds open the clearing out of which can emerge ensuing dynamics of subjectification (as various ways of trying to fill in these cracks). On numerous occasions, Žižek glosses the Hegelian substance-as-subject process as a movement wherein one predicate-term amongst a multitude of predicate-terms suddenly achieves a hegemonic structuring role as a subject-term subordinating to itself the other predicate-terms.[39] This predicate-become-subject-term is thus a "concrete universal," namely, an element that forms a set of which it itself is (still) an element, an overarching genus anchored in and directly embodied by one of its own incarnate subspecies.[40] (This Hegelian-style conception of universality as dependent on how an exceptional particularity orders other particulars—the universal does not stand separately above the plane of particulars, but is itself caught up in its own movement of concrete actualization—is a recurrent Žižekian refrain.)[41] This idea of concrete universality (an idea connected to the dynamic wherein substance becomes subject) also resembles the Laclau-Mouffe concept of hegemony à la the notion that any and every universality is the outcome/product of a struggle for structural dominance in which various particulars strive against each other to establish themselves as the enveloping, framing medium (i.e., the universal) for the "articulation" of all the other particulars[42] (even though, in terms of his political commitments, Žižek, over the past few years, has forcefully distanced himself from Laclau and the "radical democracy" camp).

In *The Indivisible Remainder*, resorting to the historical example of how money went from being just one particular commodity among others to asserting itself as the universal commodity as stand-in for all other commodities, Žižek explains that "the 'becoming-subject of substance' stands for the gesture of *hubris* by means of which a mere accident or predicate of the substance, a subordinated moment of its totality, installs itself as the new totalizing principle and subordinates the previous Substance to itself, turning it into its own particular moment" (Žižek 1996b, 129). This already conjures up a basic, spontaneous intuition about the simplest form of the mind-body relationship in human beings. The body gives rise to the mind as one of its subordinated attributes (as a property or predicate of the human species' corporeal-material nature); however, in humans, the "natural" body ends up being subordinated to the more-than-natural mind, usurped by one of its offspring (a reversal betrayed, after the fact of its occurrence, by the persistent notion that one "has" a body, instead of one "being" a body). This shift of substance becoming subject is followed by subjectification processes in which certain master elements engage in the labor of (in the terms of Laclau and Mouffe) hegemonic articulation, retroactively reconfiguring the very ground of

being-substance from which they arose. This shift occurs at both the ontogenetic and phylogenetic levels.

At the phylogenetic level, meme theory offers perhaps the best illustration of the above-delineated Hegelian-Žižekian movement from
substance through subject to subjectification. As a result of the loophole-
plagued, malfunction-ridden essence of the material-corporeal foundations of human being/nature, an opportunity is presented for a particular piece of this being/nature to run amok, to assert itself hubristically
as the new dominant organizing principle of (subjective) existence—
and this because there is no preordained harmonious organic order, a
One-All of natural being, to assign each element its proper place and
thereby preemptively hold in check such possible running-amok. What
makes meme theory a productive reference here? The inventor of the
term *meme*, Richard Dawkins, defines it as a transmissible bit of imita-
tion (more precisely, a sociocultural, symbolic-linguistic unit circulating
among those entities capable of sharing and using such units).[43] Like
genes, memes are replicators, albeit replicators consisting of a different
sort of "stuff" than genetic material. Advocates of meme theory speculate
that if the behavior of the material structuring human minds is vaguely
akin to the behavior of the material structuring human bodies, specifically in the sense of operating through replication, then the algorithms
discovered via the theory of evolution as a biological process might very
well be applicable to the "evolution" of ostensibly non-biological (i.e.,
social, cultural, symbolic, and linguistic) forms. (In a way, this version
of meme theory is a reinvention of classic 1950s structuralism, in which,
instead of the structures revealed through the study of language being
generalizable for the investigation of things other than language, the
structures revealed through the study of living organisms become the
new paradigmatic templates for analyzing other phenomena.)

One perspective in evolutionary psychology regarding the relationship between memes and genes is that, originally, memes were forged as
part of the physically dictated struggle for brute survival in the conditions
of nature. The evolutionary pressures of the environment on human
organisms catalyzed the emergence of memes as part of a biologically
determined survival strategy. However, following the occurrence of this
emergence, an inertia takes hold: the memes stubbornly persist even after the initial "natural" context justifying their creation and employment
changes or vanishes completely. In short, memes are born from genes,
but subsequently come to achieve an independence from the "material"
ground of genetic factors and immediate environmental influences (this
is somewhat reminiscent of the Schellingian motif of the immanent genesis of the [thereafter] transcendent).

Another consequence of this is that one arrives at a precise, complementary inversion of Stephen Jay Gould's "exaptation." As is well known,
exaptation is when an initially useless (i.e., useless from a genetic-survival
standpoint) mutation later becomes exploitable in the organism's ongoing struggle to adapt to changing conditions. With a sudden alteration of
environmental circumstances, what was before a nonadaptive (although
not maladaptive) feature persisting as a harmless, insignificant mutation in a subpopulation of a species becomes an adaptive advantage to
those possessing this mutation.[44] By contrast, given the above model of
the gene-meme relation, one arrives at what might be called (for lack of
a better term, and in resonance with Gould's notion) "deaptation": an
initially adaptive memetic strategy later becomes useless or even counterproductive. (Incidentally, in psychoanalysis, an initially adaptive defense
or response becoming a maladaptive disorder or set of symptoms simply
by virtue of persisting for too long, well past the time of contextually
determined usefulness, is a basic feature of neurosis in general. Perhaps,
at an evolutionary-phylogenetic level, memes really are the equivalent
of what Freud designates as collective neuroses.) And yet, this memetic
strategy nonetheless strangely persists beyond the moment of its survival-
ist utility (as tradition, as heritage, as *doxa*, etc.). Exaptation represents
the trajectory, in the evolutionary scheme, from the useless to the useful,
whereas deaptation (drawn from a certain strain of meme theory) runs
in the exact opposite direction: from the useful to the useless (or even
worse, the harmful). Hence, one reaches a point, within evolutionary
theory and cognitive science, in which these accounts' own explanatory
frameworks threaten to break down and admit ignorance, a point where
the intervention of psychoanalytic metapsychology's vision of human nature (especially its concept of *Trieb*) is needed as an explanatory supplement. Assuming that it is illegitimate to treat memes as if they really
possess some magical power and mysterious intentionality of their own
apart from their actualization in and by their subjective "hosts," certain
questions arise: Why do memes seemingly take on a life of their own,
continuing to exert their influence long after their evolutionary survival
value has become negligible or even detrimentally counterproductive?
What accounts for this stubborn inertia of memetic material, this idiotic
repetitiveness displacing the interests of the living being?

Both Dawkins and Susan Blackmore (another articulate elaborator
of meme theory) allow for what is here identified as deaptation. They
each concede that memetic processes can override the interests dictated
by genetic programs, that the memetic tail can come to wag the genetic
dog[45] (neither of them accepts the extreme reductionist version of evolutionary psychology in which memetics always ultimately is driven by

genetics). In other words, memes (as socio-symbolic units) are at first, in terms of their phylogenetic origins, particular pieces forming parts of the evolutionary-genetic struggle for survival; memes then, once up and running on this basis, come to hegemonize the bio-material field of (human) nature itself, seizing this field and progressively subjugating it to a set of denaturalized structures. Isn't this movement revealed by meme theory a perfect, powerful illustration of the previously outlined Hegelian-Žižekian conception of how subject(ification) emerges from substance, for how the substantial being of nature can and does internally sunder itself in a dialectical dynamic of natural denaturalization?

According to Freudian-Lacanian psychoanalysis, in the ontogenetic scheme of things, human beings are born, thrown into this world, stranded in a prolonged state of pre-maturational helplessness.[46] That is to say, as compared with other animals, human infants spend a relatively lengthy period of time in a state in which they are utterly and completely dependent on others for the satisfaction of their basic bodily needs.[47] This physiological reality of "pre-maturation," of a primordial *Hilflosigkeit*, is responsible for humans being (as Elizabeth Grosz nicely phrases it) "naturally social,"[48] namely, biologically inclined toward a matrix of more-than-biological structures organizing what comes to be their reality. For both Freud and Lacan, human nature is naturally predisposed to the predominance of nurture over nature. Lacan proposes that the neonate, as "still trapped in his motor impotence and nursling dependence,"[49] is propelled into a series of social relations by the initial spur of its simple helplessness (these social relations being underpinned by a symbolic order as a network of codes, meanings, norms, representations, and rules shaping inter-subjective interactions—that is, an enveloping, overarching system into which the neonate is inserted/inscribed even before the actual moment of biological birth). One could view this ontogenetic pre-maturational helplessness as an instance of a deficiency or lack built into the substantial ontological foundations of human nature (as per Žižek's axiomatic notion of incomplete being as the meta/ultra-transcendental ground for the possibility of any subject[ification] whatsoever). Likewise, in the phylogenetic scheme of things (as framed from the vantage point of meme theory), certain deficiencies or lacks in the human species (i.e., the various inabilities of this type of organism to rise to the environmental challenge of survival) spur the development of memes, propelling the human creation of and dwelling within the "memosphere" (akin to Hegel's "objective spirit" or Lacan's symbolic order).

Hence, both psychoanalysis's ontogenetic and meme theory's phylogenetic perspectives on subject formation highlight a temporal trajectory from substance (physiological pre-maturation and/or survival challenges) to subjectification (socio-psychical development and/or the construction of a memosphere). And yet, doesn't this leave out of the picture the subject per se, insofar as it is distinguished from subjectification as the filling out of the void of $? (In Lacanian terms, the distinction between subject and subjectification posited by Žižek is equivalent to the difference between *sujet* and *moi* [ego] respectively.) However, the proper Žižekian question to pose here is: What about the subject ($) as neither substance nor subjectification, as the "vanishing mediator" enigmatically situated somewhere between nature and culture, between the "stuff" of tangible material being and the "stuff" of positive socio-symbolic content?

13

The Night of the World: The Vanishing Mediator Between Nature and Culture

Žižek credits Kant not only with being the first philosopher, strictly speaking—recall that he pinpoints philosophy as truly beginning with the Kantian transcendental turn (see chapter 2)—but also with being the foundational thinker of human autonomy, which is itself one of the principal concerns of philosophy.[1] And yet Žižek sees Kant as averting his gaze after peering into the abyss of freedom, of covering over what he glimpses of this rupture of negativity disrupting the supposed consistency of being. In the domains of both the phenomenal and the noumenal, the Kantian subject appears to be a wholly determined entity devoid of autonomy. Phenomenal subjectivity amounts to the individual as inserted into the cause-and-effect chains of freedomless natural mechanisms. Moreover, Kant speculates that noumenal subjectivity, if directly accessed by reflective self-consciousness (an access he deems impossible), would manifest itself as the "awful majesty" (*furchtbaren Majestät*—this is the precise phrase used in the *Critique of Practical Reason*) of a terrible Thing also bereft of agency (as a mere node in a divine network, a network akin to Spinoza's God-substance). The insinuation here is that the subject's ignorance of its inaccessible noumenal essence sustains what might well be an illusory freedom which doesn't exist at the brute ontological level. For Kant, phenomenal reality is partial and incomplete, a field of fragmentary experience constrained by the limits constitutive of the finite subject. By contrast, the noumenal Real of being *an sich* is presumed to be whole and complete, entirely at one with itself in its internal self-consistency. Although it sometimes sounds as though Kant associates transcendental autonomy with the noumenal essence of the subject-Thing, Žižek insists that there is no room for subjective freedom within the confines of the stifling ontological closure of Kant's being-in-itself: "When we imagine the Whole of reality, there is no longer any place for consciousness (and subjectivity). There are two options here: either subjectivity is an illusion, or reality is *in itself* (not only epistemologically) not-All" (Žižek 2006, 168).

Žižek's Hegel takes the latter path, opting to posit the "not-all-ness" of being—and therefore leaving open the possibility for an actually autonomous non-epiphenomenal subjectivity. This Hegelian move, Žižek argues, is the only way to leave open this possibility.[2] And Žižek makes several more moves of his own apropos this topic. He occasionally claims that the freedom of the subject-as-$ is to be located in the "parallax gap" between the noumenal and phenomenal planes, that subjective autonomy is somehow sustained by the disjunction between these strata.[3] At other times, with an inflection more obviously in line with the general thrust of his Hegelianism, he proposes that "noumenal Freedom is *nothing but* a rupture within phenomenal reality" (Žižek 1999b, 86), rather than that this freedom subsists within a second-order region of being, such as Kant's noumenal sphere (for Hegel-Žižek, "this is it," that is, there is no "other scene" utterly apart from the here and now of less than harmonious phenomenal reality). Viewed from a Hegelian-Žižekian perspective, Kant's picture of a horrible, heteronomous noumenal Real, a domain of substantial being in which everything is determined, is nothing more than a fantasy, an imaginary regression to a pre-critical Spinozism, obfuscating the ultimate inconsistency of Real being itself (and hence occluding the subject-as-$, too).[4] Žižek explains:

> Hegel . . . rejects Kant's vision of a man who, because of his direct insight into the monstrosity of the divine Being-in-itself, would turn into a life-less puppet: such a vision is meaningless and inconsistent, since . . . it secretly reintroduces the ontologically fully constituted divine totality: a world conceived *only* as Substance, *not* also as Subject. For Hegel, the fantasy of such a transformation of man into a lifeless puppet-instrument of the monstrous divine Will (or whim), horrible as it may appear, already signals the retreat from the true monstrosity, which is that of the abyss of freedom, of the "night of the world." What Hegel does is thus to "traverse" this fantasy by demonstrating its function of filling in the pre-ontological abyss of freedom—that is, by reconstituting the positive Scene in which the subject is inserted into a positive noumenal order. (Žižek 1999b, 61)

Proposed in condensed form, the claim here is that solely through "barring" the Real of the substance of material being is one really able (as Hegel demands) to think of substance also as subject (and not as an asubjective totality). Kant's fantasmatic imaginings of an encompassing ontological One-All hidden behind the veil of finite experience envisions an unbarred Real, namely, a substance that doesn't entail a subject. Furthermore, back in the 1988 text *Le plus sublime des hystériques*, Žižek emphasizes not so much the necessary link between a barred Real and the autonomy of the subject-as-$, but instead the importance of positing a barred Symbolic. The early Žižek portrays Hegel as presaging the late Lacan's insistence on the nonexistence of the big Other ("*Le grand Autre n'existe pas*").[5] He puts forward the same argument regarding the barred Symbolic (i.e., the incomplete and inconsistent big Other of the symbolic order) in relation to the abyss of freedom as he subsequently does apropos the barred Real: if the Other is presumed to be unbarred, then no space remains for anything more than a pseudo-autonomous $ reduced to the status of a residual, epiphenomenal illusion.[6] As seen via Schelling (see chapter 9), the conjunction or overlap between the barred Real and the barred Symbolic is involved in the advent of freedom (i.e., one should combine Žižek's parallel discussions of the barred Symbolic and the barred Real in relation to the topic of autonomy).

In the third book of his pre-critical *Anthropology from a Pragmatic Point of View* ("On the Faculty of Desire"), Kant presents a subsection entitled "On the Inclination to Freedom as a Passion." He distinguishes between innate/natural and acquired/cultural passions, identifying the passion of/for freedom as the most potent instance of the former.[7] The desire for absolute self-determination, for the unshackled assertion of one's will as the highest law of reality, is, according to Kant, hard-wired into the foundations of human nature (this is also an aspect of what Freud later describes as infantile primary narcissism[8]). In a footnote, Kant cites the example of babies: the cries and screams of infants often arise as an expression of their "exasperation" when faced with obstacles inhibiting a vaguely felt proto-freedom, that is, when their whims and fancies collide with points of resistance.[9] Referring to this passage in Kant's *Anthropology*, Žižek suggests:

> What the moral Law is bound to constrain is . . . not primarily our fixation on pathological objects but, rather, the "unruliness" which Kant, in his *Anthropology*, defines as the specifically human stubborn insistence, the clinging to wild egotistical freedom unbound by any constraints (discernible in young children), this impossible point of direct phenomenal appearance of noumenal freedom which has no parallel in the animal kingdom and has to be broken and "gentrified" by the pressure of education. (Žižek 1997c, 237)

Autonomy, instead of being a capacity for calm, reflective deliberation exercised by a stable, reasonable self, is a violent, "unruly" force agitating the individual from within the heart of his or her "natural" constitution. That is to say, freedom is, at least originally, a quasi-pathological impulse, a driving compulsion. It becomes a rationally mediated power solely through being domesticated by the imposed discipline of educational practices. Žižek associates this untamed autonomy with two other inter-related notions: the Freudian-Lacanian death drive and the subject-as-$ (more specifically, the subject as an X out of joint with its surrounding matrices of mediation, as something that doesn't blend into its background/environment).

At one point in *The Ticklish Subject,* Žižek hypothesizes that the subject (as not fitting into its milieu) emerges precisely through a particular "stubborn attachment."[10] What does this mean? Briefly revisiting the terrain of meme theory is again useful. In the last paragraph of *The Selfish Gene,* the book in which the concept of the meme is first put forward, Dawkins insists upon the uniqueness of human freedom. Much of his text is devoted to examining the ways in which living beings are dominated by "selfish" replicators and thereby reduced to the status of vehicles operating in the service of perpetuating the genes within them (and, in the case of humans, memes too allegedly can and do exert this sort of self-serving dominance). Dawkins even seeks to treat instances of apparent altruism as selfish rather than selfless, namely, as refined, complex strategies for genetic (or memetic) perpetuation. However, at least with human beings, the programs of these replicators aren't absolutely and finally determinative:

> Even if we look on the dark side and assume that individual man is fundamentally selfish, our conscious foresight—our capacity to simulate the future in imagination—could save us from the worst selfish excesses of the blind replicators . . . We have the power to defy the selfish genes of our birth and, if necessary, the selfish memes of our indoctrination. We can even discuss ways of deliberately cultivating and nurturing pure, disinterested altruism—something that has no place in nature, something that has never existed before in the whole history of the world. We are built as gene machines and cultured as meme machines, but we have the power to turn against our creators. We, alone on earth, can rebel against the tyranny of the selfish replicators. (Dawkins 1976, 215)

These concluding lines by Dawkins permit several Žižekian trains of thought to be clarified, especially the linkages between substance, subjectification, and subjectivity. If genes are representative of substance (as a natural materiality) and memes are representative of subjectification (as a cultural materiality), then, to employ Žižek's phrase, a stubborn attachment of genes to certain sets of memes leads to the emergence of the subject out of substance. How does this occur?

Before proceeding further, one initially must note that two related variants on the notion of the subject are deployed by Žižek: first, the

subject as a "misfit" that isn't smoothly integrated into and contained by
its environmental envelope (the variant to be dealt with in this chapter);
and second, the subject as the negativity of a void irreducible to any of
the concrete contents attempting to fill in this hole temporarily (the
variant to be dealt with in the next chapter)—in short, $-as-out-of-joint
versus $-as-empty. As per the concept of deaptation (see chapter 12),
one trajectory in which "substance becomes subject" involves genetically determined survival strategies dictating the development of and
attachments to memetic tools employed in the struggle of evolutionary
competition. But, as with Heidegger's assertion that modern man is in
the process of becoming a tool of his tools as a "standing reserve" for his
own technology (this being a key thesis of his famous essay "The Question Concerning Technology"[11]), the genetically dictated attachment to
memes threatens to usurp the guiding natural authority of the genes that
ordered this attachment in the first place. (Additionally, this dynamic of
deaptation resembles Lacan's delineation of the relationship between,
on the one hand, need, and, on the other hand, demand and desire: real
need causes the acceptance of Symbolic mediation through forcing the
articulation of demands, with this mediation then starting to function as
an effect that outgrows and retroactively comes to dominate/restructure
its cause by alienating the corporeal body of need in the "defiles of the
signifier.") With the example of the gene-meme link, all that's addressed
is the relationship between two types of replicator-substances, two kinds
of "stuff" (i.e., natural materiality and cultural materiality—the former
is the stuff of substance and the latter is the stuff of subjectification).
And yet the subject (as distinct from subjectification) arises through this
dynamic operative between (natural) substance and (cultural) subjectification, in this transition from nature to culture. However, a great deal of
further explanatory labor is necessary before it will be clear exactly what
is entailed by Žižek's characterization of the subject as the "vanishing
mediator" between nature and culture: "The subject . . . this disturbing
excess . . . is . . . a transcendental condition of culture: a kind of malfunction which acts as a necessary vanishing mediator between nature and
culture" (Žižek and Daly 2004, 80).

There are two ways in which this process of natural materiality (i.e.,
substance) becoming attached to cultural materiality (i.e., subjectification) leads to the surfacing of the subject-as-$ (both as out of joint and
empty). The first of these two ways (the way producing $-as-out-of-joint)
has to do with the fixed and rigid quality of substance's attachment to
the elements of subjectification. (The second way, to be addressed in
chapter 14, involves the emergence of $-as-empty, an emergence that
emerges out of the failure of the elements of subjectification, such as

signifiers or memes, exhaustively to interpellate and capture the negativity of the subject.) Žižek qualifies such attachments in humans as being "stubborn," thus alluding to the mysterious inertia testified to by the odd persistence of non-advantageous or disadvantageous patterns in human life (for instance, memetic configurations that continue to recur despite no longer possessing any utility in terms of the natural/rational self-interests of the organism, or childhood psychical defense mechanisms that remain mobilized in the form of an adult neurosis long after the danger to be defended against has passed). An attachment becomes stubborn particularly when it is clung to in the face of environmental pressures to change adaptively, when its maladaptive consequences simply are endured or ignored. The "object" of this stubborn attachment thus comes to stand out against its contextual background as a coagulated blockage, a point of resistance to the mundane material flow of alteration over time; this object becomes the avatar/index of something, an out-of-joint X ($), that refuses to fit in with its surroundings, a force that isn't wholly swept up into the currents of vital being's flux. Žižek links the persistence of this stubborn X to the Freudian-Lacanian *Todestrieb*—the death drive as a power of compulsive repetition embedded within the substance of being, as a "naturally" generated glitch in human nature.

In establishing a counterintuitive equivalence between the subject-as-$ and the death drive, how does Žižek understand the latter? What warrants this unconventional equation? Here's how Žižek justifies (departing from the theme of "something goes wrong" à la nature's internal malfunctioning) his identification of German idealist subjectivity with the psychoanalytic *Todestrieb:*

> The rabbit that I now pull out of my hat is that German idealism and psychoanalysis have specific terms for this malfunction: in German idealism it is absolute self-relating negativity; in psychoanalysis it is the death drive. This is at the very centre of what I am doing generally . . . What I am asserting here is that this notion of self-relating negativity, as it has been articulated from Kant to Hegel, means philosophically the same as Freud's notion of death drive—this is my fundamental perspective. In other words, the Freudian notion of death drive is not a biological category but has a philosophical dignity. (Žižek and Daly 2004, 61)

Žižek then specifies what he takes to be the crux of the Freudian concept of the death drive:

> In trying to explain the functioning of the human psyche in terms of the pleasure principle, reality principle and so on, Freud became increas-

> ingly aware of a radical non-functional element, a basic destructiveness
> and excess of negativity, that couldn't be accounted for. And that is why
> Freud posed the hypothesis of death drive. I think that death drive is ex-
> actly the right name for this excess of negativity. This, in a way, is the big
> obsession of my entire work: this mutual reading of the Freudian notion
> of death drive with what in German idealism is rendered thematic as
> self-relating negativity. (Žižek and Daly 2004, 61)

Of course, as is common knowledge, Freud formulates the vague notion of the *Todestrieb* in response to phenomena that remain seemingly
inexplicable from the standpoint of an interpretive approach centered
on the pleasure principle as the fundamental law governing the operations of the psychical apparatus (for instance, phenomena that are "beyond the pleasure principle," such as compulsive repetitions of painful
experiences or various forms of self-destructiveness—that is, phenomena that are impractical in relation to the "realistic" calculations tied to
the homeostatic balance sheet of well-being). Given that the pleasure
principle is bound up with the reality principle—ultimately, the reality
principle is just the pleasure principle as "sublimated" in relation to the
constraints of natural and cultural realities—the pursuit of happiness
at the behest of the pleasure principle would dictate adapting to the
changing circumstances of reality as the surrounding environment into
which the psyche is inserted. And yet what psychoanalysis demonstrates,
from its very inception, is that human beings are profoundly maladapted
creatures. What are neuroses if not so many different ways of remaining "stubbornly attached" to maladaptive symptom-strategies, of being
unbalanced by excessive, pathological overinvestments rendering the
individual out of synch with his or her milieu?

The later Freud's gamble (a gamble whose furthest-reaching philosophical consequences Žižek seeks to spell out) is to insist that the distinc-
tively human tendency to resist contextually defined adaptation, to cling
to dysfunctional modes of being, simply cannot be reinscribed into an
interpretive framework in which everything is reducible to the pleasure-
reality dialectic and its vicissitudes. Something forming part of the core
of human nature (i.e., the death drive as an immanent "natural" negativity) perturbs this nature from within, leading to the strangest deviations
from the paths presumably laid down by the supposedly innate orientation toward sustainable satisfaction. In his 1924 paper "The Economic
Problem of Masochism," Freud, taking stock of this puzzling inner perturbation, feels compelled to advance the thesis that the psyche, particularly during the earliest ontogenetic stages of its development, is
plagued by a "primordial masochism"; formulated more precisely, the

destructiveness of the death drive originally is turned inward (this default setting of the psyche being its primordial masochism), and the mental apparatus must find ways to deflect this destructiveness outward into the surrounding world in order to sustain itself and thrive by avoiding masochistic self-annihilation.[12] Moreover, it should already be obvious now why Žižek associates the Freudian-Lacanian *Todestrieb* with the subject's autonomy: thanks to "the death drive" (as disruptive negativity), the human individual isn't entirely enslaved to the tyranny of the pragmatic-utilitarian economy of well-being, to a happiness thrust forward by the twin authorities of the pleasure and reality principles. Breaks with this regime of narcotizing contentment are possible, a regime that lulls human beings out of their subjectivity and settles them into the slumber of conformist sleep.

However, it would be a mistake to imagine that Žižek has recourse to the notion of the *Todestrieb* as some sort of tangible, quasi-instinctual energy competing with the libido of the pleasure principle as an alternate force, a deep countercurrent (an image that seduces Freud himself). For Žižek, "death drive" names nature's dysfunctionality, rather than another kind of natural function to be included among those natural functions already acknowledged as existing:

> What psychoanalysis enables us to grasp is that death drive is a kind of inherent condition of symbolic order. To put it in slightly simplistic terms: at its most elementary, symbolization exists as a kind of secondary stop-gap measure in the sense that it consists of an attempt to patch things up when something goes terribly wrong. And what interests me is this dimension at which something goes terribly wrong . . . what interests me so much already in German idealism is the idea that with negativity (death drive) there is neither nature nor culture, but something in between. We cannot pass directly from nature to culture. Something goes terribly wrong in nature: nature produces an unnatural monstrosity and I claim that it is in order to cope with, to domesticate, this monstrosity that we symbolize. Taking Freud's fort/da example as a model: something is primordially broken (the absence of the mother and so on) and symbolization functions as a way of living with that kind of trauma. (Žižek and Daly 2004, 64–65)

The subject-as-$ is aligned with the Real, whereas subjectification corresponds to reality (i.e., the registers of the Imaginary and the Symbolic). Žižek indicates here that Imaginary-Symbolic subjectification (achieved via the introjection of and identification with various images and words) is a strategy of self-gentrification, namely, the individual's reflexive cop-

ing with the Real dimension of subjectivity within his or her core being
(an extimate dimension containing both the abyss of autonomy and the
Todestrieb). This dark, disorienting freedom without a face, lacking a rec-
ognizable human visage, is the Real subject-as-$ at its purest. And the
constituted "self" of Imaginary-Symbolic reality—subjectification could
be described as putting a human face over the void of subjective negativity so as to mask its disturbing presence—is a means of containing and
restraining this unsettling destructive power (by trying to force the con-
gealing of the restless verb-like subject, a subject incapable of succumb-
ing to reifying objectification, into the stable inertness of objectified,
noun-like forms of subjectification). In Žižek's view, Hegel's "tarrying
with the negative" means "conceiving positive being itself as materialization of Negativity—as 'metonymy of Nothing,' to use the Lacanian
expression";[13] more specifically, in this context, the "positive being" of
subjectification is the "materialization" of the subject. Subjectification
never completely succeeds at reducing the subject to an object (i.e., $
isn't a developmentally prior stage of subject formation subsequently
eclipsed by the onset of subjectifying dynamics). As with Freud's warning
not to conceive ontogenetic development as consisting of stages in which
later advances displace or obliterate earlier psychical constellations—regarding this caveat, Freud depicts the psyche with an image of the city
of Rome in which all of the city's different historical states are preserved
simultaneously in sedimentary layers[14]—Žižek stipulates that the Real
subject is continually co-present to subjectifying reality:

> This would be my fundamental model. It is this primordial dimension,
> this transcendental condition, which interests me. Why? Because of
> course this dimension is here all the time. It's not primordial in the
> sense that it happened before . . . No, it is a dimension which, as it
> were, sustains us all the time; threatening to explode. (Žižek and Daly
> 2004, 65)

There's a lot to be unpacked here (an unpacking that will occupy many of
the following paragraphs). Žižek's transcendentalism amounts to speci-
fying the conditions making possible the self-sundering of substance, the
immanent auto-disruption of natural being (and he identifies the death
drive as the primary condition for this sundering/disruption).

Jonathan Lear, in his book *Happiness, Death, and the Remainder of Life*
(2000), argues that Freud errs in the shift from the first to the second
topographies (the shift involving the introduction of the *Todestrieb*) by
positing a second underlying principle in order to account for the breakdowns and short-circuitings of the pleasure principle. Lear's contention

is that Freud veers away from accepting that there is only the dysfunctional pleasure principle (i.e., the pleasure principle and its malfunctioning), and not the pleasure principle (i.e., Eros) plus another principle
(i.e., *Todestrieb*) that accounts for those instances in which the pleasure
principle fails to assert its authority.[15] Žižek endorses this argument, and
compares it with the leap from Kant to Hegel: there is no unifying depth
(such as Kant's noumenal Real or Freud's death drive as instinctual
energy) beneath the inconsistent surface (such as Kant's phenomenal
reality or Freud's dysfunctional pleasure principle).[16] The inconsistent
surface is all there is. So the Žižekian subject (as per the equation "$$ =
death drive") is not the positive fullness of some profound second na-
ture within nature, a substantial energetic force within being itself, but,
rather, natural substance as a failed All (in this vein, Žižek characterizes
Hegel's monistic One as existing in the mode of self-blockage[17]). The pri-
mordial, archaic subject amounts to the various inexpugnable loopholes
within natural substance that prevent this substance from achieving a
harmonious internal balance.

In Žižek's view, the paradigmatic metaphor for the German idealist
subject as a *Todestrieb*-like negativity is Hegel's "night of the world" (a turn
of phrase appearing in the 1805–6 *Jenaer Realphilosophie* manuscript). He
invokes this Hegelian phrase quite often, treating it as signifying the
culminating radicalization of the modern conception of subjectivity ush-
ered in with Descartes' discovery of the cogito.[18] This nocturnal dark-
ness, the void of anonymous negativity subsisting within the heart of the
substance(s) composing human nature, is situated, by Žižek, as the van-
ishing mediator between nature and culture, the hidden hinge permit-
ting the passage from substance to subject(ification).[19]

Žižek portrays the Hegelian night of the world as a moment of mad-
ness akin to the most extreme manifestations of psychosis in which the
psyche totally withdraws from the world by contracting into itself (simi-
lar to the situation of Schelling's God in *The Ages of the World*).[20] Some
of Žižek's most elaborate reflections on this Hegelian image occur in
Enjoy Your Symptom! (a relatively early text). Both there and elsewhere,
he describes this midnight madness as facilitating the transition from
the roiling turmoil of the vortex of *Trieb* (i.e., a Real within substance)
to the gentrifying representational networks of fully constituted real-
ity (i.e., Imaginary-Symbolic subjectification).[21] Like the innate excess
of freedom hard-wired into the subject's constitutional foundations as
described by the pre-critical Kant (i.e., a wild autonomy that must be
tamed by the discipline of education in order to be made to work in
the service of reason), the Hegelian-Lacanian $ as the negativity of the
death drive—Žižek would simply assert the direct identity between this

freedom described by Kant and the subject-as-*Todestrieb*—is a disruptive factor in the natural substance of being, a factor that the signifiers of the symbolic order attempt to contain and stabilize. In fact, for Žižek, the ethereal domain of Logos, the realm of the big Other, testifies to the silent presence of this negative void in a manner analogous to how the positive content of the accretion disk around a black hole betrays the invisible point of unimaginably dense compactness creating and shaping this whirlpool of materialized, observable activity. The "spiritual" dimension of signifier-structures gives body to the psychotic negativity of the night of the world.[22] Translated into the coordinates of the distinction between nature and culture, this means that:

> man is the animal whose life is governed by symbolic fictions. *This is the way "tarrying with the negative" takes place, this is the way negativity as such acquires positive, determinate being: when the very actual life of a community is structured by reference to symbolic fictions.* (Žižek 1992a, 52–53)

Žižek proceeds to connect this to a certain Lacanian version of the death drive (a version differing from Žižek's above-mentioned gloss on the Freudian death drive): insofar as the denaturalization of nature brought about by the sociocultural overwriting of vital being involves the colonization of the living (i.e., the organic body) by the dead (i.e., the symbolic order), one could say, following Hegel and Lacan, that human life is lived under the dominance of a lifeless set of cadaverizing signifiers (for instance, memes as mental parasites).[23] Infection by virulent strains of virus-like signifiers is contracted by the individual in the process of struggling to gentrify and mask the abyssal darkness of the void of $ subsisting within substance.

Throughout his discussions of Hegel's night of the world, Žižek regularly employs the metaphor of "wiping the slate clean." The negativity of the death drive is said to wipe the slate clean through the moment of madness in which the world is withdrawn from through a centripetal movement of psychotic contraction:

> The ontological necessity of "madness" lies in the fact that it is not possible to pass directly from the purely "animal soul" immersed in its natural life-world to "normal" subjectivity dwelling in its symbolic universe. The "vanishing mediator" between the two is the "mad" gesture of radical withdrawal from reality which opens up the space for its symbolic (re)constitution. (Žižek 1999b, 35)

Stressing the necessity of hypothesizing an intermediary event flashing between natural substance and cultural subjectification, Žižek goes on to claim:

> The key point is thus that the passage from "nature" to "culture" is not
> direct, that one cannot account for it within a continuous evolutionary
> narrative: something has to intervene between the two, a kind of "vanish-
> ing mediator," which is neither Nature nor Culture—this In-between
> is silently presupposed in all evolutionary narratives . . . the Freudian
> name for this In-between, of course, is the death drive. (Žižek 1999b, 36)

Taking into account the overarching architecture of his Hegelian-
Lacanian analyses of the tripartite structure conjoining substance, subject, and subjectification, there are two problems with Žižek's description
of the subject as the negativity of the *Todestrieb* wiping the slate clean so as
to allow for ensuing processes of subjectification (i.e., of $ as a vanishing
mediator situated between natural substance and cultural subjectification). To begin with, isn't the axiomatic thesis of the Žižekian ontology
of the Real the assertion that, so to speak, the slate is always already
wiped clean? Isn't his fundamental point that substantial being isn't so
substantial after all, that (to stick with his metaphor) the slate isn't ever
full, that blank spaces of indeterminacy are scattered across the surface
of the plane of existence?

Arguably, one of Žižek's crucial contributions to a contemporary philosophical reexamination of the question of human freedom is his contention that neither natural nor cultural materiality are as functionally determinative as they sometimes appear to be. In other words, even in their
most powerful and influential forms, neither nature nor culture are up to
the task of being flawless puppet-masters constantly pulling the strings of
heteronomous human individuals, ensuring that each and every gesture
is performed in accordance with a preordained choreography. Crude
biological determinism and equally crude social constructivism share in
common the fantasy of a master (be it nature or culture) truly up to the
task of playing God, a belief in a guaranteed predestination laid out by
an omnipotent Other. Žižek maintains that philosophy after Lacan must
renounce any references to such an Other, whether cloaked in natural
or cultural guises—natural and cultural systems are both barred (i.e., no
big Other of any sort exists). Furthermore, by speaking of the *Todestrieb*-
like $ as a mediator that intervenes in order to wipe the slate clean, Žižek
risks implying that this subject is indeed a sort of force or entity unto itself (rather than being the name for the self-disruption of substance, for
its inner malfunctioning). Because being is "not all," the slate is already
(partially) wiped clean. In fully accepting the ultimate consequences of
Žižekian ontology, there is no longer any need to think in terms of an en-
ergetic agent sweeping in from elsewhere so as to erase the inert presence
of substance (in fact, one must avoid the temptation to think like this).
Instead, substance is self-effacing.

The second problem with the metaphor of the Hegelian night of the world wiping the slate clean is the emphasis on contraction as withdrawal from the world.[24] Is this contraction a withdrawal? Isn't it the opposite, namely, an overinvestment in specific features and particular elements within the world? What's being proposed here, somewhat against the grain of the Žižekian spin on Hegel's midnight madness, is a sequence in which, initially, substance develops (to use Žižek's previously cited phrase) a stubborn attachment to certain operators of subjectification (for example, genes prompt investments in memes, or the psyche's early functioning creates investments in various ideational contents [*Vorstellungen*]). This attachment is a type of condensing contraction. Then, through the establishment of such points of fixation, tensions begin to arise between these points and the remaining contextual run of things; these fixations index and embody an inertia that resists giving way in the face of environmental pressures to alter adaptively so as to fit into a temporarily given milieu. Hence, the subject emerges in its germinal mode of manifestation as an out-of-jointness with the world, as something that refuses to "go with the flow" of the rest of reality. That is to say, $-as-out-of-joint (as different from $-as-empty—see chapter 14) is the first appearance of the negativity situated in substance more than substance itself. This negativity enters into the trajectory of transition from being "in itself" (as a non-reflexive rupture immanent to substance) to "for itself" (as an explicitly thematized dynamic) via the stubborn attachment of substance to specific operators of subjectification (i.e., via natural materiality contracting itself, through overinvestment, into particular elements of cultural materiality). This complicates the placement of the subject as a mediator: $ doesn't simply come between substance and subjectification as a linear-chronological middle stage; rather, $-as-in-itself is already present within substance (as the deathly negativity of substance's self-disruptiveness), and $-as-for-itself (which initially appears as exceptional elements of subjectification that are out of joint with the rest of reality) doesn't come to light until after substance has passed into subjectification.

At this juncture, it is fortuitous to remember that Dawkins, in his acknowledgment of freedom's power to defy the selfish replicators shaping human being, mentions the faculty of imagination as integral to this autonomy. Interestingly, Žižek's most sustained recent discussion of the Hegelian night of the world focuses on the German idealist notion of the transcendental imagination (as the capacity to disassemble and reassemble the givens of experiential reality, a capacity emblematic of subjectivity). In Kant's *Critique of Pure Reason* (particularly the A version of the "Transcendental Deduction"), imagination serves to bridge the gap between the perceptions of intuition and the conceptions of the understanding. That is to say, Kantian transcendental imagination is responsible for harmonizing the two faculties of intuition and the understanding. This power of the subject forges a cohesive, cognizable experiential unity by bringing together disparate fragments of reality. More specifically, by both filling in the holes in the fabric of experience (by mentally furnishing missing bits of information implied by partial experiential pieces) and by maintaining the continuity of experience over time (by holding before the mind's eye the no-longer and the not-yet in the midst of the now), imagination binds together what would otherwise be an incomprehensible, fractured chaos, a totally disorganized, broken-up mess.[25] Imagination assists in associatively bringing together the multitude of disparate phenomena, thus helping to make knowledge possible.[26] The mental activity of imagining what isn't present—to imagine is to envision what isn't present—is a crucial part of what makes the present itself sensible.

On Žižek's reading, the Hegelian thematic of the night of the world draws attention to the obverse of this synthesizing power of the transcendental imagination as depicted by Kant. The imagination is also willing and able to butcher and dissect reality, to tear it to pieces:

> Kant's notion of imagination silently passes over a crucial "negative" feature of imagination: obsessed as he is with the endeavour to synthesize, to bring together the dispersed manifold given in intuition, Kant passes over in silence the opposed power of imagination emphasized later by Hegel—namely, imagination *qua* the "activity of dissolution," which treats as a separate entity what has effective existence only as a part of some organic Whole. This negative power also comprises Understanding and Imagination. (Žižek 1999b, 29)

The ability to analyze (i.e., literally to break something down into its constituent elements) is a peaceful, mitigated version of the raw, spontaneous impulse violently to decompose the presence of what is. Proceeding to cite both Hegel's *Jenaer Realphilosophie* description of the nocturnal abyss of subjectivity and the paragraph in the preface to the *Phenomenology of Spirit* that refers to spirit's "magical power" of "tarrying with the negative," Žižek then identifies the night of the world with the imagination as a dispersing dynamic that shatters synthetic unities:

> What better description could one offer of the power of imagination in its negative, disruptive, decomposing aspect, as the power that disperses continuous reality into a confused multitude of "partial objects,"

spectral apparitions of what in reality is effective only as part of a larger organism? Ultimately, imagination stands for the capacity of our mind to dismember what immediate perception puts together, to "abstract" not a common notion but a certain feature from other features. To "imagine" means to imagine a partial object without its body, a colour without shape, a shape without a body: "here a bloody head—there another white ghastly apparition." This "night of the world" is thus transcendental imagination at its most elementary and violent—the unrestrained reign of the violence of imagination, of its "empty freedom" which dissolves every objective link. (Žižek 1999b, 30)

Žižek steers toward the conclusion that the fractured, fragmentary multitude synthesized by the Kantian imagination isn't an asubjective or pre-subjective givenness of pure phenomena, but rather the Hegelian imagination as the unruly freedom of the inborn, violent tearing apart of the givenness of phenomena: "This pre-synthetic 'multitude' is what Hegel describes as the 'night of the world,' as the 'unruliness' of the subject's abyssal freedom which violently explodes reality into a dispersed floating of *membra disjecta*" (Žižek 1999b, 33). To translate this into now-familiar terms, the Hegelian imagination is the subject as the nocturnal *Todestrieb* breaking apart the sphere of being (i.e., the restlessness of negativity), whereas the Kantian imagination is subjectification as the endeavor to "heal the wound" inflicted upon reality by the Hegelian imagination.[27] One hears echoes here of a line Žižek sometimes cites from Wagner's *Parsifal:* "The wound can only be healed by the spear that smote it."[28] Additionally, there is a structural homology with Hegel's figure of the "beautiful soul" (another Hegelian notion frequently referenced by Žižek): just as the beautiful soul denounces a disorder in the world that this soul fails to recognize as its own handiwork, so too does the imagination (à la its Kantian side) wrestle with a chaos that it itself is responsible for creating (à la its Hegelian side). At the level of imagination, subjectivity fights itself, taming an anarchic wildness that it introduces into the order of things. Also, recall Hegel's recasting of Kant's distinction between understanding and reason (see chapter 11): both imagination and the understanding involve the subjectively mediated dismemberment of phenomena, the carving up of the flesh of experience. And, as noted, Žižek reads Hegel as celebrating this potent bastardizing violence, instead of seeking to transcend it through gaining access to a mystical, placid heaven of all-encompassing notional unity serenely standing above the fray of lived immanence (i.e., Hegel's Absolute is not an abstract universal One transcending the concrete particular

Many). The imagination is the involuntary disassembling and reassembling of reality, an automatically occurring autonomous activity transpiring within the core of a human being (and related to the innate passion for freedom spoken of in Kant's *Anthropology*). Additionally, it should be observed that these Žižekian reflections resonate slightly with Melanie Klein's distinction between the primitive "paranoid position" (i.e., the Hegelian imagination as the death-drive-driven night of the world) and the subsequent "depressive position" (i.e., the Kantian imagination as the construction of whole objects and recognized others).[29]

Žižek's interpretation of the German idealist thematic of the transcendental imagination leads him to implications that reconnect with some of the most basic motifs of his ontology and attendant theory of the subject. (What's more, his manner of stating these implications makes it possible to avoid the aforementioned problems arising from certain descriptions he offers of $ as a nocturnal psychosis wiping the slate clean as a vanishing mediator between nature and culture.) In what follows, Žižek explicitly disavows the conception of Hegel's night of the world as a simple void, an empty abyss:

> Kant, in his *Critique of Pure Reason*, elaborates the notion of "transcendental imagination" as the mysterious, unfathomable root of all subjective activity, as a "spontaneous" capacity to connect sensible impressions that precedes rational synthesis of sensible data through a priori categories. What if . . . Hegel is indicating a kind of even more primordial power of "pre-synthetic imagination," of *tearing apart* sensible elements out of their context, of *dismembering* the immediate experience of an organic Whole? It would therefore be too hasty to identify this "night of the world" with the Void of the mystic experience: it designates, rather, its exact opposite, that is, the primordial Big Bang, the violent self-contrast by means of which the balance and inner peace of the Void of which mystics speak are perturbed, thrown out of joint. (Žižek 1999b, 31)

Apropos the transcendental imagination, Žižek describes the unbalancing of reality as a result of the intervention of both the Hegelian and Kantian sides of the imagination. The Hegelian disassembling imagination disrupts and scatters whatever comes before it as given in being, and the Kantian assembling imagination struggles to impose order on the chaos thus introduced. The synthetic unification of the plane of phenomena is achieved, by the Kantian imagination, solely through the "unbalanced" privileging of certain fragments of this field over others, through selecting singular segments of reality to function as (in the parlance of Laclau and Mouffe) hegemonic articulators of the field of reality to which these segments belong (this also calls to mind Žižek's handling of the Hegelian concrete universal—see chapter 12). So there's no need to resort to myths of creation ex nihilo; even though Žižek's language frequently suggests otherwise, it's not that there is literally some original void out of which everything emerges. On the contrary, the lack of an a priori substantial fullness of being—this absence of any ontological closure provided by a harmonious and whole One-All is precisely what the Žižekian subject-in-itself really is—means that there's nothing to hold in check an excessive contraction into isolated elements of existence, an overinvestment in disproportionately privileged elements that come to serve as operators of subjectification. There's no preordained natural balance that would prevent the unbalancing introduced into reality by the subject's conflicts with itself (conflicts exemplified by the subjectifying syntheses of the Kantian side of the imagination waging a war for stabilization against the violent disruptiveness of the Hegelian imagination—this struggle between binding and unbinding is Žižek's German idealist rendition of Freud's story of Eros versus the *Todestrieb*).

If the spontaneity of the transcendental imagination is one of the zero-level fundamental features of subjectivity—this imagination is divided against itself, being simultaneously a destructive and creative dynamic—then it is responsible for disturbing the presupposed balance of substance sans subject. The Kantian imagination (as the agent of subjectification) injects an asymmetry into existence by creating concrete universals in its fight against the disorder arising from the Hegelian imagination (i.e., from the subject's tearing apart of the texture of experience). The price of each new effectuated synthesis is the introduction of a distorting disproportionality that imposes order by elevating select particulars to the status of structuring universals (with these select particulars being drawn from the set of other determinate particulars to which those selected as structuring universals belong too): "Every synthetic unity . . . imposes as unifying feature some 'unilateral' moment that 'breaches the symmetry'" (Žižek 1999b, 33). The example of the gene-meme relationship again assists with rendering these reflections a little more tangible. Memes are just one of many elements available for utilization in the gene-driven evolutionary struggle for survival. And yet, memes come to enjoy a hegemonic privilege with respect to all other elements at the disposal of genetic substance. Genes (i.e., nature) give rise to memes (i.e., culture)—to be more precise, nature gives rise to culture when the memes run amok and achieve a disproportionate degree of structuring priority in relation to the ontological ground of genes out of which the memes grew and which the memes come to reconfigure after the fact of their genesis.

In the opening monologue to the documentary film *Žižek!*, Žižek attempts to encapsulate the basic contours of his general philosophical outlook in terms similar to those he resorts to when describing the Hegelian dynamic of substance becoming subject. He again succumbs to the temptation to evoke this recurrent image of "the Void," a primordial nothingness out of which existence somehow explodes:

> What would be my . . . spontaneous attitude towards the universe? It's a very dark one. The first one, the first thesis would have been a kind of total vanity: there is nothing, basically. I mean it quite literally . . . ultimately there are just some fragments, some vanishing things. If you look at the universe, it's one big void. But then, how do things emerge? Here I feel a kind of spontaneous affinity with quantum physics, where, you know, the idea there is that the universe is a void, but a kind of positively charged void—and then particular things appear when the balance of the void is disturbed. And I like this idea spontaneously very much . . . the fact that it's not just nothing; things are out there. It means something went terribly wrong, that what we call creation is a kind of a cosmic imbalance, cosmic catastrophe, that things exist by mistake.

In Žižek's essay "Quantum Physics with Lacan" (contained as a sort of appendix in his 1996 book on Schelling, *The Indivisible Remainder*), he already makes this same point:

> The ontological implication of quantum cosmology and its notion of "vacuum fluctuation" is that "something exists" at all only in so far as the universe is "out of joint." In other words, the very existence of the universe bears witness to some fundamental disturbance or lost balance: "something" can emerge out of "nothing" (the vacuum) only via a broken symmetry. (Žižek 1996b, 227)

In the sprit of the later Schelling (as per the half-told theosophical tale of the *Weltalter* drafts), Žižek employs a grand metaphor of cosmic proportions to describe what transpires at the smaller scale of ontogenetic subject formation. Bringing this, so to speak, back down to earth, one can read these remarks as condensing a series of concepts and themes already encountered here. Two of these conceptual-thematic threads are especially important: first, the processes of subjectification are set in motion when loopholes or short circuits generated by conflicts within substance prompt or support contractive investments into operators of subjectification; and second, these operators of subjectification, in their function as concrete universals, introduce an asymmetrical ordering of the field of phenomena, an unbalanced new synthesis of reality. And, as Žižek repeatedly emphasizes, this established "new order" of reality always can be destroyed by the subject which created it, since the negativity of $ isn't ever entirely sublated by the subjectifying orders it establishes.[30] (This negativity, as a set of virtual potentialities perpetually ready to break out of Imaginary-Symbolic systems through the events of acts, haunts the actuality of every Imaginary-Symbolic system.) The subject-subjectification dialectic is "created" because "something went terribly wrong" at the level of substance. What's more, this malfunctioning occurs because substance is shot through with openings for possible deviations from its "normal" functioning (perhaps these openings, as a lack of closure/fullness at the heart of being, are what Žižek is getting at with this motif of the void, instead of problematically referring to some sort of Nirvana-like cosmic nothingness). For Žižek, true subjectivity is a kind of catastrophic imbalance that shouldn't exist, a monstrous ontological mutation that comes to be as an outgrowth of antagonisms and tensions immanent to the being of human nature.

Why does Žižek keep invoking this figure of the void? Moreover, how (and with what degree of seriousness) should one take these occasional references to quantum physics in conjunction with his syntheses of German idealism and psychoanalysis? Thus far, an adequate amount of interpretive ground has not yet been covered to present an exhaustive, satisfying explanation of this still-enigmatic link between $-as-out-of-joint and $-as-empty (such an explanation is formulated in the next chapter). There is indeed a link between, on the one hand, the imbalance introduced by the excessive contraction of substance into concrete universals as operators of subjectification (operators which incarnate a stubbornness that doesn't conform to its enveloping environs) and, on the other hand, the shift wherein the restless negativity within substantial being (i.e., $-as-in-itself) comes to light as an X incapable of being reduced to the positivity of either the stuff of substance or the stuff of subjectification (i.e., $-as-for-itself, instances of which include the Cartesian cogito, the Kantian noumenal subject-Thing, and the Lacanian subject of enunciation). However, before taking these additional explanatory steps, there is a philosophical upshot to Žižek's employment of quantum physics (an upshot at stake in his references to other branches of the natural sciences as well, such as cognitive neuroscience and evolutionary theory) that shouldn't be missed. This point pertains to the nature of his materialism, and is best gotten at by bringing Kant and Badiou to bear on the discussion here.

Kant writes the *Critique of Pure Reason* relatively soon after mathematics begins showing its enormous power as the "language of nature" in terms of the achievements of Newtonian physics. However, Kant couldn't have foreseen the quantum revolution of the twentieth century, and it's becoming more and more apparent that his epistemology is unable adequately to address and measure continuing developments in such areas as the modern sciences. For instance, nowadays, if a student takes a course in quantum physics, the professor's opening remarks usually include a stern warning about how to engage with the material. Students are instructed to adhere strictly to the letter of the mathematical formulas, to remain entirely at the level of numbers, variables, and structured relations. They are told not to make (or at least, to avoid as much as is humanly possible) any attempts to visualize or imagine the object-correlates of the equations, since their efforts at conjuring up mental images of subatomic particles merely result in misleading or outright contradictory depictions: objects that can be in two places at once, objects that are both waves and particles, and so on. This is a far cry indeed from Kant's ostensible limits of possible experience and the accompanying insistence upon grounding knowledge exclusively in terms of its connection with (actual or potential) experiential referents. As is well known, Kant, in the *Critique of Pure Reason,* proceeds first from a "transcendental aesthetic" and then to a "transcendental dialectic." That is, he begins by discussing how legitimate forms of knowledge involve the relations between sensible intuitions and the concepts of the understanding, and then subsequently endeavors to show that the employment (by reason) of the concepts of the understanding beyond the bounds of such experience invariably leads to antinomies as irresolvable intellectual deadlocks and impasses.[31]

If a philosophically inclined quantum physicist were today to write a sequel to the first *Critique,* it would be a mirror-image inversion of Kant's masterpiece. Rather than concluding, as Kant does, with a dialectics of pure reason, it would conclude with a dialectics of sensible intuition. The anti-Kantian message of quantum physics is simply this: pure mathematical formulas provide unmediated access to the brute material Real of things themselves as they really are (in Kant's language, numerical ideas of reason furnish a direct manifestation of things-in-themselves as the ultimate yet ephemeral quantum "substance" of material reality). However, any attempt to translate this mathematized Real into perceptual constructs (in Kant's language, imaginable or perceivable objects of macro-level sensory experience) produces untenable antinomies for human thought (i.e., experiential/sensible, as opposed to rational, contradictions).

Although Badiou's bold identification of ontology with mathematics—for Badiou, ontology is mathematics[32] (and not, as per historical tradition, the province of philosophy)—doesn't amount to a straightforward endorsement of the preceding speculations about a scientifically inspired inversion of Kantian epistemology, he nonetheless moves in a similar and equally timely direction. Badiou bemoans the fact that, in the current intellectual state of affairs, mathematics generally has been reduced to nothing more than a form of "knowledge" (*savoir*), a strictly instrumental manner of reasoning. Whereas the ancient Greeks explored the rapport between being and number (thus indicating a profound link between ontology and mathematics), the dominant contemporary view is that mathematics is just an epistemological tool or mediating ideational interface whose use-value is determined primarily by its employment with respect to specific object-referents (i.e., an employment allowing for calculating, measuring, predicting, tallying, etc.). Badiou designates this referential relation between concepts and experientially given entities by the term *savoir* (i.e., knowledge as opposed to "truth" [*vérité*]). Obviously, Kant's concerns, as articulated in the first *Critique*, bear principally upon knowledge (in other words, the focus there is epistemological, as opposed to ontological). What Badiou and a certain camp within quantum physics have in common is that both are willing to decide—this decision is, in a way, a kind of wager—that mathematics, instead of being relegated to the idealist status of a constructed conceptual superimposition upon the substrate of phenomenal experience, is the most direct and unmediated disclosure of being possible (the only one available, and one that demands bypassing the "interference" of sensible intuitions).

During the course of explaining his justifications for treating ontology and mathematics as equivalent, Badiou himself invokes the example of contemporary physics. For Badiou, ontology, as mathematical, is indifferent to the specificity of what is presented in terms of particular beings: "Pure presentation, as such, abstracting all reference to 'that which'— which is to say, then, being-as-being, being as pure multiplicity—can be thought only through mathematics" (Badiou 1998, 126). Under the regime of number, the "what" of incarnated presentation can be anything whatsoever, since number grasps the multiplicity of beings in nothing more than their mere being per se, irrespective of their differentiating attributes, predicates, or qualities.[33] In the context of a conversation in which he explains these very points, Badiou notes that "physics, which is to say the theory of matter, is mathematical. It is mathematical because, as the theory of the most objectified strata of the presented as such, it necessarily catches hold of being-as-being through its mathematicity" (Badiou 1998, 127). He then stipulates that, nonetheless, a difference must be recognized between his sense of ontology and mathematized quantum physics: whereas the former is absolutely and serenely indifferent to every manner of determinate content (it deals only with "the pure multiple" as such, independent of considerations concerning what it's a multiple of), the latter directs itself toward a specific (albeit fundamental and ultimate) "that," namely, matter.[34] Badiou proceeds, despite this caveat, to acknowledge the proximity of his mathematical ontology to modern science:

> The more you decompose the concept of matter into its most elementary constituents, the more you move into a field of reality which can only be named or identified with increasingly complex mathematical operations. "Matter" would simply be, immediately after being, the most general possible name of the presented (of "what is presented") . . . Matter, in the sense in which it is at stake in physics, is matter as enveloping any particular presentation—and I am a materialist in the sense that I think that any presentation is material. If we consider the word "matter," the content of the word "matter," matter comes immediately after being. It is the degree of generality immediately co-present to ontology. The physical situation will then be a very powerfully mathematised situation and, in a certain sense, more and more so, the closer it comes to apprehending the smallest, most primordial elements of reality. (Badiou 1998, 128)

The matter spoken of by today's physicists, an almost entirely mathematized matter, is akin to number itself in its supremely general, all-encompassing applicability with respect to existent entities. As such, this new notion of matter (unlike the perceivable macro-level objects of the Newtonian physical world) "comes immediately after being" as the most universal of names for what is, as something "immediately co-present to ontology." Furthermore, Badiou insinuates that the spontaneous ontology of the scientists (to paraphrase Althusser) entails a desubstantialization of being that resembles his own handling of being qua being (*l'être en tant qu'être*). Normally, from an everyday perspective, the substantiality of material "stuff" appears to stand in stark contrast to the fleeting formal status of intangible numbers. And yet Badiou's remarks above hint at a sort of Hegelian convergence of opposites taking place in contemporary physics: the closer one approaches the elementary constituents of materiality itself, the more mathematical this materiality becomes. In its most basic and reduced form, substance seemingly becomes insubstantial; matter appears to become immaterial. This is a consequence of the (mathematical) reasoning processes of theoretical physics being forced, by virtue of the development of their own rational apparatuses, to cut sensible intuition out of the picture of the material Real. The traditional, quotidian sense of substantiality withdraws as part of this scientifically driven recession of sense, leaving behind nothing but numbers as the sole markers for the smallest constituents of matter.

Žižek's interest in quantum physics principally concerns its effect of dematerializing matter, of desubstantializing substance. Given that his own materialism, as organized around a Schellingian-Hegelian ontologization of Kant, posits an acosmism in which the ground of (human) being is incomplete and inconsistent (i.e., a groundless ground [*Grund* as *Ungrund*]), Žižek wants to avoid conceiving of the fundamental stuff of material reality as a kind of compact weightiness, a closed, saturated fullness of concrete existence.[35] Žižekian substance is a perforated materiality deprived of the density of closed completion:

> Since the radical materialist stance asserts that there is no World, that the World in its Whole is Nothing, materialism has nothing to do with the presence of damp, dense matter—its proper figures are, rather, constellations in which matter seems to "disappear," like the pure oscillations of the superstrings or quantum vibrations . . . Materialism is not the assertion of inert material density in its humid heaviness—*such* a "materialism" can always serve as a support for Gnostic spiritualist obscurantism. In contrast to it, a true materialism joyously assumes the "disappearance of matter," the fact that there is only void. (Žižek 2004c, 24–25)

When Žižek speaks of the void, what he sometimes has in mind is an intangible web of virtual possibilities (akin to the fleeting and ethereal domain of microscopic quantum events and processes) that becomes a fully constituted reality (i.e., created material nature as per vulgar philosophical conceptions of macroscopic matter) if and when the symmetrical balance of this web is disturbed through one virtual possibility being endowed with greater weight than the others. The virtuality of possibility thereby "collapses" into the reality of actuality. But what prompts the collapse of this intangible virtual web? What catalyzes the falling out of something (i.e., the reality of actuality as substantial being with material heft) from nothing (i.e., the virtuality of possibility as an insubstantiality within substantial being more than substantial being itself)? Here is where things obviously reconnect with the Hegelian topic of the rapport between substance and subject.

In Žižek's eyes, there is a Hegelian lesson to Heisenberg's famous uncertainty principle. Instead of reading this principle in a Kantian fashion (i.e., the irreducible, unavoidable effect of the observer on the observed establishes a barrier or limit preventing direct observational access to the pure physical Real as it exists unsullied by the interference of observation), Žižek prefers to pull the dialectical trick of transubstantiating an obstacle blocking access to the Thing into the very Thing itself. From this perspective, Heisenberg's uncertainty principle represents (in perhaps a quite loose and metaphorical way) the Hegelian-Žižekian ontological proposition that subject is not separate from substance. Rather, subject is substance staring back at itself; the eye of the observing individual, an eye forming a part of the universe it sees, is, in a certain sense, the universe casting a glance over itself. The subject is that part of substance carrying out the self-objectification of substance, a self-objectification in which substance transforms itself. More specifically, with this example from quantum physics, Žižek contends that subjectivity's effect on the particles it observationally reflects upon isn't a matter of Kantian-style external reflection either remaining confined within its own reality apart from material nature or introducing falsifying distortions into the field of Real being. On the contrary, the reflection of subjectivity, rather than being wholly external to what it observes, is inscribed directly into the ontological structure of the Real being of material nature itself.[36] In other words, the refraction of the object by the subject's gaze isn't simply just subjective interference; this refraction is (also) a facet of the object's own essence.

Briefly examining some remarks contained in *The Parallax View* (2006) will help make sense of the conclusion Žižek draws in the final paragraphs of *The Indivisible Remainder* (the 1996 book that ends with the essay "Quantum Physics with Lacan") regarding the philosophical connection between his musings about quantum physics and German idealist conceptions of human freedom. Revisiting his 1996 reflections on this topic almost a decade later, he asks, "Is not the shift from substantial Reality to (different forms of) Event one of the defining features of modern sciences?" and, in response to this question, again emphasizes that "quantum physics posits as the ultimate reality not some primordial elements but, rather, a kind of string of 'vibrations,' entities which can only be described as desubstantialized processes" (Žižek 2006, 165)—or, as he reiterates this later in the same text, "the lesson of quantum physics" is that "solid material reality" isn't the most elementary and fundamental grounding layer of natural substance.[37] Soon after repeating his insistence that quantum physics points to a matter deprived of any philosophically traditional image or notion of materiality, Žižek frames the contemporary difference between idealism and materialism thus:

> It is here, in this terrain, that we should locate today's struggle between idealism and materialism: idealism posits an ideal Event which cannot

be accounted for in the terms of its material (pre)conditions, while
the materialist wager is that we *can* get "behind" the event and explore
how Event explodes out of the gap in/of the order of Being. (Žižek
2006, 166)

Immediately following this succinct delineation of the distinction between these two philosophical poles, he refers to Schelling's *Weltalter*
project—which brings the present analysis underway here back to the
conclusion of "Quantum Physics with Lacan" in *The Indivisible Remainder:
An Essay on Schelling and Related Matters*. Therein, the later Schelling and
the "related matter" of quantum physics converge via the subject-as-$ as
the negativity of Real being's inner inconsistency (in metaphorical terms
borrowed from quantum physics, $ as the "void" of indeterminate and
not yet actualized virtual possibilities) both preceding the advent of fully
constituted actual reality and lingering on after this advent as the ineliminable remaining possibilities for negating the actuality of this reality:

> The emergence of human freedom can be accounted for only by the
> fact that nature itself is not a homogenous "hard" reality—that is to
> say, by the presence, beneath "hard" reality, of another dimension of
> potentialities and their fluctuations: it is as if, with human freedom, this
> uncanny universe of potentialities re-emerges, comes to light. (Žižek
> 1996b, 230)

At the level of an ontogenetic account of subject formation formulated
vis-à-vis German idealism and Lacanian theory, one could say that subjectification is the process wherein the indeterminacy of the subject-as-$
(more precisely, $-as-in-itself but not yet for-itself) is collapsed into a cer-
tain determinate configuration, a set of specified identificatory coordinates (i.e., particular key images and words as anchors of an identity mir-
rored back to the subject by select fragments of its surrounding milieu).
This movement of subjectification can be treated here as analogous to
the quantum dynamic whereby possible virtuality becomes actual reality. However, through another process yet to be explained (see chapter
14), events transpire when actual reality presents an opportune opening for the resurfacing of the possible virtuality eclipsed by this reality's
emergence. These events making possible the resurgence of possibilities buried within Real being (but obfuscated with the crystallization of
Imaginary-Symbolic reality) are the moments when $ switches from being
in-itself to becoming for-itself. For Žižek, subjective freedom amounts to
the return of the repressed Hegelian night of the world, the reappearance within reality of the Real foreclosed by reality and its accompanying

labors of subjectification. Žižekian freedom is an anonymous autonomy, a faceless power of negativity ready, willing, and able to cancel any and every congealed given within the state of the status quo.

Elsewhere in *The Parallax View*, Žižek turns his critical attention to cognitive science and evolutionary psychology. Without going into much detail regarding this newly opened theoretical front (involving a Hegelian-Lacanian engagement with bodies of literature previously considered by many to be utterly incompatible with both modern philosophy and psychoanalysis), it's worth observing that biology, and not just physics, provides Žižek with a means to ground his assertions that a materialist theory of a non-epiphenomenal transcendental subjectivity is feasible insofar as material being itself isn't reducible to a stifling ontological closure in which everything is determined in advance by a seamlessly integrated set of factors and forces. Perhaps better than anything else in the world, the human brain exemplifies the basic structural dynamic of dialectical materialism (a point convincingly and masterfully demonstrated by Catherine Malabou[38]). That is to say, the neuronal (as the electrochemical materiality of the central nervous system's folded matter) gives rise to the mental (as the experiential dimension of lived reality, including both the self and the entire reality of which it's aware). But mental dimensions come to exert a reciprocal influence back upon the neuronal substrates from which they arose. In short, the physical contours of the brain not only shape experience, but, inversely, the brain literally is sculpted by the contents of experience which it indisputably plays a central role in constituting/generating. In German idealist terms that risk sounding somewhat primitive and anachronistic in the context of discussing neurological facts, with the example of the human central nervous system in particular, the Ideal emerges from the Real, and thereafter the Ideal begins to reshape this same Real. As Žižek astutely observes, crude versions of idealism and materialism either downplay or neglect the brain's material plasticity. He asserts that "the new brain sciences" are "dialectical" insofar as they highlight "the infinite plasticity of the brain":

> This plasticity is displayed in three main modes: plasticity of development, of modulation, and of reparation. Our brain is a historical product, it develops in interaction with the environment, through human praxis. This development is not prescribed in advance by our genes; what genes do is precisely the opposite: they account for the structure of the brain, which is open to plasticity . . . Vulgar materialism and idealism join forces against this plasticity: idealism, to prove that the brain is just matter, a relay machine which has to be animated from outside,

> not the site of activity; materialism, to sustain its mechanical determin-
> ist vision of reality. This explains the strange belief which, although it is
> now empirically refuted, persists: the brain, in contrast to other organs,
> does not grow and regenerate; its cells just gradually die out. This view
> ignores the fact that our mind does not only reflect the world, it is part
> of a transformative exchange with the world, it "reflects" the possibilities
> of transformation, it sees the world through possible "projects," and this
> transformation is also self-transformation, this exchange also modifies
> the brain as the biological "site" of the mind. (Žižek 2006, 209)

The living matter of the nervous system is simultaneously constituting
(i.e., it generates all the mental states of lived experience) and constituted (i.e., these thus-generated mental states reflexively alter this same
generative matter)—and the same holds for mind in relation to brain
(i.e., the mental states of lived experience are likewise both constituting
and constituted). Clearly, the human brain illustrates that natural matter
isn't necessarily an inert, solid density operating in a totally determined
mechanistic mode. This is why partisans on both sides of stale, standard-
ized variations on the hackneyed disagreements between idealism and
materialism tend to ignore the brain's material malleability. Such motivated ignorance sustains both the reductionist agenda of mechanistic
materialists as well as the theoretical identities of the idealists who define themselves through opposition to these reductionistic materialists
as straw-men adversaries.

Along these lines, Daniel Dennett rightly insists that the "deterministic" position according to which the evolved physical brain is absolutely
central to human nature in all its richness—this position, of which Dennett is an articulate advocate, grants enormous importance to the life sciences in a philosophical explanation of the various features of the mental apparatus—isn't tantamount to a radical reductionism in which no
room is left for agency or selfhood, for anything resembling autonomous
subjectivity. In the case of the human central nervous system, determinism doesn't amount to a negation of freedom, to an eliminative denial
of individual flexibility and spontaneity. Why not? One way of putting
the answer (echoing Sartre) is that human beings are condemned to be
free, determined to be autonomous (whether they like it or not).[39] More
precisely, evolution designed the folded matter of the brain to be plastic,
to shape and reshape itself in response to the world of experience as its
dialectical partner. The neuroscientist Joseph LeDoux explains:

> Most systems of the brain are plastic, that is, modifiable by experience,
> which means that the synapses involved are changed by experience . . .

> Plasticity in all the brain's systems is an innately determined characteris-
> tic. This may sound like a nature-nurture contradiction, but it is not. An
> innate capacity for synapses to record and store information is what al-
> lows systems to encode experiences. If the synapses of a particular brain
> system cannot change, this system will not have the ability to be modified
> by experience and to maintain the modified state. As a result, the organ-
> ism will not be able to learn and remember through the functioning of
> that system. All learning, in other words, depends on the operation of
> genetically programmed capacities to learn. Learning involves the nur-
> turing of nature. (LeDoux 2002, 8–9)

Echoing LeDoux, Dennett similarly points out that "there is no paradox
in the observation that certain phenomena are *determined* to be change-
able, chaotic, and unpredictable, an obvious and important fact that
philosophers have curiously ignored" (Dennett 2003, 90). He adds that
"there are things whose *natures* change over time, so determinism does
not imply a fixed nature" (Dennett 2003, 91). And human beings, with
their malleable mental matter, are the epitome of such creatures designed by nature to have redesignable natures: "Our natures aren't fixed
because we have evolved to be entities *designed* to change their natures
in response to interactions with the rest of the world" (Dennett 2003,
93). These crucial insights, proposed by a fierce defender of contemporary cognitive science as underpinned by biology and neurology, arguably cry out for a return to German idealist conceptions of nature as a
spiritual(izable) substance (conceptions arrived at by this modern philosophical tradition through, at least in part, critiques of prior mechanistic
sorts of materialism). Don't Dennett's remarks call to mind Schelling's
notion of the material ground of human nature as a groundless ground,
a determined indeterminacy (a notion Žižek regularly invokes with the
phrase "the abyss of freedom")? Or isn't this designed capacity for rede-
signing, a capacity built into the physical seat/substrate of subjectivity, an
empirical exemplification of Žižek's depiction of Hegelian substance-as-
subject (i.e., the raw substance of the brain already harbors within itself
the potential for the actualization of variable subjectifying structures,
structures through which a dialectical movement is animated between,
for lack of better terms, the material and the more-than-material)?

In the context of this discussion, a Žižekian approach would demand
including an additional inflection regarding the substantial underbelly
of subjectivity. Not only is the human brain preprogrammed to be repro-
grammed, but what's more, the number and intricacy of both its own
physical features and the codes of socio-symbolic programs it will come
to run make conflicts, deadlocks, and short circuits inevitabilities. What

the level of intra-neuronal architecture (a sprawling network of billions of interconnected nodes) and the level of interface between this architecture and its "other" as the matrix of mediated mental experience (a matrix mediated by multiple linguistic and representational networks) share in common is a mind-boggling degree of complexity. And (as asserted in chapter 12) the likelihood of antagonisms and contradictions arising between elements of complex systems, be they material or more-than-material, increases correlative to the increased degree of these systems' complexity.

In *Freedom Evolves,* Dennett also talks about, in conjunction with his corrective recasting of biological determinism, the relation between chance and causation. Pondering the category of events without causes, he reaches for the case of tossing a coin:

> A coin flip with a fair coin is a familiar example of an event yielding a result (heads, say) that properly *has no cause* . . . Have you ever wondered about the apparent contradiction involved in using a coin flip as a generator of a random event? Surely the result of a coin flip is the *deterministic* outcome of the total sum of forces acting on the coin: the speed and direction of the release that imparts the spin, the density and humidity of the air, the effect of gravity, the distance to the ground, the temperature, the rotation of the earth, the distance to Mars and Venus at that time, and so forth. Yes, but this total sum has no predictive patterns in it. That is the point of a randomizing device like a coin flip, to make the result uncontrollable by making it sensitive to so many variables that no feasible, finite list of conditions can be singled out as the cause. (Dennett 2003, 85)

Dennett proceeds to claim that a coin toss (as a procedure for generating a random digital result), rather than "absorbing all the micro-variation in the universe," actually "amplifies it, guaranteeing that the unimaginably large sum of forces acting at the moment will tip the digitizer into one of two states, heads or tails, but with no salient necessary conditions for either state."[40] This example curiously resembles Freud's concept of the dream-navel (as glossed previously in chapter 12): just as the navel of a dream results in the absence/deficit of meaningful interpretation by flooding the interpreter with a superabundance of too much potential meaning to be interpreted, so too does the unique event of a particular coin toss thwart the isolation of a single cause (or even a limited number of enumerable causes) for its either-or outcome by this event being (like the navel) a point of ultra-dense hyper-condensation (in this case, the unique event of the coin toss is a moment in which an incalculable number of causal factors converge, condensing their influences so as to produce one digital state rather than the other). In short, there's always a result produced when a coin is flipped, but it's impossible to say what caused the coin to come up heads or tails in a given particular instance. The excessiveness of too many causes forces the appearance of a blank (i.e., the absence of a single cause or finite list of causes) in explanatory narratives.

A few pages after considering this example of tossing a coin, Dennett invokes the (Kantian) notion of the finitude of epistemological subjectivity: "Every finite information-user has an epistemic horizon; it knows less than everything about the world it inhabits, and this unavoidable ignorance guarantees that it has a *subjectively* open future. Suspense is a necessary condition of life for any such agent" (Dennett 2003, 91). The idea here is that one of the "guarantees" of human autonomy (as, at a minimum, the sense of being free, believing that one inhabits a world of multiple possibilities) is the impossibility of adopting a God's-eye view of being as an exhaustively integrated One-All. The epistemic agent's inability (an inability illustrated by the example of tossing a coin) to discern a cohesive totality of the myriad forces and variables bearing upon it as a being situated in the world provides it with sufficient "breathing room" (or, as per the title of an earlier book by Dennett, "elbow room"), letting it feel as though it's able to sustain life by inhaling the bracing fresh air of autonomy.

In response to this, Žižek likely would play Hegel to Dennett's Kant. In other words, Dennett hints at something Kant speculates about in the *Critique of Practical Reason:* if a finite human epistemic agent were somehow miraculously to overcome the limitations of its finitude and achieve direct insight into its true, essential nature (for Dennett, the sum total of causal influences shaping its being), such knowledge would deprive this agent of its feeling or sense of being free (for Kant, if the subject comes to know itself as a noumenal Thing, it turns into a lifeless puppet bereft of autonomy). Dennett thus insinuates, despite his caveats elsewhere cautioning against such an insinuation, that seeing things from the impossible God's-eye view would indeed reveal every single being and event to be a predetermined outcome of the universe as a vast nexus of causal influences. For Žižek, apart from keeping in mind the pointlessness of imagining this impossible divine perspective, one must avoid falling prey to the fantasy that, beneath the veil of appearances as the superficial façade of reality, a harmonious organic unity of natural cogs and components hums away, smoothly churning out a continuous, uninterrupted material substratum of existence (just as, for Hegel, Kant dogmatically assumes that the Real of noumena behind phenomena is devoid of an-

tinomies and contradictions, that the supposed subject hidden behind
the mask of the phenomenal-empirical "self" would suffocate through
drowning in the immanence of being). The Žižekian universe is one in
which there is no big Other entirely up to the task of exerting an invariably active deterministic control over the order of things. In fact, the
groundless ground of his Otherless ontology could be described as (to
borrow the title of Milan Kundera's book) "the unbearable lightness of
being." (In a somewhat similar vein, G. K. Chesterton, whose book *Orthodoxy* is frequently referenced by Žižek, views the causally closed cosmos
of the deterministic/mechanistic materialist as "about the smallest hole
that a man can hide his head in"[41]—in other words, the notion of being
as a fixed, predictable One-All, a seamless flow of causes and effects, is a
seductively comforting image hiding something very unsettling.)

There is always the temptation, thanks to this "unbearable lightness"
(a description also appropriate apropos the Schellingian abyss of freedom), to posit, whether implicitly or explicitly, the existence of a big
Other governing the incomprehensibly complex workings of natural,
cultural, and natural-cultural systems. Žižek's revolutionary recasting of
the notion of human freedom is tied to his (to put it in Lacanese) traversing the fantasy of there being a big Other of any type whatsoever,
namely, an ultimate Master-guarantor with sufficient determining authority to orchestrate an integrated and synthesized functioning of the
multiple strata of being. Both the Real and the Symbolic are barred, that
is, they never achieve the status of systems in which all potential bugs
and loopholes are eliminated so as to prevent disruptions of natural or
cultural patterns of determinism. The multiple strata of being and their
architectural arrangements are much more fragile and precarious than
one tends to imagine. (In solidarity with Dennett, evolution discloses
this fragility and precariousness too—evolutionary theory, unlike other
sciences such as physics, lacks predictive power precisely because of the
central role of numerous kinds of contingency in the unfolding of its
algorithms.)

Kant's critical-transcendental turn attempts to escape the sterile impasse between empiricism and rationalism in which his modern philosophical predecessors got bogged down. Similarly, Žižek aims to break
out of the forced choice of a false dilemma presented by the oversim-
plifying debates between unsophisticated varieties of materialism (i.e.,
a monistic ontology according to which consciousness, mind, subjectivity, and so on are dismissed as mere epiphenomena with respect to the
sole reality of mechanistic matter) and idealism (i.e., a dualistic ontology
according to which an immaterial plane of being enjoys an absolutely
independent existence with respect to the concrete reality of mechanis-

tic matter). His attempts to cast a shadow of doubt over this persistent and pervasive image-notion of matter as mechanistic (attempts involving Schelling, Hegel, quantum physics, and cognitive science, among other resources) are an integral component of the general endeavor to formulate a materialist theory of the subject. More specifically, this theory of subjectivity suggests that dualistic idealism's parallax split between immanent materiality and transcendent more-than-materiality emerges out of a properly reconceived version of monistic materialism's substance. Žižek's Schellingian-Hegelian ontology allows for charting the immanent genesis of the transcendent, for preserving the parallax split of idealism without conceding that an ideal plane of immateriality eternally transcends what transpires at the level of the material Real. This transcendental materialism (as an account of a more-than-material yet non-epiphenomenal subject derived from a specific ontology of the Real) requires a reworked conception of the very nature of the substance of being.

Consequently, what Žižek proposes is an ephemeral, aleatory materialism in which the autonomous negativity of subjectivity is able to move from an "in itself" status as substance's inner inconsistency (i.e., as a not-yet-subjectified subject) to a "for itself" status in which a clear contrast is visible between itself and its various enveloping matrices of mediation (i.e., as a subjectified subject). Events of Real and/or Symbolic structural breakdown are essential possibility conditions for this transition from $-as-in-itself to $-as-for-itself. In fact, $-as-in-itself could be construed as designating structural breakdown within the Real of being's substance, whereas $-as-for-itself (as will be seen in the next chapter) refers to an out-of-jointness that gradually traces the contours of an X which doesn't have an appropriate place anywhere in Imaginary-Symbolic reality. As such, this homeless misfit tends to achieve an explicitly thematized prominence during those occurrences when reality suffers from some sort of structural breakdown—that is, when, in Lacan's language, the clay feet of the big Other become apparent, when this Other is revealed to be barred through it becoming clear that, as it were, the emperor wears no clothes. $-as-in-itself is the vanishing mediator as condition of possibility for the passage of nature into culture. The ontogenetically primordial signs of this passage are stubborn attachments to particular operators of subjectification (i.e., fragments of the sociocultural milieu of the symbolic order); these points of contractive condensation create concrete universals hegemonically articulating the rest of the field in which these points are embedded, and also highlight a death-drive-like resistance to going with the flow of the run of things (a resistance that brings into focus $-as-out-of-joint).

However, the mystery remains regarding how the subject transitions from, first, its initial state of being the "in itself" *Todestrieb* subsisting within nature more than nature itself, to, second, its early manifestations via maladaptive fixations upon operators of subjectification (i.e., $-as-out-of-joint), to, third, its full-fledged "for itself" status as the void of an X without anchoring in any particular operators of subjectification offered by Imaginary-Symbolic reality (i.e. $-as-empty—à la, for instance, the Cartesian cogito, the Kantian subject-Thing, the Schellingian abyss of freedom, and the Lacanian subject of enunciation). The transitional step from two to three (from $-as-out-of-joint to $-as-empty) is parallel to the progress of a Lacanian analysis. The analysand goes from a position in which he or she is burdened with symptoms (i.e., stubborn points of jammed-up inertness anchored by the master signifiers of this subject's subjectifying structure) to a state where these master signifiers (along with the symptom-laden subjection they dictate) loosen their enthralling grip and fall away like the layers of a peeled onion (as the result of "traversing the fantasy" and confronting the extimate core of one's psychical-subjective being behind, beneath, or beyond the signifiers of subjectifying identifications). This faceless X lacking a place in Imaginary-Symbolic reality, a void which comes to appear as such after the shift from nature (i.e., substance) to culture (i.e., subjectification), is nothing other than the subject as Hegel's night of the world, the inhuman darkness glinting within the pupils of each individual person. Its genesis has everything to do with time.

Spirit Is a Bone: The Implosion of Identification

Despite his potentially misleading descriptions of the void-like subject (à la the withdrawal from reality by Hegelian midnight madness) as a mediator between natural substance and cultural subjectification (i.e., as sequentially coming before subjectification), Žižek acknowledges that, ontogenetically speaking, subjectification is primary. Subjectification is brought about by identification with particular attributes, features, qualities, and so on (in short, predicates) presented by the external medium/ order of socio-symbolic reality. And $ becomes an empty negativity for itself only after the taking-on of a series of determinate identifying predicates (or, in Lacanese, specific signifiers representing subjectivity). With reference to Lacan's conception of the subject, Žižek comments that "the subject of the signifier is a retroactive effect of the failure of its own representation; that is why the failure of representation is the only way to represent it adequately" (Žižek 1989, 175). As he later elaborates:

> "Contradiction" designates the antagonistic relationship between what I am "for the others"—my symbolic determination—and what I am "in myself," abstractedly from my relations to others. It is the contradiction between the void of the subject's pure "being-for-himself" and the signifying feature which represents him for the others, in Lacanian terms: between $ and S₁. More precisely, "contradiction" means that it is my very "alienation" in the symbolic mandate, in S_1, which retroactively makes $—the void which eludes the hold of the mandate—out of my brute reality. (Žižek 1993, 131)

In other words, $ is an *après-coup* product of the passage of substance into the mediation of master signifiers, namely, S_1s as concrete universals, as privileged nodes structuring the field of socio-symbolic subjectification. These S_1s are those representational units (signifiers, memes, and so on) that achieve a hegemonic status, determining the articulation of the individual's identity insofar as this identity consists of concrete contents fleshing out a recognizable human self (i.e., the objectified ego [*moi*] as characterized by Lacan). Master signifiers are operators of subjectification. In Žižek's account of subject formation, ego-level subjectifying identification must first fail in order for the void of $ to be illuminated.

Returning to Lacan is crucial before continuing further along the present course of speculative exploration. Of special interest here is Lacan's notion of the "unary trait" (*trait unaire*), a notion based on the role of "*ein einziger Zug*" (a unique feature) in the account of identification put forward by Freud in his 1921 study *Group Psychology and the Analysis of the Ego*. According to Freud, the identifications constitutive of both the material and organization of the ego are guided by investments in particular characteristics of those significant others functioning as important libidinal objects; the psyche of the identifying individual latches onto these features/traits, internalizing or "introjecting" the ideationally detachable signifier-like marks of the identity of the significant other with whom this psyche identifies itself.[1] Thus, the ego, as the "self" or "I" of the individual psyche, is built up from a series of identifications with others. In *The Ego and the Id* (1923), Freud famously proposes that "the character of the ego is a precipitate of abandoned object-cathexes and . . . it contains the history of those object-choices" (*SE* 19:29). Phrased somewhat differently, the ego is cobbled together using bits and pieces borrowed from the trans-individual matrix of subjective relations.

In the same session of the eighth seminar (a session Jacques-Alain Miller entitles "*L'identification par 'ein einziger Zug'*") where he emphasizes that, in the mirror stage, Symbolic identification catalyzes and conditions Imaginary identification (i.e., the visual imago is identified with by the child due to the verbally mediated promptings to do so by his or her adult others, rather than Imaginary identification developmentally preceding Symbolic identification—see chapter 5), Lacan introduces his concept of the unary trait. This introduction is foreshadowed in the previous years of *le Séminaire* by other concepts such as, most notably, the quilting point (*point de capiton*) spoken of in the third seminar on the psychoses.[2] What's more, when the late Lacan revisits the question of psychosis in the twenty-third seminar, his concept of the *sinthome*, as the symptom without which the structure of the subject would disintegrate, also bears a certain resemblance to this notion of *le trait unaire*.[3] What does Lacan say about identification in this session of his eighth seminar on the topic of transference? He begins by observing that the default ontogenetic point of departure for subject formation must be an initial state involving anxiety, longing, and unrest (an observation already made, as seen, by both Schelling and Hegel, each of whom likewise contends that substance becomes subject because this ground of being is agitated from within by the restless negativity of a primordial discontent):

> In effect, if one starts from the notion of original narcissism, perfect as regards libidinal investment, if one conceives of the primordial object as primordially included by the subject in the narcissistic sphere, as a primitive monad of enjoyment [*jouissance*], to which is identified . . . the infant nursling [*nourrisson*], one has difficulty seeing what would be able to lead to a subjective way out [*sortie subjective*]. (*SVIII* 410)

Portraying infantile "primary narcissism" as a blissful state of oblivious perfection in which the libidinal economy is unperturbed by deep dissatisfactions and inherent inadequacies (i.e., depicting the starting condition of human existence as being that of a "primitive monad of enjoyment") makes it almost impossible to explain why individuals would ever strive to exit from this archaic Garden of Eden. What could possibly motivate an entity contentedly enclosed in the confines of its own idiotic happiness to struggle spontaneously to pull itself out of this solipsistic womb of well-being? In order to account for the excursion into subjectivity/subjectification ("*une sortie subjective*"), it is necessary to posit a zero-level state of subject formation pervaded by negativity (in particular, by negative affects generated by the libidinal economy). The infant's condition of anxiety-inducing helplessness and abject dependency predisposes him or her to capitulate to the implicit and/or explicit demands coming from others (plus the Other) to accept an alienating identity mediated by foreign images and words.

As already noted (in chapter 5), Lacan stipulates that one important aspect of *le trait unaire* is its role as a stabilizer of the field of identifications (those aspects of the unary trait having to do with the libidinal dynamics of drive and desire aren't explicitly addressed here). More specifically, unary traits are ideals internalized from the milieu of the big Other as the symbolic order, namely, coordinates shaping the contours of identification.[4] Several times, Lacan stresses that the ego-ideals of the subject are grounded on such traits.[5] In fact, he treats the ego in its entirety as an infinitely receding ideal; in the essay on the mirror stage, the imago-gestalt depicts an impossible, unattainable wholeness, a placid, integrated unity that forever eludes the subject gazing upon this captivating, seductive image. Consequently, Lacan usually ends up claiming that the unary trait (impressed upon the individual by those early significant others embodying the order of the Other) underpins the entire edifice of the ego.[6] This claim goes hand in hand with his insistence that the magical mirror-stage moment of identification with the reflected *moi*-image is sparked into occurring by the child's parental figures encouraging and validating such identification (the key signifiers involved in this encouragement and validation are instances of *le trait unaire*).[7] The familial big Other is thus, through the signifying resources it bestows upon the nascent subject-to-be, the first guarantor of the cohesiveness of a self-identity, of legitimated and recognized personhood. For instance, in the tenth seminar, Lacan reminds listeners of his recent shift of emphasis (initiated in the eighth seminar) as regards the mirror stage (to repeat, the Symbolic comes before and molds the formations of the Imaginary, rather than, as Lacan's pre/proto-structuralist musings on the role of the mirror in ego construction sometimes are erroneously interpreted, the Imaginary register being a stage prior to the developmental accession to the register of the Symbolic).[8] Later on during the same session containing this reminder, Lacan declares identification with the unary trait of the Symbolic (and not the imago-gestalt of the Imaginary) to be the primary identification (i.e., that which erects the skeletal scaffolding of identity), with the mirror then furnishing a phenomenal/experiential content to this identity—an identity which thereafter continues to rely on the big Other for sustaining "authentication."[9] He concisely summarizes this in the nineteenth seminar:

> The unary trait is the support of what I departed from under the name of the mirror stage, that is to say, imaginary identification . . . everything I have said, wrote, inscribed in graphs, schematized in an optical model on one occasion, where the subject is reflected in the unary trait and where it is only from there that he locates himself as ideal-ego—all of that insists precisely on the fact that imaginary identification operates via a symbolic mark. (*SXIX* 5/10/72)

The unary trait as a "symbolic mark" is the genuine underlying mechanism behind the phenomenal experience of relating to specific images as avatars of self-identity. If the imago-gestalt of the ego as constituted within the register of the Imaginary is a sort of picture, then, it could be said, the laws of perspective structuring this picture are laid down in advance by the apparatus of the symbolic order.

In order better to concretize Lacan's concept of the unary trait, it is useful briefly to turn to two linguistic examples of this concept: proper names (as treated by Saul Kripke in terms of his concept of the "rigid designator") and personal pronouns (as treated by Emile Benveniste in terms of his concept of the "shifter"). These two elements of language both serve as the Symbolic avatars of subjective identity, supposedly representing the inner kernel of singular selfhood. So why are Kripke and Benveniste, apart from the historical fact that Lacan refers to each of them (once to Kripke and multiple times to Benveniste), relevant to understanding the Lacanian account of identification as arising from the subject's relationship to signifiers as unary traits? Hopefully, in the course of succinctly explaining Kripke's rigid designators and Benveniste's shifters, the answer soon will become obvious to anyone even vaguely familiar with Lacan's ideas.

Opposing himself to what he dubs the Frege-Russell theory of naming, Kripke asserts that proper names have nothing to do with the describable features of the named object (i.e., its qualitative properties). A name is neither a condensed description of a given thing nor a placeholder for the bundle of attributes exhibited by this thing. And, as he points out, names retain their function independently of the various (and variable) qualities of their named objects. Kripke illustrates this with the example of the name of the city Dartmouth (he borrows this example from John Stuart Mill).[10] When this city was first baptized with the name "Dartmouth," a descriptive role was envisioned: when named, the city was located at the mouth of the river Dart. However, what happens if and when the course of the river Dart changes and Dartmouth is no longer located at the mouth of the river? Does the name "Dartmouth" cease making sense? Kripke responds in the negative: it's because proper names are not descriptions of the qualitative properties of particular objects that such changes in these properties fail to disrupt the naming capacity of the proper name as rigid designator. A name is a proper name when it designates "rigidly," namely, when its designation no longer depends on a descriptive relation to its designated/named referent.

For Kripke, prior to the act of naming, there is no essential Thing, no inaccessibly deep substantial core, uniting clusters of describable attributes. He states:

> If a quality is an abstract object, a bundle of qualities is an object of an even higher degree of abstraction, not a particular. Philosophers have come to the opposite view through a false dilemma: they have asked, are these objects *behind* the bundle of qualities, or is the object *nothing but* the bundle? Neither is the case; this table is wooden, brown, in the room, etc. It has all these properties and is not a thing without properties, behind them; but it should not therefore be identified with the set, or "bundle," of its properties, nor with the subset of its essential properties. Don't ask: how can I identify this table in another possible world, except by its properties? I have the table in my hands, I can point to it, and when I ask whether *it* might have been in another room, I am talking, by definition, about *it*. I don't have to identify it after seeing it through a telescope. If I am talking about it, I am talking about *it*.
> (Kripke 1972, 52–53)

The "it" Kripke emphatically refers to in this passage is not simply an entity in the external world. He repeatedly mentions the table as something which he "talks" about. This is quite important. According to Kripke's theory of naming, proper names are rigid designators to the extent that they designate the same thing in "all possible worlds." For instance, one can imagine a possible world in which Nixon lost the 1968 election; the name "Nixon" is the fixed point of reference permitting the hypothetical substitution of differing descriptive predicates.[11] Consequently, the self-sameness of an object's identity, whether this "it" is a table or Richard Nixon, is established by virtue of the rigidity of the name allowing for the substitution of alternate definite descriptions:

> A possible world isn't a distant country that we are coming across, or viewing through a telescope. Generally speaking, another possible world is too far away. Even if we travel faster than light, we won't get to it. A possible world is *given by the descriptive conditions we associate with it* . . . "Possible worlds" are *stipulated*, not *discovered* by powerful telescopes. There is no reason why we cannot *stipulate* that, in talking about what would have happened to Nixon in a certain counterfactual situation, we are talking about what would have happened to *him*. (Kripke 1972, 44)

In Kripke's view, the identity of an object amounts to its "transworld" self-sameness. But given that one can never actually reach a world other than one's own, this modal identity across worlds is itself existent solely through its means of stipulation (i.e., the cognitive-linguistic act of substituting alternate descriptions, such as "lost the 1968 election" in place of "won the 1968 election"). Consequently, anything resembling a thing-in-itself (i.e., an object independent of its descriptive features or a subject independent of its predicates)—recall how Kant's first *Critique* insists that the noumenal subject (i.e., the non-presence of the inaccessible subject-Thing focused on by Žižek) is a *Ding an sich* for a self-consciousness necessarily routed through the matrix of phenomenal experience[12]—is an effect of rigid designation.

Kripke proposes that names become rigid designators at a specific moment of time which he calls the event of "fixing a reference."[13] In the beginning, a name may very well refer to what it names in a descriptive fashion; returning to a previous illustration, the name "Dartmouth" was initially a description of the city thus named, since the city was at the mouth of the river Dart when the event of it being named "Dartmouth" first occurred. However, once "Dartmouth" is taken as the name of the city (i.e., once the reference is fixed), this original reliance on the determinate, empirical qualities of the named object becomes irrelevant.

Once a reference is fixed, the city Dartmouth will forever after be rig-idly designated as "Dartmouth," no matter what changes the descrip-tive properties of the city subsequently undergo (even if the river later shifts course, the name "Dartmouth" still refers to the same city). And, of course, the same holds for a person's proper name in relation to the person named by it.

What about personal pronouns? Benveniste portrays them as what he calls "linguistic shifters." Unlike many other units of language, such pro-nouns perform their functions exclusively to the extent that they have no fixed signifieds outside of their immediate contexts of usage:

> Pronouns are distinguished from all other designations a language ar-ticulates in that *they do not refer to a concept or to an individual.* There is no concept "I" that incorporates all the *I*'s that are uttered at every moment in the mouths of all speakers . . . *I* refers to the act of individual dis-course in which it is pronounced, and by this it designates the speaker. It is a term that cannot be identified except in what we have called elsewhere an instance of discourse and that has only a momentary refer-ence. (Benveniste 1971, 226)

"I" is the emptiest of words. It is continually being attached and reat-tached to an incalculable number of momentary referents, but never weds itself to any of these transitory correlates. On the one hand, not only can a potentially infinite number of speakers situate themselves as the signified of this signifier, but the ever-changing individual speaker also repeatedly identifies him/herself with this pronoun. On the other hand, each particular enunciator (ever-changing over time) who places him/herself under the aegis of this word never subsists in the mode of an objectively stable signified corresponding to the invariability of the material signifier "I." In other words, the iterability of this signifying unit—the pronoun "I" is materially the same signifier even though the enunciative acts employing it continually shift as utterly unique temporal moments—creates a mirage of unity and continuity across the concat-enations of utterances in which it features.

Apropos the subjectivity of the *parlêtre*, both proper names as rigid designators and personal pronouns as iterable shifters participate in cre-ating this mirage. The rigidity of the proper name's designating func-tion generates the impression of there being some X thus named (i.e., a subject-term) that isn't at all equivalent or reducible to its contingent, variable qualities (i.e., predicate-terms). Additionally, the "I" as linguistic shifter reinforces this same impression; however, it does so by virtue of its referential fluidity (i.e., its ability to refer to any first-person enunciator whatsoever regardless of the particular attributes and properties of each enunciator, including the changing attributes and properties of the "same" individual person-enunciator over time). These two types of special signifiers (i.e., names and pronouns as unary traits) form the true bedrock of the feeling of trans-temporal identificatory self-sameness (with respect to Lacanian theory, the temporally volatile body image of the Imaginary *moi* is underpinned by the Symbolic *je*, more specifically, the unary traits structuring the vicissitudes of identification).

So, translating the preceding back into now-familiar terms, *le trait unaire* can be characterized as an operator of subjectification as quilting, hegemonic master signifier (Lacan himself treats the unary trait as closely related to the concept-matheme S_1[14]). It behaves like a Hegelian-Žižekian concrete universal, striving (in vain) definitively to "one-ify" the fragmentary field of experiential elements.[15] These S_1s of subjectifying identification establish a certain constancy of self-sameness over time, the (illusory) sense of an enduring ipseity. In the ninth seminar on identification (a seminar focused on the intimate interrelationship between the subject and the signifier), Lacan, extending his reflections from the closing sessions of the previous year's seminar, links the concept of the unary trait to the modern philosophical notion of subjectivity. He identifies *le trait unaire* as a minimal, simplistic "structural trait" (i.e., an insignia or mark) that serves as a "guarantor" of the Cartesian cogito as "vanishing subject"[16] (just as the rigid designator and linguistic shifter fabricate, each in their own way, a misleading sense that there's an ineffable yet existent trans-temporal constancy to self-identity). In the 1960 *écrit* "The Subversion of the Subject and the Dialectic of Desire in the Freudian Unconscious" (a text dating from the same period as the ninth seminar), Lacan advances the same thesis: "Consciousness is based on the ego-ideal as unary trait (the Cartesian cogito does not fail to recognize this)" (Lacan 2006o, 685). As he asserts several sessions later during the ninth seminar, this maximally minimal trait, this bare insignia or mark, succeeds at being an inscription/trace that evokes the presence of subjectivity without relying on reference to a wealth of concrete empirical features; this trait achieves an "extreme reduction . . . of all the opportunities for qualitative difference"[17] (hence the similarity with, in particular, Kripke's definition of proper names as rigid designators). Lacan therefore concludes that "it is from the effect of the signifier that the subject as such emerges" (*SIX* 12/6/61). In other words, identification with the unary trait engenders the cogito-like subject, instead of this subject having genetic or transcendental priority in relation to the particular contents of identification (such as unary traits). That is to say, there is no a priori void of non-empirical subjectivity timelessly preceding identificatory investments in operators of subjectification (features, insignias, marks, traits, etc.) presented by the individual's socio-symbolic milieu.

Further on in the ninth seminar, Lacan states that "the subject himself in the final analysis is destined for the thing" insofar as he must pass through the defiles of the big Other, thereby being submitted to this Other's Law.[18] In saying that, by virtue of the always already active mediation of the big Other, the subject "is destined for the thing," Lacan echoes Kant. In conceding that the noumenal "I" is impossible to encounter in an isolated state—one only ever glimpses it through the distorting effects of intuition's inner sense—Kant proposes that his version of the cogito is just as much a thing-in-itself as any substantial entity supposedly existing beyond the limits of possible experience. The Kantian subject-as-Thing (i.e., the X of "I or he or it, the thing that thinks") is a condition of possibility preceding any and every phenomenal "I," every accessible form of identification available to self-consciousness.

Opposing himself to both Kant and Descartes (to the extent that the Cartesian vision of subjectivity can be said to presage Kant's own portrayal of it), Lacan reverses the hierarchy between cogito-like, a priori subjectivity and the ostensibly a posteriori predications of said subject. In the Lacanian schema, the signifiers of the symbolic order preexist the advent of the enunciative mechanism (i.e., $ as the contentless subject of enunciation). The nothingness of this psychoanalytic cogito, this "empty spot" forever at odds with the big Other, is generated ex nihilo by the catalytic introduction of determinate predications of identity (i.e., operators of subjectification as signifiers—more specifically, as unary traits).[19] Succinctly stated, the predicate is prior to the subject, and not the other way around. Žižek accepts Lacan's reversal of the modern philosophical assumption according to which the subject precedes its predicates, arguing that this reversal is a core contention central to the Hegelian-Lacanian model of subjectivity.

During a discussion of identity as conceived of by Freud and Lacan, Badiou, in his *Court traité d'ontologie transitoire,* makes some passing remarks about the status of the proper name in relation to subjectivity: "In the beginning, there is but a letter if we maintain that a proper name is the position of a letter-signifier in the Subject economy. As such the proper name is empty; it says nothing" (Badiou 2006, 150). The proximity to Kripke is again striking ("the proper name is empty"). What about Žižek? How is any of this relevant to understanding his Hegelian-Lacanian theory of the subject? From a Žižekian perspective, the subject per se (i.e., the empty $, negativity-for-itself) isn't to be identified directly with the signifier as unary trait, that is, the proper name or personal pronoun freed from being bound by the task of description to concrete, qualitative empirical features as referents. The effects that such signifiers have on structures of identity pertain to the dimension of subjectification and not to the subject proper.

However, through a Lacanian appropriation of Kripke and Benveniste, a glaring discrepancy becomes visible between, on the one hand, the contentless invariability of the signifier (as the unary traits of rigidly designating names or linguistically shifting pronouns) and, on the other hand, the ceaseless variability of content designated by the signifier (as the continually shifting surfaces of experiential reality). Although this discrepancy is structural, it achieves a level of explicit thematization—it goes from being in-itself to for-itself—over time. And when this structural gap finally reveals itself in its naked negativity, the empty-subject-as-for-itself is born. In Žižek's terms, Lacan's unary traits, Kripke's rigid designators, and Benveniste's linguistic shifters all would be examples of operators of subjectification, namely, master signifiers of identification hegemonically articulating the substance of human being (i.e., imposing order onto the destructive anarchy of the primordial Kantian-Hegelian night of the world, the chaos introduced into being by the abyssal autonomy of the de-synthesizing and re-synthesizing imagination at war with itself, an imagination fighting the imbalance that it itself introduces into the world). By contrast, the subject ($-as-for-itself) names the very gap between these stabilizing operators of subjectification and the unstable flux of lived experience, a flux that these operators never fully succeed in stabilizing. Additionally, despite running the risk of stating the obvious at this juncture, it must be noted that the subject, defined as this gap, cannot come into being until the instability of substance already has passed into the order of subjectification. Stated with reference to Lacan's mirror stage, the revelation of one's cogito-like subjectivity (i.e., one's status as an anonymous, faceless nobody, as a void irreducible to any and every possible determinate content) through dis-identification with the externally mediated *moi* of the ego ("That's not me!") requires a prior moment of identification with this reflected imago-gestalt ("That's me!").

The Žižekian subject emerges from the failure of subjectifying identifications. Žižek, in *For They Know Not What They Do* (arguably the most extensive single treatment of Hegel in his entire corpus), repeatedly makes this exact point. After mentioning the temporal structure of a time lag separating the subject-term from its predicate-term—this lag inevitably intervenes in the diachronic unfolding of any statement, including statements of identity (with the tautological statement "A = A" being the epitome of self-identity as a thing's identity with itself)—he states:

Therein consists . . . the Hegelian conception of identity: identity of an
entity with itself equals the coincidence of this entity with the empty
place of its "inscription." We come across identity when predicates fail.
Identity is the surplus which cannot be captured by predicates—more
precisely (and this precision is crucial if we want to avoid a misconcep-
tion of Hegel), identity-with-itself is *nothing but* this impossibility of
predicates, *nothing but* this confrontation of an entity with the void at
the point where we expect a predicate, a determination of its positive
content . . . Identity-with-itself is thus another name for absolute (self-
referential) negativity, for the negative relationship towards all predicates that define one's—what?—*identity*. In so far as, in Hegel, absolute
negativity constitutes the fundamental feature of subjectivity, we could
add that "A = A" offers us the shortest possible formulation of the identity of substance and subject: subject is substance reduced to the pure
point of negative relationship towards its predicates; substance in so far
as it excludes all the wealth of its contents. In other words, it is a totally
"desubstantialized" substance whose entire consistency lies in the refusal
of its predicates. (Žižek 2002a, 36–37)

Given the concerns of the present critical analysis, what's important here
is Žižek's acknowledgment that the void of $-as-emptiness-for-itself, of
the subject specifically as self-relating negativity (rather than the non-
self-relating negativity of $-as-in-itself, as the conflicts and inconsistencies
within substance), is a result produced through the eventually apparent inability of operators of subjectification finally and exhaustively to
establish a satisfyingly stable identity, an adequate representation of an
unchanging self ("We come across identity when predicates fail"). Or
as Žižek subsequently declares, "*the very act of reflection as failed constitutes retroactively that which eludes it*" (Žižek 2002a, 86). This declaration
surfaces during the course of a discussion in which he challenges the
straw-man caricature of Hegel attacked by deconstruction, namely, the
image of Hegelian philosophy as an idealist "theory of everything" in
which alienation, contingency, heterogeneity, singularity, and so on are
dismissed pretentiously as deceptive appearances behind which lurks
the synchronic conceptual network of an ahistorical, eternal *Geist*.
    Žižek aims to refute the notion that Hegel's model of the subject is
one in which self-consciousness is capable of achieving a perfect transparency to itself, of reflexively transubstantiating itself from the opacity
of finite immanence into the clarity of infinite transcendence. He refers
to Rodolphe Gasché's Derridean engagement with German idealist depictions of self-conscious subjectivity: if the mirror is taken to be the metaphorical figure for the power of self-reflection, then the title of Gasché's

book (*The Tain of the Mirror*) signals his pinpointing of those spots on the
reflective surface where reflection fails (i.e., those moments when the
subject encounters the alterity of an asubjective opacity, a "tain," rather
than its own self-image).[20] Žižek alleges that this title phrase ("the tain
of the mirror") alone already betrays a fundamental misunderstanding
lying at the base of Derridean readings of Hegel.[21] He explains:

> Hegel knows perfectly well that reflection always fails, that the subject
> always encounters in a mirror some dark spot, a point which does not re-
> turn him his mirror-picture—in which he cannot "recognize himself." It
> is, however, precisely at this point of "absolute strangeness" that the sub-
> ject (the subject of the signifier, $, not the imaginary *ego*, caught in the
> mirror-relationship $m–i(a)$) is inscribed into the picture. The spot of the
> mirror-picture is thus strictly constitutive of the subject; the subject *qua*
> subject of the look "is" only in so far as the mirror-picture he is looking
> at is inherently "incomplete"—in so far, that is, as it contains a "patho-
> logical" stain—the subject is correlative to this stain. (Žižek 2002a, 89)

Once again, it is obvious that, viewed at the level of temporal-genetic
structuring, subjectification as the mirroring moment of reflective identification (i.e., the construction/constitution of an ego through the gesture of exclaiming "That's me!" in relation to externally given images
and words) precedes the advent of the subject per se (i.e., $ as an X that
emerges following the failure of the gesture of identification). So a crucial question at this point is: Why does subjectifying identification fail?
Asked differently, why must every enthusiastic "That's me!" inevitably be
followed by a "That's not me!" as a subsequent moment? Before responding to this question, yet another question still remains to be answered
(a query posed several times in chapter 13): How does the subject-as-$
move from being in-itself (i.e., an acephalous, death-drive-like negativity,
in substance more than substance itself, prompting investments in operators of subjectification as imposers of order on substance's own inner
chaos) to becoming for-itself (i.e., a self-relating negativity irreducible
to either its natural or cultural surroundings, a homeless misfit lacking
a delineable positive identity)? In other words, how does $ shift from,
first, its initial manifestations via maladaptive, stubborn attachments to
subjectifying elements (i.e., $-as-out-of-joint) to, second, its later status
as an anonymous, faceless void incapable of collapsing itself into these
same subjectifying elements (i.e., $-as-empty)?

The ontogenetic path of Hegelian-Žižekian subject formation is structured thus: $-as-in-itself → subjectification and the correlative surfacing
of $-as-out-of-joint → $-as-for-itself-emptiness. The first transition (from

$-as-in-itself to subjectification and the correlative surfacing of $-as-out-of-joint) occurs when substance-as-subject (in the sense of the being of human nature as a conflict-saturated vortex of drives, as an internally agitated "not all" already containing within itself the clearing/opening out of which will burst forth the ensuing dynamics of subject formation) undergoes subjectification (i.e., the excessive embracing of operators of subjectifying identification, namely, unary traits as master signifiers organizing, in the mode of concrete universals, ego-level selfhood) in an effort to overcome its own unstable state of existence, to stabilize the violent flux of the unsynthesized experiential field (a field traversed by the Hegelian imagination as the night of the world, the groundless, excessive freedom immanent to substance in the form of human being). This initial shift produces $-as-out-of-joint since, through subjectifying identifications with S_1 elements, a maladaptive inertia makes its presence felt. Žižek defines the *Todestrieb* quite broadly: "death drive" is the name for whatever it is in human nature that makes possible those events when a human being is more than a mere biological organism, insofar as this being can and does deviate from patterns of self-preservative adaptation in relation to its enveloping environs. In Žižek's vocabulary, this controversial psychoanalytic term designates the antagonism-inducing "dis-integration" in human nature (whether as the inherent lack of coordinated synthesis due to this life-form's incredible degree of complexity or the destructive tendencies of the psyche's spontaneous imaginative activity) prompting unbalancing overinvestments in privileged operators of subjectification that found a hegemonic "new order" aiming to tame and domesticate the disharmonious cacophony of primordial substance-as-subject (a primordiality along the lines of Schelling's vortex of *Trieb* as the barred Real of human nature). $-as-in-itself (i.e., primordial substance-as-subject) latches onto anchoring unary traits and thereby submits itself to subjectification through identification with these traits ("That's me!"). These operators of identificatory subjectification are drawn from the surrounding symbolic order, the individual's sociocultural matrix of mediation. However, such emblems of identification come to be clung to after they have outlived their purpose or usefulness (à la the trajectory of deaptation—see chapter 12). They may even be held to fiercely in the face of adverse consequences, retained in a "masochistic" manner to the extent that the individual pays a price for such fidelity to these exceptional elements of his or her universe of signifiers. Thus, thanks to the inertia of said elements, a maladaptive out-of-jointness begins disclosing itself.

Now the increasingly manifest inadequacies of the thus-embraced operators of subjectification lead to the second transition (from $-as-out-of-joint to $-as-for-itself-emptiness—or from identification to dis-identification due to the failure of identification). It's at precisely this point that the question of why subjectifying identification fails becomes especially pressing. One part of the answer already has been put forward earlier (see chapter 5): in the example of the Lacanian mirror stage (with the imago-gestalt being a crucial operator of subjectifying identification), the image reflected back to the subject's gaze gradually proves to be unsatisfactory as a herald of a constant, enduring "I" or self since the body framed by the mirror is a piece of mortal flesh subjected to the ravages of time, an ever-changing lump of matter caught up in the cycles of generation and corruption. Hence, a kind of temporal negativity turns what at first appears to be a permanent, stable representation, an adequate self-identification, into the opposite, namely, a reflected glimpse of the individual's fleeting, impermanent being, his or her transitory finitude. However, what about identification at the level of the Symbolic rather than the Imaginary? Aren't unary traits, those special units of the symbolic order such as proper names (as rigid designators) and personal pronouns (as linguistic shifters), immune to the ravages of time? Doesn't the individual's submission to (as Lacan describes it) "mortifying cadaverization" through accepting lifeless signifiers as the core constituents of her subjectivity defend her against temporal negativity? Perhaps surprisingly, Lacan's response is an emphatic "No."

Although Lacan's concept of *le trait unaire* seemingly suggests that certain master signifiers assimilated through the processes of identification set up a thereafter stable and unchanging unity of identity over time, he warns against this impression. In the ninth seminar, Lacan protests that identification with the unary trait doesn't result in some sort of "unification," the erection of a synthetic oneness.[22] Years later, in the nineteenth seminar, he insists that "the unary trait has nothing to do with the 'There is the One' . . . the unary trait is that by which repetition as such is marked. Repetition does not found any 'All' " (*SXIX* 5/10/72). Why does Lacan counterintuitively oppose repetition (in this case, the iterability of those signifiers functioning as unary traits) and any unifying One? Isn't repetition indicative of an unchanging continuity, a static Sameness? Simply put, a central axiom of Lacanian theory is the contention that perfect, pure repetition (as reinstantiation of the Same) is impossible: "In its essence repetition as repetition of the symbolic sameness is impossible" (Lacan 1970, 192). Even within the register of the Symbolic alone, at the level of iterable signifying units (such as unary traits), alteration over time is inevitable and unavoidable—and this for structural reasons inherent to the logic of the signifier (in particular, each repeated instance of a given signifier-like mark [A] introduces, if nothing else, a minimal difference between its occurrence in a diachronic sequence and other occurrences of the same mark elsewhere in this sequence [A_1 versus A_2]).[23] Succinctly stated, repetition engenders difference.[24] Just as the living body giving rise to the ego's imago ends up incarnating, despite having been latched onto as an emblem of enduring self-sameness over time, the fleeting, transitory nature of a finite being utterly at the mercy of temporal negativity, so too do the supposed constants of Symbolic operators of identificatory subjectification fail at their task of warding off transformation in and by temporality.

In several places, Lacan links together the logic of the signifier, the impossibility of repetition, the unary trait as anchor of identification, and time.[25] Signifiers are inseparable from temporal dimensions insofar as, in Lacanian theory, they always are situated in diachronically unfolding chains of more than one signifier. With reference to basic sentential syntax—a sentence is a chain of signifiers enchained together over time—signifiers functioning as subject-terms (for example, proper names or personal pronouns) have predicate-terms (i.e., other signifiers) hooked onto them at subsequent moments in the unfurling of sentences. Although both proper names (as per Kripke) and personal pronouns (as per Benveniste) are empty as independent of any particular characteristics or features serving as empirical referents, these unary traits (S_1) repeatedly take on, from moment to moment, a dizzying, shifting array of different (and differentially determining) relationships with other signifying elements (S_2, S_3 . . .). Despite superficial appearances to the contrary, there is an amazing degree of fragile, unstable volatility to signifier-mediated subjectification. Over time—repetition cannot be separated from temporality as its necessary medium—all signifiers, including those elevated to the status of concrete universals organizing stages of subjectification, unavoidably are caught up in various destabilizing, transformative diachronic dynamics.

Additionally, it mustn't be forgotten that the ground zero (or, as it were, zero ground) of human nature, the being-substance out of which the movement of subject formation arises, is, according to psychoanalysis, a fractured, fragmented foundation. That is to say, analytic thought, dispensing with the fantasy of the "paradise lost" of an original, harmonious, and natural wholeness grounding being human, proposes that the very base of a human's being is afflicted by antagonisms between different components and functions of its libidinal economy. The Freudian version of Hegelian-Žižekian substance-as-subject is the notion that the archaic vortex of drives is a raging maelstrom in which the "natural" ground of human being is at war with itself. Due to this factor alone, it would seem to follow that the various subjectifying identifications dic-

226

THE SEMBLANCE OF SUBSTANCE AND THE SUBSTANCE OF
SEMBLANCE (HEGEL–ŽIŽEK)

tated by this roiling mass of conflicting tendencies would be potentially
inconsistent with each other as well as subject to possible disruptive
destruction. Hence, with the diachronic-temporal movement of subject
formation, multiple competing operators of subjectification, operators
vying for the position of hegemonic articulator of the terrain of ego-
level identity (i.e., the self or "I" of the *moi*), come and go in an ongoing, perpetually shifting struggle. Furthermore, this unstable struggle
for hegemony among operators of subjectification helps to reveal the
ultimate contingency and impermanence of any and every ego-level
constellation. This revelation thus assists in leading from $-as-out-of-
joint (à la stubborn attachment to subjectifying elements) to $-as-empty
(à la a void that comes to be explicitly thematized for itself with the
realization of the contingent, impermanent status of all *moi* configurations). Additionally, since a series of comings and goings of operators of
subjectification (i.e., unary traits as master signifiers of identification)
is necessary before the subjectifying ego shows itself to be fleeting and
fragile, time is again an indispensable ingredient of this crucial aspect
of subject formation.

As already explained, Žižek, in line with Lacan, distinguishes between
sujet (i.e., the subject-as-$) and *moi* (i.e., the ego). Whereas the latter des-
ignates the individual's "substantial identity," his or her sense of selfhood
as determined by identifications with select portions of the surrounding experiential and socio-symbolic milieu, the former is an imageless,
nameless X, an ineffable yet palpable abyss first glimpsed by Descartes
and his philosophical successors. Speaking of Hegel's "negation of negation," Žižek defines the subject as whatever survives the cataclysm of
losing one's substantial identity (i.e., the destruction of one's *moi*):

> The "negation of negation" is not a kind of existential sleight of hand by
> means of which the subject pretends to put everything at stake, but ef-
> fectively sacrifices only the inessential; rather, it stands for the horrifying
> experience which occurs when, after sacrificing everything I considered
> "inessential," I suddenly realize that the very essential dimension for the
> sake of which I sacrificed the inessential is already lost. The subject does
> save his skin, he survives the ordeal, but the price he has to pay is the loss
> of his very substance, of the most precious kernel of his individuality.
> More precisely: prior to this "transubstantiation" the subject is not a sub-
> ject at all, since *"subject" is ultimately the name for this very "transubstantia-
> tion" of substance* which, after its dissemination, "returns to itself," but not
> as "the same." (Žižek 1996b, 126)

He continues:

It is all too easy, therefore, to be misled by Hegel's notorious propositions concerning Spirit as the power of "tarrying with the negative," that is, of resurrecting after its own death: in the ordeal of absolute negativity, the Spirit in its particular selfhood *effectively dies,* is over and done with, so that the Spirit which "resurrects" *is not the Spirit which previously expired* . . . When . . . Hegel asserts that the Spirit is capable of "tarrying with the negative," of enduring the power of the negative, this does not mean that in the ordeal of negativity the subject has merely to clench his teeth and hold out—true, he will lose a few feathers, but, magically, everything will somehow turn out OK . . . Hegel's whole point is that the subject *does NOT survive* the ordeal of negativity: he *effectively* loses his very essence, and passes over into his Other. One is tempted to evoke here the science-fiction theme of changed identity, when a subject biologically survives, but is no longer the same person—that is what the Hegelian transubstantiation is about, and of course, it is this very transubstantiation which distinguishes Subject from Substance: "subject" designates that X which is able to survive the loss of its very substantial identity, and to continue to live as the "empty shell of its former self." (Žižek 1996b, 126–27)

The dissolution or annihilation of the "stuff" constituting the *moi* presents the chance for catching sight of the *sujet,* this *je ne sais quoi* invariably out of synch with any and every identificatory element of the ego-self (moreover, this $-as-empty becomes visible only after the creation and destruction of a subjectified "I"). However, what's especially interesting here is that Žižek refuses to treat the negativity of anonymous, faceless subjectivity as an invariant transcendental constant, a timeless structural function unaffected by the hustle and bustle of the empirical-phenomenal world (this is how both the Cartesian and Kantian non-empirical subjects are characterized). Perhaps the Hegelian-Žižekian $ is more a variable than a void.

Picking up a thematic thread touched on earlier, Žižek's dematerialization of matter (in particular, his desubstantialized substance as the basis for a materialist theory of an emergent more-than-material subjectivity) dovetails with one of the oldest philosophical motifs in the history of ideas. To some extent, it could be said that the most cutting-edge contemporary sciences (quantum physics, first and foremost) are, in a way, resonating with certain notions and themes at the very heart of Plato's metaphysics. The foundational Platonic distinction between the visible realm (as the tangible yet inessential domain of constantly changing material entities) and the intelligible realm (as the intangible yet essential domain of eternally unchanging immaterial ideas), especially as

conveyed via the famous "allegory of the cave," entails the assertion that
the intelligible is what really enjoys the heft of real being, whereas the
visible amounts to nothing more than a pale, shadowy reflection of the
intelligible.[26] This flies strikingly in the face of everyday common sense.
From the vulgar, quotidian standpoint of the non-philosopher, the material entities encountered through the sensory-perceptual capacities of
the body appear to have the greatest amount of reality; these are things
that one can stub one's toe on, objects with a dense, inert presence that
one can bump up against. By contrast (and again from a mundane perspective), ideas seem to be the dim, degraded semblances of material
entities (rather than, as Plato has it, vice versa); these abstract ideational
categories are devoid of genuine ontological weight, being mere coordinates on a rarified, ephemeral logical-conceptual grid projected onto
the solid ground of material being. So, already with Platonic metaphysics, the world of matter loses its apparent firmness and substantiality.
Material being turns out to be a dematerialized dance of shadows, an
insubstantial parade of (epi)phenomena.

In a sense, the reason for Plato's counterintuitive reversal of the
standard assignment of degrees of ontological weight to the perceptual
(which discloses the visible realm) and the conceptual (which discloses
the intelligible realm) is quite simple. Taking mathematics as the exem-
plary model discipline for the production of true knowledge in all areas
of inquiry, Plato insists that any and every truth, as true, must be eternal
and unchanging (for example, two plus two will always equal four, and a
triangle will always have three sides whose angles add up to 180 degrees).
So, since the visible realm displayed to perception is an ever-changing
flux in which nothing stands still—material existence is the Heraclitian
river into which one cannot step twice—truth, as eternal and unchanging, isn't to be found within the mad dance of this domain dominated
by temporal negativity. Because of continual alteration over time, what
seems most substantial to quotidian, non-philosophical common sense
(i.e., matter as perceived stuff) is, in actuality, insubstantial. Temporality
robs material being of its seemingly hefty solidity.

Of course, neither Hegel nor Žižek are idealists or metaphysical
realists in the manner of Plato. They reject the contention, central to
Platonic philosophy, that a supersensible heaven of ideational beings,
a transcendent realm of universal categories or sets, truly exists on its
own as a timeless plane separated off from the hurly-burly of immanent
historical-material reality. Nonetheless, this passing reference to Plato
here is important for no other reason than that it points toward a possible bridge between two theoretical topics: the immateriality of matter
and the negativity of time. This perforated, aleatory materiality is a cru-

cial notion for Žižek's transcendental materialist account of subjectivity, an account of the immanent genesis of the transcendent according to which the subject is both generated out of substance and ontogenetically comes to achieve an autonomy with respect to its substantial ground. The move of advancing the thesis that the insubstantiality of substance is nothing other than temporality has an Ockham's-razor sort of appeal. This move enables the various facets and features of Žižekian Hegelianism to be brought together elegantly in a coherent, systematic fashion. However, a few more steps must be taken before this becomes fully apparent.

Along with "substance as subject" and the "night of the world," another Hegelian philosophical phrase repeatedly cited and interpreted by Žižek is Hegel's strange assertion that "the spirit is a bone" (from the section on "Observing Reason" in the *Phenomenology of Spirit*).[27] In fact, these three phrases ("substance as subject," "night of the world," and "spirit is a bone") serve as nodal quilting points for Žižek's reflections on Hegel. Much could be said about the Hegelian critique of physiognomy and phrenology, both in terms of its historical significance and its potential relevance to today's debates about the relationship between mind and body. However, what's of interest in the current context is Žižek's appropriation and employment of this odd-sounding "infinite judgment" (i.e., a proposition bringing together two apparently distant and unrelated concepts). On one occasion, Žižek reads Hegel's phrase "substance as subject" alongside "the spirit is a bone," treating both as almost identical examples of the infinite judgment:

> It is not enough to say that there is a "lack of identity" between Substance and Subject—if we do only that, we still presuppose Substance and Subject as two (positive, identical) entities between which there is no identity; the point is rather that *one of the two moments (Subject) is none other than the non-identity-with-itself of the other moment (Substance)*. "The Spirit is a bone" *means that* bone itself can never achieve complete identity with itself, and "Spirit" is none other than that "force of negativity" which prevents bone from fully "becoming itself." (Žižek 2002a, 119)

In this passage, Žižek links Hegel's phrenological infinite judgment to the theme of being as "not all," to a materialism grounded on a groundless ground. Matter (i.e., bone) is incapable of closing in upon itself as an unperturbed ontological oneness; instead, substance is internally agitated and disturbed by reflexive processes (i.e., spirit) immanent to its very being. However, through this reading, it actually sounds as though Žižek turns this Hegelian judgment on its head. That is to say, Žižek's pe-

culiar brand of Hegel-inspired materialism, based as it is on a dematerialized materiality, is committed to the claim that, as it were, "the bone is a
spirit" (i.e., matter, at least the kind of matter than can produce subjects
out of itself, is never simply inert substantial density, but rather something traversed by restless spiritual negativity within its inner core).

As Žižek observes, the equation of the soul of subjectivity with an utterly lifeless piece of inactive matter simply sounds ridiculous.[28] Isn't it
impossible to capture the intangible activity of the ever-mobile subject
within the confines of the most vulgar of materialist perspectives, a perspective according to which the truth of subjectivity is an underlying
passive inertness? Žižek's response to this question is that the genuine
subject per se ($) is this very incompatibility between subject-term (i.e.,
spirit) and predicate-term (i.e., bone):

> The proposition "the Spirit is a bone" provokes in us a sentiment of radi-
> cal, unbearable contradiction; it offers an image of grotesque discord, of
> an extremely negative relationship. However . . . it is precisely thus that
> we produce its speculative truth, because *this negativity, this unbearable*
> *discord, coincides with subjectivity itself,* it is the only way to make present
> and "palpable" the utmost—that is, self-referential—negativity which
> characterizes the spiritual subjectivity. We *succeed* in transmitting the
> dimension of subjectivity *by means of the failure itself,* through the radical
> insufficiency, through the absolute maladjustment of the predicate in
> relation to the subject. (Žižek 1989, 207)

As he adds a few pages later, "the subject is strictly correlative to its own
impossibility; its limit is its positive condition" (Žižek 1989, 209). Hence,
for Žižek, subjectivity isn't to be identified as the spirit opposed to the
bone, but instead as the very opposition between immaterial spirit and
material bone. The absurdity of Hegel's phrenological formula succeeds
in highlighting the futile absurdity of trying to attach, with the fixity of a
once-and-for-all finality, specific, determinate predicates to the spiritual
negativity of the subject:

> Our first reaction to Hegel's "The spirit is a bone" is "But this is sense-
> less—spirit, its absolute, self-relating negativity, is the very *opposite* of the
> inertia of a skull, this dead object!"—however, this very awareness of the
> thorough incongruity between "spirit" and "bone" *is* the "Spirit," its radi-
> cal negativity. (Žižek 2000f, 30)

This formula's failure adequately and satisfactorily to reflect/represent
subjectivity is precisely the same failure that defines the essence (or lack

thereof) of the Hegelian-Žižekian $-as-empty. The subject truly emerges through the coming to light of the unsuturable gap between itself and its multiple possible operators of identificatory subjectification—the upshot here being that all such operators are ultimately "bones" (in Lacan's language, subjectification amounts to the progressive "cadaverization" or "corpsification" of $, its "fading" into the lifelessness of objectified, reified identities mediated by skeletal structures consisting of signifier-like elements).

Žižek's reading of Hegel's discussion of phrenology makes clear yet again that the subject-for-itself, as an explicit, self-relating negativity devoid of any concrete determinateness (i.e., $-as-empty), surfaces only after the implosion of identification. The "That's not me!" dis-identification bringing into view the void of $ occurs following several unsuccessful attempts at establishing lasting forms of "That's me!" identification. Of course, this is quite consonant with the basic spirit of Hegelian dialectical philosophy, given that, for Hegel, truth is reached not by avoiding error, but rather precisely by passing through error; the key insights of dialectics require that certain mistakes must be made before these insights disclose themselves. There are no shortcuts, no safe paths allowing for errors/mistakes to be bypassed in the progress toward subsequent stages of philosophical reflection (in this vein, bypassing the false ultimately blocks further movement in the direction of the true).

So it is with the Žižekian delineation of subject formation: the void of the pure self-reflexive negativity of $-as-empty doesn't reveal itself until after the unfolding of a series of failed attempts to conceal this void through processes of identificatory subjectification. In other words, the faceless anonymity of the cogito-like subject is not, as Žižek sometimes insinuates, an a priori structural emptiness preexisting the sequences of subjectifying identifications that try in vain to fill up this hole in the fabric of constituted reality.[29] Rather, this hole is gradually hollowed out through the increasingly apparent contingency of all operators of subjectification, a contingency that becomes apparent solely through the rise and fall of various temporarily hegemonic master signifiers of identity jostling with and displacing one another. In short, the more frantic is the "mad dance of identification," the more visible is the identityless void of $. To paraphrase Marx, when all solid identities melt into air, the subject as devoid of any solid identity begins to emerge (hence the increasing timeliness, rather than outdated irrelevance, of the modern Cartesian-Kantian-Hegelian depiction of the subject in a postmodern world of increasingly malleable and plastic modes of subjectifying identifications—Žižek stresses that the cogito-as-$ attains greater degrees of prominence with the growing "multicultural" awareness of multiple varieties of communal identities,[30] an awareness on the rise in the world of globalized advanced capitalism).

What's more, this point concerning the subject's birth out of the ashes of subjectification subtly differentiates Žižek from Laclau and Mouffe. The "radical democratic" model of hegemony advanced by Laclau and Mouffe (as indebted to Claude Lefort's quasi-structuralist, vaguely Lacanian analysis of what distinguishes democracy from non-democratic governing arrangements) involves there being the form of an empty place structurally preexisting the content of the hegemonic articulator-elements temporarily occupying this place. Politically speaking, the locus of power in a democratic system is a node defined by the structure of the laws and institutions of that system, rather than an individual person such as a monarch or dictator; in a democracy, the place of power and the person occupying this place must never be allowed to fuse together, with the time-limited nature (limited by terms in office) of the person's occupation of this place being an indispensable means for maintaining this separation.[31] Commenting on the "peculiarity of modern democracy," Lefort notes that "of all the regimes of which we know, it is the only one to have represented power in such a way as to show that power is an *empty place*" (Lefort 1988, 225). By contrast, the properly conceived Žižekian version of the rapport between form and content in the logic of hegemony (as per his Hegelian theory of the dialectic between subject and subjectification) stipulates that the empty place (i.e., the void of $-as-for-itself-emptiness) only comes into fully effective existence out of and after a multitude of destructive, violent wars for dominance have been waged among those articulator-elements (i.e., $-as-out-of-joint, as a series of stubborn attachments to operators of subjectification) competing for the status of hegemonic concrete universal (S_1). Succinctly stated, Žižek's Hegelian subject as empty place isn't a static a priori given that precedes hegemonic struggles—along these lines, Žižek accuses Laclau of being a closet Kantian due to a perceived structural formalism in the latter's radical democratic model of hegemony[32]—but instead is a genetic outcome or product arising as a subsequent result from hegemonic struggles (however, more recent discussions of Lefort, universalism, and populism between Laclau and Žižek have further complicated this picture).

To return to the guiding thread of the discussion here, what about the Žižekian reading of Hegel's "spirit is a bone"? In his essay "The Phrenology of Spirit," Mladen Dolar contributes his own detailed examination of this perplexing phrenological infinite judgment. As is the case with Žižek too, Dolar's reading initially strikes one as a somewhat heterodox interpretation of Hegel. Dolar insists that the yawning chasm separating "spirit" (i.e., subject) from "bone" (i.e., predicate) in the phrenological

infinite judgment is an antinomic gap that cannot be sublated dialectically. Like Žižek, he argues that this gap is the very index of the genuine
actuality of subjectivity proper:

> The self-conscious subject of Reason could not find itself in anything
> positive, but this bit of the contingent, immediate being represented by
> the bone demonstrates precisely the fact that the impossibility of find-
> ing itself *is* the subject, it is coextensive with it. If it could embody itself
> as something positive, it would cease to be a subject, it would turn into
> a lifeless Thing. If the subject is just this impossibility of being anything
> positive, then the phrenological proposition, "the Spirit is a bone," is the
> positive demonstration of this impossibility. (Dolar 1994a, 69)

From an orthodox exegetical perspective, Hegel's idealism is centered
on the assertion that thinking and being are one (contra, for instance,
Kant's transcendental idealism, according to which the cognizing activities of the epistemic agent are separate from the ontological stuff of the
inaccessible noumenal realm). Viewed in this traditional light, the stages
of dialectical progress mapped by Hegel amount to successively closer
approaches to the truth that thinking and being, subject and object, are
inextricably intertwined in an inseparable union; the ultimate *Aufhebung*
is the dialectical dissolution of the very distinction between subjective
ideality and objective reality. And yet Dolar proceeds to propose that
Hegel's conception of subjectivity requires the dialectical sublation of
the thinking-versus-being opposition remaining incomplete and unfinished. In other words, the subject remains only for so long as the antinomic divide separating the spirit of negativity from the bone of matter is
sustained by something that successfully resists the absorbing undertow
of the *Aufhebung*. Dolar maintains:

> The Hegelian subject is subject only in so far as "all substance" is not
> subject; a certain non-subjectifiable point is "the condition of possibility"
> of the subject. If the subject could get rid of it, dissolve it in the dialecti-
> cal movement, if it could recognize itself in it or appropriate it, it would
> cease to be a subject. The infinite judgment denotes this impossibility.
> (Dolar 1994a, 71–72)

Žižek echoes this line of argumentation:

> So we have here the structure of the Moebius strip: the subject is correla-
> tive to the object, but in a negative way—subject and object can never
> "meet"; they are in the same place, but on opposite sides of the Moebius
> strip. Or—to put it in philosophical terms—subject and object are iden-

tical in the Hegelian sense of the speculative coincidence/identity of
radical opposites: when Hegel praises the speculative truth of the vulgar
materialist thesis of phrenology "The Spirit is a bone," his point is not
that the spirit can actually be reduced to the shape of the skull, but
that there is a spirit (subject) only in so far as there is some bone (some
inert material, non-spiritual remainder/leftover) that *resists* its spiritual
sublation-appropriation-mediation. (Žižek 2000f, 28–29)

Both Dolar and Žižek are committed to a theory of subjectivity according to which the subject (more specifically, the fully constituted subject
as a for-itself emptiness) is a forever-alienated X, a homeless misfit, inherently incapable of finding a proper place within the domains of either nature or culture. In fact, this barred S ($), in its various guises
and manifestations, is the factor responsible for the barring of both the
Real ($-as-in-itself is the immanent negativity perturbing the "not all"
of being's conflict-riddled substance) and the Symbolic ($-as-for-itself
is the impossible-to-represent void defying reduction to the mediating
sociocultural terms of the big Other—$-as-self-reflexive-negativity is, in
a sense that dovetails nicely with Hegel's equation of the spirit with a
bone, the proverbial "bone in the throat" of the symbolic order). Consequently, Dolar and Žižek insist that there is always a stain/tain, a spot
of opacity, on the surfaces of nature and culture interfering with the
otherwise smooth two-way flow of dialectical reflection between thinking and being, between subject and object. Without this opaque obstacle
(i.e., bone), subjectivity would lose itself through full immersion in the
immediacy of being; the subject would be drowned in and by the completeness of a self-enclosed substance (i.e., a subjectless substance).[33] An
internal limit to the movement of *Aufhebung* preserves the (non-)being
of $. Both Dolar and Žižek regard the genuine Hegelian gesture con-
densed in the infinite judgment of his phrenological formula to be the
sudden transformation of the subject's failure to find itself amidst the
debris of the world into a success (i.e., the lack of adequate externally
mediated representation by concrete entities is subjectivity at its purest
insofar as instances of this lack present the subject with chances to grasp
itself self-reflexively as a negativity irreducible to representation). The
idea of finally surmounting the division between the spirit of subjectivity
and the bone of objectivity is a pseudo-Hegelian (rather than properly
Hegelian) notion.

15

The Parallax of Time: Temporality and the Structure of Subjectivity

A further interpretive twist can and should be grafted onto Hegel's "the spirit is a bone." Phrenology focuses on one sort of bone in particular, namely, the human skull. Furthermore, a footnote in *Tarrying with the Negative* draws attention to a phrase that occurs in the final paragraph of the *Phenomenology of Spirit:* "the Calvary of absolute Spirit" (*die Schädelstätte des absoluten Geistes*).[1] Žižek notes that the literal translation of *Schädelstätte* is "the site of skulls."[2] Following this observation, he suggests:

> The infinite judgment "spirit is a bone (a skull)" acquires thereby a
> somewhat unexpected dimension: what is revealed to the Spirit in the
> backwards-gaze of its *Er-Innerung,* inwardizing memory, are the scattered
> skulls of the past "figures of consciousness." The worn-out Hegelian
> formula according to which the Result, in its abstraction from the path
> leading to it, is a corpse, has to be inversed once again: this "path" itself
> is punctuated by scattered skulls. (Žižek 1993, 269)

Žižek aims to invert the perspective in which the concluding moment of the dialectical progress of consciousness from sensuous certainty to absolute knowing charted by Hegel in the *Phenomenology* appears to be a lifeless, static totality (i.e., absolute knowledge as an achieved state of rest, a motionless notional eternity that has kicked away the disposable ladder of negativity-driven existence so as serenely to distance itself from the temporal flux of living immanence). Instead, the figures of consciousness that precede the moment of absolute knowing are what is dead and inert, amounting to so many reified (yet inevitably liquidated) partial positions adopted by the restless subject of the dialectic. Put differently, Žižek's point here is that absolute knowing isn't a bone or skull as frozen stability. On the contrary, absolute knowing, as the self-relating of pure negativity, entails the insight that there is no such position of conclusive stability; the reconciliation achieved by absolute knowing amounts to the acceptance of an insurmountable incompleteness, an irresolvable driving tension that cannot finally be put to rest through one last *Aufhebung.*[3] Consequently, the preceding figures/moments of the dialectical process reveal themselves to be unsuccessful attempts to congeal this absolute negativity into lifeless, static forms (i.e., these preceding figures/moments, and not the culminating finale of absolute knowing, are bones/skulls).

However, what about the theme of death that this image of the skull obviously calls to mind? Given this imagistic evocation, one could say that the Hegelian metaphor of the skull is shaped by yet another dialectical convergence of opposites: this inert, static object, this remainder silently testifying to a now-dead former life, (also) represents its opposite, namely, the frantic, kinetic march of time, the fragile insubstantiality of a finite existence exposed to a mortality inseparable from relentless temporal negativity. The skull is a lifeless, motionless object that simultaneously embodies the rapidly moving life of subjectivity (insofar as this subject is essentially mortal as subjected to the ceaseless passage of time—in Heideggerian parlance, *Dasein* as a "being-towards-death"). So Hegel's phrenological infinite judgment "spirit is a bone" signifies, in a highly condensed mode, the truth that subjective spirituality is a temporalized mortal finitude alienating itself within a series of reified figures. The opposition that converges in the evocative image of the skull, an image of both kinetic life and static death, is an opposition internal to and constitutive of *Geist* as temporal negativity.

Žižek's ontology of the Real and corresponding transcendental materialist theory of subjectivity involve (at least) three central notions: first, nature as the barred Real of dematerialized matter, as being bereft of the massiveness of weighty self-enclosure à la a totally consistent One-All (i.e., substance as already an in-itself subject, $ as *Todestrieb*-like negativity); second, culture as the barred Symbolic of the inconsistent big Other (i.e., the symbolic order, the mediating milieu of identificatory subjectification, as containing ineliminable loopholes and short-circuiting points of potential dysfunctional breakdown); and third, the movement of the monistic One (i.e., the conflict-ridden substance of [human] being) becoming the dualistic Two (i.e., mind versus body, transcendental versus empirical, noumenal versus phenomenal, ontological versus ontic, etc.), a Two refracting the One into a series of incommensurable parallax splits (i.e., subjective negativity as separating off from and thereby transcending its immanent material-ontological ground, establishing itself as the second-order self-relating negativity of a for-itself void). The relatively simple theoretical gesture of directly identifying the subjective negativity focused on by Žižek with temporality has the tempting appeal of tying together the above notions into an elegant systematic unity as well as enabling the vexed issue of the relationship between transcendentalism and materialism to be readdressed productively. Accepting the equation "$\$$ = temporal negativity" permits one to see both how subject is immanent to substance and why it is that any and every subjectifying identification is vulnerable to failure. That is to say, this equation clarifies the perhaps still-enigmatic ontogenetic process of transubstantiation leading from $\$$-as-in-itself as the death drive (construed as the name for the inner inconsistency of the ontological foundation of human nature, namely, the conflict-plagued libidinal economy as the point of departure for the trajectories of subject formation) through $\$$-as-out-of-joint (an out-of-jointness generated by an unbalanced investment in and fixation upon privileged operators of subjectification) to $\$$-as-for-itself as the void of self-relating negativity (an abyssal emptiness opening up through the successive implosions of subjectifying identifications).

As observed previously, Plato equates the visible realm of tangible entities with ceaseless change over time. He contends that the essence (or, more accurately, essencelessness) of material being, a dimension disclosed via the sensory-perceptual powers of the physical body, is nothing other than a puppet theater of dematerialized, shadowy pseudo-things deprived of genuine ontological heft. This lack of true weight is arguably due to the fact that all tangible entities are subject to the ravages of time, the cycles of generation and corruption. Plato's visible realm is traversed by temporal negativity. And this unstable plane of continual fluctuation is stabilized through the invocation of an eternal, unchanging "other world" of immortal ideational beings, namely, Platonic ideas. Žižek's Hegelian materialism tacitly redeploys this Platonic notion of materiality as insubstantial—but of course, without endorsing, alongside this redeployment, Plato's objectionable idealist metaphysical realism (i.e., the assertion that a transcendent supersensible realm of immateriality forever exists in and of itself apart from the immanence of unstable material being). The ultimate insubstantial substance of Platonic material (non-)being is time-as-becoming (as per the opposition between enduring being and transitory becoming), that is, temporal negativity as the constantly inconstant flux of alteration. Time is what prevents the visible realm from closing in upon itself through satisfactorily achieving the completion of a lasting harmonious balance expressible in the form of mathematical-style eternal and unchanging truths; immanent material being is self-sundering, split from within by temporality as its intrinsic essence(lessness). If one opts to appropriate this Platonic philosopheme and correspondingly to treat the ideational stabilization of this time-ravaged phenomenal whirlpool in a Hegelian-Žižekian fashion—any posited supersensible world, whether as (to take two obvious examples) Plato's intelligible realm of the forms or Kant's noumenal domain of things-in-themselves, is a secondary genetic by-product as reactionary response to the anarchy of appearances—then one already has in place the rudiments of an account for the transition from the *Todestrieb*-like subject-as-in-itself (i.e., substance as subject insofar as substance is split from within by temporal negativity) to subjectification (i.e., the taming and domesticating of this negativity immanent to phenomenal materiality through the synthesizing intervention of, for instance, the Platonic soul's access to ideas/forms or the Kantian unification of the fragmented field of experience via the concepts of the understanding, the ideas of reason, and the activity of the imagination).

Furthermore, one could sketch another line of argumentation (a line branching off from Plato's recourse to mathematics) for the ultimate equivalence of materiality and temporality: the fact that pure mathematics perhaps provides the sole manifestation of eternal and unchanging truths hints at this equivalence. That is to say, pure mathematics refers to no determinate, specified "what"; it is not constrained by references to particular empirical-ontic entities (as already seen, this is a point also made by Badiou in the course of justifying his transferral of responsibility for the formulation of a fundamental ontology from philosophy to mathematics—more specifically, to set theory). Only in removing themselves from every relation to material being(s) do mathematical truths attain a status exempting them from the fluctuating ravages of time's incessant passage (as truths true in all times and all places). This directly implies that materiality is fundamentally temporal in nature, since a reference or relation to it prohibits the formulation of utterly timeless truths.

Consequently, the somewhat counterintuitive becoming-insubstantial of substance (i.e., the Žižekian dematerialization of matter discerned in, among other sources, quantum physics, cognitive science, and, arguably, Platonic metaphysics too) again thrusts itself forward. The hyperactive vortex of material nature becomes almost immaterial when looked at in light of its inability to crystallize anything lasting and permanent. (Recent discussions in scientific circles suggest that, on the grandest of cosmic time scales, even the fundamental laws of physics, those features of the material universe supposedly enjoying the status of invariant constants, have changed before and will change again. Maybe, in the terms of the simplest fundaments of a Hegel-influenced fundamental ontology, the only constant is the lack of constancy, the only invariant is continual variance, etc.) Thanks to an absolute refusal of ties to any spatiotemporal "this" or "that," to the hyperactive vortex of material nature, the conceptions of mathematics (as opposed to the ever-changing perceptions of the sensing body immersed in the flows of the visible realm) calmly establish themselves as enduring and fixed coordinates. Thus, at least in Plato's eyes, these mathematical "entities" appear to be more substantial, more ontologically hefty, than anything material (a perspective demanding the inversion of a certain quotidian view according to which material being is a hard, durable substratum and, by contrast, numerical conceptual structures are ephemeral ideational abstractions leading nothing more than a weightless phantom existence within the human mind as artificial but useful constructs). Žižek's repeated invocations of the figure of the void hence become more comprehensible against this background: at the most foundational level, the apparent firmness and solidity of material being conceals an underlying, unstable insubstantiality (with the insubstantiality of dematerialized matter ultimately being due to the ceaseless restlessness of temporal negativity). Bringing into consideration the dimension of time, one can say (following Žižek) that the entire universe really is, in a very basic sense, a spectacular dance of the void in which fragmentary, vanishing things (all things being fragmentary and vanishing) come and go at an incalculable number of varying rates of speed.

Similarly, the dialectical movement of Hegel's *Science of Logic* well and truly departs starting from the category of "becoming" as perpetually changing existence. The categories of "being" and "nothing," upon considered analysis, turn out to be false starts. The genuine beginning per se is becoming as the convergence of the opposites of being and nothing. Pure being as such is an empty abstraction devoid of anything determinate. Therefore, it converges with nothing.[4] However, Hegel warns that being and nothing are not simply synthesized here as two previously external categories, since this supposed externality is shown to be a false, fictional abstraction.[5] Likewise, being and nothing are brought together (i.e., unified) in a conflicting, discordant tension (i.e., separated) within becoming, so, as a paradoxical unity-in-diversity, they are neither entirely the same nor completely different.[6]

For Hegel, the movement of becoming is a result of the inextricable intertwining of being and nothing. In other words, Hegelian becoming is simultaneously the dynamic of being passing into nothing and of nothing passing into being. This two-way dynamic is driven by, among other factors, temporal negativity. The unstoppable movement of time is the passage of nothing into being that forces being to pass into nothing by negating any and every congealed configuration of being(s). This negation by time guarantees that everything apparently solid will, whether sooner or later, melt into air. And yet this air is never empty, but rather is always filled anew with other partial, unsuccessful solidifications. Hegel's ontology is one in which all actually existing things are crystallized objectifications of the antagonism between being and nothing. Everything with actual ontological status is in a state of becoming as a materialization of the dialectical oscillation between being and nothing. Consequently, in this ontology, there is neither brute being as inert raw matter (i.e., subjectless substance) nor pure nothing as entirely dematerialized negativity (i.e., substanceless subject)—substance always involves the subject and vice versa (consequently, Hegelian ontology is neither idealist nor materialist in the traditional senses of these philosophical labels). As Hegel repeats, all of existence is an "impure" admixture of these abstract poles: "Nowhere in heaven or on earth is there anything which does not contain within itself both being and nothing" (Hegel 1969, 85), and correlatively but conversely, nowhere in heaven or on earth is there being by itself or nothing by itself. And again, he maintains that "*there is nothing which is not an intermediate state between being and nothing*" (Hegel 1969, 105).

It is necessary once more to return to Žižek's vehement insistence on the notion of finitude as utterly central to Hegelian thought. If, as Hegel asserts, everything is immersed in the moving waters of becoming, then one legitimately can claim that everything is finite as limited in and by time. However, this temporal finitude is, at the same time, the Absolute with a capital A as such—and this because of Hegel's absolutization of finitude à la Kant, his denial that there is a seamlessly consistent Elsewhere (i.e., a timeless cosmic One-All, whether as Plato's heaven of ideas/forms or Kant's contradiction-free noumenal Real) transcending the immanence of being as "not all" (i.e., being as an incomplete inconsistency shot through with antagonistic contradictions). Unstable immanence is the Absolute precisely because, with the Hegelian ontological radicalization of Kantian epistemological acosmism, there is no stable transcendence above and beyond this immanence. An essential aspect of the realization of "absolute knowing" achieved by a finally self-relating *Geist* is this spirit's appreciation of its unqualified immersion within the flowing flux of temporalized being-as-becoming. In a manner relevant to the present analysis, Jean-Luc Nancy elegantly summarizes the basic gist of Hegel's treatment of substance as subject (or, one could say, of matter as spirit). He clarifies this thus:

> The pure element of sense or of truth—what Hegel calls "concept" or "grasp" from the point of view of its activity and the "idea" from the point of view of its presentation—is the element of "spirit," which names infinite relation itself, the step out of self into the other of all reality. This "life of the spirit" is not something separate; it is not a spirituality that floats above and beyond materiality. It is nothing—or simple abstraction—as long as it remains considered in itself as if it were outside the world of effectivity. It is the breath of spirit, but this breath is not an

immateriality: on the contrary, it is the unsettling of matter inseparable from matter itself, the sensible insofar as it senses, is sensed, and senses itself. It names the restlessness and awakening of the world, immanence always already tense, extended and distended within itself as well as out-side itself; space and time, already, as the ex-position of every position. (Nancy 2002, 19)

Nancy adds: "Spirit is not something separate—neither from matter nor from nature, neither from the body, from contingency, nor from the event—because it is itself nothing other than separation. It is separation as the opening of relation" (Nancy 2002, 19). Substance is subject—and given that subject doesn't transcend substance, subject is also substance (i.e., an immanent feature of substance)—insofar as substance is a mo-nistic One split from within by a reflectivity/reflexivity internal to its own being (what Nancy quite aptly describes as "the unsettling of matter inseparable from matter itself, the sensible insofar as it senses, is sensed, and senses itself"). Each individual consciousness really is the natural material universe staring back at itself through the eyes of something immeasurably smaller in relation to it than a grain of sand; the human gaze actually is the universe gazing upon itself in and through a finite part of itself.

What's more, fully accepting the Hegelian radicalization of the Kant-ian notion of finitude requires that the individual view him/herself as entirely immanent to material nature as (in)substantial being. However, doing so in a properly Hegelian fashion doesn't lead to any sort of stan-dard version of reductive materialism (in which accepting this imma-nence of subject to substance entails admitting the epiphenomenal, il-lusory status of subjectivity). Put differently, viewing oneself as immanent to nature doesn't (just) mean that one is therefore wholly natural in a banal, straightforward fashion (as, for instance, Newtonian mechanis-tic matter thoroughly determined by physical cause-and-effect laws). It (also) means that, in a manner of speaking, nature itself is unnatural, that the entire category of nature (as matter, substance, etc.) must be re-thought if the reflectivity and reflexivity embodied by human beings is to be included within the monistic One of the natural material universe (a One without an Other as a transcendent Beyond or Elsewhere). The un-avoidable philosophical price to be paid for naturalizing human being is the reciprocal denaturalizing of material being so as to accommodate the former type of being within the latter. The capacity for (self-)relating "within nature more than nature itself," this immanent reflectivity/re-flexivity (i.e., substance as subject), is precisely what creates the multiple parallax effects dividing the One from itself into Two (or more).

One of the intrinsic powers of this capacity for reflexive reflection embedded within the being of substance itself (the capacity that drives the ontogenetic trajectory of subject formation out of substance) is what philosophy, from Aristotle to the present, refers to as "imagination" (recall here both Žižek's musings about the rapport between the Kantian synthetic imagination and the Hegelian destructive imagination as well as Richard Dawkins's linking of exceptional human autonomy with the ability to imagine times other than the present—see chapter 13). In book 3 of *De Anima* (particularly chapter 10), Aristotle, in the course of delineating the abilities and features of the intellective faculty of the soul (the faculty possessed by human beings as "rational animals," setting them apart from all other soul-endowed living beings), ties the workings of the intellect, especially its practical function of planning long-term courses of future action, to an awareness of times other than the present. Whereas perception (the perceptive faculty of the soul possessed by all sentient beings, animals as well as humans) is riveted to the immediacy of the given here and now, the intellect, aided and abetted by the imagination's ability to envision entities and occurrences that do not exist in the directly perceived present, is free to range over an expanse of possibilities vastly exceeding the actual now accessible to perception. (Aristotle distinguishes between sensory imagination, which he declares both animals and humans to possess—this type of imagination is the involuntary mental imaging of objects of desire that gets roused into action by appetites for food, sex, and the like—and rational imagination as the assistant of the intellect, which only reason-endowed beings possess.)[7] Drawing on the reservoir of past perceptual traces retained by memory, the imagination is at liberty to reassemble these traces into novel configurations, some of which point toward possible futures of concern to the intellect.

For Aristotle, the soul (*psuchê*, the etymological origin of Freud's "psyche") is a set of dynamics driven by desires (i.e., appetites). Different desires correspond to different faculties of the soul (Aristotle lists five faculties: nutritive, propagative, perceptive, locomotive, and intellective). In book 3, chapter 10 of *De Anima,* Aristotle discusses the relation between appetency and the intellect. He distinguishes between practical intellect (i.e., the part of the intellect concerned with figuring out the best ways to go about satisfying the desires of the other faculties of the soul besides the intellect itself) and speculative intellect (i.e., the part of the intellect concerned with its own self-satisfaction, namely, with gratifying the natural curiosity, the hard-wired desire to understand for the sake of understanding itself, forming an essential aspect of the desires moving any intelligent being—Aristotle names this purely intellectual appetite "rational wish").[8] Both the practical and speculative portions of the intellect can and do come into conflict with the appetitive influences of the other faculties of the soul. Aristotelian "reason," as the combined workings of the intellect and the (rational as opposed to sensory) imagination, often finds itself pulling in different directions than those "irrational," non-intellectual desires clamoring for immediate gratification. Aristotle asserts that reason's cognizance of time is precisely what gives rise to the conflict between it and the noisy rabble of other appetites: "Now desires arise which are contrary to one another, and this occurs whenever reason and the appetites are opposed, that is, in those animals which have a perception of time" (Aristotle 1991, 97). Unlike other sentient beings confined to the immediacy of the here and now present (i.e., non-human animals), human beings, as possessing the intellective as well as perceptive faculty of soul, live in several times simultaneously. And dwelling in multiple times creates conflicts at the level of the appetites and desires moving this sort of temporalized living being.

Jumping forward into more recent philosophical history, both the young Schelling and the early Heidegger propose, in similar yet distinct ways, regrounding theories of subjectivity as well as fundamental ontology on the idea of time.[9] The doctrine of the soul outlined by Schelling in his 1802 dialogue *Bruno* (a doctrine with some striking resemblances to that of Aristotle) foreshadows essential aspects of Heidegger's analytic of *Dasein* (as sketched in *Being and Time* [1927], *The Basic Problems of Phenomenology* [1928], and *Kant and the Problem of Metaphysics* [1929]).[10] Like the young Schelling, the early Heidegger characterizes the transcendence particular to being human not in the standard philosophical terms according to which this transcendent dimension amounts to a timeless, frozen eternity (such as an immortal soul à la Plato or a transcendental or noumenal "I" à la Kant); for Heidegger, the transcendent dimension of subjectivity-as-*Dasein* is nothing other than its temporal "ecstasis," namely, its constant exceeding of its present "there" (*Da*), its continual stretching beyond the now.[11] *Dasein* never simply lives within the immediacy of the here and now. Its being spills over into other times; more accurately, its genuine being is this very spilling over. *Dasein* exists within several different temporal registers all at the same time. Additionally, Heidegger doesn't just temporalize human being via his analytic of *Dasein*. At the more general level of fundamental ontology, he goes so far as to assert that being is time—the ontological questions of philosophy arise because *Dasein* is the (temporal) being for whom its own being is a question—at least insofar as temporality (as the transcendental basis making possible the being of *Dasein* as such) forms the ultimate frame/ horizon for the construction of any possible ontology by *Dasein*.[12] Contra the Platonic tradition within the history of philosophy in its various guises and instantiations, being cannot be kept separate from time, left serenely untouched by the movements of temporality.

Jacques-Alain Miller maintains that "what animates philosophical discourse" (more specifically, a certain "traditional" philosophy ultimately indebted to Plato) is a concern with "sheltering being from time. It is this effort which gave birth to the fabulous concept, the extraordinary myth of eternity" (Miller 2005, 17). Miller proceeds to proclaim that Heidegger's groundbreaking philosophical breakthrough consists in the temporalization of being:

> This sheltering of being outside time is certainly crucial, since the precise innovation Heidegger introduced in philosophy was the opposite— proposing the conjunction of time and being. Always dominant was the notion that what exists is outside time because time introduces negativity: it introduces disappearance, wear and tear, aging, death, decline. Freud referred to La Rochefoucauld's phrase: one cannot look death in the face any more than the sun. One might also say that this is true also of time, that there is also (we invent this) a *horror temporis,* a horror of time. (Miller 2005, 17)

The fact that mortality is granted such a central role in Heidegger's analytic of *Dasein* (in his famous discussion of being-towards-death from division 2, section 1 of *Being and Time*) is no accident. Confronting the traditional philosophical *horror temporis* and traversing this horror so as to temporalize both being and human being requires assigning mortal finitude a privileged place as a structuring factor in the temporalized existence of subjectivity. Miller's remarks also gesture in the direction of the topic of time in psychoanalysis. In speaking of a "horror of time," Miller subtly hints that certain aspects of temporality might best be situated in the Lacanian register of the Real.[13]

On first glance, it perhaps seems as though Lacan, falling into the trap Bergson denounces as the "spatialization of time" (i.e., the problematic reduction of time to quantifiable points on lines or circles),[14] treats time as a strictly Symbolic construct. In his early work of the 1940s and his late work of the 1970s, he compares temporality to spatio-synchronic structures, whether these structures are the carefully contrived game-theoretic rules of a prisoners' dilemma (as per the 1946 essay "Logical Time and the Assertion of Anticipated Certainty: A New Sophism") or the mathematically delineable surfaces of topology (as per the twenty-sixth seminar of 1978–79 on "Topology and Time").[15] However, especially considering Lacan's nuanced reflections on the causality of "traumatic" (or, more broadly, psychically significant) events (i.e., the *tuché* of the Real) in relation to the unconsciously encoded effects of these same events (i.e., the *automaton* of the Symbolic) as presented in his deservedly celebrated eleventh seminar of 1964, the superficial impression that sees Lacanian time as a construction entirely situated within the register of the Symbolic must be discarded. Certain fundamental facets of time/temporality belong to the Real.[16]

Žižek's relatively recent revisions to his depiction of the Lacanian Real underscore that this register isn't to be conceived of as akin to the Kantian noumenal sphere of substantial yet inaccessible things-in-themselves. Instead, he stresses that the Real is, when all is said and done, nothing more than the inconsistency of experiential reality, an inconsistency that prompts the positing of Kantian-style transcendent registers behind or beyond the incompletely synthesized plane of immanent phenomena (a positing that lends a false sense of consistency to inconsistent reality by hypothesizing the deeper being of a substantial fullness as a Real beneath reality). The Žižekian Real surfaces when a multitude of incompatible perspectives appear to compete with each other for access to and articulation of a true Thing as an objective point of reference undistorted by this play of partial perspectives. The genuine nature of the Real is properly apprehended when one realizes that, at least in given instances of a particular sort, there is no such objective point of reference, no pre/non-perspectival Thing grounding the play of partial perspectives. This Real is touched upon solely through the self-shattering of perspective itself, through the internal splitting of the field of phenomena into a series of incommensurable parallaxes; it's the name for the inner blockage or obstacle within reality that thwarts this experientially accessible plane of immanence from bringing its multiple perspectival manifestations together into a consistent, unified One-All.[17]

The history of philosophical efforts, beginning with the thinkers of ancient Greece and running up through today, to establish the "real" essence of the thing called "time" strongly indicates that this thing is an instance of the Žižekian Real as irreversible, irreparable parallax-splitting. As soon as one tries to pin down what time in the singular is (i.e., Time as such), or even what each of its parts amounts to as an isolated, distinct category (i.e., past, present, and future), one finds that the temporal "object" of inquiry in question refuses to be pinned down; the times of time repeatedly divide into multiple and seemingly irreconcilable modes/structures. For example, when reflected on, the present-as-now splits into (at a minimum) an eternal presence of full being (i.e., only the now exists, and neither the past nor the future possess any actual ontological status of their own) versus a continually disappearing noth-

ingness (i.e., the now is nothing more than the ephemeral vanishing
mediator between the past and the future). Overall, one could propose
that each of the three dimensions of time (i.e., past, present, and future)
contains within itself this same tripartite division: the past is composed
of the past-past, the present-past, and the future-past; the present is composed of the past-present, the present-present, and the future-present;
the future is composed of the past-future, the present-future, and the
future-future—and each of these nine subcategories would likely multiply even further upon sustained examination (they each can be construed as designating several different phenomena). Žižek proposes
that the Lacanian Real is configured in exactly this way: the Real divides
into the Real-Real, the Symbolic-Real, and the Imaginary-Real (just as
the Symbolic and the Imaginary both refract the three registers [Real,
Symbolic, and Imaginary] within themselves too).[18] Time as such, as the
indivisible, essential X of a Thing hidden behind and grounding these
multiple manifestations of temporality, doesn't exist. Time exists only as
this layered juxtaposition of irreducibly different parallax planes.

Furthermore, with regard to Lacan's register theory, one could maintain that different forms of temporality correspond to each of the three
registers. There is Real time, Symbolic time, and Imaginary time. Interestingly, a similar parallax split arises within each of the temporalities
corresponding to these three Lacanian registers; within each, there's
an antinomic division between, on the one hand, the timelessness of
a repetitive inertia or stasis and, on the other hand, the time of a non-
repetitive becoming or genesis. Not only, as already noted, does Lacan
insist that perfect repetition is impossible due to the fact that repetition
itself invariably engenders difference—correlatively but inversely, with
his one-liner "*Y a d'l'Un*" (There is the One),[19] he suggests that an exceptional element (i.e., the One) repeatedly resurfaces within the differentiating stream of ever-flowing times. In other words, for Lacan, there is
neither timeless repetition without temporal difference nor vice versa.
How does this relate to the three registers of the Real, the Symbolic,
and the Imaginary? Real time is simultaneously a cyclical (a)temporality
paying no heed whatsoever to other modes of temporality as well as the
absolute negativity of pure flux. Symbolic time is simultaneously the im-
mobility of interminably repeatable signifiers as well as the diachronic
dynamics continually subjecting these same signifiers to ongoing alteration. Imaginary time is simultaneously the frozen, quasi-immortal images
of the ego's imago-gestalt as well as the visible reflection of the all-too-
mortal body of flesh displayed by these same mirror images. Delineating
and exploring these Lacanian temporalities in anything close to a satisfactory fashion would be a task requiring a lengthy book unto itself.

One aspect of the Real dimension of time already has been alluded to here apropos Hegelian ontology in relation to the Žižekian distinction between subjectification (i.e., the positive someone) and the subject (i.e., the negative no one): temporal negativity, as the ceaseless restlessness of a movement whose effects appear through the transitory nature of all things as subjected to the cycles of generation and corruption, resists being congealed into stable forms of determinate representation. In particular, subjectification entails the crystallization of reified edifices of identity, edifices built out of inert, lifeless elements (i.e., the "bones" of the spirit as unary traits, etc.). In their very static inertness, these operators of subjectification fail to reflect the ever-mobile negativity of the voidlike subject-as-$. Miller's reflections on Lacanian time are again valuable here. Referring to Lacan's oft-repeated thesis according to which "the signifier is what represents the subject for another signifier," Miller extracts the implications contained within this compact statement:

> Hegel defined the essential subjectivity of time. While space is used objectively, subjectivity is essentially temporal. This is what Lacan asserted. It's what we deal with every day, except that we represent it spatially when we say: "the subject is between the signifiers, it is in the interval." (Miller 2005, 38–39)

Miller continues:

> But, in fact, what's in play here is the temporal order of the signifying chain. In order to simplify I would say: between the past signifier and the future signifier, between the signifier of before and the signifier of after, the barred subject in the Lacanian sense gathers in all the paradoxes of the Aristotelian now. Moreover, one cannot better inscribe the subjective negativity than by writing $, and by describing it, this subject, as an evasive, fugitive being, disappearing, which is effectively an entirely temporal status of the subject . . . What Lacan calls the subject is the temporalization of the signifying pair, which causes the subject to be transported in the signifying chain. (Miller 2005, 39)

How does accepting the formula declaring that "the signifier is what represents the subject for another signifier" lead to a theory of subjectivity in which the subject is a thoroughly temporalized function-movement, the insubstantial (non-)entity of a strange, unfamiliar event ontology based on time rather than being (or, one could say, on being as time)? What does temporality have to do with the subject of the signifier? The explanation itself will take some time here.

Two interrelated Saussurean structuralist axioms inform Lacan's definition of the signifier as that which represents the subject for another
signifier. First, Lacan emphasizes that signifiers are caught up in both
diachronic dynamics and synchronic structures; temporal as well as
spatial differentiation is essential to the status of the signifier.[20] Second,
Lacan insists that signifiers come in sets of two or more signifiers; both
synchronic and diachronic differentiation depend on the existence of
more than one element, the minimal signifying battery being S_1 and S_2.[21]
As Jean-Claude Milner explains, Lacanian signifiers are always situated in
"chains," namely, diachronic concatenations of multiple signifying units
(with each unit differentially determining and being determined in turn
by the other units within the chain in which it's embedded).[22] Similarly,
in the sixteenth seminar, Lacan notes that having a chain of two or more
signifiers is requisite for the coming into being of the subject; there must
be a (temporal-diachronic) movement from S_1 to S_2 in order to produce
the event of $.[23]

Paul-Laurent Assoun pinpoints the first appearance of the formula
"the signifier is what represents the subject for another signifier" in
Lacan's 1960 *écrit* "The Subversion of the Subject and the Dialectic of
Desire in the Freudian Unconscious."[24] Therein Lacan asks, "Once the
structure of language is recognized in the unconscious, what sort of subject can we conceive of for it?" and begins laying out his answer with
reference to the signifier "I" as a linguistic shifter (à la Benveniste).[25]
However, regarding this "I"-as-shifter, he quickly warns that "it designates
the enunciating subject, but does not signify him" (Lacan 2006o, 677).
What does Lacan have in mind with this distinction between "designating" and "signifying"? As is well known, during this period of his teaching in the early 1960s, Lacan forges a distinction between the "subject
of enunciation" (*sujet de l'énonciation*) and the "subject of the utterance"
(*sujet du énoncé*); the former is the verb-like speaking subject setting in
motion diachronically unfolding chains of signifiers, whereas the latter
is the noun-like spoken subject subjected to being determined by uttered chains of signifiers (or, as Lacan later phrases this distinction in his
1973 essay "*L'étourdit*," there is a difference between the "saying" [*dire*] of
enunciation and the "said" [*dit*] of the utterance[26]). Translated into the
more philosophical language of Žižek's Hegelian Lacanianism, enunciating subjectivity is the anonymous, faceless subject unable to encounter
a satisfactory representational reflection of itself at the level of subjectifying utterances—and this because it is the insubstantiality of temporal
negativity, an empty variable forever on the move through the alienating
universe of the comparatively less mobile symbolic order of static signifiers.

So the "I" as linguistic shifter, the first-person pronoun, is the signifying element belonging to the dimension of the subject of the utterance that "designates the subject insofar as he is currently speaking" (i.e., the subject of enunciation as whoever or whatever is speaking at a given present moment).[27] It should briefly be noted that the "I"-as-shifter can and sometimes does signify (rather than merely designate) the subject of enunciation, but not necessarily in all instances in which it's used (sometimes it just designates anonymously an uttering-at-time-t). Now Lacan proceeds to clarify the difference between the enunciating subject being signified rather than being designated vis-à-vis the phenomenon of the *ne explétif* in French grammar. He alleges that many grammarians erroneously dismiss this grammatical device as "sheer whimsy,"[28] as a superfluous, excessive bit of insignificant linguistic window dressing. By contrast, Lacan, having carefully distinguished between the two sides of the subject of the signifier (i.e., enunciation versus utterance), maintains that the occurrence of an instance of the *ne explétif* in a sentence signals a moment in which the subject of enunciation brings itself into view through the *ne* as a subtle indicator of how it positions itself with respect to the meaning of the signifying content uttered. Bruce Fink helpfully compares the French *ne explétif* to certain employments of the English word *but* (as in, for example, "I can't help but think that . . . " or "I cannot deny but that . . . "). Fink contends that the French *ne* and the English *but* are each means of expressing an attitude of ambivalence toward the meaningful content of the sentence uttered (an attitude coloring the position of the subject of enunciation) without, for all that, disrupting or repudiating the literal meaning of the sentence per se as the sense established in the form of an utterance.[29] Philippe Van Haute claims that the occurrence of the *ne explétif* makes for the difference between, in its absence, the "impersonal" phenomenon of a simple assertive sentence in which the subject of enunciation's intention-to-signify coincides with (or collapses/fades into) the thus-established position of the subject of the utterance, and, in its presence, the "personal" phenomenon of indicating, through the *ne*, an affectively inflected distance between the speaker (i.e., enunciation) and the significance of what the speaker spoke (i.e., utterance).[30] The signifier *ne* or *but* marks, within the uttered sentence, the enunciator's unease with what he or she uttered. Consequently, for Lacan, an "I" is "designated" when there is no gap indicated between enunciation and utterance, whereas an "I" is "signified" when there is indeed a gap indicated between enunciation and utterance.

Much later in "The Subversion of the Subject," Lacan introduces his thereafter interminably repeated mantra concerning the subject's rapport with signifiers. He states:

> My definition of the signifier (there is no other) is as follows: a signifier
> is what represents the subject to another signifier. This latter signifier is
> therefore the signifier to which all the other signifiers represent the sub-
> ject—which means that if this signifier is missing, all the other signifiers
> represent nothing. For something is only represented to. (Lacan 2006o,
> 693–94)

Lacanian theory maintains that the minimal signifying structure is the chain $S/S_1 \rightarrow S'/S_2$. Additionally, these two signifiers aren't equal. As later defined by Lacan in the seventeenth seminar, S_1 is the master signifier (i.e., the arbitrary point of departure for signifying chains), and S_2 is the matheme standing for the various other signifiers charged with the task of, so to speak, fleshing out S_1. These S_2s labor to elaborate a network of content (as "knowledge" [*savoir*]) on the basis of the (contingent) anchoring provided by S_1.[31] In the passage quoted immediately above, "the signifier to which all the other signifiers represent the subject" would seemingly be the master signifier. And one would expect here that this master signifier would be the subject-term of a sentence as a proper name or personal pronoun. However, in reference to the left-to-right diachronic movement of the sentence from one signifier (S/S_1) to another (S'/S_2), Lacan indicates that the "latter signifier" (S'/S_2) is what quilts together the chain of signifiers in the mode of a *point de capiton*. The master signifier (S_1) merely represents "for" or "to" other signifiers (S_2s), and these other signifiers have, as it were, the final word. These latter signifiers, as situated at the point of punctuation bringing a given sentential utterance to a close, determine the meaningful status of the initial subject-term (S_1) initiating the utterance (a determination swiftly transpiring after the fact of the initial subject-term having been pronounced). Once the chain of two or more signifiers as a sentential utterance has been "punctuated" (i.e., brought to a close), the subject of the utterance is constituted at the expense of the subject of enunciation (the latter tends to disappear behind the façade of the former—in the language of Lacan's eleventh seminar, the enunciator fades into the alienating medium of the utterance[32]). This uttered dimension of subjectivity is the subject as subjected to the signifier, a dimension (to resort to a neologism from Lacan's teachings of the 1970s, a *dit-mension* [said-dimension, dimension of the said][33]) that Lacan insists is constitutive of subjectivity as such. In Žižekian parlance, the punctuating closure of an utterance brings about an effect of subjectification, a reifying freezing of $ into the congealed inertness of meaning through the fleshing out of S_1 (as the [in principle] empty proper name as rigid designator or personal pronoun as linguistic shifter) by a plethora of S_2s. Or, in

Žižek's Hegelese, the "spirit" of the subject of enunciation finds itself confronting the alterity of an external spectacle of itself as subjected to the "bone" of an utterance (with this experience of the alienating gap between enunciation and utterance bringing into view the empty void of $ thanks to the sharply contrasting discrepancy of this very gap).

Of course, the reason for the "master" signifier's dependence on its supposedly subordinated S_2s is depicted in the "Graph of Desire" as constructed and explained in "The Subversion of the Subject." The minimal, rudimentary framework of this graph is a "cell" consisting of two intersecting trajectories: one, a left-to-right trajectory running from S/S_1 to S'/S_2; and two, a horseshoe-shaped right-to-left trajectory starting below S'/S_2 and curving upwards first through S'/S_2 and then passing downwards through S/S_1.[34] The first trajectory (from S/S_1 to S'/S_2) charts the chronological movement of a chain of signifiers (say, a sentence) as it unfurls over linear time. The second trajectory (for Lacan, from Δ to $, or, as Fink has it, from *a* as "lost being" to $ as "alienated subject of meaning"[35]) maps a movement in the opposite direction, namely, the retroactive temporality specific to signifying dynamics (i.e., Freud's *Nachträglichkeit* and Lacan's *après-coup*).

This retroactive temporality is the reason why the S_1 master signifier is always a false, failed master. Its apparent signifying authority is a misleading illusion.[36] In discussing the "discourse of the master" during the seventeenth seminar, Lacan refers to Hegel's famous "lordship and bondage" dialectic from the *Phenomenology of Spirit*.[37] As is common knowledge, Hegel proposes that the master, despite having socio-symbolic authority and a correlative monopolizing possession of physical things, ultimately is dependent on the slave; the slave is more of a genuine subject than the master, insofar as it's the slave who humanizes the material world by transforming it through his or her work[38] (the master doesn't work, and hence doesn't externalize his subjective being by negating, through the activity of labor, the objective being of the given world—Lacan's Hegelian master, Alexandre Kojève, dwells at length on this stage of the dialectic in the *Phenomenology*).

What is involved in the master's discourse as delineated by Lacan? Each of Lacan's four discourses (of the master, university, hysteric, and analyst) embodies a four-part skeletal structure. The top half of the structure runs left to right from the position of the "agent" (*l'agent*) to the position of the "other" (*l'autre*), and the bottom half of the structure runs right to left from the position of the "product" (*la production*) to the position of the "truth" (*la vérité*).[39] Significantly, in Lacan's discourse theory, the truth is situated beneath the agent's position—meaning, for Lacan, that the supposed locus of agency in any discourse is a "semblance" (*sem-*

blant), that is, an illusory appearance of volitional control covering over
an underlying X as the obfuscated truth of this agent-position.[40] In the
discourse of the master, the agent is S_1, the other is S_2, the product is *a*,
and the truth is $ (i.e., S_1, the master signifier as the operator of subjec-
tifying identification, is a false agent whose semblance of mastery masks
$, namely, the subject as ineliminable, dissatisfied dis-identification with
any and every form of subjectification). Both Fink and Žižek identify the
discourse of the master as a fundamental point of departure for Lacan's
theory of the four discourses, since this "primary discourse" represents
the general condition of the Lacanian subject as alienated in and by signifiers.[41] And Lacan himself speaks of the discourse of the master as depicting what's involved in the axiomatic formula according to which "the
signifier represents a subject for another signifier" (*SXVIII* 1/13/71).
Can all this be made somewhat more straightforward?

Given that Lacan is a psychoanalyst theorizing, at least in part, for the
sake of practicing analytic clinicians, the situation of being in analysis is a
good concrete example to start with in the context of this rather abstract
exposition here. The conscious speaking individual intends to "master"
her speech, to control the flow of discourse so as successfully to convey
a certain meant meaning as the consciously intended sense she has in
mind when speaking. In talking about herself, with self-reference being
linguistically signaled through S_1s such as the proper name and first-
person pronoun, the analysand articulates utterances; she constructs discursive chains, sentential sequences reducible to the elementary form
of $S/S_1 \rightarrow S'/S_2$. Moreover, the conscious endeavor to master one's discourse, to control one's speech along the lines of one's conscious signifying intentions, involves the syntax of grammar as well as the semantics
of verbal content. The punctuation, scansion, and timing of utterances
are integral components shaping the meanings produced through the
use of language.

In analysis, there are two factors confounding this effort at maintaining conscious mastery over speech—one that isn't specific to the analytic situation and another that is. For all speaking beings, and not just
analysands, language is as much something that speaks them as something that they speak. In particular, taking into account the inevitable,
unavoidable slipperiness of signifiers, the meaning of the words and
phrases one uses is impossible to control totally and completely; thanks
to the multifaceted nature of the signifying resources of natural languages, there will always be unintended "surplus" meanings generated
in and by select utterances that one produces. At certain points in one's
discourse, "slips" will occur where a disjunction surfaces between one's
conscious intention-to-signify and what one's complete articulated ut-

terance actually ends up signifying. One of Freud's interpretive gambles is to hypothesize that instances of such disjunctions reveal repressed thoughts, that failures of the conscious intention-to-signify are successes for unconscious ideas seeking expression;[42] in Lacanese, lapses of the ego's mastery over speech are openings through which speaks the subject of the unconscious, the *sujet* usually eclipsed by the *moi*. This points to the second factor confounding the effort at maintaining conscious mastery over speech, a factor specific to analysis. Part of the analyst's job, as an attentive interpreter attuned to the muffled voice of the murmuring unconscious, is to listen for these possible lapses, these slips as disruptions of the analysand's discourse of mastery (as mastery of discourse). By drawing the attention of the analysand to such phenomena as plays on words and double-meanings latent within her associative utterances (i.e., instances exhibiting an unintended, uncontrolled discrepancy between the intention-to-signify and the signification actually generated), the analyst hopes to attune the analysand's ear to something other than the ego's predictable, carefully scripted monologue. Furthermore, the Lacanian analyst also tracks, in addition to the semantics of verbal content, the punctuation, scansion, and timing operative within the dimensions of grammar and syntax. These dimensions too can and should be put to precise interpretive use. The intervention of the analytic act in relation to the analysand's $S/S_1 \rightarrow S'/S_2$ chains (an act aiming to derail the ego's supposed domination of speech) ought to highlight the bottom half of the discourse of the master, namely, both the product (a) and truth ($) of this discourse.

During the years immediately following his 1960 introduction of the definition of the signifier as that which represents the subject for another signifier, Lacan repeatedly strives to clarify the meaning and implications of this axiomatic proposition (an effort at clarification carried out primarily in the ninth through eleventh seminars [1961–64], as well as in the *écrit* "Position of the Unconscious" [a text delivered orally at the 1960 Bonneval colloquium, but rewritten in 1964 and then included in the 1966 *Écrits*]). In the ninth seminar, Lacan contrasts the sign with the signifier: the sign represents something for or to someone (i.e., signs, as meaningful combinations of signifiers and signifieds, are involved in inter-subjective discursive communication in which the communicating partners understand each other), but the signifier doesn't represent something for or to someone.[43] Why not? There are two reasons for this contrast with the sign: one, the subject of enunciation is neither a "something" represented (i.e., enunciating subjectivity is an ephemeral, vanishing insubstantiality, not a stable, reified "something") nor (as already explained at length here) is it adequately represented by the signifiers constituting the subject of the utterance; and two, the other (in this case, S_2) for whom one signifier (S_1) inadequately represents the subject is not a "someone," another person as a partner in communication, an anthropomorphic alter ego situated in the register of the Imaginary (instead, in this instance, the addressee or receiver is another signifier-structured locus situated in the register of the Symbolic, belonging to the order of the big Other).

This latter point regarding the alterity addressed by the signifier is hinted at by Lacan's reformulation of the contrast between sign and signifier a year later in the tenth seminar: "The sign is that which represents something for someone, whereas the signifier is that which represents a subject for a signifier-being" (SX 77). That to which a signifier represents a subject is not an ordinary human interlocutor, but rather a "signifier-being" (*être signifiant*). As he puts it later:

> The definition of a signifier is that it represents a subject not for another subject but for another signifier. This is the only definition possible of the signifier as different from the sign. The sign is something that represents something for somebody, but the signifier is something that represents a subject for another signifier. (Lacan 1970, 194)

In the eleventh seminar, Lacan provides an example to concretize what he has in mind in terms of this contrast between the Imaginary other (i.e., the inter-subjective "somebody" receiving the signs of communication emitted by the ego as master of its conveyed meanings) and the Symbolic Other (i.e., the trans-subjective "signifying being" of other signifiers [S_2s] with which certain signifiers [S_1s] link up to produce subjectifying effects). He refers to something akin to the Rosetta stone:

> Now, what is a signifier? I have been drumming it into you long enough not to have to articulate it once again here. A signifier is that which represents a subject. For whom?—not for another subject, but for another signifier. In order to illustrate this axiom, suppose that in the desert you find a stone covered in hieroglyphics. You do not doubt for a moment that, behind them, there was a subject who wrote them. But it is an error to believe that each signifier is addressed to you—this is proved by the fact that you cannot understand any of it. On the other hand you define them as signifiers, by the fact that you are sure that each of these signifiers is related to each of the others. And it is this that is at issue with the relation between the subject and the field of the Other. (SXI 198–99)

The signifiers of this desert stone—the individual who encounters these yet-to-be-decoded hieroglyphs must relate to them as signifiers rather than meaningful signs, since he or she doesn't know what they mean—don't simply address another human being (if that were the case, then whoever comes across this stone ought to be able to grasp the sense of its inscribed marks). In order to become the addressee of the stone's signifiers, the individual must "subject" him/herself to the Symbolic big Other in which these signifiers have their place; simply put, he or she needs to be transformed into a specific sort of signifying being (*être signifiant*) by learning the lost code so as to decipher the hieroglyphs. Only by inhabiting the network of this long-past symbolic order can one gain access to the significance of these silent, stony traces. The decoder becomes another type of signifying being (as opposed to human being) and, as situated within this alien Other's constellation of signifiers, is thereby able to entertain a relationship to the signifiers displayed by this strange desert object. Žižek offers another illustration of this notion. Borrowing from the setting of a hospital, he describes the medical charts posted at the end of the patients' beds in a way precisely analogous to Lacan's above-quoted image of the stone adorned with hieroglyphs. The doctors addressed by these charts aren't addressed as mere human beings or individual persons (i.e., as Imaginary others) but instead as bearers of an impersonal body of medical-scientific knowledge, a trans-subjective matrix of signifier-encoded expertise (i.e., as incarnations of a Symbolic big Other).[44]

How does this long detour through Lacan's delineation of the rapport between subject and signifier in the early 1960s lead back to the topic of time? What role does temporality play in this rapport? By 1964 Lacan begins spelling this out. In the eleventh seminar, referring to "the unconscious as . . . something that opens and closes," he remarks, "The subject is this emergence which, just before, as subject, was nothing, but which, having scarcely appeared, solidifies into a signifier" (*SXI* 199). He describes this same opening-and-closing movement as a "temporal pulsation,"[45] which he also characterizes as the "open sesame" of the unconscious (i.e., the fact that there are specially timed windows of opportunity, windows that quickly open and close during the diachronic unfolding of associations, for overhearing the underlying speech of the *sujet* stifled by the superficial uttered discourse of the *moi*).[46] In "Position of the Unconscious," Lacan states:

> The register of the signifier is instituted on the basis of the fact that a signifier represents a subject to another signifier. That is the structure of all unconscious formations: dreams, slips of the tongue, and witticisms. The same structure explains the subject's original division. Produced in the locus of the yet-to-be-situated Other, the signifier brings forth a subject from a being that cannot yet speak, but at the cost of freezing him. The

ready-to-speak that *was to be* there—in both senses of the French imper-
fect "*il y avait*," placing the ready-to-speak an instant before (it was there
but is no longer), but also an instant after (a few moments more and it
would have been there because it could have been there)—disappears,
no longer being anything but a signifier. (Lacan 2006p, 713)

Lacan employs an almost disorienting manipulation of verb tenses in this
passage to allude to a complex, dynamic interaction between the *après-
coup* (i.e., what will have been) and the future anterior (i.e., what was to
have been). This passage can and should be elucidated by returning to
some of the conceptual/terminological resources of Lacanian theory
laid out earlier. The "readiness-to-speak" that Lacan refers to here can
be taken as roughly equivalent to the subject of enunciation, and the
subsequent subjected condition of being "solidified" or "frozen" by signifiers can be taken as roughly equivalent to the subject of the utterance. Arguably, the subject of the utterance involves two inextricably
intertwined temporal trajectories: one, the linear, chronological movement from S/S_1 to S'/S_2; and two, the backward, retroactive movement
from S'/S_2 to S/S_1. With the completion of this second movement (i.e.,
the after-the-fact "hooking" of the meaning established through subsequent S_2s back onto the initial S_1), the utterance immediately passes over
from the indeterminacy of underway temporal kinesis (as the process of
enunciating) to the determinacy of completed de-temporalized stasis (as
the subjectifying product uttered). Expressed in the terms proposed in
"Position of the Unconscious," the temporal kinesis of enunciation "was
to be" instantiated by the signifiers mobilized in the form of an utterance; however, these signifiers (as Lacan later phrases it in "*Radiophonie*")
"cadaverize" or "corpsify" this being-as-becoming, transforming it into a
lifeless skeleton.[47]

Additionally, in the above quotation from "Position of the Unconscious," Lacan suggests that there is an illusion to be aware of here. It's
not that a fully constituted subject of enunciation preexists its alienation
in and through the signifiers constituting the subject of the utterance.
The notion that there "was to have been" a determinate intention-to-
signify subsequently betrayed and derailed by its flawed translation into
signifying units is an *après-coup* illusion of perspective (albeit an *après-
coup* phenomenon different from the retroactive time internal to the
signifying chains shaping the subject of the utterance). This future anterior ("was to have been") subject of enunciation wasn't actually present
before the betrayal/derailing of an ill-formed, indeterminate "want-to-
speak" that doesn't achieve a self-relating clarity until after a contrast

is established between it and its inadequate representation via uttered signifiers. Expressed in a relatively simple manner, for Lacan, individuals figure out what they desired to say (but what can only be "half-said" [*midit*][48] by them in an incomplete, partial fashion) exclusively after failing adequately to say whatever "it" was. That is to say (resorting to several Lacanian mathemes to be explained in detail below), the uttered signifiers retroactively turn an asubjective X (i.e., Δ/a as the presupposed state prior to the articulation of the utterance) into a subject proper (\$) by instituting an unsuturable "cut" between Δ/a and the utterance itself as a structure symbolized by Lacan as $S/S_1 \rightarrow S'/S_2$. \$ is the gap between Δ/a and $S/S_1 \rightarrow S'/S_2$, a gap that, after the fact of its having been generated by the passage of Δ/a into $S/S_1 \rightarrow S'/S_2$, makes it deceptively seem as though \$ (i.e., the self-relating negativity of the fully constituted subject of enunciation, rather than the proto/a-subjective Δ/a) always already was there to begin with, as the prior intention-to-signify inadequately rendered by the signifiers actually spoken. One of Žižek's caveats regarding Hegel's notion of negation is pertinent in this context. Žižek remarks that "*the Spirit to whom we return, the Spirit that returns to itself, is not the same as the Spirit that was previously lost in alienation*" (Žižek 1996b, 123). He then goes on to compare Hegelian negation and Lacanian symbolic castration (reading the latter as the passage of "S" as the pre-Symbolic "substance of drives" into the matrix of the big Other, a passage that produces the result of \$ as "the void of negativity"—of course, the matheme S readily can be replaced by Δ/a).[49] Just as the *Aufhebung* of Hegel's dialectic preserves the previously destroyed state of *Geist* solely insofar as this *Geist* is radically transformed into something different than it was, so too does the "castrating" routing of Δ/a through $S/S_1 \rightarrow S'/S_2$ preserve this thus-negated Δ/a exclusively as \$.

What about this flurry of Lacanian mathemes? How are they to be understood? Moreover, how do they help reveal the absolutely essential rapport between subjectivity and temporality? The subject of enunciation is rendered both as the vector running from Δ to \$ in the elementary cell of the "Graph of Desire" from "The Subversion of the Subject" (1960) and as the bottom half of the discourse of the master (i.e., a as product and \$ as truth) from the seventeenth seminar (1969–70). From the ontogenetic perspective of psychoanalytic metapsychology, the movement from Δ to \$ represents the entry into language, the individual's transition from a state of not being mediated by the signifiers of the big Other (Δ) to the condition, following "symbolic castration," of being submitted to and split by Symbolic mediation (\$).[50] With reference to Lacan's related recasting of the psychoanalytic conception of the libidinal economy via the need-demand-desire triad, Δ is Real need (i.e., the corporeal causes agitating the body of the living being) which, when passed through the utterance of Symbolic demand addressed to another $(S/S_1 \rightarrow S'/S_2)$, yields \$ as the split subject of desire (i.e., the unsatisfied remainder of the passage of need into demand, as per Lacan's equation stating that desire is what results when need is subtracted from demand[51]). Lacan qualifies this by saying that Δ as the purely non-Symbolic condition of lived bodily immediacy (i.e., the raw Real of brute need) is a myth (albeit a necessary fiction for metapsychology) since, of course, both the individuals being analyzed by analysts as well as the analytic theorists theorizing about conceptions of subjectivity are enveloped by Imaginary-Symbolic reality. Lacan would also add that the "pre-verbal" infant is thrown into a language-saturated social universe, a preexistent world that has prepared a place for him or her even before the moment of birth. Prior to his or her ability to mentally register and self-reflectively appreciate its effects, the symbolic order nonetheless shapes the being of the human child.[52] Language is already there, even before it's acquired.

From the more here and now perspective of the psychoanalytic clinic dealing with the already-developed adult individual, the analyst's repeated interpretive disruptions of the ego-directed movements from S/S_1 to S'/S_2 gradually produce the awareness of an insistent "something" (i.e., a) that doesn't fit smoothly into the narrative constructed by the flow of conscious speech, and eventually force a confrontation with the truth that it is impossible to eliminate the gap between, on the one hand, $S/S_1 \rightarrow S'/S_2$ and, on the other hand, a. This gap is \$ as the discordance between positions of enunciation (involving both the needy "subjugated asubject" [*l'assujet*][53] as Δ, the being subjugated to need, and the desiring subject-as-\$) and the inevitably alienating results of the utterances enunciated $(S/S_1 \rightarrow S'/S_2)$. In other words, \$ isn't just, as implied earlier, the dynamic, kinetic subject of enunciation as opposed to the inert, static subject of the completed utterance. Rather, \$ names the out-of-synch discordance, the structural incompatibility, between these two sides of signifier-mediated subjectivity.

The top half of the discourse of the master $(S_1 \rightarrow S_2)$ can be treated as equivalent to the subject of the utterance, and correspondingly, the bottom half of this discourse (\$ // a) can be treated as equivalent to the subject of enunciation. The chains of S_1s and S_2s constituting subjectifying utterances form closed circuits involving two reciprocally related temporal trajectories: a left-to-right linear movement followed by an ensuing right-to-left retroactive movement (i.e., chronological time and *après-coup* time). However, \$ and a, the two constituents/facets of enunciating subjectivity, each can be construed as standing for two other temporal modalities foreclosed from (and yet still affecting) the proac-tive-retroactive time circuit of $S_1 \rightarrow S_2$. As hinted above in the compari-sons drawn between the elementary cell of the "Graph of Desire" (from "The Subversion of the Subject") and the discourse of the master (from the seventeenth seminar), the four components S, S', Δ, $ (1960) and S_1, S_2, a, $ (1969–70) are approximately interchangeable respectively. So a can be read, in one sense, as standing for Δ as Real need—from a theoretical perspective privileging temporality, as the turbulent flux of a durational lived time not measurable by the regularity of the cyclically recurring numerical markers of the big Other's clocks. This Δ/a, as the ceaseless changes and shifts emanating from the forever lost immediacy of a vital being inescapably permeated by pure temporal negativity as the relentless march of mortal-making time, propels the individual it buffets to enter into the circuit $S/S_1 \rightarrow S'/S_2$ (and thus to be subjected to the combined operations of chronological and *après-coup* time). Incidentally, there is a certain vaguely Platonic thrust to one aspect of this opposition between Δ/a (as linked to the body) and $S/S_1 \rightarrow S'/S_2$ (as linked to lan-guage): contrary to vulgar common sense, according to which language is associated with the lightness of conceptual transparency and body with the heaviness of non-conceptual opacity, signification is the level of dense, hard, reified inertness (i.e., the de-temporalized stasis of uttered signifiers) and corporeality is the level of ephemeral, fleeting, insubstan-tial dynamism (i.e., the temporalized genesis of material becoming).

The outcome of the passage of Δ/a through $S/S_1 \rightarrow S'/S_2$ is the gen-esis of $, the latter obeying a staccato temporality, an evental time of abrupt flashes winking in and out of existence. $ unpredictably comes to light on rare occasions, suddenly rupturing the surface of Imaginary-Symbolic reality only at those moments when the $S/S_1 \rightarrow S'/S_2$ circuits fail effectively to conceal their discord with Δ/a. Clinically speaking, psychoanalysis strives for the "precipitation of subjectivity," the catalyz-ing of the exceptional event of $ becoming a self-relating negativity, by interfering with the ways in which the $S/S_1 \rightarrow S'/S_2$ circuits cover over the discrepancies between themselves and "something other" as both Δ/a and $ (i.e., the two sides of the subject of enunciation). Along these lines, Žižek, in his handling of Lacan's theory of the four discourses, claims that the figure of the hysteric (a position depicted via Lacan's "discourse of the hysteric" in which $ is the agent, S_1 is the other, S_2 is the product, and a is the truth) is the position from which this discrepancy between Δ/a and $S/S_1 \rightarrow S'/S_2$, a discrepancy normally masked by the imposture of the master's discourse, is felt.[54] The figure of the master is "hystericized" when she loses the certainty of being equal to her signifier-mediated selfhood as established in the big Other, when she begins to doubt and question whether the signifying units of the symbolic order provide a sufficient guarantee of identity.[55] Similarly, on several occasions, Žižek asserts that the figure of the hysteric, conceived in this manner, stands for subjectivity as such, for the subject per se as $-as-for-itself (i.e., the X that lacks a place in the symbolic order and experiences all signifiers representing it as inadequate and problematic).[56] He proposes that "the subject 'is' only through its confrontation with the enigma of *Che vuoi?* ('What do you want?') insofar as the Other's desire remains impenetrable, insofar as the subject doesn't know what object it is for the Other" (Žižek 1997a, 79). Since the hystericized master loses the confidence of being equal to the $S/S_1 \rightarrow S'/S_2$ subjectifying identifications established within the sphere of the Symbolic big Other, she becomes $—in the terms of Lacan's discourse theory, $ displaces S_1 from the agent position—through facing the (unsolvable) mystery of what she is in relation to this Other ("*Che vuoi?*"). Therefore, Žižek concludes, "the hysterical subject is the subject *par excellence*" (Žižek 2004b, 144). One could say that the discourse of the master is grounded on a gesture of identification ("That's me!"), whereas the discourse of the hysteric is grounded on a gesture of dis-identification ("That's not me!").

Once again translating this discussion back into the parlance of the Hegelian-Žižekian ontology and attendant theory of subjectivity developed at length above, $\Delta/a = $-as-in-itself (i.e., the raw temporal negativity pervading natural substance), $S/S_1 \rightarrow S'/S_2$ = subjectification (i.e., the proactive-retroactive temporal dialectic structuring cultural subjectification), and $ = $-as-for-itself (i.e., the intermittent eventual temporality of the neither-natural-nor-cultural subject as an inhuman misfit). But moving in a somewhat different direction than Žižek, subjectivity as such, defined from the most overarching philosophical-theoretical perspective, should be redefined as the less-than-synthesized "not all" ensemble of these three incommensurable, out-of-synch temporal modalities. Certain varieties of contemporary music help render this vision of the subject more tangible: temporalized subjectivity is like a recording of multiple layered soundtracks each running at different rhythms and rates. Sometimes the result might be a pleasing song whose audible harmony creates a seemingly synthesized sound successfully lulling the listener into forgetting that a multitude of juxtaposed tracks brings about this mellifluous effect; at other times, the layering of these multiple tracks running at different time-speeds results in a disharmonious cacophony, making the listener painfully aware of the fragmented multitude involved.

This image of the subject is, in a certain fashion, a transformative psychoanalytic appropriation of the Heideggerian analytic of *Dasein*. Heidegger conceives of *Dasein* as a simultaneous dwelling within a plurality of registers of temporality (as the various forms of temporal "ec-stasis"). Through its "ecstatic" temporal transcendence-in-immanence (i.e., its multiple modes of excessively stretching beyond its here and now *Da* from within this *Da* itself), *Dasein* always ex-ists in several differ-ent times all at once. The crucial psychoanalytic twist to be added here amounts to the introduction of the motif of conflict, a motif central to Freudian and Lacanian thought, into this picture: the multiple temporal modes constitutive of subjectivity can and do come into conflict with each other; they don't blend together to compose an organic unity. One could even go so far as to argue that these antagonistic temporalities are the ultimate motor forces behind the libidinal economy, that the drives and desires moving human being arise along the fissures and fault lines between (to put it in Hegelian-Žižekian terms) the time of substance (Δ/a), the time of subjectification $(S/S_1 \rightarrow S'/S_2)$, and the time of the subject ($). Drives and desires aren't simply quotas of energetic force welling up from the brute corporeality of a primitive id. Rather, they are the aftershocks generated by the repeated collisions of incompatible temporal dynamics.[57]

Is there, however, a way to circumnavigate back from here to the topic of Hegel's philosophy and Žižek's Lacanian reading of it? Hegel himself provides the means for doing so. Žižek contends that one of the reasons he's licensed to Lacanianize Hegel is that Hegelian logic is, in fact, a "logic of the signifier."[58] Hegel's remarks about language at the begin-ning of the preface to the second edition of his *Science of Logic* (remarks Žižek alludes to[59]) indeed seem to support this contention:

> The forms of thought are, in the first instance, displayed and stored in human *language*. Nowadays we cannot be too often reminded that it is *thinking* which distinguishes man from the beasts. Into all that becomes something inward for men, an image or conception as such, into all that he makes his own, language has penetrated, and everything that he has transformed into language and expresses in it contains a category—con-cealed, mixed with other forms or clearly determined as such, so much is logic his natural element, indeed his own peculiar *nature*. If nature as such, as the physical world, is contrasted with the spiritual sphere, then logic must certainly be said to be the supernatural element which permeates every relationship of man to nature, his sensation, intuition, desire, need, instinct. (Hegel 1969, 31–32)

Lacan himself could not have written a more Lacanian passage than this. Hegel clearly maintains that humans are profoundly dissimilar to "beasts" as living beings belonging to the natural world. Humans are,

instead, conceptual-linguistic beings (as Lacan puts it, the human individual is a speaking being [*parlêtre*]). In other words, humans are beings
whose "nature," shot through as it is with the pervasive influences of
Symbolic structures "penetrating" and "permeating" right down to the
foundational libidinal bedrock of bodily existence, is thoroughly denaturalized as compared with that of other creatures in the animal kingdom.
(Speaking from the perspective of the neurosciences, LeDoux describes
the acquisition of language as a "revolution" as opposed to an "evolution,"[60] namely, as human nature's sharp break with nature abruptly occurring within and out of nature itself.) Hegel even hints that humanity's
immersion in language entails the existence of unconscious dimensions:
the "categories" shaping conceptually-linguistically mediated reality can
be "concealed" or "mixed with other forms," thus suggesting that individuals often are unaware of the structuring effects of the signifiers invisibly molding their own being and that of their world.

In *The Sublime Object of Ideology*, Žižek argues that language plays a
central role in Hegel's *Phenomenology of Spirit* (and not just in his later
Logic). He claims:

> Language is, of course, the very medium of the "journey of conscious-
> ness" in *Phenomenology*, to such a point that it would be possible to define
> every stage of this journey, every "figure of consciousness," by a specific
> modality of language; even in its very beginning, in the "sense-certainty,"
> the dialectical movement is activated by the discord between what con-
> sciousness "means to say" and what it effectively says. (Žižek 1989, 210)

Žižek refers here to the opening section of the *Phenomenology* on "Sense-
Certainty: Or the 'This' and 'Meaning.'" Therein Hegel describes the
condition of consciousness situated as the originary starting point of
the dialectical process. In the supposed beginning, there is just "sense-
certainty," namely, the pure immediacy of unfiltered lived experience;
consciousness is at one with the here and now of the world disclosed to
it.[61] The "This" in Hegel's subtitle for the section of his text describing
this opening stage of the dialectic is the always-particular here and now to
which sense-certainty is experientially glued. And the "Meaning" Hegel
also mentions in this same subtitle is the intention of consciousness to
express or signify this here and now via linguistic means, to convey the
content of its experience in the form of language. As soon as consciousness attempts to carry out this intention, thereby diverting experiential
content through linguistic form, a disjunctive gap emerges between what
it "meant to say" (i.e., the particular here and now) and what it actually
says (i.e., the universal "here and now").[62]

The intervention of time in this process is crucial (in fact, Hegel uses the example of the "now" here). Consciousness as sense-certainty is fixated upon singularity as the unique now-points of its fluctuating field of immediate experience, whereas what this consciousness conveys through symbolizing this singularity is something entirely other, that is, iterable symbols indifferent to the uniqueness of this singularity. Linguistic articulation channels particular immediacy into universal mediation, derailing, for instance, the unique non-conceptual now into the generic conceptual "now"[63] (in Lacanian mathemes, Δ / a is derailed into $S/S_1 \rightarrow S'/S_2$). Phrased in a deceptively simple fashion, the Hegelian dialectic begins with a chasm opening up between things and words.

Consistent with his general interpretive picture of Hegel's philosophy, Žižek is careful to depict the dialectic as celebrating this divorce between things and words, this discrepancy between what is meant and what is said. He insists that Hegel isn't interested in overcoming or suturing this gap; the dialectic doesn't culminate in a synthetic reconciliation "healing the wound" of this split that arises between the particular and the universal. Rather, the culmination of the dialectic, properly conceived, is the realization that this wound neither can nor should be healed. What's more, Hegelian "absolute knowing" doesn't accept this disjunction with a defeated sigh of resignation. Instead, it enthusiastically embraces the power of negativity introduced into reality through the internal rupturing of the idiotic, sterile enclosure of consciousness as solipsistic sense-certainty. Žižek maintains, apropos "the abyss which separates 'things' from 'words,'" that "Hegel . . . perceives it as the Spirit's supreme accomplishment, he sees in it the Spirit's 'infinite' power to disengage itself from the immediacy of what is simply given, to break up its organic unity" (Žižek 1992a, 54). That is to say, what consciousness initially perceives as a failure is seen from the concluding perspective of the *Phenomenology* as a success.

The implications of this, given the ground laid above, easily can be rendered in precise Lacanian terms. Those who misread Hegel as the proponent of an Absolute in which the negativity of difference is finally submitted to the totalizing closure of a seamless One-All erroneously engage with his philosophy as a version of the discourse of the master. As Žižek notes, the hallmark of the master's discourse is the pretense of establishing perfect equivalence between enunciation and utterance[64] (for example, denying any mismatch whatsoever between what is meant and what is said). As read by both Lacan and Žižek, Hegel is "the most sublime of hysterics."[65] In other words, Hegel's philosophical discourse is centered on $ as the full realization of the gap between Δ / a and $S/S_1 \rightarrow S'/S_2$, the subject as the dynamic, productive movement of negativity

made possible by the unsuturable parallax splits rupturing consciousness from within.

However, Žižek warns against another possible misreading that his
own critiques of the misreading of Hegel's philosophy as an instance of
the discourse of the master risk encouraging. He cautions that "it is not
sufficient to conceive Hegel as the 'thinker of negativity,' as the philosopher who displayed the bacchanalian dance of Negativity which sweeps
away every positive-substantial identity" (Žižek 2002a, 73). Just as Lacan
underscores, on various levels, that temporal difference is inextricably
intertwined with atemporal repetition, so too are the time of the kinetic
negative and the timelessness of the static positive entirely bound up with
each other in Hegelian dialectics. Žižek observes that Hegel is equally
concerned with the inevitable succession of forms in and through which
the "mad dance of the negative" concretizes itself, achieving a transitory synthetic stability (i.e., the succession of one-ifying master signifiers
[S_1s] temporarily "quilting" the fluctuating, contradiction-suffused field
in which the negative circulates).[66] In fact, the trajectory of negativity's
restless movement is shaped by the specific ways in which its finite, inert
coagulations break apart. Viewed from this angle, the negative is the
name for the failed self-stabilization of all figures of consciousness, for
the internally generated implosion of any and every subjectifying identification with positive conceptual-linguistic forms. The Hegelian-Žižekian
subject emerges when this failure or implosion of identificatory subjectification is itself directly identified with as the sole oneness of the subject,
when the negative gesture of dis-identification with all positive identities
is recognized as the only genuine identity: "The 'One' of Hegel's 'monism' is thus not the One of an Identity encompassing all differences,
but rather a paradoxical 'One' of radical negativity which forever blocks
the fulfillment of any positive identity" (Žižek 2002a, 69). Žižek adds a
page later: "The key 'reversal' of the dialectical process takes place when
we recognize in what first appeared as a 'condition of impossibility'—as
a hindrance to our full identity, to the realization of our potential—the
condition of the possibility of our ontological consistency" (Žižek 2002a,
70).

Repeating a point made much earlier here, failure comes first
(see chapter 1). One of the key dialectical features of Žižek's Hegel-
influenced theory of subjectivity is that the "error" of identifying with
operators of subjectification (i.e., Δ/a passing into $S/S_1 \rightarrow S'/S_2$) is absolutely necessary for the subsequent productive genesis of the subject as
the void of self-relating negativity ($\$$). Without the prior "misstep" of the
"fall" into the defiles of mediating words and images—this misstep/fall
sets up the possibility for the collapse of the specific subjectifying identi-

fications thereby established—subjectivity proper cannot come into full-fledged existence.

Finally, this returns the discussion to the relationship between Kant and Hegel, a multifaceted philosophical relationship whose various nuances are utterly essential to the ongoing evolution of Žižek's work. Although, over the course of the past several years, Žižek periodically has criticized his earliest writings for being too Kantian, he quite recently appears to be calling for another return to Kant. With reference to his new philosophical motif of "parallax," he seemingly reverses his tendency to favor Hegelian dialectics over Kantian transcendentalism:

> When confronted with an antinomic stance in the precise Kantian sense of the term, one should renounce all attempts to reduce one aspect to the other (or, even more, to enact a kind of "dialectical synthesis" of the opposites). One should, on the contrary, assert antinomy as irreducible. (Žižek 2004d, 256)

Despite how this might sound, Žižek is neither endorsing a traditional, orthodox Kantianism nor repudiating his own version of Hegelianism. According to the Žižekian theory of the subject, the void of cogito-like subjectivity, whether as Kant's subject-Thing or Hegel's night of the world, arises out of a preceding series of failed forms of subjectification. Hence, unlike Kant, Žižek doesn't depict this empty X simply as an a priori given, as part of an ahistorical, eternally present transcendental structure unrelated to the dialectical interactions between multiple (and often conflicting) strata of reality. $ is an end-result rather than a beginning-origin, a non-empirical/ahistorical subject-term generated out of prior empirical/historical predicate-terms. The Kantian antinomy between the noumenal and the phenomenal, fracturing the subjective individual into timeless and temporal dimensions, is treated by Kant as an obstacle to the individual becoming reflectively acquainted with the essential *an sich* kernel of his or her being (i.e., the unavoidable routing of self-consciousness through the matrix of phenomenal experience bars reflexive access to oneself as a noumenal entity). And, as seen, Žižek contends that Hegel's move in response to this isn't to "dialectically synthesize" this split so as to posit a perfectly transparent form of actualized self-consciousness, but rather to proclaim that subjectivity is nothing other than the negativity of the very split between different, incommensurable strata.[67] In other words, Žižek's Hegel "asserts antinomy as irreducible." The Hegelian-Žižekian subject as a pure negativity immanently circulating within the plane of reality is nothing other than an effect of the antinomies inherent to this plane.[68]

In a sense, what Hegel (and Schelling too) accomplishes is an explicit temporalization of Kantian subjectivity, an account of the immanent empirical/historical genesis of the thereafter non-empirical/ahistorical transcendent(al). Of course, with Žižek's Hegelianism, it's conceded that certain fundamental ontological conditions of possibility must always already be in place—the principal condition is the notion of substance as subject, namely, being as an incomplete and inconsistent "not all" (i.e., subject-as-in-itself, as Δ/a)—in order for there to be the potential for the subject-as-for-itself (\$) to arise and achieve a self-relating actuality. Moreover, the Hegelian Žižek appears to admit that the subject-as-in-itself inevitably enters into processes of subjectification (i.e., from Δ/a to $S/S_1 \rightarrow S'/S_2$); these are processes in which an illusorily consistent and stable ego, a *moi* as opposed to a *sujet*, is created through identification with the empirical/historical contents of whatever happens to be the surrounding sociocultural milieu at the time. Ego-level identificatory subjectification tends to obfuscate the ineliminable discordance between Δ/a and $S/S_1 \rightarrow S'/S_2$, creating a false feeling of harmony in which the avatars of identity (drawn from and determined by the Symbolic space of the big Other) pretend satisfactorily to sublate the underlying agitation and discontent motivating the acceptance of this alienating mediation. The master signifiers of subjectifying identification deceptively make it seem as though the "stuff" constituting the *moi* is the natural, necessary reflection of the essential being of the individual. \$ arises when this appearance of natural necessity breaks down.[69]

So one could say that both the subject-as-in-itself (Δ/a) as well as the transition from this substance as subject to subjectification ($S/S_1 \rightarrow S'/S_2$) are, for Žižek, conditions of possibility for the potential genesis of the subject-as-for-itself (\$). But to be more precise, the former (Δ/a) is an ontological condition of possibility, whereas the latter (i.e., the often obfuscated but always underlying discord between Δ/a and $S/S_1 \rightarrow S'/S_2$), due to the fact that the operators of subjectification are elements of a particular sociocultural context as a specific big Other, is (at least in terms of its content) a historical condition of possibility for the emergence of \$ (\$ designates the moment when the ultimately unbridgeable chasm between Δ/a and $S/S_1 \rightarrow S'/S_2$ is accepted and embraced as such, rather than repudiated in favor of the fantasy that this gap can be sutured). In *The Indivisible Remainder*, Žižek explains how Hegel's handling of the distinction between the ahistorical universal and the historical particular is distinctive in a very important respect:

> The Hegelian approach to universality differs from the standard one:
> the standard approach is concerned with the historicist problem of the

effective scope of a universal notion (is a notion truly universal, or is its validity actually constrained to a specific historical epoch, social class, etc.?), whereas Hegel asks exactly the opposite question: how, in what precise historical conditions, can a "neutral" universal notion emerge at all? (Žižek 1996b, 215)

In a later piece, Žižek uses this explanation of Hegel's distinctiveness apropos this issue to establish a clear contrast with Kant's rigid partitioning of the transcendental (as an ahistorical universal dimension) and the empirical (as a historical particular dimension):

> It is crucial to defend the key *Hegelian* insight directed against the Kantian position of the universal a priori frame distorted by empirical "pathological" conditions . . . The question is . . . how, through what violent operation of exclusion/repression, does this universal frame itself emerge? With regard to the notion of hegemony, this means that it is not enough to assert the gap between the empty universal signifier and the particular signifiers that endeavour to fill its void—the question to be raised is, again, how, through what operation of exclusion, does this void itself emerge? (Žižek 2000c, 257–58)

Although, in these two quoted passages, Žižek doesn't explicitly mention his theory of the subject, the implications of the above remarks for that theory ought to be glaringly obvious at this point. On Žižek's reading, Hegel doesn't repudiate the Kantian notion of there being a universal side of subjectivity irreducible to empirical gentrifications at the level of culture, history, politics, society, and so on; the negativity of the Hegelian subject is this very irreducibility. What bothers Hegel about Kant is, instead, the unforgivable absence of any sustained examination of when and how, under what particular circumstances, the universal negativity of subjectivity comes to light in and for itself—in short, when and how a trans-phenomenal subject explodes out of the domain of phenomena so as to posit itself as such. This doesn't happen under just any conditions and in just any circumstances.

In *The Plague of Fantasies*, Žižek clearly formulates the consequences of the Hegelian conceptualization of universality for an account of subjectivity. He states:

> What Hegel draws attention to is the fact that actual Universality is not only the abstract content common to all particular cases, but also the "negative" power of disrupting each particular content. The fact that the Subject is a Universal Being means that . . . I become "universal" only

through the violent effort of disengaging myself from the particularity of
my situation . . . Subjectivity and universality are thus strictly correlative:
the dimension of universality becomes "for itself" only through the "in-
dividualist" negation of the particular context which forms the subject's
specific background. (Žižek 1997c, 222)

Perhaps the most basic philosophical thesis here is the assertion that
there is indeed a universality incarnated within each and every individual, but that this universal dimension isn't to be found at the level of any
of the contents latched on to by individuals as constitutive of their subjectifying identities. These identities, inextricably bound up with different
communities and groups as their "specific background," are not what
grants access to an X that is irreducible to sociohistorical particularity.
What individuals share in common above and beyond their inevitably
differing forms of subjectification is the impossibility (an impossibility
theorized by Lacan from myriad angles) of ever completely and exhaustively collapsing their entire being into these forms of subjectification; all
individuals are "alienated" in relation to their externally mediated selves,
and this alienation within their own subjective structure is the extimate
trans-individuality "in them more than themselves." Only through a gesture of dis-identification via negating the particular contents of ego-level
subjectifying identifications is this universal negativity able to shift from
latent potentiality (i.e., $-as-in-itself) to manifest actuality (i.e., $-as-for-
itself): "*Only an entity that is in itself hindered, dislocated—that is, one that
lacks its 'proper place,' that is by definition 'out of joint'—can immediately refer to
universality as such*" (Žižek 1994b, 146).

From Žižek's perspective, the crucial questions raised by this Hegelian-
Lacanian reconsideration of the nature and status of subjectivity, questions facing both clinical psychoanalytic practice and revolutionary political thought, are: How does one precipitate the emergence of the subject
out of subjectification? Under what precise (clinical or political) conditions can individuals be made undeniably aware of the discrepant gap
between Δ/a and $S/S_1 \rightarrow S'/S_2$, a gap they are called upon to put to work
in different ways? Or, to recall the earlier proposed musical metaphor
employed so as to clarify the image of the subject ($) as (in)consisting
of multiple varying-speed temporal tracks, how does one get people to
stop being seduced into a stupor by the anesthetizing sounds of over-
synthesized siren songs, to unplug from fantasies of eliminating the disharmonious discord constitutive of subjectivity, and start listening to the
sounds of a new sort of music?

Conclusion: The Unbearable Lightness of Being Free

According to Badiou, philosophy always thinks under conditions—that is to say, philosophizing is an activity driven by evental impacts forcing it to move along certain truth-trajectories.[1] In *Manifesto for Philosophy*, Badiou confesses that the situation-specific socioeconomic processes of contemporary capitalism form an immanent condition of possibility (as a "historic medium"[2]) for his ontology of the pure multiple-without-One, of the infinite infinities of being qua being (*l'être en tant qu'être*). The frenetic Heraclitian flows of perpetually mobile virtual capital, flows eroding any fixed and stable solidity, reveal something fundamental about being as such. In other words, the historical particularity of today's late capitalism simultaneously discloses an essential aspect of the more-than-historical ontological domain.[3] Badiou explains:

> If one takes "nihilism" to mean desacralization, Capital, whose planetary reign is beyond any doubt—"technology" and "Capital" being only paired off in an historic sequence but not in the concept—is certainly the only nihilistic potency of which men have succeeded in being the inventors as well as the prey. (Badiou 1999, 56)

He continues:

> Yet, for Marx, and for us, desacralization is not in the least nihilistic, insofar as "nihilism" must signify that which declares that the access to being and truth is impossible. On the contrary, desacralization is a *necessary condition* for the disclosing of such an approach to thought. It is obviously the only thing we can and must welcome within Capital: it exposes the pure multiple as the foundation of presentation; it denounces every effect of One as a simple, precarious configuration; it dismisses the symbolic representations in which the bond found a semblance of being. That this destitution operates in the most complete barbarity must not conceal its properly *ontological* virtue. (Badiou 1999, 56–57)

Through, as Ray Brassier describes it, global capital bringing about a "universal unbinding"[4] (à la Marx's "all that is solid melts into air" or "deterritorialization" as per Deleuze and Guattari), thought is stimulated to envision being qua being as an insubstantial mad dance of the Oneless multiple, instead of as a dense, hefty materiality closed in upon itself in static idiocy. Capitalism conditions a radical reconsideration of the very (in)substantiality of the Real.

In addition to serving as the spur for a rethinking of ontology, the dynamics of capital present the opportunity for apprehending and appreciating intrinsic facets of the skeletal structure of subjectivity itself (given that Badiou treats subjectivity as arising from always-unique events and their power to subjectify individuals in a manner akin to moments of interpellation—Badiouian subjects are invariably subjects of specific evental ruptures, rather than there being a single form of subjectivity in general[5]—he wouldn't, as will be done here, opt to exploit capitalism in order to discern and sketch the contours of an overarching theory of a general, nonspecific subject). Within the framework of capitalism and its marketplaces, an aggregate of multiple individuals generates, in a bottom-up fashion (i.e., through the horizontal, lateral interactions between these individuals), a set of economic patterns that eventually take on a life of their own, patterns that, as it were, come to transcend the individuals constituting the aggregate and achieve a relative self-relating autonomy—hence the "alienating" effects of capital identified by Marx, the fact that its movements and migrations cease to be regulated by the interests of those responsible for generating it (in Schellingian terms, one could describe this facet of Marxian alienation as the virtual existence of capital arising from and breaking with the material ground of labor). Once again, the motif of the immanent genesis of the transcendent resurfaces here (a motif already delineated by previous portions of this project in relation to Schelling, Hegel, and meme theory, among other points of reference). However, whereas traditional Marxist thought insists upon the possibility of revolutionarily reversing such alienation at the macro-level of socioeconomic relations, a capitalist-inspired account of micro-level subjectivity (an account also heavily indebted to Lacan and Žižek) requires supplementing dialectical materialism with transcendental materialism by insisting on the existence of certain sorts of irreversible alienation (such as, most notably, the Lacanian notion of the constitution of the subject in and by the alienating mediation of signifiers[6]).

Prior to explaining the differences between dialectical and transcendental materialism, it's important first to pose the questions and problems to which the transcendental materialist theory of the subject is an answer/solution. In his 1958 *écrit* "The Direction of the Treatment and the Principles of Its Power," Lacan declares that the object of psychoanalysis ("our particular subject matter") is "*antiphusis*" (anti-nature).[7] Years later, in a session of the twenty-fourth seminar, Lacan again makes reference to a "counter-nature" (*contre-nature*), maintaining there that this is a notion easier to comprehend than what is imprecisely signified by the term *nature*.[8] Analysis deals with something other than nature, with something opposed to or set against that which is commonly identified as natural. At this stage in his teaching (the quasi-structuralist phase during the 1950s), it isn't difficult to guess what Lacan means by this. Given that human nature, as the specific nature with which psychoanalysis occupies itself, is shot through with non-natural influences, analysts are restricted to handling manifestations of a denaturalized nature.[9] And of course, the reason why human nature is (from an analytic perspective) invariably denaturalized is that individuals are submerged in a world of images and signifiers from their earliest beginnings onwards. What's more, Lacan repeatedly emphasizes that the big Other, as a non-natural symbolic order, precedes the birth of the individual, preparing in advance a place for him or her in a system obeying rules other than the laws of nature. Thanks to these representational mediators and their central role in the processes of subjectification, the Lacanian subject exists as a (non-)being alienated from its corporeal-material substratum.

But what allows for these Imaginary-Symbolic structures to take root in the first place? What permits them to colonize bodies, to overwrite the being of individuals and thereby denaturalize their natures? Why aren't these structures, often involving modifications apparently moving in directions contrary to the presumed default trajectories of the libidinal economy, rejected by this economy in a manner analogous to failed organ transplants? An incredibly important philosophical-theoretical issue of direct concern to Freudian-Lacanian psychoanalytic metapsychology is at stake here: the very conditions of possibility for the genesis of the subject, for the ontogenetic emergence of a being situated on the plane of *antiphusis*. One might be tempted to respond to these questions by insisting that, as far as Freud and Lacan are concerned, an external imposition, coming from an Other (whether this Other be the Freudian Oedipal family unit or the Lacanian symbolic order), is solely responsible for fashioning unnatural subjectivity out of natural animality, for transubstantiating an organic being with instincts and needs into a speaking being with drives and desires. The (symbolic) "castration" dictated by the socio-structural *Umwelt* is, according to this response, a transformative traumatic blow descending upon the individual from elsewhere. However, human nature must be, in its intrinsic essence, configured in such a way as to be receptive to this blow and its repercussions. In other words, it must be in the nature of this particular nature to be open to and capable of undergoing the dynamics of denaturalization involved in the processes of subjectification. A psychoanalytically influenced theory of the subject that fails to furnish a basic delineation of human nature as the precondition for the genesis of subjectivity is groundless, incapable of explaining a foundational dimension of its object of inquiry.

In the later seminars of the 1970s, a series of somewhat cryptic remarks testifies to Lacan's awareness of the need to redefine nature itself in order to account for why human nature is predisposed to being thoroughly altered by the denaturalizing mediation of socio-symbolic structures. In both the twenty-first and twenty-fourth seminars, Lacan contends that nature is far from being entirely natural.[10] However, this isn't just a slightly reworded reiteration of his earlier remarks from the 1950s about humanity's denaturalized nature. Rather than grounding his assertions here by invoking the externally imposed intrusion of images and significrs as the ultimate cause of the denaturalization involved in subjectification, Lacan takes the additional step of pointing to something within nature itself that inclines it in the direction of its own effacement. In the twenty-third seminar, Lacan posits that "nature distinguishes itself by not being one" ("*la nature se spécifie de n'être pas une*" [*SXXIII* 12]). That is to say, nature (at least human nature) should not be envisioned as an integrated organic wholeness, a coordinated sphere of components interrelating according to the laws of an eternally balanced harmony.

In fact, Lacan's contemporaneous meditations on the nonexistence of the *rapport sexuel* (sexual relationship)[11] are directly tied to these broader reflections on the nature of nature. One of the rudimentary lessons of psychoanalysis is that the sexual is never simply sexual. Hence, the notion of the *rapport sexuel* is bound up with a whole series of motifs and implications concerning matters seemingly far removed from the carnal interactions between males and females. The (nonexistent) sexual relationship, as Lacan repeatedly insists, is the paradigm for the pervasive themes of harmony and wholeness that color, at a global level, fundamental conceptualizations regarding the essence of reality and material being.[12] "*Il n'y a pas de rapport sexuel*" implies, among other things, that balanced coordination is missing, that nature, within the realm of human existence, is anything but a harmonious and whole One-All. As Lacan expresses it in the seventeenth seminar, nature doesn't "copulate" so as to generate the fictitious, perfected unity of a spherical totality.[13] This fractured field of material being is an aspect of the barred Real (corresponding to Lacan's barred Other as the inconsistent, contradiction-riddled symbolic order).

What are the consequences of these reflections regarding the disharmonious "not-wholeness" of (human) nature? More specifically, how is this barred Real relevant to a theory of subjectivity informed by psychoanalysis? The late Lacan provides only a few hints. At one point, he identifies "liberty" (*liberté*) with "the non-existence of the sexual relationship,"[14] which, in light of the above, can be understood as indicating that the freedom enjoyed by the autonomous subject is made possible by the lack of an integrated organic foundation as the grounding basis of this subject's being. Similarly, several years later, Lacan speaks of nature as not all that natural due to being internally plagued by "rottenness" (*pourriture*), by a decay or defect out of which culture (as *antiphusis*) bubbles forth (*bouillonner*).[15] Viewed thus, human nature is naturally destined for denaturalization. Put differently, more-than-material subjectivity immanently arises out of the dysfunctionality of a libidinal-material ground.

Žižek's creative synthesis of German idealism and Lacanian psychoanalysis enables the argument to be advanced that certain properties of an asubjective, heteronomous libidinal-material foundation (as the barred Real of human nature) function as fundamental conditions of possibility for the ontogenesis of subjective autonomy (as a transcendence of this same "natural" foundation). These properties are the meta-transcendental conditions for the event of the advent of the transcendent(al) subject-as-$. A psychoanalytic theory of subjectivity informed by German idealism is able to contend that, strange as it may sound, autonomy immanently emerges out of heteronomy as an excess or surplus that cannot be reinscribed back within the ontological register out of which it grew. As Lacan indicates in his later seminars, the freedom of autonomous subjectivity is possible only if being is inherently incomplete and internally inconsistent, asymmetrical and out of joint with itself.

For the sake of rigorous clarity and precision, it must be asked at this juncture: What is the difference between, on the one hand, dialectical materialism and, on the other hand, what is referred to throughout this project as "transcendental materialism" (as in the transcendental materialist theory of subjectivity made possible by Žižek's synthesis of German idealism and Lacanian psychoanalysis)? Invoking Badiou here is again useful. In a seminar from February 7, 1977, contained in the 1982 text *Théorie du sujet*, Badiou presents a table succinctly portraying the basic differences between five philosophical paradigms: subjective metaphysical idealism, objective metaphysical idealism, dialectical idealism, metaphysical materialism, and dialectical materialism.[16] Two columns of the table run next to each of these five paradigmatic types: a column under the heading "thought" (*pensée*) and a column under the heading "being-in-itself" (*être-en-soi*). In the row for type one (i.e., subjective metaphysical idealism), a circle closing in upon itself is drawn under the heading "thought" and the area beneath the heading "being-in-itself" is crossed out (indicating that this philosophical type represents something along the lines of Berkeley-style solipsism). In the row for type two (i.e., objective metaphysical idealism), a circle closing in upon itself is drawn under the heading "thought," but with an arrow connecting it to a point of reference under the heading "being-in-itself" (indicating that this philosophical type represents models involving a correspondence between the mental representations of subjective cognition and the material entities of objective reality). In the row for type three (i.e., dialectical idealism), a circle closing in upon itself starts from a point in the domain of "thought," moves through the domain of "being-in-itself," and returns to its initial point of departure in "thought" (this philosophical type obviously depicts an orthodox, textbook conception of Hegelianism). In the row for type four (i.e., metaphysical materialism), the area beneath the heading "thought" is crossed out and there is only a relation between points under the heading "being-in-itself" (indicating that this philosophical type represents varieties of severely reductive eliminative or mechanistic materialisms in which the existence of everything associated with subjectivity is either denied outright or dismissed as merely epiphenomenal). Finally, there is the fifth type of philosophical paradigm depicted in Badiou's table, namely, dialectical materialism—its visual schema is one in which a spiral starting from a point in "being-in-itself" loops back and forth between "being-in-itself" and "thought." That is to say (borrowing language from classical German idealism), the core dynamic of dialectical materialism is one in which the ground of the immanent material Real gives rise to the existence of the transcendent more-than-material Ideal (in Lacanian terms, Imaginary-Symbolic reality), with the transcendent more-than-material Ideal then coming to exert a transformative influence altering the immanent material Real—with the thus-altered Real then proceeding to transform the Ideal which altered it, and so on indefinitely. In short, rendered in this way, dialectical materialism posits an oscillating interaction between "thought" (i.e., the Imaginary-Symbolic subject) and "being-in-itself" (i.e., the asubjective Real). Through this posited interaction, it asserts that a constant, continual process of reciprocal modification links disparate orders/registers. The Imaginary-Symbolic subject of *pensée* and the asubjective Real of *être-en-soi* remain tethered to each other—subjectivity never achieves a self-relating autonomy in relation to its ontological underbelly.

Apropos Badiou's five types of philosophical paradigms, transcendental materialism would be a sixth possible position. In terms of his two-column table, transcendental materialism would be depicted as an arrow moving from a point of departure under the heading "being-in-itself" and crossing over into the area under the heading "thought." But instead of looping back into "being-in-itself" (as in dialectical materialism), this trajectory departing from the ground of the immanent material Real and entering into the space of the transcendent more-than-material Ideal doesn't return to the domain in which its point of departure is situated. There's no going back; this process of genesis is a one-way street (as in, for example, the ontogenetic event of language acquisition— once acquired, language cannot normally be un-acquired). The break induced by the more-than-material subject splitting off from its material origins is irreparable, opening up an impossible-to-close gap, a non-dialecticizable parallax split. The transcendental materialist theory of the subject is materialist insofar as it asserts that the Ideal of subjective thought arises from the Real of objective being, although it is also simultaneously transcendental insofar as it maintains that this thus-generated Ideal subjectivity thereafter achieves independence from the ground of its material sources and thereby starts to function as a set of possibility conditions for forms of reality irreducible to explanatory discourses allied to traditional versions of materialism.

However, before saying more, it should be admitted that, despite present appearances to the contrary, dialectical materialism and transcendental materialism are not diametrically opposed, mutually exclusive paradigms as regards theorizing the nature and formation of subjectivity. (In his 1975 text *Théorie de la contradiction*, Badiou defines dialectical materialism properly conceived as a doctrine according to which, despite the acknowledged fact that the material generally occupies a dominant structuring position in the order of things, there is a negativity that can and does contradict this structuring materiality.[17] Transcendental materialism affirms both that this more-than-material negativity arises from materiality and that this negativity, once generated, subsequently remains, at least in part, separate from and irreducible to its material base/ground.) Although the very rift itself created by the rupture between the Ideal of subjective thought and the Real of objective being is incapable of being healed/sealed by any sort of reconciling *Aufhebung*, there are indeed facets of more-than-material subjectivity that are entangled in reciprocal, oscillating configurations of movement with material being (as per dialectical materialism), as well as facets of subjectivity that subtract themselves from and achieve autonomy in relation to this being (as per transcendental materialism).

The transcendental materialist theory of the subject outlined here can be elucidated further through recourse to, perhaps surprisingly, the interlinked genres of Anglo-American analytic philosophy of mind and contemporary cognitive science. In his seminal paper "Mental Events,"

Donald Davidson advocates adopting, with respect to the infamous mind-body problem, a position he dubs "anomalous monism." (It's worth noting that Mark Solms, the best-known advocate of contemporary "neuropsychoanalysis," endorses Davidson's position—Solms [along with his coauthor, Oliver Turnbull] refers to it as "dual-aspect monism"—in his efforts to combine neuroscience and metapsychology.)[18] According to Davidsonian anomalous monism, mind (subject) and body (being) aren't ontologically different in kind; there is only one sort of substance (hence "monism") rather than, as per Descartes, *res cogitans* versus *res extensa*. But, Davidson insists, the monistic One he presupposes here necessarily refracts itself into two utterly distinct and separate planes of epistemological access: a plane that can be described in physical terms (i.e., terms that stick strictly to a third-person language with no reference to first-person inner mental states) and a plane that can be described in mental terms (i.e., terms that refer to first-person beliefs, desires, intentions, etc., in subjective agents). The latter plane, he contends, cannot be reduced descriptively to the former plane. In other words, the language of the mental cannot, through some unimaginable procedure of translation, be replaced by the language of the physical (as per the fantasy of eliminative materialism and related perspectives on the mind-body problem).[19] So although Davidson concedes the monism of standard versions of materialism (i.e., at the level of fundamental ontology, there is only matter and nothing more), he denies that this ontological concession can and should force an abandonment of mind-body dualism at the epistemological level: "Anomalous monism resembles materialism in its claim that all events are physical, but rejects the thesis, usually considered essential to materialism, that mental phenomena can be given purely physical explanations" (Davidson 1980, 214).

One could argue that Davidson articulates anomalous monism in the mode of a static analysis. More specifically, he treats the refractive splitting of the monistic One into the dualistic Two as a quasi-factual given, with no questions asked about whether and how this split might be something genetic (i.e., an emergent phenomena produced rather than just given). Admittedly, there is indeed support for Davidson's silent assumption of this givenness coming from certain sectors of developmental psychology (for instance, the thesis of Paul Bloom's recent book *Descartes' Baby* is that human beings are "natural Cartesians,"[20] namely, "natural-born dualists"[21] who are thrown into this world at birth hard-wired with an automatic, spontaneous disposition/tendency to divide up reality into physical bodies and mental souls[22]). However, both psychoanalytically and philosophically, there are a series of significant problems with Davidson's implicit and Bloom's explicit claim that full-blown dualism is always already in place. Moreover (Bloom and developmental psychology aside), Davidson tacitly denies any ontological status to the dualistic Two, since this split is relegated to being the fashion in which the monistic One (deceptively) appears; the dualistic Two seems to be nothing more than an epistemological necessary illusion. A transcendental materialist theory of subjectivity inspired, in particular, by Lacan and Žižek challenges the supposition of the static givenness of the dualistic Two as well as the notion that this Two is simply an epistemological appearance devoid of the weight of ontological status.

In *The Emergent Self*, William Hasker proposes and defends an account of what he calls "emergent dualism."[23] Hasker's position stipulates both that the brain gives rise to the mind (i.e., the mind emerges from the brain) and that there is a distinction to be recognized between brain and mind (i.e., the emergence of mind from brain establishes a genuine duality—hence "emergent dualism").[24] But, Hasker adds, once generated, the mind can and does exert a reciprocal guiding and transformative influence upon the brain from which it arises: "So the power attributed to matter by emergent dualism amounts to this: when suitably configured, it generates a field of consciousness . . . and *the field of consciousness in turn modifies and directs the functioning of the physical brain*" (Hasker 1999, 195). It's not just that the brain creates and shapes the mind; the mind folds itself back upon the brain, reshaping its own material ground[25] (a mind-driven reshaping of the brain which, one could presume, would then correlatively alter the same mind performing the reshaping). In essence, this amounts to a dialectical materialist model of mind.

Along related lines relevant to the present discussion, in an insightful essay entitled "*Des neurosciences aux logosciences*," François Ansermet underscores the crucial, significant implications of the biological fact of the neuroplasticity of the human central nervous system (this plasticity being what, in Hasker's emergent dualism schema, allows the mind that emerged from the brain to sculpt the malleable physical contours of this same brain). However, instead of speaking in terms of "mind"—by "mind" Hasker simply means the field of consciousness as awareness/cognizance—Ansermet refers to the "subject" (this terminological difference will turn out to be more than merely that). He elaborates:

A place seems to be made for the subject—more precisely for its very possibility—at the very heart of the laws of the organism. It is hence that the neurosciences no longer have the power to eclipse psychoanalysis. The phenomenon of plasticity necessitates thinking the subject within the very field of the neurosciences. If the neuronal network contains in its constitution the possibility of its modification; if the subject . . .

participates in this network's formation, in its realization; in short, if one acknowledges the concept of plasticity—one is obliged to introduce in the field of the neurosciences the question of uniqueness and therefore diversity. (Ansermet 2002, 377)

Echoing Hasker's thesis regarding the reciprocal causal powers of the mind with respect to the brain, Ansermet, emphasizing "the fact of plasticity," proposes that "one even comes to conceive of a psychical causality capable of shaping the organism!" (Ansermet 2002, 377). Ansermet's stance involves two key claims. First, when it comes to the matter constituting the neurological apparatus (matter that forms anything but a tightly closed field fully and exhaustively saturated by causally determining forces), the Hegelian dictum "substance is subject" holds precisely because the malleable plasticity of this special kind of materiality intrinsically harbors the potential for facilitating and undergoing processes of phenomenological and structural subjectification creating more-than-corporeal forms of subjectivity. (Moreover, as Ansermet goes on astutely to observe, given that the plastic brain is designed by nature to be redesigned by nurture insofar as humans are "genetically determined not to be genetically determined,"[26] the neurologically hard-wired "default of determinism" guarantees, at the brute material level, that spaces are cleared and held open for an autonomous subject[27]—see also chapter 13.) Second, both Hasker and Ansermet insist that the mind or subject isn't epiphenomenal, that the dialectical interaction between the parts of the dualistic Two is a properly ontological process and not just an illusory epistemological appearance distorting the subsisting being of an underlying, unperturbed monistic One.

Before turning to the pressing topic of epiphenomenalism, the implications of the above-noted terminological difference between Hasker and Ansermet—Hasker speaks of the "mind" whereas Ansermet speaks of the "subject"—must be articulated. It would seem that Hasker's emergentism is a model in which, once the right kind of material body is created (i.e., a body with the sort of neurological hardware found sitting inside human skulls), the sentient mind as field of consciousness automatically arises (in this sense, Hasker is quite close to the Aristotelian account of the body-soul relationship as delineated in *De Anima*). Perhaps one could call this a non-genetic emergentism, since, by contrast with psychoanalytic accounts of the temporally elongated ontogenetic emergence of various psychical structures coming to create a full-fledged subject (a subjectivity that isn't simply equivalent to consciousness as awareness), the sentient mind as field of consciousness pops into existence if and when the appropriate corporeal substratum is in place. This is one of the main reasons why Ansermet's choice of the term *subject* rather than *mind* is important: The emergentism proposed in transcendental materialism's model of subject formation, a model influenced by Kant and post-Kantian German idealism combined with Freudian-Lacanian psychoanalytic metapsychology, is genetic rather than, as with Hasker, instantaneous—and this because subjectivity, as opposed to mere conscious awareness, involves complex constellations of images, words, identifications, and dis-identifications. In short, a bodily brain becomes (the seat of) a subject (a subject straddling the lines between consciousness and the unconscious) over time and only through the intervention of a variety of mechanisms operative within the surrounding trans-individual milieu of Imaginary-Symbolic reality. As Žižek explains in *The Parallax View*, "it is not enough to talk about the parallel between neuronal and mental, about how mental is grounded in neuronal, about how every mental process has to have its neuronal counterpart, and so forth" (Žižek 2006, 210–11). Instead, he insists that "the real question, rather, is . . . how does the emergence/explosion of the mental *occur at the level of the neuronal itself?*" (Žižek 2006, 211)—that is, the now-familiar problem of how a more-than-material transcendence arises out of a material immanence.

Apropos the psychoanalytic approach to cognitive neuroscience, André Green justifiably warns that identifying signifying activities at work in and supported by the brain doesn't license one to speak of these significations as being contained within and emerging out of the brain itself.[28] Consequently, although the Lacanian subject of signifiers plays on cerebral surfaces—Lacan describes language as straddling the brain like a spider[29]—these subjectifying signifiers are inscribed on neural matter by an external symbolic order (and the Freudian-Lacanian portrayal of the ontogenetic starting point of the trajectory of human subject formation as an anxiety-suffused state of pre-maturational helplessness coupled with a conflict-ridden psychical apparatus explains why such potentially subjectifiable beings indeed accept the inscriptions of these mediating, structuring elements impressed upon them from without[30]—see also chapter 14). Additionally, these signifiers enjoy their own dynamics of structured interaction between themselves, dynamics obeying a logic that isn't directly and entirely controlled by the neuronal networks of the central nervous system. If anything, especially given Lacan's insistence on the materiality of the signifying chains shaping the psyche—this doctrine of the material signifier (see also chapter 7) is one of the reasons why a Lacanian approach to signifier-mediated subjectivity would object to treating the gap separating mind/subject from brain/body as merely a deontologized epistemological appearance[31]—the interactive operations between multitudes of signifiers as ideational representations (*Vorstellungen*) wire and rewire the neuronal networks running these operations.

For Hasker, the mind of emergent dualism isn't epiphenomenal precisely because of the dialectical materialist bi-directional movement of reciprocal, determining influential currents flowing between mind and brain: "The mind is not merely the passive, epiphenomenal resultant of brain activity; instead, the mind actively influences the brain at the same time as it is being influenced by it" (Hasker 1999, 193). However, in relation to the transcendental materialist theory of the subject as constructed by this project, there is another argument against epiphenomenalism that absolutely must be mentioned here, an argument alluded to by Kant in the third section of his *Grounding for the Metaphysics of Morals*. Therein Kant compares and contrasts his speculative/theoretical philosophy (à la the *Critique of Pure Reason*) with his practical/moral philosophy. A self-created problem he faces in this context is that the previously established speculative/theoretical distinction between noumenal and phenomenal subjectivity stipulates that the latter bars access to the former. More precisely, since self-consciousness is always and necessarily routed through the matrix of phenomenal spatiotemporal experience, the noumenal dimension of the subject remains an unknowable thing-in-itself, an X inaccessible to reflective acquaintance and therefore unable to serve as a subject-term to which specific, determinate predicate-terms could be attached via theoretical judgments (such as the predicate-terms *autonomous* and *free*). The phenomenal subject is mired in the "world of sense," a freedomless reality situated entirely under the governance of strict cause-and-effect laws.[32] So if self-consciousness is restricted to knowing itself solely at the phenomenal level, then how can it be sure it's autonomous/free at the noumenal level? What licenses attributing autonomy/freedom to the subject, given that the epistemologically accessible side of this subject is situated in the heteronomous regime of the sensible?

Kant has several answers to these troubling queries. But in relation to the analysis underway here in which the issue of epiphenomenalism is at stake, there is one Kantian answer that is of particular interest. He suggests that the fact of simply being able to conceive of oneself as free—for Kant, given reason's ineradicable cognizance of logical and temporal modalities of possibility, one cannot truly avoid or deny the idea of being a free agent capable of realizing various possibilities for things being otherwise than as they are—is sufficient for actually being free:

> Now I say that every being which cannot act in any way other than under the idea of freedom is for this very reason free from a practical point of view. This is to say that for such a being all the laws that are inseparably

bound up with freedom are valid just as much as if the will of such a being could be declared to be free in itself for reasons that are valid for
theoretical philosophy. (Kant 1993b, 50)

He attaches a footnote to these crucial remarks:

> I adopt this method of assuming as sufficient for our purposes that free-
> dom is presupposed merely as an idea by rational beings in their actions
> in order that I may avoid the necessity of having to prove freedom from
> a theoretical point of view as well. For even if this latter problem is left
> unresolved, the same laws that would bind a being who was really free
> are valid equally for a being who cannot act otherwise than under the
> idea of its own freedom. Thus we can relieve ourselves of the burden
> which presses on the theory. (Kant 1993b, 50)

Of course, later in the same section of this text as well as in the subsequent *Critique of Practical Reason*, Kant goes on to "prove freedom from a
theoretical point of view," to argue that there indeed exists a "transcendental freedom" belonging to the essence of the noumenal subject.[33]
But, as he points out in the passages above, such a proof isn't necessary
to "relieve . . . the burden" resulting from the portrait of the split subject
painted in the *Critique of Pure Reason;* all he requires is that there be an
idea of freedom (as an empty regulative ideal), the mere conception of
being free and nothing more. Why is this true?

To insist, as many materialists do, that mind and subjectivity are epiphenomenal as ineffective, residual illusions secreted by a thoroughly
physical reality is to ignore something that becomes incredibly obvious
upon a single moment of genuine reflection: even if the idea of being an
autonomous subject is an illusion, it's an illusion that actually steers one's
cognition and comportment—and thus shapes and reshapes one's very
being (including the components of one's material constitution itself).
Borrowing again from Alenka Zupančič (see chapter 4), this amounts
to acknowledging that there's something Real to the illusion, that the
idea of being free is Real, even if it cannot be rendered as a concept of
the understanding anchored by reference to an empirical, phenomenal
reality.[34] Succinctly put, believing oneself to be an autonomous subject
is, if nothing else, a self-fulfilling prophecy, a virtual epiphenomenon
with the strange power to become an actual phenomenon. In this vein,
Žižek proposes that "subject is appearance itself, brought to its self-
reflection; it is *something that exists only insofar as it appears to itself*" (Žižek
2006, 206). (He then proceeds to link this proposal with the enigma of
freedom, arguing that the question "How is a free act possible?" amounts

to asking *"How can appearance exert a causality of its own?"* [Žižek 2006, 206].) Additionally, in combined Kantian and Lacanian terms, the Real of this illusion is impossible in two senses: it is impossible to prove as an empirically verifiable piece of substantiated data and it is impossible to exorcise decisively as a specter forever haunting human beings' self-conceptions (and, Kant maintains, so long as this ideational specter lingers around—at most, this ghost can be repressed but not destroyed—individuals cannot divest themselves of the burden of their transcendental freedom insofar as a phantom idea is enough to make autonomy real).

In his 1946 *écrit* "Presentation on Psychical Causality," Lacan not only calls for a "return to Descartes" (see chapter 5) but also offers a critique of typical, vulgar ways of opposing idealism and materialism in relation to the notion of the epiphenomenal. He delcares:

> Of course, I wince a tad when I read that "for dualism" (still Cartesian, I presume) "the mind is a mind without existence," remembering as I do that the first judgment of certainty that Descartes bases on the consciousness that thinking has of itself is a pure judgment of existence: *cogito ergo sum.* I also get concerned when I come across the assertion that "according to materialism, the mind is an epiphenomenon," recalling as I do that form of materialism in which the mind immanent in matter is realized by the latter's very movement. (Lacan 2006e, 129)

Lacan alleges that ideal subjectivity à la the Cartesian cogito has a definite sort of existence instead of being an unreal, ephemeral ethereality. He then proceeds to hint at a variety of materialism (and not idealism) in which this subject immanently realizes itself within a material milieu.

Later in "Presentation on Psychical Causality," Lacan remarks that "if a man who thinks he is a king is mad, a king who thinks he is a king is no less so" (Lacan 2006e, 139). Lacan's basic point here is that, regardless of whether one is a king who believes himself to be a king or a lunatic who believes himself to be a king, the subject's identifications at the level of Imaginary-Symbolic reality (i.e., the world of images and words) are fictional, virtual constructs, insubstantial ideals that nonetheless are much more than mere epiphenomena insofar as these ideals entail structuring effects that reverberate throughout the entirety of the individual's multilayered being. This thesis regarding subjectifying identification justifies a reversal of the Lacanian one-liner according to which truth has the structure of a fiction.[35] Fiction has the structure of a truth: more-than-material subjectivity isn't a false, fictional epiphenomenon since it literally (re)structures the very being of the individual. (As Lacan puts it subsequently in this 1946 text, there is a "law of our becoming" commanding one to "Become such as you are"[36]—that is to say, false virtual identifications become true actual identities through fiction remaking true being in its own image.) Lacan goes on to maintain that an intimate rapport conjoins madness and freedom: both madness and freedom are possibilities for a human being due to "the permanent virtuality of a gap opened up in his essence."[37] Thanks to the mediating matrix of images and words in which the psychical individual is alienated, he or she becomes unglued from a direct referential relationship to the brute, raw immediacy of "what there is." This crack that opens up between, one could say, the virtual and the actual—the mirror stage is the primal scene of this gap's emergence (and likewise, in Hegel's *Phenomenology of Spirit*, this begins with sensuous certainty's efforts to articulate its experience)—liberates the individual psyche from a slavish adhesion to the surface of things. And yet, at the same time, this liberation from immediate reality, this negativity making possible subjectivity as such, also makes possible the complete collapse of reality characteristic of the most extreme forms of psychotic psychopathological phenomena.

Given the background role played in "Presentation on Psychical Causality" by Lacan's reflections on the mirror stage, it is clear now how these remarks on idealism, materialism, epiphenomenalism, freedom, and madness fit together: first, the material constitution of the human organism propels this being into accepting and internalizing sets of foreign images and words; second, these sets of foreign images and words thereby open up the negativity of a gap in the human organism between actual materiality and virtual more-than-materiality; and third, this gap between the actual and the virtual is the source of both freedom and madness. Thus, Lacan here understands himself to be proposing a model for the material genesis of a non-epiphenomenal, more-than-material subject (akin to the cogito, and yet linked to a certain materiality). In his much-referenced discussion of "the passion of the Real," Badiou, citing the concept of "misrecognition" (*méconnaissance*) from Lacan's mirror stage, proposes that there is a "power of misrecognition" (*puissance de la méconnaissance*) and furthermore that "there is a function of misrecognition that makes it such that the abruptness of the real operates only in fictions, montages, and masks" (Badiou 2005c, 76–77), a formulation clearly echoing the Lacanian motif of truth structured as a fiction. This "power of misrecognition" can be construed as what generatively produces a Real of illusions, as what makes the emergent virtual constellations supporting processes of subjectification more than an empty theater of fantasmatic shadows cast by the elements of a substantial physical substratum. In Lacanian theory, the images and words of the surrounding reality-matrix that the human organism is pushed into embracing by the material catalysts of its "natural" constitution start establishing between themselves cross-resonating patterns determined by their own intra-systemic logics (this is closer to Francisco Varela's notion of emergent properties[38] than to Hasker's variety of emergentism). When facets of a supposedly "epiphenomenal" field begin interacting with each other according to laws internal and specific to this field itself, epiphenomena are no longer epiphenomena.

At this juncture, transcendental materialism as conceived herein can now be precisely defined as a dialectical materialist dynamic that comes into play after the emergence of an undialecticizable dualistic split between the material and the more-than-material, a split whose resistance to cancellation by dialectical sublation is best expressed via the irreducibility constraint of anomalous/dual-aspect monism (however, contra the apparent implications of anomalous/dual-aspect monism, this split isn't epiphenomenal, since both sides of the antagonism/discrepancy between the material and the more-than-material enjoy a degree of ontological heft). Thus far, this delineation of a transcendental materialist theory of subjectivity (as distinguished from standard dialectical materialism, the anomalous monism of Davidson, and the emergent dualism of Hasker) has, in Žižek's terms, limited itself to addressing the distinction between the substance of the corpo-Real and Imaginary-Symbolic subjectification, without touching upon the subject per se (as per the Žižekian distinction between subject and subjectification—see part 3). In "The Subversion of the Subject and the Dialectic of Desire in the Freudian Unconscious," Lacan perplexingly declares that "it is precisely because desire is articulated that it is not articulable" (Lacan 2006o, 681). Likewise, in the contemporaneous seventh seminar of 1959–60, he claims that "the essential dimension of desire" resides in the fact that "it is always desire in the second degree, desire of desire" (SVII 14). As is well known, Lacanian desire is structured by the mediation of signifiers (i.e., it is "articulated"). And desire being articulated in and by signifiers is what opens up the possibility for infinite reflexive regressions (in the form of "Do I desire to desire what I desire?" as second-plus-order desires). Hence, desire isn't "articulable" as capable of being stated with a decisive, straightforward finality, since its very articulation through signifying structures and their dynamic diachronic movements (an articulation introducing reflexive regressions) liquidates any such "the buck stops here" finality. In being articulated by signifiers, desire becomes a mysterious, ineffable *je ne sais quoi*, an enigmatic X incapable of being pinned down in relation to specific desired object-contents as stable referents.

One of Žižek's recent portrayals of the Lacanian subject of the signifier in the context of an analysis of the nature of freedom resonates strongly with the preceding comments on desire as defined by Lacan. Žižek states:

> We should take Lacan's term "subject of the signifier" literally: there is, of course, no substantial signified content which guarantees the unity of the I; at this level, the subject is multiple, dispersed, and so forth—its unity is guaranteed only by the self-referential symbolic act, that is, "I" is a purely performative entity, it is the one who says "I." This is the mystery of the subject's "self-positing," explored by Fichte: of course, when I say "I," I do not create any new content, I merely designate myself, the person who is uttering the phrase. This self-designation nonetheless gives rise to ("posits") an X which is not the "real" flesh-and-blood person uttering it, but, precisely and merely, the pure Void of self-referential designation (the Lacanian "subject of the enunciation"): "I" am not directly my body, or even the content of my mind; "I" am, rather, that X which has all these features as its properties. The Lacanian subject is thus the "subject of the signifier"—not in the sense of being reducible to one of the signifiers in the signifying chain ("I" is not directly the signifier I, since, in this case, a computer or another machine writing "I" would be a subject), but in a much more precise sense: when I say "I"—when I designate "myself" as "I"—this very act of signifying adds something to the "real flesh-and-blood entity" (inclusive of the content of its mental states, desires, attitudes) thus designated, and the subject is that X which is added to the designated content by means of the act of its self-referential designation. It is therefore misleading to say that the unity of the I is "a mere fiction" beneath which there is the multitude of inconsistent mental processes: the point is that this fiction gives rise to "effects in the Real," that is to say, it acts as a necessary presupposition to a series of "real" acts. (Žižek 2006, 244–45)

Both the first-person pronoun "I" as a Benvenistean linguistic shifter and the proper name as a Kripkean rigid designator (see chapter 14) enunciated by the "flesh-and-blood" individual not only establish the skeletal frameworks upon which empirical personal identities (i.e., types of subjectification) will be patched together—they also, as Žižek suggests here, bore a hole, hollow out an empty space, in the fabric of reality. As with Lacanian desire, the positive articulations of subjectification simultaneously generate an impossible-to-articulate negativity as an X detached from and out of joint with both nature (as the barred Real) and culture (as the barred Other). What's more, this anonymous, faceless misfit ($) starts wandering around Imaginary-Symbolic reality, bending and warping the fields in which it is an internally excluded element.

The process Žižek describes in the passage quoted immediately above, a process in which the subject-as-$ arises out of signifiers as a medium of subjectification, relies on the lack of a unifying closure in the symbolic order, namely, the fact that the big Other is barred because its own internal constituents and their laws create, one could say, a chaotic, broken-up hall of mirrors in which reflexive regressions potentially stretch out to infinity. And prior to this entrance into the defiles of the symbolic order's signifying batteries (an entrance creating both subjectification and the subject), a barred Real (as the anxiety-laden, conflict-perturbed corpo-Real) propels the human organism into the arms of this barred big Other. The subject-as-$ is a by-product of both the barred Real and the barred Symbolic.

However, what does this have to do with the topic of autonomy? In *Žižek! The Movie*, Žižek, after posing the perennial question "What is philosophy?" proclaims that, rather than being a preposterous exercise in asking unanswerable questions about absolute Truth with a capital T, "philosophy is a very modest discipline. Philosophy asks a different question, the true philosophy: How does a philosopher approach the problem of freedom?" One of the most striking features of Žižek's oeuvre is his attempt to think together two seemingly incompatible senses of being a subject: on the one hand, the subject as an overdetermined effect of subjection (whether as the dupe of ideology as per Marxism or as the plaything of the unconscious as per psychoanalysis); on the other hand, the subject as an unpredictable upsurge of freedom (whether as the force of negativity uncovered by Kant, Schelling, and Hegel or as the correlate of Lacanian acts and Badiouian events). The paradoxical recto and verso of the Žižekian subject amounts to this: individuals, usually unconscious of their true subjectivity, are simultaneously more heteronomous and more autonomous than they (want to) believe or know.

Of course, Marxist theories of ideology, psychoanalytic conceptions of the unconscious, and the accumulating data about human material nature divulged by cognitive neuroscience and evolutionary psychology all seemingly present serious challenges nowadays for anyone who wishes to defend the idea of some sort of autonomous subjectivity. In light of what is presently known regarding the deterministic influences operative at historical, psychical, and biological levels, is there space left for a subject that could be said to be free in any meaningful sense? Žižek's work uniquely enables answering this question with a carefully qualified "yes."

Being free is a transitory event arising at exceptional moments when the historical, psychical, and biological run of things breaks down, when the determining capacities of natural and cultural systems—these systems are never actually the seamless networks of unfaltering determination (i.e., big Others) they so often inaccurately appear to be—are temporarily suspended as a result of deadlocks and short circuits being generated within and between these multifaceted, not-whole systems. Individuals are able to exploit the thus-generated (and perhaps rare) openings for autonomy thanks to having a constitution riddled with conflicts (this being what Žižek is getting at when he describes the dimension of the event as exploding out of the domain of the drives[39]). This quest to formulate a joint philosophical-psychoanalytic theory of autonomous subjectivity leads Žižek to a profound reconsideration of the very ontological foundations of materialism—what ultimately enables the event of subjective freedom is the fact that material being itself is already perforated by irreducible antagonisms and inconsistencies. What is being proposed here, in Žižek's wake, is a depiction of subjectivity as a transient transcendence made possible by an underlying ontology of an Otherless, barred Real. This absence of any One-All is an incredibly light being whose burden can be harder to bear than the immobilizing weight of the entire world.

Notes

Two sets of abbreviations are used for citing certain works in both the text and notes. All citations of Freud are references to the *Standard Edition*, which is abbreviated as *SE*, followed by the volume number and the page number (*SE* #:#). The abbreviation system for Jacques Lacan's seminars is a little more complicated. All seminars are abbreviated *S*, followed by the Roman numeral of the volume number. For those seminars available in English (seminars one, two, three, seven, eleven, and twenty), the page numbers given are of the volumes published by W. W. Norton and Company. For those seminars published in French in book form but not translated into English (seminars four, five, eight, ten, sixteen, seventeen, and twenty-three), the page numbers refer to the French editions published by Éditions du Seuil. As for the rest of the seminars, the dates of the seminar sessions (month/day/year) are listed in place of page numbers.

Preface

1. Žižek 2001a, 269; Žižek 2002d, 68.
2. Badiou 2000a, 11–12, 13.
3. Žižek 2002a, xi.
4. Žižek 1999c, ix.
5. Gigante 1998, 153–54, 166.
6. Derrida 1981, 95–96.
7. Foucault 1984, 118–19.
8. *SXVII* 139; Lacan 2006d, 106.
9. Wolin 1993, ix–x.
10. Žižek 2002b, 158.
11. Žižek 2001b, 9.

Chapter 1

1. Frank 1989, 25.
2. Johnston 2002, 425–26.
3. Frank 1989, 295–96, 305.
4. Lacan 2006b, 76.
5. Lacan 2006b, 80.

6. Johnston 2003a, 72–73.
7. Dolar 1998, 12; Le Gaufey 1996, 48–49, 226.
8. Žižek 1998c, 263–64.
9. Žižek 1999b, 183.

Chapter 2

1. Žižek 1999c, viii–ix.
2. Žižek 1998a, 3–4.
3. Žižek 2000b, 111–12; Žižek 2000g, 26–27.
4. Žižek 1998c, 263–64; Žižek 1999b, 304.
5. Žižek 1996b, 124.
6. Žižek 1989, 205–6.
7. Kay 2003, 1–2, 28, 45.
8. Žižek 1994b, 185; Balibar 1991, 89–90; Vaysse 1999, 196.
9. Žižek 1993, 3.
10. Žižek 2000e, ix.
11. Žižek 1993, 14.
12. Žižek 1994b, 186; Žižek 1998c, 265.
13. Žižek 1997c, 121.
14. *SVII* 139; Miller 1994, 75–76.
15. Kant 1965, 547 (A 666/B 694).
16. Kant 1965, 533–34 (A 664–65/B 672–73); Žižek 2000c, 234–35; Žižek 2001a, 205, 209.
17. Žižek 1989, 6.
18. Žižek 2002a, 217.
19. Žižek 2002a, xxv.
20. Žižek 1999g, 291–92; Žižek 1999h, 308.
21. Kant 1965, 332 (A 347/B 405); Žižek 1994b, 143–44.
22. Žižek 1997c, 208.
23. Schelling 1994a, 120.
24. Breazeale 1995, 88; Žižek 1997a, 44–45; Žižek 1999b, 44–45.
25. Žižek 1997b, 136.
26. Beiser 1987, 124.
27. Žižek 1997b, 136.
28. Fichte 1982, 33, 109, 116–17, 122.
29. Breazeale 1995, 93.
30. Fichte 1982, 191.
31. Vaysse 1999, 233.
32. Breazeale 1995, 99; Neuhouser 1990, 48–49.
33. Žižek 1989, 169; Johnston 2001, 414–15.
34. Lacan 2006h, 342.
35. Schelling 1936, 16–17, 18.

Chapter 3

1. Žižek 1997c, 237.
2. Žižek 1998a, 7.
3. Kay 2003, 23.
4. Hegel 1977c, 18–19 (§32).
5. Žižek 2000i, 231, 239–40.
6. Laplanche and Pontalis 1973, 376–77.
7. *SE* 14:76.
8. Žižek 2000a, 36.
9. Clark 1996, xi, 54, 62–63.
10. *SXI* 177, 197–98, 199; Lacan 2006p, 719–20; Miller 2001a, 29.
11. *SXI* 204–5; Miller 2000, 26; Verhaeghe 1998, 168.
12. *SE* 14:305.
13. Žižek 1994b, 116; Žižek 1995, 208; Žižek 2001c, 81–82; Žižek 2002b, 152.
14. Žižek 1997a, 22–23; Žižek 1997c, 66.
15. Žižek 1997a, 24.
16. Žižek 1999b, 267.
17. Žižek 2002b, 144–45; Žižek 2002a, lxxiii.
18. *SX* 105, 187–88.
19. Kristeva 1982, 2, 3–4, 5, 11.
20. Heidegger 1962, 281–82, 282–83.
21. Kant 1978, 24–25, 26.
22. Kant 1965, 161–62 (B 146–47), 171 (B 161), 208–9 (B 218–19); Kant 1977, 43–44, 58–59.
23. Žižek 2000c, 256.
24. *SIX* 5/23/62; *SXVII* 142–43; Lacan 2001e, 405; Lacan 1978.
25. *SXX* 79.
26. *SE* 20:129–30.
27. *SXXI* 12/18/73.
28. *SII* 211.
29. *SIII* 179–80.
30. *SXXII* 4/8/75.
31. *SXXIII* 125.
32. *SV* 465.
33. Lacan 1990b, 107.
34. Lacan 2001f, 451.
35. *SE* 14:186–87.
36. Lacan 2006g, 316; Lacan 2001g, 549.
37. *SXVII* 142.
38. Copjec 1994, 24–25, 25–26, 27–28; Kay 2003, 88–89.
39. Kant 1965, 396 (A 426–27/B 454–55).
40. Kant 1965, 455 (A 517/B 545).
41. Kant 1965, 194–95 (B 156); Zupančič 1996, 52–53.
42. Kant 1965, 389 (A 350–51).
43. Baas 1998, 249; Poissonnier 1998, 204; Safouan 2001a, 12–13.

Chapter 4

1. *SXVII* 118–19.
2. Žižek 1999b, 59–60.
3. Žižek 1999b, 163–64.
4. Laplanche and Pontalis 1986, 19.
5. Laplanche and Pontalis 1986, 27.
6. *SE* 14:290.
7. Milner 1995, 68–69.
8. Žižek 1994a, 26; Kant 1965, 108 (A 71–73/B 97–98).
9. Žižek 1992b, 262.
10. *SIII* 321.
11. *SIII* 81, 190–91.
12. Ragland 1995, 102.
13. Lacan 1977, 38–39; Žižek 2001b, 100.
14. Muller 1980, 147, 156.
15. *SE* 5:357.
16. *SXIII* 12/15/65.
17. *SE* 14:296.
18. *SE* 20:93–94, 135–36.
19. Brown 1959, 127–28; Becker 1973, 107.
20. Rank 1958, 124–25.
21. Rank 1958, 116.
22. Žižek 1997a, 80; Žižek 1996a, 117.
23. Žižek 1996a, 94.
24. Plato 2002, 104 (lines 67b–e).
25. Žižek 1996b, 110–11.
26. Heidegger 1962, 280.
27. Heidegger 1962, 281.
28. Žižek 2001b, 169.
29. *SE* 21:64–65.
30. Zupančič 2001, 141–42.

Chapter 5

1. *SE* 10:232–33.
2. Schneiderman 1983, 145.
3. Leclaire 1980, 109–10.
4. Green 2000b, 169–70, 180.
5. Žižek 1993, 76.
6. Žižek 1997c, 123.
7. *SVII* 320.
8. Lacan 2001e, 409.
9. Lacan 2006b, 76; Lacan 2006c, 90.
10. Lacan 2006b, 76; Johnston 2000, 63–64.
11. Boothby 2001, 135–36, 138, 140.

12. Miller 2001b, 35.
13. *SII* 238.
14. Lacan 2006b, 76, 79.
15. Lacan 2005b, 41.
16. Kojève 1947, 372–73.
17. *SI* 178, 242–43.
18. *SVII* 248.
19. Safouan 1983, 60.
20. Johnston 2000, 66.
21. *SXX* 17; Miller 2001a, 21.
22. Žižek 2002b, 107.
23. *SE* 14:120; *SE* 18:28–29.
24. Lacan 2006b, 76.
25. Johnston 2003b, 227–28.
26. Lacan 1966, 93.
27. Lacan 2006e, 133.
28. *SE* 1:169–70.
29. *SVIII* 415–16; *SX* 42; *SXII* 2/3/65.
30. *SVIII* 417–18, 443–44, 460.
31. *SXXIII* 150, 154.
32. Van Haute 2002, xv–xvi.
33. Žižek 2000d, v–vi.
34. *SX* 326, 328–29.
35. *SXI* 53–54, 54–55.
36. *SXI* 128.
37. *SXI* 126.
38. *SXI* 70, 77, 80.
39. *SE* 4:111; *SII* 157; Johnston 2005a, 242–43.
40. *SXVIII* 6/16/71; *SXX* 3.
41. *SVIII* 427.
42. *SE* 18:28–29.
43. Žižek 1999b, 198.
44. Badiou 1992, 66; Badiou 2006, 30; Badiou 2000b, 296.
45. Badiou 2005a, 391, 432; Badiou 1991, 26; Badiou 2003c, 87; Gillespie 1996, 60.
46. Badiou 2005a, 23–24, 24–25, 93–94.
47. Badiou 2005a, 52, 69.
48. Hallward 2003, 65–66, 100–101.
49. *SXVIII* 1/20/71.
50. Žižek 1999b, 59–60.
51. Žižek 2004c, 125–26.
52. Johnston 2005b, 340–41.

Chapter 6

1. Žižek 2004c, 58.

2. Žižek 1999b, 276–77.
3. Žižek and Daly 2004, 65–66.
4. Žižek 1996b, 8; Žižek 1997a, 4; Myers 2003, 39.
5. Žižek 1999b, 88.
6. Žižek 1988, 225.
7. Žižek 1997c, 208.
8. Žižek 1996b, 7.
9. Žižek 1992a, 49–50.
10. Johnston 2003a, 59, 60–61.
11. Žižek 1994b, 129.
12. Johnston 2003b, 228, 230.
13. *SXXIII* 137–38.
14. Žižek 1997a, 18; Žižek 2002d, 22; Žižek 2004a, 34.
15. Kant 1965, 161 (B 145); Johnston 2003a, 57–58, 59.
16. Bowie 1993, 163.
17. Žižek 1994b, 129–30; Žižek 2001c, 10.
18. Schelling 1936, 16–17.
19. Bowie 1993, 140.
20. Žižek 1996b, 100.
21. Žižek 2004c, 58.
22. Schelling 2000, 60–61; Žižek 1996b, 28–29.
23. Žižek 1988, 227–28; Žižek 1996b, 8–9.
24. Žižek 2002b, 167; Žižek 2004c, 23.
25. Žižek 2001b, 95; Žižek 2004a, 32.
26. Žižek 1996b, 53.
27. Schelling 1936, 86–87.

Chapter 7

1. Žižek 2000f, 86.
2. Žižek 1997a, 24.
3. Žižek 1997a, 103.
4. Schelling 2002, 19.
5. Schelling 2002, 22.
6. Schelling 2000, 20, 49.
7. Žižek 2001c, 96.
8. Schelling 1994c, 202.
9. Schelling 2002, 54.
10. Schelling 2000, 31–32, 63.
11. Schelling 2000, 21.
12. Schelling 2000, 48.
13. Schelling 2002, 27.
14. Schelling 2002, 72.
15. Schelling 2000, 27–28.
16. Schelling 2000, 20, 92.

17. Žižek 1997a, 82, 84–85.
18. Žižek 1997a, 80–81.
19. Schelling 1994c, 237.
20. Schelling 2002, 34.
21. Schelling 2002, 34–35.
22. Schelling 2002, 35, 36–37.
23. Schelling 2000, 62.
24. Schelling 2002, 39–40.
25. Žižek 1997a, 46; Žižek 1999e, 73.
26. Schelling 1966, 65, 123; Schelling 1984, 180; Johnston 2003b, 230–31.
27. Žižek 1996b, 112, 152; Žižek 2004c, 75.
28. Schelling 1994a, 120.
29. Žižek 1997b, 136.
30. Lacan 2001b, 137–38; Lacan 2001c, 199.
31. *SII* 82.
32. *SIX* 1/10/62.
33. *SXIV* 5/10/67.
34. Derrida 1987, 464.
35. *SXXIV* 4/19/77.
36. *SXVI* 88–89, 90.
37. Lacan 2006m, 580.
38. Žižek 2002a, 53.
39. Žižek 2004c, 142.
40. Johnston 2005b, xxxi–xxxii, 374–75.
41. Schelling 1994c, 206–7.
42. Schelling 1994c, 200.
43. *SE* 21:65–66, 66–67, 68.
44. Schelling 2000, 5–6.
45. Schelling 2000, 11.
46. Žižek 1996b, 19.

Chapter 8

1. Schelling 2000, 16.
2. Schelling 1994c, 207–8; Schelling 2000, 31.
3. *SE* 19:236–37, 238–39.
4. Schelling 2000, 22–23.
5. Žižek 2000f, 93–94.
6. Žižek 1988, 221.
7. Žižek 1988, 229.
8. Žižek 1997a, 14–15.
9. *SXVII* 101–2.
10. Žižek 1988, 224.
11. Schelling 2000, 49.
12. Žižek 1997a, 29.

13. Derrida 1992, 13–14.
14. Žižek 1997a, 37–38.
15. *SE* 14:148–49, 180–81; *SE* 20:94.
16. *SE* 1:231, 270–71, 279; *SE* 3:220, 255.
17. Žižek 1996b, 47.
18. Zupančič 2000, 28, 39; Zupančič 2001, 35, 46.

Chapter 9

1. Kant 1993a, 76–77; Kant 1993b, 8–9.
2. Žižek 2004c, 25–26.
3. Žižek 1992a, 35–36; Žižek 1997a, 41.
4. Žižek 1999b, 318.
5. Žižek 1988, 222–23.
6. Kant 1960, 32.
7. Allison 1990, 40; Allison 1995, 13.
8. Schelling 1936, 44–45, 47–48; Žižek 1999f, 272–73.
9. Žižek and Daly 2004, 135.
10. Vaysse 1999, 269–70.
11. Johnston 2005b, 340–41.
12. Žižek 2004c, 24–25.
13. Badiou 2005a, 173–74.
14. Žižek and Daly 2004, 60, 94.
15. Žižek and Daly 2004, 59.
16. Žižek and Daly 2004, 64–65.
17. Žižek 1996b, 73.
18. Žižek 1988, 77.
19. Heidegger 1985, 60.
20. Hallward 2003, xxxii, 167.
21. Badiou 2003a, 131.
22. Hallward 2003, 144.
23. Schelling 1994c, 225.
24. Althusser 1994, 130–31, 135–36.
25. Aristotle 1999, 35 (book 3, chapter 3, §10).
26. Kant 1993a, 3, 6.
27. Schelling 1936, 3, 24.
28. Johnston 2003b, 229, 241–42.
29. *SE* 7:148.

Chapter 10

1. Žižek 1997a, 37–38.
2. Žižek and Daly 2004, 75–76.
3. Žižek 2000c, 221.

Chapter 11

1. Žižek 1991, 37; Žižek 1996b, 121–22; Žižek 2000g, 29; Žižek 2003b, 79–80; Žižek and Daly 2004, 63.
2. Žižek 1994b, 35.
3. *SII* 192–93; Lacan 2006a, 35.
4. Žižek 1989, 61–62; Žižek 2002a, 169.
5. Žižek 2001b, 101.
6. Žižek 1999b, 86.
7. Žižek 1999b, 113.
8. Žižek 2002a, 145.
9. Hegel 1975, 76–77 (§48).
10. Žižek 2002a, xcvi.
11. Hegel 1969, 56.
12. Žižek 2002a, 217; Žižek 1993, 19; Žižek 2004c, 60.
13. Žižek 2002a, 67.
14. Hegel 1977c, 490–91 (§805), 491–92 (§806–7).
15. Žižek 1993, 245–46; Žižek 2002a, xxv.
16. Hegel 1977a, 90–91.
17. Hegel 1977b, 66.
18. Žižek 2002a, 159–60.
19. Žižek 2002a, 157–58; Žižek 1999b, 85–86.
20. Fichte 1982, 148.
21. Fichte 1982, 247, 252; Fichte 1965, 82.
22. Schelling 1994a, 100.
23. Schelling 1994a, 101.
24. Schelling 1994a, 102.
25. Hegel 1969, 47.
26. Hegel 1977b, 76–77.
27. Hegel 1969, 36, 62.
28. Hegel 1990, 65 (§33).
29. Žižek 1989, 172; Žižek 1993, 20.
30. Hegel 1977a, 173.
31. Kant 1965, 27 (B xxvi–xxvii).
32. Hegel 1977b, 89.
33. Hegel 1977c, 87–88 (§144).
34. Hegel 1969, 489.
35. Žižek 1996b, 160; Žižek 1999b, 196–97.
36. *SXI* 103, 111–12.
37. Žižek 1993, 39, 245–46.
38. Hegel 1969, 507.
39. Hegel 1969, 489.
40. Hegel 1990, 92 (§88).
41. Žižek 2002a, 58–59.
42. Hegel 1969, 490–91.
43. Žižek 1989, 214; Žižek 2002a, 58.

44. Žižek 1993, 38; Žižek 1996b, 139; Žižek 2002a, xlix–l.
45. Žižek 2002a, xxx.
46. Heidegger 1962, 236, 400, 435.
47. Žižek 2004d, 259.
48. Žižek 1989, 213; Žižek 2000h, 172–73.

Chapter 12

1. Lacan 1990a, 6.
2. Žižek 2001c, 80–81; Žižek 2002a, xxvii–xxviii.
3. Žižek 2002d, 31–32; Žižek 2003b, 67.
4. Žižek 1988, 77.
5. *SXX* 93.
6. Žižek 2003b, 69–70.
7. Žižek 1993, 128–29.
8. *SE* 12:219; *SE* 14:231.
9. Fichte 1982, 189.
10. Fichte 1982, 191.
11. Schelling 1994b, 75.
12. Schelling 1984, 136; Hegel 1977a, 156.
13. Schelling 1984, 147.
14. Schelling 1984, 199.
15. Schelling 1984, 208.
16. Žižek 1996b, 112.
17. Schelling 1994b, 85.
18. Hegel 1969, 46.
19. Kant 1965, 22 (B xvi–xvii).
20. Schelling 1994a, 102.
21. Brown 1977, 94–95.
22. Žižek 1996b, 58.
23. Schelling 1994b, 87.
24. *SE* 4:111.
25. *SE* 5:525.
26. *SE* 18:273.
27. Žižek 1992a, 53.
28. Žižek 1993, 153–54.
29. Žižek 2003b, 28.
30. Žižek 2005e, 216–17.
31. Žižek 1993, 128.
32. Žižek 2005b, 28–29; Žižek 2002a, 94–95.
33. Žižek 1999b, 159–60.
34. Žižek and Daly 2004, 58.
35. Žižek and Daly 2004, 61.
36. Heidegger 1962, 103–4, 105–6.
37. Damasio 2003, 164.

38. Žižek 2002a, 119.
39. Žižek 2002a, 42.
40. Žižek 2002a, 43.
41. Žižek 2002a, 43–44, 46; Žižek 2005d, 74; Žižek 1999b, 92, 100–101, 102–3; Žižek 2003b, 87.
42. Laclau and Mouffe 2001, 138–39, 143–44, 193.
43. Dawkins 1976, 206.
44. Gould and Vrba 1982, 4, 6.
45. Dawkins 1976, 207–8, 213; Blackmore 1999, 79–80, 99–100, 235.
46. *SE* 20:154–55, 167.
47. Lacan 2001a, 33–34.
48. Grosz 1990, 33.
49. Lacan 2006b, 76.

Chapter 13

1. Žižek 2003b, 54.
2. Žižek 2004c, 58.
3. Žižek 2004c, 42; Žižek 2004d, 258, 259–60.
4. Žižek 1999a, 26.
5. Žižek 2005b, 27.
6. Žižek 2005b, 31; Žižek 2005c, 41, 55.
7. Kant 1978, 175.
8. *SE* 23:150–51.
9. Kant 1978, 176.
10. Žižek 1999b, 104.
11. Heidegger 1993, 332.
12. *SE* 19:163–64.
13. Žižek 2002a, 144.
14. *SE* 21:69–70.
15. Lear 2000, 80–81, 84–85.
16. Žižek 2003b, 70–71.
17. Žižek 2002a, 69.
18. Žižek 1999b, 2.
19. Žižek 1994b, 145.
20. Žižek 1997a, 9; Žižek 2000f, 81–82; Žižek 2001a, 77.
21. Žižek 1992a, 53; Žižek 1999b, 55.
22. Žižek 1992a, 50–51.
23. Žižek 1992a, 51–52, 54.
24. Žižek 1998c, 258.
25. Kant 1965, 133 (A 101–2), 144 (A 120).
26. Kant 1965, 144–45 (A 121–22).
27. Žižek 1999b, 32.
28. Žižek 1993, 171.
29. Klein 1964, 61–62; Klein 1975, xiii–xiv.

30. Žižek 1992a, 66.
31. Kant 1965, 24 (B xix–xx).
32. Badiou 2005a, 6; Badiou 2004, 37–38; Badiou 2006, 40.
33. Badiou 2005a, 28; Badiou 2006, 36; Hallward 1998, 89–90.
34. Badiou 2005a, 7; Badiou 1998, 127.
35. Žižek 1996b, 230–31.
36. Žižek 1996b, 211.
37. Žižek 2006, 239.
38. Malabou 2004, 127, 141, 146–47, 159, 161–62, 162–63, 164.
39. Sartre 1956, 439, 484–85.
40. Dennett 2003, 85.
41. Chesterton 1995, 28.

Chapter 14

1. *SE* 18:106–7, 116.
2. *SIII* 267–68.
3. *SXXIII* 94.
4. *SVIII* 417–18; Lacan 2006l, 567.
5. *SIX* 2/28/62; *SXI* 256.
6. *SXII* 2/3/65.
7. Lacan 2006l, 567–68, 569; *SXI* 256–57; Safouan 2001b, 179–80.
8. *SX* 42.
9. *SX* 52.
10. Kripke 1972, 26.
11. Kripke 1972, 41.
12. Kant 1965, 331 (A 345–46/B 404).
13. Kripke 1972, 57–58.
14. *SXVI* 394.
15. *SIX* 11/29/61, 12/13/61.
16. *SIX* 11/22/61.
17. *SIX* 12/6/61.
18. *SIX* 3/28/62.
19. *SIX* 11/15/61.
20. Gasché 1986, 6, 238.
21. Žižek 2002a, 89.
22. *SIX* 11/29/61.
23. Johnston 2005b, 153, 320.
24. Dor 1992, 84, 87, 91–92; Safouan 2001b, 189–90.
25. *SXIV* 2/15/67; *SXVI* 121, 126–27.
26. Plato 1992, 189 (lines 517b–c).
27. Hegel 1977c, 208 (§343).
28. Žižek 1989, 207.
29. Žižek 1989, 194.
30. Žižek 2005a, 11–12.

31. Lefort 1988, 225, 228; Laclau and Mouffe 2001, 186–87.
32. Žižek 2000b, 111–12.
33. Žižek 1992a, 87–88.

Chapter 15

1. Hegel 1977c, 493 (§808).
2. Žižek 1993, 269.
3. Žižek 1993, 26.
4. Hegel 1969, 82–83.
5. Hegel 1969, 96.
6. Hegel 1975, 131 (§88).
7. Aristotle 1991, 98.
8. Aristotle 1991, 96–97.
9. Johnston 2003b, 241–42.
10. Johnston 2003b, 228–29.
11. Heidegger 1962, 401–2; Heidegger 1982, 301–2, 307, 314–15, 318.
12. Heidegger 1982, 323–24.
13. Martin-Mattera 2002, 99–100.
14. Bergson 1910, 104–5, 128–29.
15. Johnston 2005b, 24–25, 35, 55–56.
16. Johnston 2005b, 25, 42–43, 55, 77.
17. Žižek 2003b, 78–79.
18. Žižek 2001c, 82; Žižek and Daly 2004, 69; Žižek 2004c, 102–3.
19. *SXIX* 4/19/72.
20. *SVI* 11/12/58.
21. *SXIX* 2/3/72.
22. Milner 2002, 144–45, 146.
23. *SXVI* 379–80, 380–81.
24. Assoun 2003, 80.
25. Lacan 2006o, 677.
26. Lacan 2001f, 449, 452–53.
27. Lacan 2006o, 677.
28. Lacan 2006o, 677.
29. Fink 1995, 39–40.
30. Van Haute 2002, 41–42.
31. *SXVII* 11–12.
32. *SXI* 207–8, 218, 236.
33. Lacan 2001f, 452; Lacan 1990a, 9.
34. Lacan 2006o, 681–82.
35. Fink 2004, 116.
36. *SXVIII* 1/20/71.
37. *SXVII* 101–2, 167.
38. Hegel 1977c, 117–18 (§193–95), 118–19 (§196).
39. Lacan 2001e, 447.

40. Verhaeghe 2001a, 22.
41. Fink 1998, 31; Žižek 1998b, 75; Žižek 1999d, 28; Žižek 2004b, 133.
42. *SE* 6:61.
43. *SIX* 12/6/61.
44. Žižek 1998b, 74–75; Žižek 2004b, 132–33.
45. *SXI* 207.
46. Lacan 2006p, 711.
47. Lacan 2001e, 409.
48. Lacan 2001f, 452.
49. Žižek 1996b, 123.
50. Fink 2004, 114–15; Van Haute 2002, 21–22.
51. Lacan 2006m, 580.
52. *SV* 218–19.
53. *SV* 189.
54. Žižek 1999d, 28–29.
55. Žižek 2004b, 133–34.
56. Žižek 2002b, 192–93; Žižek 2004b, 144.
57. Johnston 2005b, xxxi–xxxii.
58. Žižek and Salecl 1996, 25.
59. Žižek 1999b, 87.
60. LeDoux 2002, 197–98.
61. Hegel 1977c, 58 (§90).
62. Hegel 1977c, 60 (§97).
63. Hegel 1977c, 59–60 (§95–96); Žižek 2002a, 160–61.
64. Žižek 2004b, 134.
65. *SXVII* 38.
66. Žižek 2002a, 51–52, 78; Žižek 1994b, 46–47; Žižek 1996b, 47–48.
67. Žižek 1996b, 124.
68. Žižek 2002a, 47–48; Žižek 1993, 23.
69. Žižek 2002a, 189.

Conclusion

1. Badiou 2005b, 14.
2. Badiou 1999, 58.
3. Badiou 1990, 4–5, 6.
4. Brassier 2004, 52.
5. Badiou 1991, 25, 27; Badiou 2001, 44; Badiou 2003b, 56; Badiou 2003d, 175.
6. *SXI* 207, 210.
7. Lacan 2006k, 514.
8. *SXXIV* 4/19/77.
9. *SIV* 254.
10. *SXXI* 5/21/74; *SXXIV* 5/17/77.
11. *SXX* 6–7, 9, 12.

12. *SVIII* 117; *SXVIII* 2/17/71; *SXIX* 3/3/72.
13. *SXVII* 36.
14. *SXVIII* 2/17/71.
15. *SXXIV* 5/17/77.
16. Badiou 1982, 135.
17. Badiou 1975, 77–78, 80.
18. Solms and Turnbull 2002, 56–57.
19. Davidson 1980, 216–17, 221–22, 225.
20. Bloom 2004, xii.
21. Bloom 2004, xiii.
22. Bloom 2004, 24.
23. Hasker 1999, 194.
24. Hasker 1999, 189–90.
25. Hasker 1999, 190–91.
26. Ansermet 2002, 378.
27. Ansermet 2002, 383.
28. Green 1995, 45.
29. Lacan 2005a, 46.
30. Johnston 2006, 34–35, 36–37.
31. Lacan 2001d, 224.
32. Kant 1993b, 52–53.
33. Kant 1993b, 53–54, 54–55; Kant 1993a, 57–58.
34. Zupančič 2002a, 52.
35. Lacan 2006i, 376; Lacan 2006n, 625; Lacan 2006o, 684.
36. Lacan 2006e, 145.
37. Lacan 2006e, 144.
38. Varela 1995, 216.
39. Žižek and Daly 2004, 137.

Works Cited

Agamben, Giorgio. 2004. *The Open: Man and Animal.* Translated by Kevin Attell. Stanford: Stanford University Press.

Allison, Henry E. 1990. *Kant's Theory of Freedom.* Cambridge: Cambridge University Press.

———. 1995. "Spontaneity and Autonomy in Kant's Conception of the Self." In *The Modern Subject: Conceptions of the Self in Classical German Philosophy.* Edited by Karl Ameriks and Dieter Sturma. Albany: State University of New York Press. 11–45.

Althusser, Louis. 1994. "Ideology and Ideological State Apparatuses (Notes Towards an Investigation)." In *Mapping Ideology.* Edited by Slavoj Žižek. London: Verso. 100–140.

Ansermet, François. 2002. "*Des neurosciences aux logosciences.*" In *Qui sont vos psychanalystes?* Edited by Nathalie Georges, Jacques-Alain Miller, and Nathalie Marchaison. Paris: Éditions du Seuil. 376–84.

Aristotle. 1991. *De Anima.* Translated by R. D. Hicks. Buffalo, N.Y.: Prometheus Books.

———. 1999. *Nicomachean Ethics.* Translated by Terence Irwin. Indianapolis: Hackett.

Assoun, Paul-Laurent. 2003. *Lacan.* Paris: Presses Universitaires de France.

Baas, Bernard. 1998. *De la chose à l'objet: Jacques Lacan et la traversée de la phénoménologie.* Louvain: Peeters.

Badiou, Alain. 1975. *Théorie de la contradiction.* Paris: François Maspero.

———. 1982. *Théorie du sujet.* Paris: Éditions du Seuil.

———. 1990. "*L'entretien de Bruxelles.*" *Les temps modernes,* 526:1–26.

———. 1991. "On a Finally Objectless Subject." Translated by Bruce Fink. In *Who Comes After the Subject?* Edited by Peter Connor and Jean-Luc Nancy. New York: Routledge. 24–32.

———. 1992. "*Le (re)tour de la philosophie* elle-même." In *Conditions.* Paris: Éditions du Seuil. 57–78.

———. 1998. "Politics and Philosophy: An Interview with Alain Badiou (with Peter Hallward)," *Angelaki* 3, no. 3 (December):113–33.

———. 1999. *Manifesto for Philosophy.* Translated by Norman Madarasz. Albany: State University of New York Press.

———. 2000a. *Deleuze: The Clamor of Being.* Translated by Louise Burchill. Minneapolis: University of Minnesota Press.

———. 2000b. "*L'existence et la mort.*" In *Philosopher T2: Les interrogations contempo-*

raines, matériaux pour un enseignement. Edited by Christian Delacampagne and Robert Maggiori. Paris: Fayard. 293–302.

———. 2001. *Ethics: An Essay on the Understanding of Evil.* Translated by Peter Hallward. London: Verso.

———. 2003a. "Beyond Formalisation: An Interview (with Peter Hallward and Bruno Bosteels)." Translated by Bruno Bosteels and Alberto Toscano. *Angelaki* 8, no. 2 (August): 111–36.

———. 2003b. "Philosophy and Desire." In *Infinite Thought: Truth and the Return of Philosophy.* Edited and translated by Oliver Feltham and Justin Clemens. London: Continuum. 39–57.

———. 2003c. "Philosophy and Psychoanalysis." In *Infinite Thought: Truth and the Return of Philosophy.* Edited and translated by Oliver Feltham and Justin Clemens. London: Continuum. 79–90.

———. 2003d. "Ontology and Politics: An Interview with Alain Badiou." In *Infinite Thought: Truth and the Return of Philosophy.* Edited and translated by Oliver Feltham and Justin Clemens. London: Continuum. 169–93.

———. 2004. "Philosophy and Mathematics: Infinity and the End of Romanticism." In *Theoretical Writings.* Edited and translated by Ray Brassier and Alberto Toscano. London: Continuum. 21–38.

———. 2005a. *Being and Event.* Translated by Oliver Feltham. London: Continuum.

———. 2005b. *Handbook of Inaesthetics.* Translated by Alberto Toscano. Stanford: Stanford University Press.

———. 2005c. *Le siècle.* Paris: Éditions du Seuil.

———. 2006. *Briefings on Existence: A Short Treatise on Transitory Ontology.* Translated by Norman Madarasz. Albany: State University of New York Press.

Balibar, Étienne. 1991. *"Lacan avec Kant: L'idée du symbolisme."* In *Lacan avec les philosophes.* Edited by Bibliothèque du Collège International de Philosophie. Paris: Éditions Albin Michel. 87–97.

Bataille, Georges. 1988. *Inner Experience.* Translated by Leslie Anne Boldt. Albany: State University of New York Press.

Becker, Ernest. 1973. *The Denial of Death.* New York: Free Press.

Beiser, Frederick. 1987. *The Fate of Reason: German Philosophy from Kant to Fichte.* Cambridge, Mass.: Harvard University Press.

Benveniste, Emile. 1971. "Subjectivity in Language." In *Problems in General Linguistics.* Translated by Mary Elizabeth Meek. Coral Gables: University of Miami Press. 223–30.

Bergson, Henri. 1910. *Time and Free Will: An Essay on the Immediate Data of Consciousness.* Translated by F. L. Pogson. Kila, Montana: Kessinger. Reprint.

Blackmore, Susan. 1999. *The Meme Machine.* Oxford: Oxford University Press.

Bloom, Paul. 2004. *Descartes' Baby: How the Science of Child Development Explains What Makes Us Human.* New York: Basic Books.

Boothby, Richard. 2001. *Freud as Philosopher: Metapsychology After Lacan.* New York: Routledge.

Bowie, Andrew. 1993. *Schelling and Modern European Philosophy: An Introduction.* New York: Routledge.

Brassier, Ray. 2004. "Nihil Unbound: Remarks on Subtractive Ontology and Thinking Capitalism." In *Think Again: Alain Badiou and the Future of Philosophy.* Edited by Peter Hallward. London: Continuum. 50–58.

Breazeale, Daniel. 1995. "Check or Checkmate?: On the Finitude of the Fichtean Self." In *The Modern Subject: Conceptions of the Self in Classical German Philosophy.* Edited by Karl Ameriks and Dieter Sturma. Albany: State University of New York Press. 87–114.

Brown, Norman O. 1959. *Life Against Death: The Psychoanalytic Meaning of History.* Hanover, N.H.: Wesleyan University Press and University Press of New England.

Brown, Robert F. 1977. *The Later Philosophy of Schelling: The Influence of Boehme on the Works of 1809–1815.* Lewisburg, Pa.: Bucknell University Press.

Chesterton, G. K. 1995. *Orthodoxy.* San Francisco: Ignatius.

Clark, William C. 1996. *Sex and the Origins of Death.* Oxford: Oxford University Press.

Copjec, Joan. 1994. "Sex and the Euthanasia of Reason." In *Supposing the Subject.* Edited by Joan Copjec. London: Verso. 16–44.

———. 2004. *Imagine There's No Woman: Ethics and Sublimation.* Cambridge, Mass.: MIT Press.

Dalto, Silvana. 2002. "The Origin of the Subject from the Perspective of Freud's Scientific Materialism." Translated by Luke Thurston. In *The Pre-Psychoanalytic Writings of Sigmund Freud.* Edited by Gertrudis Van de Vijver and Filip Geerardyn. London: Karnac. 215–25.

Damasio, Antonio. 2003. *Looking for Spinoza: Joy, Sorrow, and the Feeling Brain.* New York: Harcourt.

Davidson, Donald. 1980. "Mental Events." In *Essays on Actions and Events.* Oxford: Oxford University Press. 207–25.

Dawkins, Richard. 1976. *The Selfish Gene.* Oxford: Oxford University Press.

Dennett, Daniel C. 2003. *Freedom Evolves.* New York: Viking.

Derrida, Jacques. 1981. "Plato's Pharmacy." In *Dissemination.* Translated by Barbara Johnson. Chicago: University of Chicago Press. 61–171.

———. 1987. "*Le facteur de la vérité.*" In *The Post Card: From Socrates to Freud and Beyond.* Translated by Alan Bass. Chicago: University of Chicago Press. 411–96.

———. 1992. "Force of Law: The 'Mystical Foundation of Authority.'" Translated by Mary Quaintance. In *Deconstruction and the Possibility of Justice.* Edited by Drucilla Cornell, Michel Rosenfeld, and David Gray Carlson. New York: Routledge. 3–67.

Descartes, René. 1993. *Meditations on First Philosophy.* Translated by Donald A. Cress. Indianapolis: Hackett.

Dolar, Mladen. 1993. "Beyond Interpellation." *Qui Parle* 6, no. 2 (Spring/Summer): 75–96.

———. 1994a. "The Phrenology of Spirit." In *Supposing the Subject.* Edited by Joan Copjec. London: Verso. 64–83.

———. 1994b. "*Das Vermächtnis der Aufklärung: Foucault und Lacan.*" Translated by Lydia Marinelli. In *Wo Es war: Kant und das Unbewußte.* Vienna: Turia und Kant. 7–30.

————. 1996. "At First Sight." In *Gaze and Voice as Love Objects*. Edited by Renata Salecl and Slavoj Žižek. Durham, N.C.: Duke University Press. 129–53.

————. 1998. "Cogito as the Subject of the Unconscious." In *Cogito and the Unconscious*. Edited by Slavoj Žižek. Durham, N.C.: Duke University Press. 11–40.

Dor, Joël. 1992. *Introduction à la lecture de Lacan, Tome II: La structure du sujet*. Paris: Denoël.

Dostoyevsky, Fyodor. 2003. *"Notes from Underground" and "The Double."* Translated by Jessie Coulson. New York: Penguin Books.

Eagleton, Terry. 2001. "Enjoy!" In "A Symposium on Slavoj Žižek: Faith and the Real." *Paragraph* 24, no. 2 (July): 40–52.

————. 2003. "Alain Badiou." In *Figures of Dissent: Critical Essays on Fish, Spivak, Žižek and Others*. London: Verso. 246–53.

Fichte, J. G. 1965. *The Vocation of Man*. Translated by William Smith. La Salle, Ill.: Open Court.

————. 1982. *The Science of Knowledge*. Translated by Peter Heath and John Lachs. Cambridge: Cambridge University Press.

Fink, Bruce. 1995. *The Lacanian Subject: Between Language and Jouissance*. Princeton, N.J.: Princeton University Press.

————. 1998. "The Master Signifier and the Four Discourses." In *Key Concepts of Lacanian Psychoanalysis*. Edited by Dany Nobus. New York: Other Press, 29–47.

————. 2004. *Lacan to the Letter: Reading* Écrits *Closely*. Minneapolis: University of Minnesota Press.

Foucault, Michel. 1984. "What Is an Author?" Translated by Josué V. Harari. In *The Foucault Reader*. Edited by Paul Rabinow. New York: Pantheon Books. 101–20.

Frank, Manfred. 1989. *What Is Neostructuralism?* Translated by Sabine Wilke and Richard Gray. Minneapolis: University of Minnesota Press.

Freud, Sigmund. *The Standard Edition of the Complete Psychological Works of Sigmund Freud*. 24 vols. Edited and translated by James Strachey, in collaboration with Anna Freud, assisted by Alix Strachey and Alan Tyson. London: Hogarth Press and the Institute of Psycho-Analysis, 1953–74.

————. "Some Points for a Comparative Study of Organic and Hysterical Motor Paralyses." *SE* 1:155–72.

————. "Extracts from the Fliess Papers." *SE* 1:173–280.

————. "The Aetiology of Hysteria." *SE* 3:187–221.

————. "Abstracts of the Scientific Writings of Dr. Sigm. Freud 1877–1897." *SE* 3:223–57.

————. *The Interpretation of Dreams*. *SE* 4–5.

————. *Three Essays on the Theory of Sexuality*. *SE* 7:123–245.

————. "Notes Upon a Case of Obsessional Neurosis." *SE* 10:151–318.

————. "Formulations on the Two Principles of Mental Functioning." *SE* 12:213–26.

————. "On Narcissism: An Introduction." *SE* 14:67–102.

————. "Instincts and Their Vicissitudes." *SE* 14:109–40.

————. "Repression." *SE* 14:141–58.

———. "The Unconscious." *SE* 14:159–215.

———. "A Metapsychological Supplement to the Theory of Dreams." *SE* 14:217–35.

———. "Thoughts for the Times on War and Death." *SE* 14:273–302.

———. "On Transience." *SE* 14:303–7.

———. "The 'Uncanny.'" *SE* 17:217–56.

———. *Beyond the Pleasure Principle. SE* 18:1–64.

———. *Group Psychology and the Analysis of the Ego. SE* 18:65–143.

———. "Medusa's Head." *SE* 18:273–74.

———. *The Ego and the Id. SE* 19:1–66.

———. "The Economic Problem of Masochism." *SE* 19:155–70.

———. "Negation." *SE* 19:233–39.

———. *Inhibitions, Symptoms and Anxiety. SE* 20:75–175.

———. *Civilization and Its Discontents. SE* 21:57–145.

———. "An Outline of Psycho-Analysis." *SE* 23:139–207.

Gasché, Rodolphe. 1986. *The Tain of the Mirror: Derrida and the Philosophy of Reflection.* Cambridge, Mass.: Harvard University Press.

Gigante, Denise. 1998. "Toward a Notion of Critical Self-Creation: Slavoj Žižek and the 'Vortex of Madness.'" *New Literary History* 29, no. 1 (Winter): 153–68.

Gillespie, Sam. 1996. "Hegel Unsutured: An Addendum to Badiou." In *Umbr(a): Badiou.* Edited by Sam Gillespie and Sigi Jöttkandt. Buffalo, N.Y.: Center for the Study of Psychoanalysis and Culture, SUNY. 57–69.

Gould, Stephen Jay, and Elisabeth S. Vrba. 1982. "Exaptation—A Missing Term in the Science of Form." *Paleobiology* 8, no. 1:4–15.

Green, André. 1995. *La causalité psychique: Entre nature et culture.* Paris: Éditions Odile Jacob.

———. 2000a. "*L'originaire dans la psychanalyse.*" In *La diachronie en psychanalyse.* Paris: Les Éditions de Minuit. 41–85.

———. 2000b. "*Le temps et l'autre.*" In *Le temps éclaté.* Paris: Les Éditions de Minuit. 157–83.

Grosz, Elizabeth. 1990. *Jacques Lacan: A Feminist Introduction.* New York: Routledge.

Hallward, Peter. 1998. "Generic Sovereignty: The Philosophy of Alain Badiou." *Angelaki* 3, no. 3 (December):87–111.

———. 2003. *Badiou: A Subject to Truth.* Minneapolis: University of Minnesota Press.

Hasker, William. 1999. *The Emergent Self.* Ithaca, N.Y.: Cornell University Press.

Hegel, G. W. F. 1969. *Science of Logic.* Translated by A. V. Miller. Amherst, Mass.: Humanity Books.

———. 1975. *Logic: Part One of the Encyclopedia of the Philosophical Sciences.* Translated by William Wallace. Oxford: Oxford University Press.

———. 1977a. *The Difference Between Fichte's and Schelling's System of Philosophy.* Translated by H. S. Harris and Walter Cerf. Albany: State University of New York Press.

———. 1977b. *Faith and Knowledge.* Translated by Walter Cerf and H. S. Harris. Albany: State University of New York Press.

———. 1977c. *Phenomenology of Spirit.* Translated by A. V. Miller. Oxford: Oxford University Press.

———. 1990. *Encyclopedia of the Philosophical Sciences in Outline.* Edited by Ernst Behler. Translated by Steven A. Taubeneck. New York: Continuum.

Heidegger, Martin. 1962. *Being and Time.* Translated by John Macquarrie and Edward Robinson. New York: Harper and Row.

———. 1982. *The Basic Problems of Phenomenology.* Translated by Albert Hofstadter. Bloomington: Indiana University Press.

———. 1985. *Schelling's Treatise on the Essence of Human Freedom.* Translated by Joan Stambaugh. Athens: Ohio University Press.

———. 1993. "The Question Concerning Technology." Translated by William Lovitt. In *Basic Writings.* Edited by David Farrell Krell. New York: HarperCollins. 307–41.

Horstmann, Rolf-Peter. 2000. "The Early Philosophy of Fichte and Schelling." In *The Cambridge Companion to German Idealism.* Edited by Karl Ameriks. Cambridge: Cambridge University Press. 117–40.

Johnston, Adrian. 2000. "Rigid 'I,' Modal Subject: Miller, Kripke, and the Suture of Rigid Designation." *Clinical Studies: International Journal of Psychoanalysis* 5, no. 2:51–72.

———. 2001. "The Vicious Circle of the Super-Ego: The Pathological Trap of Guilt and the Beginning of Ethics." *Psychoanalytic Studies* 3, no. 3/4 (September/December): 411–24.

———. 2002. "The Exception and the Rule." *Continental Philosophy Review* 35, no. 4 (December): 423–32.

———. 2003a. "The Genesis of the Transcendent: Kant, Schelling, and the Ground of Experience." *Idealistic Studies* 33, no. 1 (Spring): 57–81.

———. 2003b. "The Soul of *Dasein*: Schelling's Doctrine of the Soul and Heidegger's Analytic of *Dasein*." *Philosophy Today* 47, no. 3 (Fall): 227–51.

———. 2005a. "Intimations of Freudian Mortality: The Enigma of Sexuality and the Constitutive Blind Spots of Freud's Self-Analysis." *Journal for Lacanian Studies* 3, no. 2:222–46.

———. 2005b. *Time Driven: Metapsychology and the Splitting of the Drive.* Evanston, Ill.: Northwestern University Press.

———. 2006. "Ghosts of Substance Past: Schelling, Lacan, and the Denaturalization of Nature." In *Lacan: The Silent Partners.* Edited by Slavoj Žižek. London: Verso. 34–55.

Kant, Immanuel. 1960. *Religion Within the Limits of Reason Alone.* Translated by Theodore M. Greene and Hoyt H. Hudson. New York: Harper and Row.

———. 1965. *Critique of Pure Reason.* Translated by Norman Kemp Smith. New York: Saint Martin's Press.

———. 1977. *Prolegomena to Any Future Metaphysics.* Translated by Paul Carus. Revised by James W. Ellington. Indianapolis: Hackett.

———. 1978. *Anthropology from a Pragmatic Point of View.* Translated by Victor Lyle Dowdell. Carbondale: Southern Illinois University Press.

———. 1993a. *Critique of Practical Reason.* Translated by Lewis White Beck. New Jersey: Prentice-Hall.

———. 1993b. *Grounding for the Metaphysics of Morals.* Translated by James W. Ellington. Indianapolis: Hackett.

Kay, Sarah. 2003. *Zizek: A Critical Introduction.* Cambridge: Polity.

Klein, Melanie. 1964. "Love, Guilt and Reparation." In Melanie Klein and Joan Riviere, *Love, Hate and Reparation.* New York: W. W. Norton. 55–119.

———. 1975. *The Psycho-Analysis of Children: The Writings of Melanie Klein,* vol. 2. Translated by Alix Strachey. New York: Free Press.

Kojève, Alexandre. 1947. *Introduction à la lecture de Hegel.* Edited by Raymond Queneau. Paris: Gallimard.

Kripke, Saul A. 1972. *Naming and Necessity.* Cambridge, Mass.: Harvard University Press.

Kristeva, Julia. 1982. *Powers of Horror: An Essay on Abjection.* Translated by Leon S. Roudiez. New York: Columbia University Press.

Lacan, Jacques. 1966. *"Le stade du miroir comme formateur de la fonction du Je telle qu'elle nous est révélée dans l'expérience psychanalytique."* In *Écrits,* Paris: Éditions du Seuil. 93–100.

———. 1970. "Of Structure as an Inmixing of Otherness Prerequisite to Any Subject Whatever." In *The Structuralist Controversy: The Languages of Criticism and the Sciences of Man.* Edited by Richard Macksey and Eugenio Donato. Baltimore: Johns Hopkins University Press. 186–200.

———. 1977. "Desire and the Interpretation of Desire in *Hamlet.*" Edited by Jacques-Alain Miller. Translated by James Hulbert. In *Yale French Studies* 55/56, *Literature and Psychoanalysis: The Question of Reading: Otherwise.* Valencia, Spain: Artes Gráficas Soler, S.A. 11–52.

———. 1978. *"Le rêve d'Aristote."* Unpublished manuscript. http://www.ecole-lacanienne.net/documents/1978-06-01.doc

———. 1990a. "Television." Translated by Denis Hollier, Rosalind Krauss, and Annette Michelson. In *Television/A Challenge to the Psychoanalytic Establishment.* Edited by Joan Copjec. New York: W. W. Norton. 1–46.

———. 1990b. "Responses to Students of Philosophy Concerning the Object of Psychoanalysis." Translated by Jeffrey Mehlman. In *Television/A Challenge to the Psychoanalytic Establishment.* Edited by Joan Copjec. New York: W. W. Norton. 107–14.

———. 1990c. "The Other Is Missing." Translated by Jeffrey Mehlman. In *Television/A Challenge to the Psychoanalytic Establishment.* Edited by Joan Copjec. New York: W. W. Norton. 133–35.

———. 2001a. *"Les complexes familiaux dans la formation de l'individu: Essai d'analyse d'une fonction en psychologie."* In *Autres écrits.* Edited by Jacques-Alain Miller. Paris: Éditions du Seuil. 23–84.

———. 2001b. *"Discours de Rome."* In *Autres écrits.* Edited by Jacques-Alain Miller. Paris: Éditions du Seuil. 133–64.

———. 2001c. *"Problèmes cruciaux pour la psychanalyse: Compte rendu du Séminaire 1964–1965."* In *Autres écrits.* Edited by Jacques-Alain Miller. Paris: Éditions du Seuil. 199–202.

———. 2001d. *"Petit discours à l'ORTF."* In *Autres écrits.* Edited by Jacques-Alain Miller. Paris: Éditions du Seuil. 221–26.

———. 2001e. *"Radiophonie."* In *Autres écrits.* Edited by Jacques-Alain Miller. Paris: Éditions du Seuil. 403–47.

———. 2001f. *"L'étourdit."* In *Autres écrits.* Edited by Jacques-Alain Miller. Paris: Éditions du Seuil. 449–95.

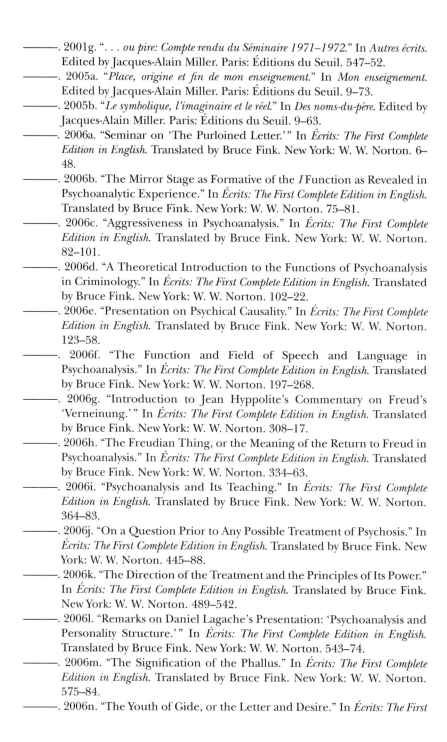

———. 2001g. "... *ou pire: Compte rendu du Séminaire 1971–1972.*" In *Autres écrits.* Edited by Jacques-Alain Miller. Paris: Éditions du Seuil. 547–52.

———. 2005a. "*Place, origine et fin de mon enseignement.*" In *Mon enseignement.* Edited by Jacques-Alain Miller. Paris: Éditions du Seuil. 9–73.

———. 2005b. "*Le symbolique, l'imaginaire et le réel.*" In *Des noms-du-père.* Edited by Jacques-Alain Miller. Paris: Éditions du Seuil. 9–63.

———. 2006a. "Seminar on 'The Purloined Letter.'" In *Écrits: The First Complete Edition in English.* Translated by Bruce Fink. New York: W. W. Norton. 6–48.

———. 2006b. "The Mirror Stage as Formative of the *I* Function as Revealed in Psychoanalytic Experience." In *Écrits: The First Complete Edition in English.* Translated by Bruce Fink. New York: W. W. Norton. 75–81.

———. 2006c. "Aggressiveness in Psychoanalysis." In *Écrits: The First Complete Edition in English.* Translated by Bruce Fink. New York: W. W. Norton. 82–101.

———. 2006d. "A Theoretical Introduction to the Functions of Psychoanalysis in Criminology." In *Écrits: The First Complete Edition in English.* Translated by Bruce Fink. New York: W. W. Norton. 102–22.

———. 2006e. "Presentation on Psychical Causality." In *Écrits: The First Complete Edition in English.* Translated by Bruce Fink. New York: W. W. Norton. 123–58.

———. 2006f. "The Function and Field of Speech and Language in Psychoanalysis." In *Écrits: The First Complete Edition in English.* Translated by Bruce Fink. New York: W. W. Norton. 197–268.

———. 2006g. "Introduction to Jean Hyppolite's Commentary on Freud's 'Verneinung.'" In *Écrits: The First Complete Edition in English.* Translated by Bruce Fink. New York: W. W. Norton. 308–17.

———. 2006h. "The Freudian Thing, or the Meaning of the Return to Freud in Psychoanalysis." In *Écrits: The First Complete Edition in English.* Translated by Bruce Fink. New York: W. W. Norton. 334–63.

———. 2006i. "Psychoanalysis and Its Teaching." In *Écrits: The First Complete Edition in English.* Translated by Bruce Fink. New York: W. W. Norton. 364–83.

———. 2006j. "On a Question Prior to Any Possible Treatment of Psychosis." In *Écrits: The First Complete Edition in English.* Translated by Bruce Fink. New York: W. W. Norton. 445–88.

———. 2006k. "The Direction of the Treatment and the Principles of Its Power." In *Écrits: The First Complete Edition in English.* Translated by Bruce Fink. New York: W. W. Norton. 489–542.

———. 2006l. "Remarks on Daniel Lagache's Presentation: 'Psychoanalysis and Personality Structure.'" In *Écrits: The First Complete Edition in English.* Translated by Bruce Fink. New York: W. W. Norton. 543–74.

———. 2006m. "The Signification of the Phallus." In *Écrits: The First Complete Edition in English.* Translated by Bruce Fink. New York: W. W. Norton. 575–84.

———. 2006n. "The Youth of Gide, or the Letter and Desire." In *Écrits: The First*

Complete Edition in English. Translated by Bruce Fink. New York: W. W. Norton. 623–44.

———. 2006o. "The Subversion of the Subject and the Dialectic of Desire in the Freudian Unconscious." In *Écrits: The First Complete Edition in English.* Translated by Bruce Fink. New York: W. W. Norton. 671–702.

———. 2006p. "Position of the Unconscious." In *Écrits: The First Complete Edition in English.* Translated by Bruce Fink. New York: W. W. Norton. 703–21.

Lacan, Jacques. The Seminars:

———. *The Seminar of Jacques Lacan, Book I: Freud's Papers on Technique, 1953–1954.* Edited by Jacques-Alain Miller. Translated by John Forrester. New York: W. W. Norton, 1988.

———. *The Seminar of Jacques Lacan, Book II: The Ego in Freud's Theory and in the Technique of Psychoanalysis, 1954–1955.* Edited by Jacques-Alain Miller. Translated by Sylvana Tomaselli. New York: W. W. Norton, 1988.

———. *The Seminar of Jacques Lacan, Book III: The Psychoses, 1955–1956.* Edited by Jacques-Alain Miller. Translated by Russell Grigg. New York: W. W. Norton, 1993.

———. *Le Séminaire de Jacques Lacan, Livre IV: La relation d'objet, 1956–1957.* Edited by Jacques-Alain Miller. Paris: Éditions du Seuil, 1994.

———. *Le Séminaire de Jacques Lacan, Livre V: Les formations de l'inconscient, 1957–1958.* Edited by Jacques-Alain Miller. Paris: Éditions du Seuil, 1998.

———. *Le Séminaire de Jacques Lacan, Livre VI: Le désir et son interprétation, 1958–1959.* Unpublished typescript.

———. *The Seminar of Jacques Lacan, Book VII: The Ethics of Psychoanalysis, 1959–1960.* Edited by Jacques-Alain Miller. Translated by Dennis Porter. New York: W. W. Norton, 1992.

———. *Le Séminaire de Jacques Lacan, Livre VIII: Le transfert, 1960–1961.* Edited by Jacques-Alain Miller. Paris: Éditions du Seuil, 2001.

———. *Le Séminaire de Jacques Lacan, Livre IX: L'identification, 1961–1962.* Unpublished typescript.

———. *Le Séminaire de Jacques Lacan, Livre X: L'angoisse, 1962–1963.* Edited by Jacques-Alain Miller. Paris: Éditions du Seuil, 2004.

———. *The Seminar of Jacques Lacan, Book XI: The Four Fundamental Concepts of Psycho-Analysis, 1964.* Edited by Jacques-Alain Miller. Translated by Alan Sheridan. New York: W. W. Norton, 1977.

———. *Le Séminaire de Jacques Lacan, Livre XII: Problèmes cruciaux pour la psychanalyse, 1964–1965.* Unpublished typescript.

———. *Le Séminaire de Jacques Lacan, Livre XIII: L'objet de la psychanalyse, 1965–1966.* Unpublished typescript.

———. *Le Séminaire de Jacques Lacan, Livre XIV: La logique du fantasme, 1966–1967.* Unpublished typescript.

———. *Le Séminaire de Jacques Lacan, Livre XV: L'acte psychanalytique, 1967–1968.* Unpublished typescript.

———. *Le Séminaire de Jacques Lacan, Livre XVI: D'un Autre à l'autre, 1968–1969.* Edited by Jacques-Alain Miller. Paris: Éditions du Seuil, 2006.

———. *Le Séminaire de Jacques Lacan, Livre XVII: L'envers de la psychanalyse, 1969–*

1970. Edited by Jacques-Alain Miller. Paris: Éditions du Seuil, 1991.

———. *Le Séminaire de Jacques Lacan, Livre XVIII: D'un discours qui ne serait pas du semblant, 1971.* Unpublished typescript.

———. *Le Séminaire de Jacques Lacan, Livre XIX: . . . ou pire, 1971–1972.* Unpublished typescript.

———. *Le Séminaire de Jacques Lacan, Livre XIX: Le savoir du psychanalyste, 1971–1972.* Unpublished typescript.

———. *The Seminar of Jacques Lacan, Book XX: Encore, 1972–1973.* Edited by Jacques-Alain Miller. Translated by Bruce Fink. New York: W. W. Norton, 1998.

———. *Le Séminaire de Jacques Lacan, Livre XXI: Les non-dupes errent, 1973–1974.* Unpublished typescript.

———. *Le Séminaire de Jacques Lacan, Livre XXII: R.S.I., 1974–1975.* Edited by Jacques-Alain Miller. In *Ornicar?* 2, 3, 4, 5 (1975).

———. *Le Séminaire de Jacques Lacan, Livre XXIII: Le sinthome, 1975–1976.* Edited by Jacques-Alain Miller. Paris: Éditions du Seuil, 2005.

———. *Le Séminaire de Jacques Lacan, Livre XXIV: L'insu que sait de l'une-bévue s'aile à mourre, 1976–1977.* Edited by Jacques-Alain Miller. In *Ornicar?* 12/13, 14, 15, 16, 17/18 (1977–79).

Laclau, Ernesto, and Chantal Mouffe. 2001. *Hegemony and Socialist Strategy: Towards a Radical Democratic Politics.* London: Verso.

Laplanche, Jean, and Jean-Bertrand Pontalis. 1973. *The Language of Psycho-Analysis.* Translated by Donald Nicholson Smith. New York: W. W. Norton.

———. 1986. "Fantasy and the Origins of Sexuality." In *Formations of Fantasy.* Edited by Victor Burgin, James Donald, and Cora Kaplan. New York: Methuen. 5–34.

La Rochefoucauld, François, duc de. 1959. *Maxims.* Translated by Leonard Tancock. New York: Penguin Books.

Lazarus, Sylvain. 1996. *Anthropologie du nom.* Paris: Éditions du Seuil.

Lear, Jonathan. 2000. *Happiness, Death, and the Remainder of Life.* Cambridge, Mass.: Harvard University Press.

Leclaire, Serge. 1980. "Jerome, or Death in the Life of the Obsessional." Translated by Stuart Schneiderman. In *Returning to Freud: Clinical Psychoanalysis in the School of Lacan.* Edited by Stuart Schneiderman. New Haven, Conn.: Yale University Press. 94–113.

LeDoux, Joseph. 2002. *Synaptic Self: How Our Brains Become Who We Are.* New York: Penguin Books.

Lefort, Claude. 1988. "The Permanence of the Theologico-Political?" In *Democracy and Political Theory.* Translated by David Macey. Minneapolis: University of Minnesota Press. 213–55.

Le Gaufey, Guy. 1996. *L'incomplétude du symbolique: De Réne Descartes à Jacques Lacan.* Paris: E.P.E.L.

Malabou, Catherine. 2004. *Que faire de notre cerveau?* Paris: Bayard.

Martin-Mattera, Patrick. 2002. *"Temps et réalité psychique."* In *Fondations subjectives du temps, avec un index du temps chez Lacan.* Edited by August Morille and

Patrick Martin-Mattera. Paris: L'Harmattan. 79–100.

Miller, Jacques-Alain. 1994. *"Extimité."* Translated by Françoise Massardier-Kenny. In *Lacanian Theory of Discourse: Subject, Structure, and Society.* Edited by Mark Bracher, Marshall W. Alcorn, Jr., Ronald J. Corthell, and Françoise Massardier-Kenny. New York: New York University Press. 74–87.

———. 2000. "Paradigms of *Jouissance.*" Translated by Jorge Jauregui. *Lacanian Ink* 17 (Fall): 10–47.

———. 2001a. "Lacanian Biology and the Event of the Body." Translated by Barbara P. Fulks. *Lacanian Ink* 18 (Spring): 6–29.

———. 2001b. "The Symptom and the Body Event." Translated by Barbara P. Fulks. *Lacanian Ink* 19 (Fall): 4–47.

———. 2005. "Introduction to the Erotics of Time." Translated by Barbara P. Fulks. *Lacanian Ink* 24/25 (Winter/Spring): 8–43.

Milner, Jean-Claude. 1995. *L'oeuvre claire: Lacan, la science, la philosophie.* Paris: Éditions du Seuil.

———. 2002. *Le périple structural: Figures et paradigme.* Paris: Éditions du Seuil.

Muller, John P. 1980. "Psychosis and Mourning in Lacan's *Hamlet.*" *New Literary History* 12, no. 1 (Autumn): 147–65.

Myers, Tony. 2003. *Slavoj Žižek.* New York: Routledge.

Nancy, Jean-Luc. 2002. *Hegel: The Restlessness of the Negative.* Translated by Jason Smith and Steven Miller. Minneapolis: University of Minnesota Press.

Neuhouser, Frederick. 1990. *Fichte's Theory of Subjectivity.* Cambridge: Cambridge University Press.

Plato. 1992. *Republic.* Translated by G. M. A. Grube. Revised by C. D. C. Reeve. Indianapolis: Hackett.

———. 2002. *Phaedo.* In *Five Dialogues: Euthyphro, Apology, Crito, Meno, Phaedo.* Translated by G. M. A. Grube. Revised by John M. Cooper. Indianapolis: Hackett. 93–154.

Poissonnier, Dominique. 1998. *La pulsion de mort: De Freud à Lacan.* Paris: Points Hors Ligne.

Ragland, Ellie. 1995. *Essays on the Pleasures of Death: From Freud to Lacan.* New York: Routledge.

Rank, Otto. 1958. *Beyond Psychology.* New York: Dover.

Safouan, Moustapha. 1983. *Pleasure and Being: Hedonism from a Psychoanalytic Point of View.* Translated by Martin Thom. New York: Saint Martin's Press.

———. 2001a. *"Du réel dans la psychanalyse."* In *Dix conférences de psychanalyse.* Paris: Librairie Arthème Fayard. 11–26.

———. 2001b. *Lacaniana: Les séminaires de Jacques Lacan, 1953–1963.* Paris: Librairie Arthème Fayard.

Sartre, Jean-Paul. 1956. *Being and Nothingness: An Essay on Phenomenological Ontology.* Translated by Hazel E. Barnes. New York: Philosophical Library.

Schelling, F. W. J. 1936. *Philosophical Inquiries into the Nature of Human Freedom and Matters Connected Therewith.* Translated by James Gutmann. Chicago: Open Court.

———. 1966. *On University Studies.* Translated by E. S. Morgan. Athens: Ohio University Press.

————. 1978. *System of Transcendental Idealism.* Translated by Peter Heath. Charlottesville: University Press of Virginia.

————. 1980. "Philosophical Letters on Dogmatism and Criticism." In *The Unconditional in Human Knowledge: Four Early Essays (1794–1796).* Translated by Fritz Marti. Lewisburg, Pa.: Bucknell University Press. 156–218.

————. 1984. *Bruno, or On the Natural and Divine Principle of Things.* Translated by Michael G. Vater. Albany: State University of New York Press.

————. 1988. *Ideas for a Philosophy of Nature.* Translated by Errol E. Harris and Peter Heath. Cambridge: Cambridge University Press.

————. 1994a. *On the History of Modern Philosophy.* Translated by Andrew Bowie. Cambridge: Cambridge University Press.

————. 1994b. "Treatise Explicatory of the Idealism in the *Science of Knowledge.*" In *Idealism and the Endgame of Theory: Three Essays by F. W. J. Schelling.* Translated by Thomas Pfau. Albany: State University of New York Press. 61–138.

————. 1994c. "Stuttgart Seminars." In *Idealism and the Endgame of Theory: Three Essays by F. W. J. Schelling.* Translated by Thomas Pfau. Albany: State University of New York Press. 195–268.

————. 2000. *The Ages of the World: Third Version (c. 1815).* Translated by Jason M. Wirth. Albany: State University of New York Press.

————. 2002. *Clara, or On Nature's Connection to the Spirit World.* Translated by Fiona Steinkamp. Albany: State University of New York Press.

Schneiderman, Stuart. 1983. *Jacques Lacan: The Death of an Intellectual Hero.* Cambridge, Mass.: Harvard University Press.

Solms, Mark, and Oliver Turnbull. 2002. *The Brain and the Inner World: An Introduction to the Neuroscience of Subjective Experience.* New York: Other Press.

Van Haute, Philippe. 2002. *Against Adaptation: Lacan's "Subversion" of the Subject— A Close Reading.* Translated by Paul Crowe and Miranda Vankerk. New York: Other Press.

Varela, Francisco. 1995. "The Emergent Self." In *The Third Culture.* Edited by John Brockman. New York: Simon and Schuster. 209–22.

Vaysse, Jean-Marie. 1999. *L'inconscient des modernes: Essai sur l'origine métaphysique de la psychanalyse.* Paris: Gallimard.

Verhaeghe, Paul. 1998. "Causation and Destitution of a Pre-Ontological Non-Entity: On the Lacanian Subject." In *Key Concepts of Lacanian Psychoanalysis.* Edited by Dany Nobus. New York: Other Press. 164–89.

————. 2000. "The Collapse of the Function of the Father and Its Effects on Gender Roles." In *Sexuation.* Edited by Renata Salecl. Durham, N.C.: Duke University Press. 131–54.

————. 2001a. "From Impossibility to Inability: Lacan's Theory on the Four Discourses." In *Beyond Gender: From Subject to Drive.* New York: Other Press. 17–34.

————. 2001b. "Subject and Body: Lacan's Struggle with the Real." In *Beyond Gender: From Subject to Drive.* New York: Other Press. 65–97.

Wolin, Richard. 1993. "Preface to the MIT Press Edition: Note on a Missing Text." In *The Heidegger Controversy: A Critical Reader.* Edited by Richard Wolin. Cambridge, Mass.: MIT Press. ix–xx.

Žižek, Slavoj. 1988. *Le plus sublime des hystériques: Hegel passe.* Paris: Point Hors Ligne.

———. 1989. *The Sublime Object of Ideology.* London: Verso.

———. 1991. *Looking Awry: An Introduction to Jacques Lacan Through Popular Culture.* Cambridge, Mass.: MIT Press.

———. 1992a. *Enjoy Your Symptom!: Jacques Lacan in Hollywood and Out.* New York: Routledge.

———. 1992b. "In His Bold Gaze My Ruin Is Writ Large." In *Everything You Always Wanted to Know about Lacan (But Were Afraid to Ask Hitchcock).* Edited by Slavoj Žižek. London: Verso. 211–72.

———. 1993. *Tarrying with the Negative: Kant, Hegel, and the Critique of Ideology.* Durham, N.C.: Duke University Press.

———. 1994a. "Kant as a Theoretician of Vampirism." *Lacanian Ink* 8 (Spring): 19–33.

———. 1994b. *The Metastases of Enjoyment: Six Essays on Woman and Causality.* London: Verso.

———. 1995. "The Lamella of David Lynch." In *Reading Seminar XI: Lacan's Four Fundamental Concepts of Psychoanalysis.* Edited by Richard Feldstein, Bruce Fink, and Maire Jaanus. Albany: State University of New York Press. 205–20.

———. 1996a. "'I Hear You with My Eyes,' or The Invisible Master." In *Gaze and Voice as Love Objects.* Edited by Renata Salecl and Slavoj Žižek. Durham, N.C.: Duke University Press. 90–126.

———. 1996b. *The Indivisible Remainder: An Essay on Schelling and Related Matters.* London: Verso.

———. 1997a. "The Abyss of Freedom." In *The Abyss of Freedom/Ages of the World.* Ann Arbor: University of Michigan Press. 1–104.

———. 1997b. "Interview—with Andrew Long and Tara McGann." *JPCS: Journal for the Psychoanalysis of Culture and Society* 2, no. 1 (Spring): 133–37.

———. 1997c. *The Plague of Fantasies.* London: Verso.

———. 1998a. "Introduction: Cogito as a Shibboleth." In *Cogito and the Unconscious.* Edited by Slavoj Žižek. Durham, N.C.: Duke University Press. 1–8.

———. 1998b. "Four Discourses, Four Subjects." In *Cogito and the Unconscious.* Edited by Slavoj Žižek. Durham, N.C.: Duke University Press. 74–113.

———. 1998c. "The Cartesian Subject Versus the Cartesian Theater." In *Cogito and the Unconscious.* Edited by Slavoj Žižek. Durham, N.C.: Duke University Press. 247–74.

———. 1999a. "*The Matrix,* or Malebranche in Hollywood." *Philosophy Today* 43, supplement: 11–26.

———. 1999b. *The Ticklish Subject: The Absent Centre of Political Ontology.* London: Verso.

———. 1999c. "Preface: Burning the Bridges." In *The Žižek Reader.* Edited by Elizabeth Wright and Edmond Wright. Oxford: Blackwell. vii–x.

———. 1999d. "The Undergrowth of Enjoyment: How Popular Culture Can Serve as an Introduction to Lacan." In *The Žižek Reader.* Edited by Elizabeth Wright and Edmond Wright. Oxford: Blackwell. 11–36.

———. 1999e. "The Spectre of Ideology." In *The Žižek Reader*. Edited by Elizabeth Wright and Edmond Wright. Oxford: Blackwell. 53–86.

———. 1999f. "A Hair of the Dog That Bit You." In *The Žižek Reader*. Edited by Elizabeth Wright and Edmond Wright. Oxford: Blackwell. 268–82.

———. 1999g. "Kant with (or Against) Sade." In *The Žižek Reader*. Edited by Elizabeth Wright and Edmond Wright. Oxford: Blackwell. 283–301.

———. 1999h. "Of Cells and Selves." In *The Žižek Reader*. Edited by Elizabeth Wright and Edmond Wright. Oxford: Blackwell. 302–20.

———. 2000a. *The Art of the Ridiculous Sublime: On David Lynch's Lost Highway*. Seattle: University of Washington Press.

———. 2000b. "Class Struggle or Postmodernism?: Yes, Please!" In Judith Butler, Ernesto Laclau, and Slavoj Žižek, *Contingency, Hegemony, Universality: Contemporary Dialogues on the Left*. London: Verso. 90–135.

———. 2000c. "Da Capo Senza Fine." In Judith Butler, Ernesto Laclau, and Slavoj Žižek, *Contingency, Hegemony, Universality: Contemporary Dialogues on the Left*. London: Verso. 213–62.

———. 2000d. "Foreword: The Cartesian Body and Its Discontents." In Miran Božovič, *An Utterly Dark Spot: Gaze and Body in Early Modern Philosophy*. Ann Arbor: University of Michigan Press. v–ix.

———. 2000e. "Foreword: Why Is Kant Worth Fighting For?" In Alenka Zupančič, *Ethics of the Real: Kant, Lacan*. London: Verso. vii–xiii.

———. 2000f. *The Fragile Absolute, or Why Is the Christian Legacy Worth Fighting For?* London: Verso.

———. 2000g. "Lacan Between Cultural Studies and Cognitivism." In *Umbr(a): Science and Truth*. Edited by Theresa Giron. Buffalo, N.Y.: Center for the Study of Psychoanalysis and Culture, SUNY. 9–32.

———. 2000h. "Postface: Georg Lukács as the Philosopher of Leninism." In Georg Lukács, *A Defense of History and Class Consciousness: Tailism and the Dialectic*. Translated by Esther Leslie. London: Verso. 151–82.

———. 2000i. "The Thing from Inner Space." In *Sexuation*. Edited by Renata Salecl. Durham, N.C.: Duke University Press. 216–59.

———. 2001a. *Did Somebody Say Totalitarianism?: Five Interventions in the (Mis)use of a Notion*. London: Verso.

———. 2001b. *The Fright of Real Tears: Krzysztof Kieślowski Between Theory and Post-Theory*. London: British Film Institute.

———. 2001c. *On Belief*. New York: Routledge.

———. 2002a. *For They Know Not What They Do: Enjoyment as a Political Factor*. London: Verso.

———. 2002b. " 'I Do Not Order My Dreams.' " In Slavoj Žižek and Mladen Dolar, *Opera's Second Death*. New York: Routledge. 103–225.

———. 2002c. "The Real of Sexual Difference." In *Reading Seminar XX: Lacan's Major Work on Love, Knowledge, and Feminine Sexuality*. Edited by Suzanne Barnard and Bruce Fink. Albany: State University of New York Press. 57–75.

———. 2002d. *Welcome to the Desert of the Real!: Five Essays on September 11 and Related Dates*. London: Verso.

———. 2003a. "Liberation Hurts: An Interview with Slavoj Žižek (with Eric Dean Rasmussen)." http://www.electronicbookreview.com/thread/endconstruction/desublimation.

———. 2003b. *The Puppet and the Dwarf: The Perverse Core of Christianity.* Cambridge, Mass.: MIT Press.

———. 2004a. "Everything You Always Wanted to Know About Schelling (But Were Afraid to Ask Hitchcock)." In *The New Schelling.* Edited by Judith Norman and Alistair Welchman. London: Continuum. 30–42.

———. 2004b. *Iraq: The Borrowed Kettle.* London: Verso.

———. 2004c. *Organs Without Bodies: On Deleuze and Consequences.* New York: Routledge.

———. 2004d. "The Parallax View: Toward a New Reading of Kant." *Epoché* 8, no. 2 (Spring): 255–69.

———. 2005a. "Author's Preface: The Inhuman." In *Interrogating the Real.* Edited by Rex Butler and Scott Stephens. London: Continuum. 8–18.

———. 2005b. "Lacan—At What Point Is He Hegelian?" Translated by Rex Butler and Scott Stephens. In *Interrogating the Real.* Edited by Rex Butler and Scott Stephens. London: Continuum. 26–37.

———. 2005c. " 'The Most Sublime of Hysterics': Hegel with Lacan." Translated by Rex Butler and Scott Stephens. *Interrogating the Real.* Edited by Rex Butler and Scott Stephens. London: Continuum. 38–58.

———. 2005d. "Connections of the Freudian Field to Philosophy and Popular Culture." In *Interrogating the Real.* Edited by Rex Butler and Scott Stephens. London: Continuum. 59–86.

———. 2005e. "The Eclipse of Meaning: On Lacan and Deconstruction." In *Interrogating the Real.* Edited by Rex Butler and Scott Stephens. London: Continuum. 206–30.

———. 2006. *The Parallax View.* Cambridge, Mass.: MIT Press.

Žižek, Slavoj, and Glyn Daly. 2004. *Conversations with Žižek.* Cambridge: Polity.

Žižek, Slavoj, and Renata Salecl. 1996. "Lacan in Slovenia (An Interview with Slavoj Žižek and Renata Salecl [with Peter Osborne])." In *A Critical Sense: Interviews with Intellectuals.* Edited by Peter Osborne. New York: Routledge. 20–44.

Zupančič, Alenka. 1996. "Philosophers' Blind Man's Buff." In *Gaze and Voice as Love Objects.* Edited by Renata Salecl and Slavoj Žižek. Durham, N.C.: Duke University Press. 32–58.

———. 2000. *Ethics of the Real: Kant, Lacan.* London: Verso.

———. 2001. *Das Reale einer Illusion: Kant und Lacan.* Translated by Reiner Ansén. Baden-Baden: Suhrkamp.

———. 2002a. *Esthétique du désir, éthique de la jouissance.* Paris: Théétète Éditions.

———. 2002b. "On Love as Comedy." *Lacanian Ink* 20 (Spring): 62–79.

Index

Due to the frequency with which they are mentioned, not all references to the following figures are indexed: Sigmund Freud, G. W. F. Hegel, Immanuel Kant, Jacques Lacan, F. W. J. Schelling, and Slavoj Žižek. The same holds here for mentions of the three portions of Freud's first topography (i.e., conscious, preconscious, and unconscious) as well as Lacan's three registers (i.e., Real, Symbolic, and Imaginary). A few other frequently occurring terms that are not indexed include "dialectic" and "dialectical" (à la Hegel); "epistemology" and "epistemological"; "experience" (à la Kant); "ontogenesis" and "ontogenetic" (à la Freud); "ontology," "ontological," and "being"; and "signifier" (à la Lacan).

Hegel's texts
  Difference Between Fichte's and Schelling's System of Philosophy, The, 135
  Encyclopedia Logic, 138, 140, 262
  Encyclopedia of the Philosophical Sciences in Outline, 140
  Faith and Knowledge, 136
  Jenaer Realphilosophie, 187, 191
  Phenomenology of Spirit, xviii, 21, 49, 130–31, 136, 165, 191, 229, 235, 251, 262–63, 283
  Science of Logic, 135, 137, 140, 239, 261–62
hegemony, 173, 176, 193–94, 209, 211, 218, 220, 223, 226, 231–32
Heidegger, Martin
  Basic Problems of Phenomenology, 243
  Being and Time, 42–43, 168–69, 243–44
  being-in-the-world, 26, 169
  being-towards-death, 42–43, 52, 236, 244
  Dasein (being-there), 26, 28, 42–43, 115, 117, 168–69, 236, 243–44, 260–61
  Freud and, 25
  Kant (*Kant and the Problem of Metaphysics*) and, 243
  ontological difference (ontological and ontic), 169, 236, 238
  "Question Concerning Technology, The," 182
  ready-to-hand vs. present-at-hand, 169
  Schelling (*Schelling's Treatise on the Essence of Human Freedom*) and, 74, 107, 110, 114–15, 117, 243
  temporal ecstasis, 243, 260–61
  temporalization of being, 243–44, 260–61
  thrown-ness, 34–35, 143, 176, 258, 276
Heisenberg, Werner, 200–201
helplessness, xxiii, 47, 52, 59–60, 176, 213, 279
Heraclitus, 228, 269
historicity, 94, 118–20, 122
Horstmann, Rolf-Peter, 74
Hume, David, 73–74
Husserl, Edmund, 5

idealism, 8, 17, 146, 153, 155, 198, 221, 233
  vs. materialism, 86–88, 107–8, 143, 148–51, 164–65, 201–4, 208–9, 240, 282–83

metaphysical realism and, 228, 237
Innenwelt (inner world), 60, 87
interpellation, 112, 183, 270
inverse interpellation, 112

Jacobi, F. H., 17
Jameson, Fredric, 13

Kant, Immanuel
  antinomies, 28–30, 65, 100, 129, 148, 155, 163, 197, 207–8, 233, 246, 265
  cogito and, xxiii, 12, 15–16, 42, 56, 219
  constitutive vs. regulative, 15, 28, 31, 281
  Copernican revolution, 13, 75, 128, 131, 140, 155
  cosmological idea, 29
  critical philosophy, xvi, xxiv, 13, 15, 21, 25, 61, 70–71, 73–74, 76, 128, 133, 135, 153, 156, 161, 163–64, 208
  death/mortality and, xxiv, 22, 24–26, 28, 33, 37
  Descartes and, 10–12, 15–16, 30, 53, 56, 61, 219
  embodiment and, xxiv, 53
  empirical/psychological self, 12, 208
  finitude and, xxiv, 14–16, 22, 24, 30, 33, 129, 142, 172, 178, 207, 241
  Hume and, 73–74
  ideas of pure reason, 42
  imagination, 190–94, 220, 238, 242
  inclination, 103–4, 112
  infinite judgment, 36–37
  interest of reason, the, 15, 19, 31
  intuition/pure forms of intuition, 26, 29–30, 72, 128–29, 132–33, 142, 157–58, 191, 197–200, 219
  life and, 25, 29
  limits of possible experience, 14, 29–30, 42, 128–29, 135–36, 138, 163, 178, 197, 219
  necessary illusion, 133, 277
  negative judgment, 36–37
  neurosis and, 21–22, 24, 45, 58, 61
  noumenal and phenomenal, xiii, xxiv, 9, 13–14, 21, 30–33, 61–63, 71, 75, 114, 129, 131–33, 135–38, 140–43, 145–46, 152, 154–55, 158–59, 161–63, 178–79, 187, 207–8, 216, 219, 236, 245, 265, 280–81
  practical philosophy, 103–4, 113–14

About the Author

Adrian Johnston is an assistant professor of philosophy at the University of New Mexico at Albuquerque and an assistant teaching analyst at the Emory Psychoanalytic Institute in Atlanta. He is the author of *Time Driven: Metapsychology and the Splitting of the Drive,* also published by Northwestern University Press.